PALEO-INDIAN
ARTIFACTS

Identification
& Value Guide

Lar Hothem

COLLECTOR BOOKS

A Division of Schroeder Publishing Co., Inc.

Front cover, left to right:

Clovis point, long flute on obverse face, 2⅞", museum grade.
Stemmed lanceolate point or blade, 4⅞", unlisted.
Fluted point with multiple obverse flutes, 3⅞", museum grade.
Fluted point, 4⅝", museum grade.

Front cover, bottom:

Fluted point, 4½", museum grade.

Cover design by Beth Summers

Book design and layout by Mary Ann Hudson

COLLECTOR BOOKS
P.O. Box 3009
Paducah, Kentucky 42002-3009
www.collectorbooks.com

Copyright © 2005 Lar Hothem

Searching For A Publisher?

We are always looking for people knowledgeable within their fields. If you
feel that there is a real need for a book on your collectible subject and have a large
comprehensive collection, contact Collector Books.

The current values in this book should be used only as a guide. They
are not intended to set prices, which vary from one section of the country
to another. Auction prices as well as dealer prices vary greatly and are
affected by condition as well as demand. Neither the author nor the publisher assumes responsibility for any losses that might be incurred as a result
of consulting this guide.

CONTENTS

See page 258 for information.

ACKNOWLEDGMENTS

Thanks are due the many collectors who contributed photographs for this book, and their names are credited with the photographs. Without their kind help this book would not have been possible.

Special thanks also to Dennis Arbeiter (Rainbow Traders, P.O. Box 566, Godfrey, IL 62035) for auction photographs and results. And the following businesses and individuals contributed photographs: Back to Earth, Old Barn Auction, Gilbert Cooper, Earthworks Artifacts, Dave Summers, H. B. Greene II, John and Susan Mellyn, Michael Hough, Len and Janie Weidner, and John Baldwin.

For more information and products, the following publications and businesses are recommended:

Indian Artifact Magazine
245 Fairview Road
Turbotville, PA 17772-9063

Prehistoric Antiquities Quarterly
P.O. Box 296
North Lewisburg, OH 43060

Artifact Display Frames
Indian River Display Case Company
13706 Robins Road
Westerville, OH 43081

See page 6 for information.

There is something about Paleolithic (15,000 – 8000 BC) artifacts that intrigues archaeologists and collectors alike. No prehistoric era in North America is more talked about or studied. There's something about the first people in America — the lifeway, the tools and weapons — that is endlessly fascinating, and cannot be overlooked or set aside.

This wide appeal of Paleo artifacts springs from three aspects, their rarity and beauty and originality. Compared with those from later times, Paleo artifacts are far fewer in number. Many Paleo tools are attractive because they were finely chipped from high-grade flints, cherts, and obsidians. And, like fluted points and some blades, nothing like them exists outside the Paleo time frame.

Add to this an element of mystery, and the aura surrounding Paleo artifacts begins to be understood. How did these first hunters reach what is now America? When? No one has exact answers, although almost everyone has an opinion. All that is known for certain is that a unique lifeway (that sometimes involved killing large, now-extinct animals) once existed, and that the Paleo people roamed most of North America.

Today's collector of Indian artifacts is aware of all this. No general assemblage is complete without at least a few examples from Paleo times, and some collectors specialize in Paleo artifacts. This can be expensive in several ways. Certain fluted-base points are among the highest-priced artifacts available. One reason for these prices is that collectors like Paleo materials so much that there is often not much turnover; pieces tend to be collected and held.

Fake Paleo artifacts are common, and these days they are made correctly and aged and weathered almost to perfection. If a collector unknowingly obtains these bad pieces, his or her money is wasted and the entire collection is compromised.

None of this, however, seems to detour the pursuit of Paleo artifacts. There are dozens of collecting subclasses and probably a hundred distinct, named regional point types. So, there is something for every level of financial capability, ranging from end-scrapers (a few dollars) to uniface blades (some at a few hundred) to fluted points (some at several thousand dollars).

Collectors are aware that these objects from earliest ancient times are important. Collectors preserve the artifacts for the future, so that others also may appreciate and study them. When the worked flints are placed in a frame or display case, they are marvelous things to see. The many centuries roll away, and the distant past does not seem so far away after all.

For past books, some readers have asked the meaning of the terms *unlisted* and *museum grade*. (The value listed is what the collector/owner feels is a fair market value, or in some instances, what has been offered.) Some artifacts have "unlisted," and this simply means that for some reason, no value was assigned to that particular piece. It may have been a personal find with value other than that of a monetary figure.

"Museum grade" assumes a high value, but one that is difficult to determine and in a way is "unlisted plus." Usually this is because the artifact is highly superior in one or more respects. It is understood that truly top-grade pieces have no absolute upper limits as to what they might sell or trade for. In fact, for highly superior specimens, private transactions have involved values far higher than those listed in this book.

Also, and something non-collectors with a few artifacts do not usually consider, just because a fine 5" Paleo lance in pristine condition is listed at two thousand dollars does not automatically mean a person's 5" field-found point or blade is worth the same amount. It must be kept in mind that for any Paleo artifact, whether museum grade or not, to have a high value, it must have high quality — and unquestionable authenticity.

A few words are in order about geographic coverage of the book. The reader will note that there are more photographs of artifacts from the Midwest and East than from the West, and there are several reasons for this. The Midwest and East (especially Southeast) have more collectors than does the West. Also, there are many more Paleo artifacts in these parts, and more agriculture of the kind that has uncovered artifacts. The book coverage corresponds to the distribution and concentration of Paleo Indian artifacts in North America.

FLUTED POINTS — TYPES

The distinguishing feature of fluted points is of course the flutes. These are long wide or narrow flakes that were driven from the base toward the tip on one or both faces. All fluted points are scarce, and some types are quite rare.

There are more eastern fluted points and eastern fluted point types than western, probably because of a larger Paleo population, which eventually meant more differences. Eastern types include generalized Clovis forms, Debert (deeply concave baselines), Holcombe (often with multiple narrow flutes), Redstone (triangular), Ross County (wide, with shallow flutes), Cumberland (thick, with long flutes), and Barnes (some resemblance to Cumberlands).

As they are in the East, western types are generalized Clovis forms, plus the famous Folsom (fluted to the tip on one or both faces, extended basal ears). An interesting thing is that Clovis points — though grouped under the one name — had a variety of styles. Even points from a single kill site may have major differences in size, material, and overall form. Clovis points in the West (and in the East, for that matter) are not a single design frozen in flint but more a family of subtypes.

A fluted point tends to have a concave or incurved baseline, because the fluting platform or projection at the base center was destroyed in the process of fluting. The concavity ranges from slight to very deep, and there is some evidence that the deeper the concavity, the later the point. After the fluting process was complete, edges were ground or smoothed so that sharp edges did not cut the lashing ties. Most fluted points are neither stemmed nor notched, which gives fluted points a distinctive shape.

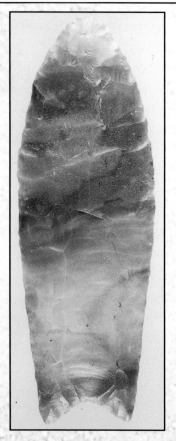

St. Louis fluted point, translucent Carter Cave (Paoli) flint in five muted hues, 4½". The obverse flute is over half of point length and the reverse flute is 3¾" long. This is simply a wonderful point in color, style, shape, size, and condition. It has a Perino COA and is from Scioto County, Ohio. *Gilbert Cooper collection.* Museum grade.

Fluted point, 3⅛", blue and cream Flint Ridge. It has a half-length obverse flute and is ex-collections Bell, Townsend, and Jack Hooks. Richland County, Ohio. *Doug Hooks collection.* $3,000.00.

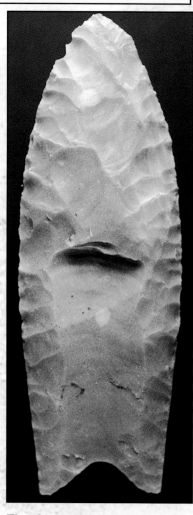

Fluted point, a very superior example, well tapered, pale gray hornstone, 3½". Fluted on both faces, it is ex-collections Barrett and Jack Hooks. Ohio. *Private collection.* $7,000.00.

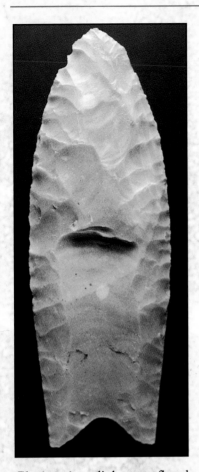

Clovis point, slight ears, fluted on both faces, 2⅞". The material is near-gem Flint Ridge translucent moss agate, and the point was found in 1998. Delaware County, Ohio. *Doug Hooks collection.* $2,500.00.

Fluted point, light gray striped blond Upper Mercer flint, 3⅞". The point has a Davis COA and exhibits the typical rather blunt Clovis tip. Summit County, Ohio. *Earthworks Artifacts.* $4,200.00.

Fluted point, ex-collection Shelton, 2¾". Glossy dark Upper Mercer, it has both Jackson and Perino COAs. It came from Owen County, Kentucky. *Earthworks Artifacts.* $2,250.00.

Fluted point, Upper Mercer in various streaks of gray, 4⅜". This exceptional point in material and size is ex-collections Cooper and Larson. It has a Perino COA and was picked up in Coshocton County, Ohio. *Earthworks Artifacts.* Museum grade.

Fluted point, Carter Cave flint in three shades, 3" long. It has a Perino COA and presents classic Clovis shape. Morgan County, Kentucky. *Earthworks Artifacts.* $2,300.00.

Fluted point, long flutes on both faces, Fort Payne chert. It is 4" long and has a Perino COA. This well-shaped point was found in the Clinch River area, Tennessee. *Earthworks Artifacts.* $4,300.00.

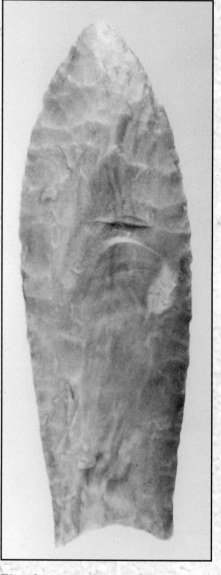

Fluted point, pale mixed Carter Cave (KY) flint, 4½". The obverse flute is 2½" long and the point has a Perino COA. This is a top piece in all considerations of quality and value. Owen County, Kentucky. *Earthworks Artifacts.* $6,000.00.

Fluted point, Flint Ridge pale gray and red, 2¼". It is ex-collection Johnson, from Marion County, Ohio. *Doug Hooks collection.* $750.00.

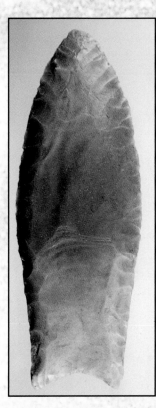

Fluted point, patinated multicolored Flint Ridge, 2¼". This example with ears is ex-collection Jack Hooks and was found in Medina County, Ohio. *Doug Hooks collection.* $1,000.00.

Fluted point, near black Upper Mercer, fluted both faces. The point is 2½", ex-collections Townsend and Jack Hooks. Fairfield County, Ohio. *Doug Hooks collection.* $1,200.00.

Fluted point, cloudy blue Indiana flint, 3" long. The obverse is fluted for nearly one-half of length, and the point came from Morgan County, Indiana. *Len and Janie Weidner collection.* Museum grade.

Hazel or Ross County fluted point, Wyandotte flint, 3⅝". This is an exceptional piece in workstyle and size, well-fluted and ex-collection Bush. It was found in Ross County, Ohio. *Len and Janie Weidner collection.* Museum grade.

Hazel or Ross County fluted point, translucent creamy gray Kaolin flint with inclusions, 4⅛" long. This excellent Paleo with tapered waist was picked up in Alexander County, Illinois. *Len and Janie Weidner collection.* Museum grade.

Ross County type fluted point, 3⁷⁄₁₆", black Kanawha flint from West Virginia. This specimen is ex-collection Copeland, from Licking County, Ohio. *Len and Janie Weidner collection.* $1,400.00.

Clovis point, wide and short obverse flute, 2½". This example was found by the owner in 1982. Kane County, Illinois. *Collection of and photograph by Duane Treest, Illinois.* $150.00 – 200.00.

Clovis point, fluted on both faces for ⅝", overall point length 2⅞". It is ex-collection Frank Squire, and was found in Wisconsin. *Collection of and photograph by Duane Treest, Illinois.* $275.00 – 500.00.

Fluted point, obverse, patinated jewel Flint Ridge, very translucent. The obverse has three flutes, and the point is 3¾" long. Points of this quality bring well over $10,000. Medina County, Ohio. *Private collection.* Museum grade.

Fluted point, reverse, single wide flute with termination ledge, point length 3¾". It has an extensive collecting history, including VandeVeer, King, Fuller, and Jack Hooks. Medina County, Ohio. *Private collection.* Museum grade.

Clovis point, 2¼", mixed chert, fluted on both faces. Well shaped, the point was picked up near Spottsville, Kentucky. *Collection of and photograph by Duane Treest, Illinois.* $450.00 – 750.00.

Clovis point, fluted on obverse face only, 2⅝". The example in chert was found in Wisconsin. *Collection of and photograph by Duane Treest, Illinois.* $150.00 – 250.00.

Fluted point, gray Onondaga (New York) flint, double flutes on obverse and single flute on reverse. It measures 2¼" and is ex-collections Frush and Jack Hooks. Perry County, Ohio. *Doug Hooks collection.* $1,200.00.

Clovis point, 3⅜", patinated unknown flint. A very fine piece, previous collectors included Dr. Kramer, Dunn, and Jack Hooks. Ohio. *Private collection.* $3,000.00.

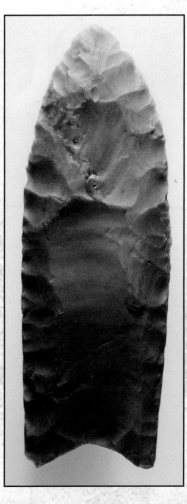

Clovis point, large flute on obverse, 3⅜". High-grade Indiana hornstone (Harrison County flint), the point is ex-collection Shipley. Fairfield County, Ohio. *Joel Embrey collection.* $4,500.00.

Clovis point, multiple obverse flutes, 3⅛". The upper blade irregularities suggest tool use for this piece, made of cream and gray Flint Ridge. Ohio. *Joel Embrey collection.* $800.00.

Clovis point, was in Quinn auction of May 4, 2002, lot 82. The material is a fossiliferous mixed chert and the obverse flute runs for three-quarters of base to tip. The bid amount includes a 10% buyer's premium for this piece, 3" long. It has a Perino COA and is from Ralls County, Missouri. *Rainbow Traders, Illinois.* $1,760.00.

Clovis fluted point, a very fine specimen, auctioned February 9, 2002, in lot 219. The final bid included a 10% buyers' premium. The clovis is thin and measures 1⅜" x 4⁵⁄₁₆". It has a Perino COA and is made of rare Excello flint, black with blue inclusions. This piece is pictured in *Tully's Flint Blades & Projectile Points*, page 23, No. 39. Oregon County, Missouri. *Rainbow Traders, Illinois.* $11,275.00.

Fluted point, Perino COA, 3" long. Very attractive, the material is Carter Cave, which changes from tan flint for the tip and upper blade to translucent orange for the lower blade and base. Fleming County, Kentucky. *Gilbert Cooper collection.* $3,000.00.

Fluted point, ex-collection Wilkins, 3⅛". With a Perino COA, the reverse flute is 1⅛" long. In patinated Upper Mercer, the point came from Ross County, Ohio. *Gilbert Cooper collection.* $1,750.00.

Fluted point, mixed blue Upper Mercer, ex-collection Wertz. The point is 2⁵⁄₁₆" and has a Perino COA. It was found in Scioto County, Ohio. *Gilbert Cooper collection.* $700.00.

Clovis fluted point (right), lot 145, thin for type, white chert and good flute. It is 3⅛" long and was found on the well-known Lincoln Hills Paleo site. (At left is an Early Archaic Hardin.) The winning bid for the Clovis included the 10% buyer's premium, and the point was sold August 23, 2003. The Clovis has a Howard COA. Jersey County, Illinois. *Rainbow Traders, Illinois.* $1,320.00.

Clovis fluted point, exceptional, lot 155, auctioned March 15, 2003, and bid figured with the 10% buyer's premium. It has double COAs, Davis and Perino, and is made of Carter Cave flint. Bath County, Kentucky. *Rainbow Traders, Illinois.* $4,675.00.

Paleo group of points, all auctioned Dec. 7, 2002. Bid values with 10% buyer's premium included. Left to right: Lot 233, Dalton, 3¾", white chert, Pike Co., Illinois. $187.00. Lot 232, Clovis, 1⅜" x 4⅛", broken and glued, from near Memphis, Tennessee. $2,750.00. Lot 234, Dalton, 4⁵⁄₁₆", Pike Co., Illinois. $412.50. *Rainbow Traders, Illinois.*

Clovis point, restored tip, blue Upper Mercer flint with a lighter inclusion. The right ear has been chipped into a graver or cutter tip. Mason County, West Virginia. *Craig Ferrell collection.* Unlisted.

Clovis point, with shaft-scraper edge, 3¾". Striped gray Upper Mercer, this elegant point is ex-collections Barrett and Jack Hooks. Ohio. *Doug Hooks collection.* $2,500.00.

Fluted point, 3⅝", Kanawha black flint with lighter inclusions. This is a very well-made point in all respects, with good size and form. Marion County, Ohio. *Len and Janie Weidner collection.* $1,700.00.

Fluted point, full obverse flute, 2¼". Nicely balanced, this Upper Mercer piece is ex-collection Copeland and was found September 21, 1963. Knox County, Ohio. *Len and Janie Weidner collection.* $900.00.

Fluted point, several shades of blue Upper Mercer, very good lines, size, condition, and workstyle. With a fine overshot flake scar two-fifths of distance from base to tip, it measures 3¾" and came from Delaware County, Ohio. *Len and Janie Weidner collection.* Museum grade.

Fluted point, high-grade Upper Mercer with colors of blue and cream, small lightning line, 3⅝". This is simply one of the better fluted points from the state. Ex-collection Copeland. Knox County, Ohio. *Len and Janie Weidner collection.* Museum grade.

Cumberland-like point, fluted both faces, 2½". The material is glossy Onondaga from New York state, and the artifact was found in Knox County, Ohio. *Doug Hooks collection.* $2,500.00.

Clovis point, lower blade edges ground, both faces fluted, small obverse flute. The example is 2⅝" long and is made of Plum Run flint. Ex-collection Jack Hooks, Lorain County, Ohio. *Doug Hooks collection.* $1,000.00.

Clovis point, two-thirds fluted, with a wide flute, restored tip. The material is Hillsdale or Greenbrier Valley chert, and the point is from a site that will be destroyed by strip mining. Logan County, West Virginia. *Craig Ferrell collection.* Unlisted.

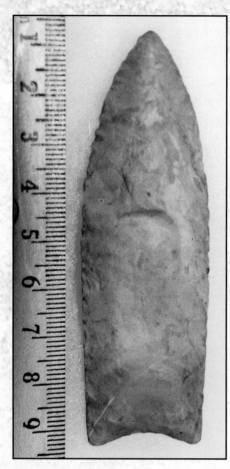

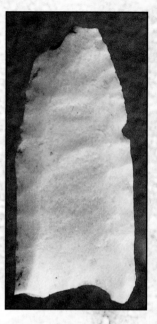

Clovis fluted point, fluted both lower faces, milky Hixton silicified sandstone (quartzite). This example was found by the owner in 1994. Kane County, Illinois. *Collection of and photograph by Duane Treest, Illinois.* $100.00 – 150.00.

Clovis fluted point, restored tip, black Zaleski flint. It is 4⅛" long, from Knox County, Ohio. *Glenn F. Witchey collection.* Unlisted.

Clovis point, classic shape with excellent form, material, and workstyle. It is fluted for three-fifths of obverse length and is in pristine condition. Made of Fort Payne high-grade flint, this is one of the better Clovis examples from the state. It came from near Chapmanville, Logan County, West Virginia. *Craig Ferrell collection.* $3,000.00.

Clovis point, fluted both lower faces, 2⅛". The small side-notches were likely added by a later culture. This point was found by the owner in 1998. Kane County, Illinois. *Collection of and photograph by Duane Treest, Illinois.* $275.00 – 500.00.

Clovis fluted point, 2¹³⁄₁₆", mixed flint of uncertain origin. Lower blade edges are ground, and the baseline has the curious indentation seen on some fluted points. Marion County, Ohio. *Jesse Weber collection; photograph by Norman's Photo, Newcomerstown, Ohio.* $425.00.

Clovis point, Ross County sub-type, mottled glossy flint that is probably Upper Mercer. Lower blade edges are ground on this example, which measures 1¼" x 3¼". Tuscarawas County, Ohio. *Jesse Weber collection; photograph by Norman's Photo, Newcomerstown, Ohio.* $1,000.00.

Fluted point, Upper Mercer flint in several shades, 3" long. The reverse has a 1" flute and lower stem edges are ground. Darke County, Ohio. *Len and Janie Weidner collection.* $1,000.00.

Fluted point, blue Upper Mercer flint, 2³⁄₁₆". Well shaped, it is fluted for about two-thirds of length. Marion County, Ohio. *Len and Janie Weidner collection.* $800.00.

Fluted Cumberland-like point, Upper Mercer mixed blue and gray, 2¼". It is ex-collection Jack Hooks and provenance is unlisted. *Doug Hooks collection.* $1,200.00.

Crowfield point, with multiple obverse flutes, dark Upper Mercer flint. It is 2½", ex-collection Tolliver. Very thin, the point came from Hocking County, Ohio. *Private collection.* $1,000.00.

Paleo point, barbed shoulders, reverse double fluted with main flute to the tip, Indiana hornstone. It is 2¼" long, ex-collection Frush. The point was found in Perry County, Ohio. *Doug Hooks collection.* $1,200.00.

Fluted Clovis point, fluted for two-fifths of length, pointed basal ears. An exceptional artifact in both workstyle and length, it is 4½" long. The Clovis was picked up near Morgantown, Butler County, Kentucky. *Len and Janie Weidner collection.* Museum grade.

Fluted point, translucent creamy Flint Ridge, Perino COA. This point is 3⅞" and has small double flutes on the obverse. Fairfield County, Ohio. *Gilbert Cooper collection.* Museum grade.

Fluted point, with shaft-scraper, 2⅞". The material is translucent milky and dark blue, probably a Flint Ridge variant sometimes seen in the Early Paleo. Broken and glued, this piece has a Perino COA and came from Scioto County, Ohio. *Gilbert Cooper collection.* $500.00.

Paleo fluted points, auctioned May 4, 2002. Values listed reflect a 10% buyers' premium. Left to right: Lot 151, Avon chert, 1⁵⁄₁₆" x 3⅛", Perino COA, Fulton County, Illinois. $1,100.00. Lot 152, 1⅛" x 3¼", strawberry Burlington, Perino COA, Scott County, Missouri. $1,375.00. Lot 153, 1⅛" x 2½", blue quartzite, Berner and Howard COAs, Jackson County, Kentucky. $880.00. *Rainbow Traders, Illinois.*

Clovis point, unknown material that may be creek cobble, 2⅜". With a wide flute for one-half of length, this specimen was found in Delaware County, Ohio. *Len and Janie Weidner collection.* $650.00.

Fluted Clovis point, attractive Flint Ridge material, 1⅜" x 3⁹⁄₁₆". It was auctioned March 15, 2003, and the figure reflects a 10% buyers' premium. The Clovis has a Howard COA and the artifact was found near Columbus, Ohio. *Rainbow Traders, Illinois.* $3,850.00.

Clovis point, 3", well-fluted, white chert, sold at auction August 23, 2003. Bid price included the 10% buyers' premium. Cooper County, Missouri. *Rainbow Traders, Illinois.* $797.50.

Clovis fluted point, sold August 23, 2003, lot 144. Made of translucent dark amber Knife River flint, it is 3⅛" long and has Howard and Amble COAs. The listed value includes a 10% buyers' premium. Southeastern Iowa. *Rainbow Traders, Illinois.* $2,310.00.

Clovis point or blade, large at 4¾" and well fluted, greatly weathered Upper Mercer flint. Ex-collections Walls and Tolliver, it came from along the Ottawa River in Allen County, Ohio. *Doug Hooks collection.* $15,000.00.

Clovis point, fluted both faces, 3½". Ground on the lower edges and made of blue Upper Mercer, it is ex-collections Beer and Jack Hooks. Richland County, Ohio. *Private collection.* $4,000.00.

Fluted point, Flint Ridge patinated multicolor, probably a Ross County type. It is 3⅛" long, ex-collections Dr. Kramer, Beers, and Jack Hooks. Ohio. *Doug Hooks collection.* $3,500.00.

Clovis point, three-fifths flute on obverse, Flint Ridge translucent blue-gray. The point is 3¼" long and is ex-collections Norm Dunn and Jack Hooks. Ohio. *Doug Hooks collection.* $2,500.00.

Clovis point, highly patinated Flint Ridge, 3" long. The obverse flute is wide and deep, and the point is ex-collections Homer Frush and Jack Hooks. Probably Perry County, Ohio. *Doug Hooks collection.* $2,000.00.

Clovis fluted point, lot 57 at the August 24, 2002 auction, once in the Nickel and Perino collections. The listed value reflects a 10% buyers' premium for this Early Paleo piece, 2¾" long. Osage County, Missouri. *Rainbow Traders, Illinois.* $825.00.

Clovis fluted point, a large and well-made example, auctioned December 7, 2002, lot 131-A. The listed figure reflects the added 10% buyers' premium. Made of Fort Payne chert, it is 1³⁄₁₆" x 4⁵⁄₁₆" and has a Perino COA. It was found near Mammoth Cave, Kentucky. *Rainbow Traders, Illinois.* $7,040.00.

Fluted Clovis point, auction date August 24, 2002, lot 61-A. Value listed includes 10% buyers' premium. This point is 1" x 3" and has Davis and Howard COAs. It is made of Carter Cave material, from Kentucky. *Rainbow Traders, Illinois.* $2,475.00.

Fluted point, high-grade mixed Upper Mercer, 3¾". The obverse narrow flute is 2¼" long. Ex-collection Wertz, it has a Perino COA. Scioto County, Ohio. *Gilbert Cooper collection.* Museum grade.

Fluted point, translucent pale tan with cream and blue Flint Ridge, 3¼". The point is ex-collection Wilkins and has a Perino COA. Brown County, Indiana. *Gilbert Cooper collection.* $1,500.00.

Fluted point, red to maroon unknown flint, 2⅝". The faces have equal flutes and the point has a Perino COA. It is from the Mt. Orab area, Brown County, Ohio. *Gilbert Cooper collection.* $1,000.00.

Fluted point, tapered lower blade, 3⅛". It has a Perino COA and the obverse flute is two-fifths of point length. This is a very well-made point, from Pickaway County, Ohio. *Gilbert Cooper collection.* Museum grade.

Fluted point, differing patinations on the faces, 4⁷⁄₁₆". It is made of Fort Payne chert and has a Perino COA. This piece was on the cover of the Wilkins sales catalog, and was found in Mercer County, Ohio. *Gilbert Cooper collection.* $4,000.00.

Ross County fluted Clovis point, Kentucky pale blue-gray flint. Nicely fluted, it is 3½" and ex-collection Rivers Anderson. The point was found southeast of Hopkinsville, Kentucky. *Len and Janie Weidner collection.* $6,500.00.

Fluted point, glossy high-grade Burlington flint, 3⅛" long. Well-chipped and symmetrical, this point was found in Callaway County, Missouri. *Len and Janie Weidner collection.* $1,200.00.

Fluted point, patinated Flint Ridge, 2½". It was found in the Baltimore area, Fairfield County, Ohio. *Len and Janie Weidner collection.* $550.00.

Fluted point, pale blue Upper Mercer with cream, tan, pink, and maroon, 3⅝". It is fluted for over one-half of the obverse. Licking County, Ohio. *Len and Janie Weidner collection.* Museum grade.

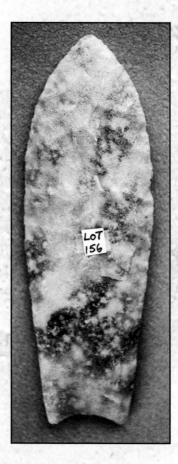

Clovis point, well-fluted, translucent flint, 1¼" long. Auctioned August 24, 2002, the bid amount included a 10% buyers' premium. Formerly in the Perino collection, this Clovis (lot 299) was found in Texas. *Rainbow Traders, Illinois.* $660.00.

Clovis point, lot 156, large and fine, sold May 24, 2003. The bid amount included a 10% buyers' premium. The point measures 1¹¹⁄₁₆" x 5¹⁄₁₆" and is made of Tallahatta Quartzite. The Clovis has Perino and Howard COAs and is from the Conecuh River area, Escambia County, Alabama. *Rainbow Traders, Illinois.* $6,600.00.

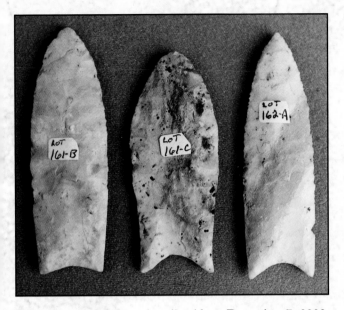

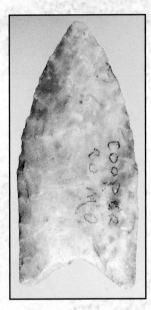

Clovis points, left to right, all sold on December 7, 2002, and each with 10% buyers' premium added. All have Motley COAs. Clovis, lot 161-B, 1¹⁄₁₆" x 3½", light-colored flint, Fulton County, Illinois. $2,035.00. Clovis, lot 161-C, 1⁵⁄₁₆" x 3⅛", flint in white, blue, gray, and tan (Avon?), Fulton County, Illinois. $2,475.00. Clovis, lot 162-A, tip rechipped, 3½" long, Union County, Illinois. $462.00. *Rainbow Traders, Illinois.*

Fluted point, high-grade translucent Upper Mercer in half a dozen shades, 3½". This extraordinary piece came from Pickaway County, Ohio. *Len and Janie Weidner collection.* Museum grade.

Fluted point, possibly Crescent Quarry flint, 2½". Resharpened size, it was found in Cooper County, Missouri. *Len and Janie Weidner collection.* $550.00.

Clovis point, auction of February 9, 2002 and lot 106, 4" long. The listed value reflects a 10% buyers' premium for this piece, which has an attractive color pattern and a Motley COA. The Clovis came from Warren County, Missouri. *Rainbow Traders, Illinois.* $3,410.00.

Barber Clovis point, fluted, auction date was December 1, 2001, figure reflects the 10% buyers' premium. Lot 141. This slender point is 2¾" long. It is made of Edwards Plateau flint and has a Howard COA. Central Texas. *Rainbow Traders, Illinois.* $605.00.

Clovis point, fluted, 2½" long. The material is cream and caramel with dark specks, possibly a Flint Ridge variety. This point came from Perry County, Ohio. *Len and Janie Weidner collection.* $700.00.

23

Clovis fluted point, lot 84, sale date May 4, 2002, bid reflected a 10% buyers' premium. The artifact, with a Perino COA, is 2¼" long and has a broad, short flute. Northern Illinois. *Rainbow Traders, Illinois.* $440.00.

Redstone point, fluted to tip on obverse, 2⅝". This point was found near mastodon bones, but the point was not with the bones. Ex-collection Hiles, it is from near Hodgenville, Larue County, Kentucky. *Jim Miller collection.* $3,500.00.

Fluted point, mottled blue Upper Mercer, 3⅝" long. It is ex-collection Vietzen and was pictured in *Indians of the Lake Erie Basin*, page 241. It was found near Elyria, Lorain County, Ohio. *Jim Miller collection.* $4,000.00.

Lanceolate point or blade, pale blue and milky Flint Ridge, 4¾" long. It has a needle tip and was found in Fairfield County, Ohio. *Len and Janie Weidner collection.* $850.00.

Clovis point, Indiana Green flint in green and white, 1⅛" x 2⅞". It has a Davis COA and came from Indiana. *Keith and Rhonda Dodge collection, Michigan.* $900.00.

Clovis point, unidentified light brown flint, 1" x 3½". The Clovis has a Davis COA and was picked up in Michigan. *Keith and Rhonda Dodge collection, Michigan.* $1,200.00.

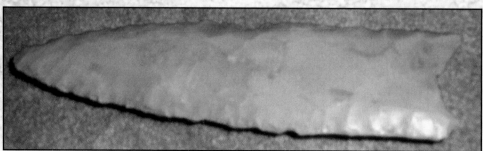

Clovis point, resharpened size, ex-collections Cunningham, Townsend, and Spaulding. The material is Bayport chert and the point measures 1⅛" x 2½". With a Davis COA, it is from Berrien County, Michigan. *Keith and Rhonda Dodge collection, Michigan.* $800.00.

Point or blade, mottled and highly translucent amber Carter Cave flint, 2¾". The obverse is fluted for about two-fifths of length and there is a narrow tip flute as well. This artifact was picked up in Hocking County, Ohio. *Len and Janie Weidner collection.* $700.00.

Redstone-like fluted point, dark high-grade flint, 2⅞" long. Basal edges on this example are heavily ground. The point was found in Kentucky. *Jim Miller collection.* $1,000.00.

Fluted point, broad obverse flute, slightly flared base corners, 3¾". It is made of dark blue Upper Mercer and was pictured in the Spring 1973 *Ohio Archaeologist.* The point was found near Loveland, probably Clermont County, Ohio. *Jim Miller collection.* $3,000.00.

Clovis point, resharpened size, 1" x 1⅞". This point has a Davis COA and is made of creamy Boyle chert. Kentucky. *Keith and Rhonda Dodge collection, Michigan.* $500.00.

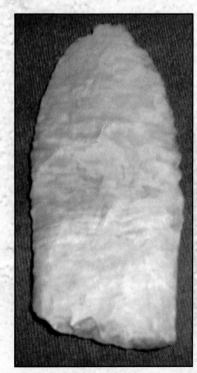

Ross County Clovis point, brown Dover chert, 1³⁄₁₆" x 2¾". With a Davis COA, it came from Trigg County, Kentucky. *Keith and Rhonda Dodge collection, Michigan.* $400.00.

Clovis point, short basal flute, glossy yellow jasper. This Clovis is ⅞" x 3⅛" and was found in Cumberland County, Pennsylvania. *Collection of and photograph by H. B. Greene II, Florida.* $700.00.

Fluted point, 5¼", mixed blue unknown flint. A very superior piece, it has a Perino COA and was found in the Ripley area, Brown County, Ohio. *Gilbert Cooper collection.* Museum grade.

Clovis point, typical short flute on obverse, multicolored material that may be petrified wood. It is 3⅝" long and was obtained by the owner's father in the Southwest. *Collection of and photograph by H. B. Greene II, Florida.* Museum grade.

Clovis point, reverse, 3⅝" x ¾", mixed glossy petrified wood, fluted for nearly three-quarters of length. This exceptional piece was acquired by the owner's father in the early 1940s. U.S. Southwest. *Collection of and photograph by H. B. Greene II, Florida.* Museum grade.

Fluted point, unknown striped golden tan and brown material that could be patinated Flint Ridge, 3⅞". This exceptional artifact is ex-collection Copeland. Licking County, Ohio. *Len and Janie Weidner collection.* Museum grade.

Clovis point, tan chert, wide and with narrow flute. It is made of quality material and is 1" x 3⅝" long. There is basal side grinding for a short distance up from the basal tips. Provenance unknown. *Collection of and photograph by H. B. Greene II, Florida.* $900.00.

Clovis point, translucent cream and pale gray flint, 3⅛". With a shaft-scraper worked in the upper right edge, it is fluted on both faces and the reverse flute is 1¾" long. Ex-collection Norbert Bingman, Southeastern Illinois. *Private collection.* Unlisted.

Clovis fluted point, resharpened size in Flint Ridge gray and red. It is 1" x 1⅞" and has about the same flute length on both faces. With a Davis COA, it is ex-collection Vietzen (1998 auction) from northern Ohio. *Gregory D. Brown collection, West Virginia.* $375.00.

Fluted point, Clovis, large and shallow flute on obverse base, 2⅝". Of mixed Upper Mercer flint, it was found in Ohio. *Mike Barron collection, Ohio.* $400.00.

Clovis fluted point, Sonora flint, found in the 1950s. Two-thirds fluted on the obverse, this large and fine Clovis is 1⁷⁄₁₆" x 4⁹⁄₁₆". It came from Cumberland County, Kentucky. *Private collection, Kentucky.* Museum grade.

Clovis fluted point, found in the 1950s in a gravel pit. This large masterpiece from Early Paleo times is beautifully chipped and fluted. It measures ¹⁵⁄₁₆" x 4¹¹⁄₁₆" and has multiple COAs. New Mexico. *Private collection, Kentucky.* Museum grade.

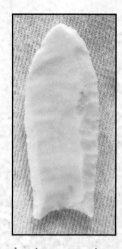

Clovis point, thin, well made, and fluted, 2⅝". High-grade Burlington was used for this piece, found in the Western Bluff area of Jersey County, Illinois. *Gregory L. Perdun collection, Illinois.* $2,600.00.

Clovis point, large obverse flute, blue Upper Mercer flint. This impressive point is 3⅝" and has a long ownership history. Ex-collections Hills, Townsend, and Jack Hooks, Delaware County, Ohio. *Private collection.* $4,000.00.

Clovis point, creamy Burlington that contains a scattering of dark specks, 2⁷⁄₁₆". The point was found in the Western Bluff area, Jersey County, Illinois. *Gregory L. Perdun collection, Illinois.* $1,400.00.

Fluted point, a very interesting piece. Though it resembles a Folsom, it was actually made from a Clovis flute spall. It is 1¹³⁄₁₆", thin, creamy Burlington, and the tip has been repointed in modern times. The point was found in the Western Bluff area, Jersey County, Illinois. *Gregory L. Perdun collection, Illinois.* Unlisted.

Fluted point, Cumberland family with full flute on obverse, 3" long. Flint Ridge material was used for this piece, translucent pale blue and cream. It is ex-collection Copeland and came from Harrison County, Kentucky. *Len and Janie Weidner collection.* Museum grade.

Fluted point, very attractive and unusual Indiana hornstone (Harrison County flint) colored in two shades of gray plus milky gray. It is 3⁵⁄₁₆" and came from Christian County, Kentucky. *Len and Janie Weidner collection.* $1,350.00.

Clovis point/tool, obverse, 1⅛" x 3⁵⁄₁₆", ⁵⁄₁₆" thick. It is made of swirled high-grade Harrison County flint (Indiana hornstone). The tip was squared in prehistoric times and beveled on one face. This piece was found by the owner in 1973. Clark County, Indiana. *Richard B. Lyons collection, Indiana.* Unlisted.

Clovis point/tool, reverse, showing the beveled tip. The Clovis has a strong basal flute on the obverse and the tip (as shown) was also fluted along one side of the face. At 3⁵⁄₁₆", this is a thin and well-chipped Clovis. Clark County, Indiana. *Richard B. Lyons collection, Indiana.* Unlisted.

Clovis point, pale blue-gray chert, 2½". This early piece is ex-collection Norbert Bingman, from southeastern Illinois. *Private collection.* $200.00.

Clovis point, wide and shallow flute on obverse, 2⅜". Translucent cream and brownish-orange flint, it is ex-collection Norbert Bingman. Southeastern Illinois. *Private collection.* Unlisted.

Ross County type fluted point, patinated Flint Ridge, 3¾". As is typical, the point is wider for length than most fluted points. Ross County, Ohio. *Len and Janie Weidner collection.* Museum grade.

Clovis point, Fern Glen flint, 2⅛". The example is in resharpened length and the point has a partial tip flute. Well-made, it came from the Western Bluff area of Jersey County, Illinois. *Gregory L. Perdun collection, Illinois.* $950.00.

Clovis point, Burlington chert with mineral deposits, 2" long. Triangular-shaped, it came from the Western Bluff area of Jersey County, Illinois. *Gregory L. Perdun collection.* $650.00 – 800.00.

Fluted point, unknown material in a light shade of gray, 1¾". It was found in the Western Bluff area, Jersey County, Illinois. *Gregory L. Perdun collection, Illinois.* $550.00 – 650.00.

Clovis point, double flutes on obverse, 2½" long. Made of light-colored Burlington, the owner obtained the point from the finder, R. Copher, in 1996. Adams County, Illinois. *Fred Smith collection, Illinois.* $300.00 – 400.00.

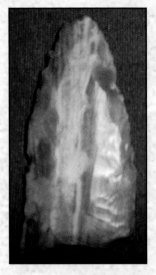

Redstone point, Tyrone gray and tan flint, 1" x 2⅛". With a Davis COA, this triangular form was found in Kentucky. *Keith and Rhonda Dodge collection, Michigan.* $400.00.

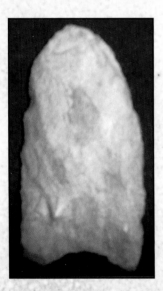

Clovis point, Indian Green flint, 1⅛" x 2⅛". Pictured in *Ohio Flint Types*, it has a Davis COA. Mercer County, Ohio. *Keith and Rhonda Dodge collection, Michigan.* $300.00.

Fluted point, translucent Carter Cave flint, double-fluting on obverse face. It is fluted nearly to the tip on both faces and is 1⅞" long. This point is thin and well made, and Folsom-like. Ex-collection Norbert Bingman, southeastern Illinois. *Private collection.* Unlisted.

Fluted Clovis, 80mm x 29mm, with one or two minor tip resharpenings. It has a Perino COA and is ex-collection Bakutis. Burlington in cream and pale gray, this very superior point was found in Pike County, Illinois. *Mike Trekell collection, Minnesota.* $2,500.00 – 3,000.00.

Clovis point, Early Paleo, near-purple Sonora flint. This piece, with an exceptionally long obverse flute, is 1¹⁄₁₆" x 3⁵⁄₁₆". The Clovis was found in Hardin County, Kentucky. *George and Elizabeth Williamson collection, Kentucky; David Davis photograph.* Unlisted.

Fluted point, possibly a Ross County type, 3¾". In creamy Flint Ridge, the base is translucent. This is a very fine point, well fluted, ex-collections Copeland, Weidner, and Coulter. Pickaway County, Ohio. *Private collection.* Museum grade.

Fluted point, high-grade Upper Mercer in four colors, 4⅜" long. It was picked up near a sawmill, where logging equipment exposed the point on the side of a rut. One of the finest points from the state, it is ex-collection Fender and was found near Chili, Coshocton County, Ohio. *Allen Selders collection.* Museum grade.

Clovis fluted point, 1⅜", glossy brown chert, wide basal flute. It is pictured in *Prehistoric American 2002*, page 47, and was found in Montgomery County, Kentucky. *Jeff Schumacher collection, Kentucky.* $125.00 – 150.00.

St. Louis Clovis point, black flint, Davis COA. The size is 1¹¹⁄₁₆" x 3" and the point came from Illinois. *Keith and Rhonda Dodge collection, Michigan.* $500.00.

Clovis point, 3" long, Tyrone flint. Found by S. Rogers, it has a Davis COA. The flute is over 2" long and the Early Paleo piece came from Clark County, Kentucky. *Jeff Schumacher collection, Kentucky.* $500.00 – 600.00.

Clovis point, long obverse flute, 4¼". Creamy Burlington was used for this exceptional Clovis, found in McDonough County, Illinois. *Dale and Betty Roberts collection, Iowa.* $2,500.00.

Fluted Clovis point, obverse, 95mm x 38mm, with several resharpenings. This big point or blade is thin for size and is well fluted on both faces. It has a Perino COA. Greenup County, Kentucky. *Mike Trekell collection, Minnesota.* $4,000.00.

Fluted point reverse, 95mm x 38mm. With a Perino COA, this is an exceptional point in fluting and width. Made of Carter Cave flint in several shades, it is from Greenup County, Kentucky. *Mike Trekell collection, Minnesota.* $4,000.00.

Clovis point, carefully chipped, thin and fluted. It is 1" x 2½" and basal edges are ground. The Clovis is made of Burlington and was a personal find of the owner. St. Louis County, Missouri. *Bob Rampani collection, Missouri.* Museum quality.

Clovis point, 2⁵⁄₁₆". Colorful translucent material that may be Alibates from Texas. Found by J. Porter, the flute is about two-thirds of obverse face and the ears are barbed. Fulton County, Illinois. *Dale and Betty Roberts collection, Iowa.* $2,000.00.

Clovis point, Ross County fluted type, 1¼" x 4½". It is made of light gray chert. This exceptional point was a creek find by the owner in 1998. St. Louis County, Missouri. *Lee Holmes collection, Missouri.* Museum grade.

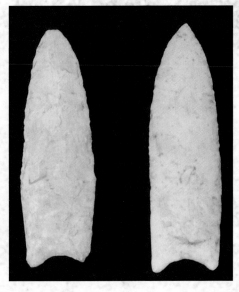

Clovis points, light-colored chert. Left, Burlington, 1⅛" x 2⅜", found in the 1940s in St. Louis County, Missouri. $350.00. Right, Burlington, ⅞" x 2⅛", found in 1984, Pike County, Illinois. $300.00. *Bob Rampani collection, Missouri.*

Clovis points, quite similar in size and fluted on both faces, both made of Burlington chert and from Missouri. Left, 1" x 3", Pike County. $250.00. Right, 1" x 3⅛", from Ralls County. $450.00. *Bob Rampani collection, Missouri.*

Clovis point, high-grade glossy cream chert, 1¹⁄₁₆" x 3¹⁄₁₆". It is fluted on both lower faces, and basal areas are ground. It is ex-collection Hopple and came from Montgomery County, Missouri. *Bob Rampani collection, Missouri.* $1,200.00.

Clovis point, fluted on both faces, glossy high-grade material. It is 1⅛" x 2½" and was found on a farm by Lloyd Rose. St. Louis County, Missouri. *Bob Rampani collection, Missouri.* $500.00.

Clovis point, gray and light cream unknown flint, 2¾". According to the previous owner, it was found by a relative on a small hillside site that also produced two rectangular Paleo blades. Fairfield County, Ohio. *Lar Hothem collection.* $550.00.

Ross County type fluted point, with wide and flat facial chipping scars, 3" long. Double-fluted at the base, the material is black semiglossy flint. This piece was found in northern Ohio. *Lar Hothem collection.* $750.00.

Clovis point, fluted on obverse, Burlington chert, ¾" x 2¼". The point was found near Amazonia, Andrew County, Missouri. *Mike George collection, Missouri; Terry Price photograph.* $225.00.

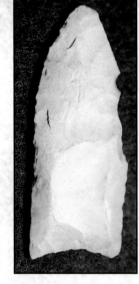

Clovis point, obverse flute, brown flint, ¾" x 2". With a possible shaft-scraper on the upper right edge, it was found near Forbes, Holt County, Missouri. *Mike George collection, Missouri; Terry Price photograph.* $200.00.

Clovis fluted point, intermingled brown and dark gray flint, wide basal flute. This is a top piece and one of the better Clovis points to come from the state. Stewart County, Tennessee. *Rodney M. Peck collection, North Carolina.* Museum grade.

Clovis point, well-shaped and artistic outline, Coshocton (Upper Mercer) mixed light-colored flint. Found in 1989, this superior point came from Brown County, Ohio. *Rodney M. Peck collection, North Carolina.* $6,000.00.

Fluted point, pale blue Upper Mercer with cream, 3¼". It is fluted for about two-fifths of obverse length and is ex-collection Copeland. This very superior point came from Perry County, Ohio. *Len and Janie Weidner collection.* Museum grade.

Ross County type fluted Clovis point, brown material that is probably Delaware County flint, ex-collection Dr. Copeland. It is sketched in *Ohio Flint Types,* page 5, and was found in Delaware County, Ohio. *Rodney M. Peck collection, North Carolina.* $2,500.00.

34

Barnes point, white Burlington, triangular shape, ¹¹/₁₆" x 1½". The Barnes has a Davis COA and was found in Illinois. *Keith and Rhonda Dodge collection, Michigan.* $450.00.

Clovis point, large and uniform obverse flute, 1" x 3⅜". Glossy cream Burlington chert was used for this fine point, which has a Davis COA. Illinois. *Keith and Rhonda Dodge collection, Michigan.* $3,000.00.

Clovis point, high-quality light Burlington chert, finely made and in top condition. This Early Paleo point is 3⅜" long and was found in the Westen Bluff area of Jersey County, Illinois. *Gregory L. Perdun collection, Illinois.* $5,500.00+.

Clovis point, creamy high-grade Burlington, 3³/₁₆". Even though this fluted point has minor tip damage, it is a fine piece. Jersey County, Illinois. *Gregory L. Perdun collection, Illinois.* $2,200.00.

Clovis point, brown glossy Harrodsburg chert, 1" x 2¹¹/₁₆". This Clovis has a Davis COA and was found in Tennessee. *Keith and Rhonda Dodge collection, Michigan.* $1,500.00.

Fluted point, thin, 3⅜". It is fluted for about two-fifths length on the obverse and for 1¼" on the reverse. This slender point is made of unknown gray and mauve flint, and is so-described in *Survey of Ohio Fluted Points No. 9*, July 1963. Ex-collection Hogue, it came from Licking County, Ohio. *Lar Hothem collection.* Museum grade.

35

Clovis point, Fort Payne tan chert, 1⅛" x 2¹⁵⁄₁₆". This Clovis has a Davis COA and was found in Tennessee. *Keith and Rhonda Dodge collection, Michigan.* $750.00.

Fluted points, once in the Kramer collection and now in the Gilcrease Museum. Note the range of materials and styles in these fine artifacts. *Photo courtesy Jan Sorgenfrei, Old Barn Auction.*

Clovis point, light and shallow obverse fluting, a large and well-chipped artifact. It is made of gray and white flint and measures 1¼" x 3¾". Provenance unknown. *Collection of and photograph by H. B. Greene II, Florida.* $900.00.

Fluted point, gray Harrison County flint, slight expansion of base corners. It measures 2⅛" and is ex-collection Norbert Bingman. Southeastern Illinois. *Private collection.* $150.00.

Clovis point, 2½", Kentucky black flint. This sturdy example is ex-collection Rice and has a Davis COA. Montgomery County, Kentucky. *Jeff Schumacher collection, Kentucky.* $400.00 – 475.00.

Clovis point, nicely fluted, resharpened size, brownish-gray chert. This piece is 1" x 1⅞" and came from Yellow Breeches Creek, Cumberland County, Pennsylvania. *Collection of and photograph by H. B. Greene II, Florida.* $100.00.

Clovis point, half-length flute, point 2¾". In milky and light tan Burlington, it came from near Biggsville, Henderson County, Illinois. *Dale and Betty Roberts collection, Iowa.* $450.00.

Clovis point, wide obverse flute, point 3⅛". It is made of creek-stained Burlington and was found by J. Baker. An excellent fluted point, it is from Davis County, Iowa. *Dale and Betty Roberts collection, Iowa.* $2,250.00.

Clovis point, fluted, dark green chert, ⅞" x 2⅛". The material appears weathered and the point has been resharpened. Haywood County, North Carolina. *Collection of and photograph by H. B. Greene II, Florida.* $175.00.

Clovis point, resharpened size, ⅞" x 1¾". Gray glossy flint was used for this artifact, found near Marion, Virginia. *Collection of and photograph by H. B. Greene II, Florida.* $300.00.

Fluted point, glossy cream Flint Ridge with blue, 2¹⁄₁₆". In resharpened size, the point was found in Pickaway County, Ohio. *Len and Janie Weidner collection.* $450.00.

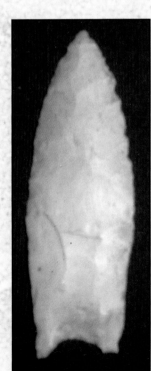

Barnes point, fluted on obverse, cream Burlington chert, ¾" x 2⅜". This point has a Davis COA and was found in Missouri. *Keith and Rhonda Dodge collection, Michigan.* $800.00.

Clovis point, very excurvate edges, brown and tan jasper. This is a very superior point in all aspects, and it came from Prince George County, Virginia. *Rodney M. Peck collection, North Carolina.* Museum grade.

37

Fluted point, high-grade streaked Upper Mercer, 4" long. Flute for two-fifths of obverse length, it has a ¾" flute on the reverse. Ex-collection Keller, the point was found in Clay Township, Knox County, Ohio. *Lar Hothem collection.* Museum grade.

Clovis point, rounded tip, brown jasper with light-colored inclusions. This fine example came from Adams Coutny, Illinois. *Rodney M. Peck collection, North Carolina.* $6,000.00.

Fluted point, fossil coral, heavily patinated, 3¼". This top example is fluted for two-thirds of obverse length, and is well chipped in a scarce material. Hillsborough County, Florida. *Len and Janie Weidner collection.* Museum grade.

Fluted point, 3" long, possibly patinated Carter Cave flint in caramel and tan. This excellent point was found in Highland County, Ohio. *Len and Janie Weidner collection.* $1,200.00.

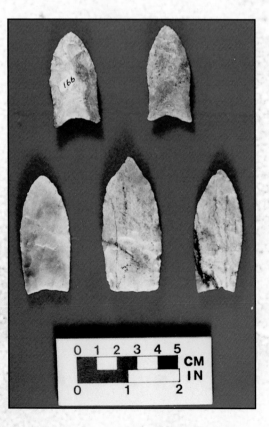

Clovis points, Cattail Creek chalcedony. All five are from a major fluted point site in Dinwiddie County, Virginia. *Rodney M. Peck collection, North Carolina.* Each, $1,000.00.

Clovis point, gray and tan hornstone, 1¼" x 2¾". It has a Davis COA and was found in Kentucky. *Keith and Rhonda Dodge collection, Michigan.* $350.00.

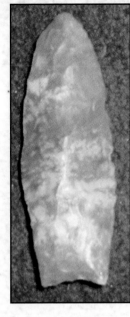

Clovis, high-grade white Burlington with darker inclusions, 1¹⁄₁₆" x 2½". This piece has a Davis COA and came from Stoddard County, Missouri. *Keith and Rhonda Dodge collection, Michigan.* $750.00.

Redstone point, large flute, Tyrone gray-striped chert, 1³⁄₁₆" x 3⅛". This piece has a Davis COA and was found in Tennessee. *Keith and Rhonda Dodge collection, Michigan.* $550.00.

Clovis point, Fort Payne gray and white chert, ¹⁵⁄₁₆" x 2⁹⁄₁₆". The Early Paleo point has a Davis COA and came from Casey County, Kentucky. *Keith and Rhonda Dodge collection, Michigan.* $850.00.

Clovis point, glossy gray hornstone, 1" x 3¼". The obverse face is double-fluted and the point has a Davis COA. Casey County, Kentucky. *Keith and Rhonda Dodge collection, Michigan.* $950.00.

Fluted point, dark blue Upper Mercer, obverse flute over half of point length, 2⅝". This piece has a Perino COA and was found in Ohio. *Gilbert Cooper collection.* $1,500.00.

Fluted point, light tan glossy Carter Cave (Paoli) flint, 3¹⁄₁₆". The point is ex-collection Wertz and there is a Perino COA. Point Pleasant, West Virginia. *Gilbert Cooper collection.* $1,500.00.

Fluted point, flared basal ears, 3" long. Dark blue Upper Mercer, the obverse has three flutes. It is ex-collection Wilkins and has a Perino COA. Warren County, Ohio. *Gilbert Cooper collection.* $1,800.00.

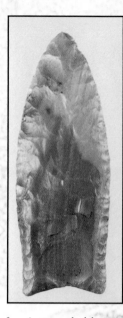

Clovis preform (left) and Clovis point. The example on left is made of Onondaga chert and the one on the right of brown Pennsylvania jasper. Both are from a well-known Paleo site in Dauphin County, Pennsylvania. Left, preform, $20.00. Right, Clovis, $800.00. *Rodney M. Peck collection, North Carolina.*

Clovis points. The materials are jasper, silicified shale, agate, and crystal quartz. All are very superior examples and from North Carolina. *Rodney M. Peck collection, North Carolina.* Each, $500.00 – museum grade.

Fluted point, probably patinated Carter Cave, 3¹⁄₁₆". It is very symmetrical, in high-grade glossy material, and it has a Perino COA. Fleming County, Kentucky. *Gilbert Cooper collection.* $2,000.00.

Fluted point, blue Upper Mercer flint, 3⅜" long. This large point was found in Bartholomew County, Indiana. *Frank Meyer collection.* $1,200.00.

Fluted point, 4¾", reverse flute 2" long. Probably found in 1961, it is ex-collection Copeland and has a Perino COA. The material is Delaware County or hornstone. Ross County, Ohio. *Gilbert Cooper collection.* Museum grade.

Fluted point, dark patinated Upper Mercer, 4" long. Slender for length, it came from Ross County, Ohio. *Frank Meyer collection.* $600.00.

Fluted point or blade, Kentucky or Indiana hornstone, 2½". The obverse has multiple flutes, the longest of which is two-thirds point length. Kent County, Michigan. *Frank Meyer collection.* Unlisted.

Paleo points, various grades of chert and flint. Top right example, 1³⁄₁₆" x 3⅜", origins indicated on frame. Top left is a Cumberland, while the others are Clovis and Clovis related. Top left Cumberland, $3,500.00; top center Clovis, $2,500.00; top right Clovis, $3,500.00; bottom center Clovis, $500.00; bases, $30.00. and $75.00 (largest); fragments, $5.00. Bottom center and bottom right are in Peck's North Carolina fluted point survey as numbers 46 and 75, respectively. *Collection of and photograph by Gary Henry, North Carolina.*

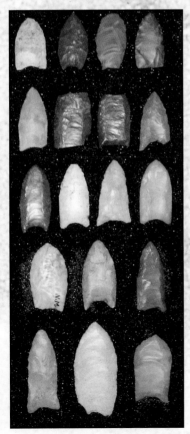

Fluted points, Western U.S., made of regional flint, chert, jasper, and agate. (Some examples are pictured elsewhere in this book). Scale, Folsom point, second row from bottom on left, 1⅝". *John and Susan Mellyn collection, Texas.* Unlisted.

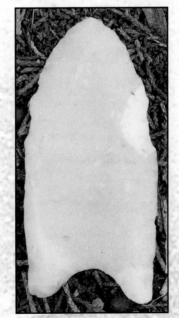

Clovis point, white flint, probably resharpened size, 2⅜". It was found in Henderson County, Kentucky. *John and Susan Mellyn collection, Texas.* $600.00.

Clovis point, barbed shoulders, white patinated flint with a few darker inclusions. It is 2½" and came from Bexar County, Texas. *John and Susan Mellyn collection, Texas.* $800.00.

Early trianglular point, 1½" long, made of petrifed palmwood. The point came from Wilson County, Texas. *John and Susan Mellyn collection, Texas.* $150.00.

Eastern fluted Clovis point, 2¼", weathered silicified shale. With a well-centered flute on the obverse face, it was found in McDowell County, North Carolina. *Collection of and photograph by Ron Harris, North Carolina.* $700.00.

Eastern fluted Clovis point, 2" long, made of clear crystal quartz, which is a native North Carolina material. This rare piece was found in the New River Basin area of Ashe County, North Carolina. *Collection of and photograph by Ron Harris, North Carolina.* $1,200.00.

Eastern fluted Clovis point, high-grade light green Rhyolite, 2⅞". This well-chipped point is nicely fluted and came from Surry County, North Carolina. *Collection of and photograph by Ron Harris, North Carolina.* $1,000.00.

Crowfield point, 2⅞", gray Indiana hornstone (Harrison County flint). Ex-collection Smith, the upper right edge has a meandering burin facet. Eastern Midwest. *Frank Meyer collection.* Unlisted.

Clovis point, resharpened, white flint, heavily ground baseline and lower side edges, 2" long. Central Texas. *John and Susan Mellyn collection, Texas.* $600.00.

Eastern fluted Clovis point, 1½", green rhyolite. This resharpened example came from Randolph County, North Carolina. *Collection of and photograph by Ron Harris, North Carolina.* $200.00.

Clovis point, damaged tip, 4" long. The obverse flute is 2¾", and the material is high-quality mottled gray and blue Upper Mercer. Ex-collection Lewis, the point came from Hocking County, Ohio. *Frank Meyer collection.* Unlisted.

Eastern Clovis point, unknown maroon chert, obverse with wide and short flute. This example was picked up in Lycoming County, Pennsylvania. *Fogelman collection.* $2,000.00.

Crowfield point, reverse with multiple flutes, 2⅜". Near-black Upper Mercer flint was used for this point, found in Auglaize County, Ohio. *Frank Meyer collection.* Unlisted.

Fluted point, light gray hornstone, ex-collections Kramer and Saunders. Edge indentations suggest knife use for this piece, 2⅜" long. Franklin County, Ohio. *Frank Meyer collection.* Unlisted.

Clovis fluted knife, St. Louis type, small base because of the tapered lower blade, light blue chert. It was found in Lycoming County, Pennsylvania. *Fogelman collection.* $1,400.00.

Holcomb type fluted point, restored tip, Upper Mercer flint from eastern Ohio. It was found in the Ohio-Pennsylvania border area. *Fogelman collection.* Unlisted.

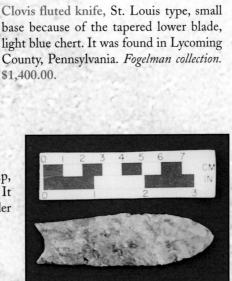

Redstone point, fluted nearly to tip, typical widest-at-base form, black chert. The example was found in Huntington County, Pennsylvania. *Fogelman collection.* $1,250.00.

Clovis point, narrow obverse flute, ground basal edges. It is 1¼" x 3¼" and is made of grayish-brown glossy chert. The Clovis was found in eastern Box Elder County, northern Utah. *Mark Stuart collection, Utah.* $450.00.

Clovis point, gray sugar quartzite, ⅞" x 2⅛". This piece is ex-collection Lyerla and was found by F. Boles ca. 1950. Northwestern Akansas. *Tom Fouts collection, Kansas.* $1,000.00.

Clovis point or blade, light-colored flint or chert, ex-collection Lyerla. This big and well-made Clovis is 1⅜" x 4¾" and was found after the 1993 flood. Cape Girardeau County, Missouri. *Tom Fouts collection, Kansas.* $2,500.00.

Clovis point, crisply fluted, 1¼" x 3¹⁵⁄₁₆", Boyle chert. It was found in 1999 by the owner and has a Davis COA. Madison County, Kentucky. *John Gibson collection, Kentucky; Tom Davis photograph.* $2,500.00.

Ross County type eastern fluted point, 3¾", highly weathered silicified shale. Fluted, this Early Paleo piece is from Johnston County, North Carolina. *Collection of and photograph by Ron Harris, North Carolina.* $850.00.

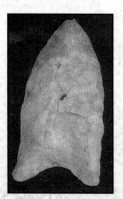

Clovis point, Early Paleo, 1¾". Has excellent patina; provenance is unlisted. *Jeff Anderson collection, Indiana.* $300.00.

Clovis point, good lines and patina, 1¾". Provenance is unlisted. *Jeff Anderson collection, Indiana.* $400.00.

Eastern Fluted point, 4", weathered silicified shale. With slight restoration, this piece is ex-collection Mabe and came from Randolph County, North Carolina. *Collection of and photograph by Ron Harris, North Carolina.* $850.00.

Crowfield point, fluted, Late Paleo, 2¼" long. Very thin, it has a small tip break and pointed basal corners. Ex-collection Swartz, it is from northcentral Ohio. *Jesse Weber collection; photograph by Norman's Photo, Newcomerstown, Ohio.* $450.00.

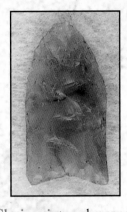

Clovis point, resharpened or retipped size, 1⅝". It is made of highly translucent vaseline Flint Ridge, a near-gem material. The owner purchased this point at an estate sale in 2000. Chandlersville area, Muskingum County, Ohio. *Jesse Weber collection; photograph by Norman's Photo, Newcomerstown, Ohio.* $800.00.

Fluted point, 2¾", ex-collection Johnston. It is made of yellow-gray patinated flint and came from Champaign County, Ohio. *Frank Meyer collection.* $300.00.

Fluted point, blue Upper Mercer, ex-collection Walls. The point is 2½", from Putnam County, Ohio. *Frank Meyer collection.* $500.00.

Fluted point, Carter Cave (Kentucky) striated flint in several colors, 2¾". This well-made and streamlined point was picked up in Hancock County, Ohio. *Frank Meyer collection.* **Museum grade.**

Fluted point, orange-brown patinated Upper Mercer, 1⅜". A well-made point, it was found in Fairfield County, Ohio. *Don Casto collection.* $750.00.

Clovis point, 1" x 2⅜", ¼" thick. On the obverse (shown) the flute is 1½", and the reverse flute is 1". Made of gray mottled Upper Mercer, it is ex-collection Vietzen. Origin unknown, but probably Ohio. *Mark Boswell collection, Colorado; photograph by Infocusphotography.com, Colorado.* $350.00.

Redstone point, Early Paleo, 1¼" x 2⅝" and 3/16" thick at base. Well patinated, there are multiple flutes on the obverse and a flute 1⅝" on the reverse. Made of tan Fort Payne, it has a Davis COA. Kentucky. *Mark Boswell collection, Colorado; photograph by Infocusphotography.com, Colorado.* $325.00.

45

Clovis points, all from Texas. Left, 1⅛" x 4½", root-beer flint with bleach patina. A very attractive point, it is ex-collection Ted Nemec Jr., Jasper County. Center, 1¼" x 5⅛", ex-collection Ted Nemec Jr. Made of gray and green Edwards Plateau, this exceptional point is from Milam County. Right, ⅞" x 3⅝", ex-collections Dwain Rogers and Dana Harper. The material is a tan flint with reddish-gold patina. Harris County. *William M. German collection, Texas; DWC Photography.* All museum grade.

Redstone point, medium-dark chert, 1⅛" x 3". The right ear was rechipped by later people in prehistoric times, as indicated by a patina difference. This was found by the owner and is in Peck's North Carolina fluted point survey as No. 425. Buncombe County, North Carolina. *Gary Henry collection, North Carolina; Bill Duyck photograph.* $1,000.00.

Redstone fluted point, bicolored quartzite, ⅞" x 2". This was found by the owner and is pictured as No. 427 in Peck's North Carolina fluted point survey. Buncombe County, North Carolina. *Gary Henry collection, North Carolina; Bill Duyck photograph.* $200.00.

Fluted point, very unusual and unknown material that is a gray and cream chert. Ex-collection Smith, it measures 2½". Midwest. *Frank Meyer collection.* $250.00.

Fluted point, orange Flint Ridge, 2⅝". It is ex-collection LaDow Johnston and came from Fairfield County, Ohio. *Frank Meyer collection.* Unlisted.

Fluted point, gray and cream Upper Mercer, ex-collection Warner. The point is 2⅞", possibly from Michigan. *Frank Meyer collection.* Unlisted.

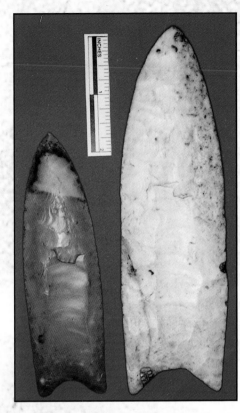

Clovis fluted points, two of the finest in North America. Left, 1⁷⁄₁₆" x 4⅝", Genuine Indian Relic Society authentication #O-14. It is made of translucent cream, pink, and red flint and is ex-collections Judge King, Dr. E. J. Bowser, and William Feldser. Pope County, Minnesota. Right, very large Clovis, Flint Ridge translucent white with tan clouding, 2" x 6½". This piece, rare in size and perfection, was found in the 1940s. Ex-collections C. L. Dine and Culveryhouse, it has Genuine Indian Relic Society authentication #B-45. Van Buren County, Michigan. *Baldwin Trust collection.* Both museum grade.

Clovis fluted points, reverse-lighted to show translucency. Left, 2" x 6½", Van Buren County, Michigan. It is pictured in *Ohio Archaeologist*, Vol. 52 No. 2, Spring 2002, page 22, and *Central States Archaeological Journal*, Vol. 49 No. 4, October 2002, page 170. Right, 1⁷⁄₁₆" x 4⅝", Pope County, Minnesota. It was featured in *Prehistoric Art-Archaeology '83*, Vol. XVIII No. 3, pages 88 – 89. While Mr. Baldwin has owned many fluted points over the years, these are the only two he has kept. *Baldwin Trust collection.* Both museum grade.

Clovis (Barnes?) point, glossy gray flint, 3⅝". The reverse flute on this example is 1⅝" long. A very fine point, it has a Perino COA and came from Clark County, Indiana. *Earthworks Artifacts.* $3,100.00.

Clovis fluted point, well-shaped and with a distinct flute, symmetrical, 3½". Harrison County flint was used for this piece, which has a Perino COA. Grant County, Indiana. *Earthworks Artifacts.* $3,000.00.

Fluted point, translucent Flint Ridge with patination, 3". The obverse flute on this point is 2" long. An exceptional point in near-gem material, it has a Perino COA and came from Fayette County, Ohio. *Earthworks Artifacts.* $2,800.00.

Redstone point, fluted for three-fourths of obverse face, 2¹⁵⁄₁₆". It is made of Ft. Payne chert and has a restored tip. Found by T. Peebles, it is ex-collection Weinstein. Colbert County, Alabama. *Bill Moody collection, Massachusetts.* $400.00.

Clovis point, 2⅜", light tan flint, ex-collection Townsend. It was found in Indiana. *Bill Moody collection, Massachusetts.* $750.00.

Clovis point, two-fifths flute on obverse, overall length 3¾". Ex-collection Frank, it is made of blue Upper Mercer flint. Delaware County, Ohio. *Bill Moody collection, Massachusetts.* $3,000.00.

Clovis point, 2¼", pale flint, ex-collection Col. Vietzen. It has a diagonal break across the flute hinge and is glued. The Clovis was found near Nelsonville, Hocking County, Ohio. *Bill Moody collection, Massachusetts.* $450.00.

Clovis point, wide and short obverse flute, 2½". The material is mixed red with cream, probably Flint Ridge. Ex-collection Vietzen, it is from Lorain County, Ohio. *Bill Moody collection, Massachusetts.* $800.00.

Ross County type Clovis point, 3⅝", river-stained coastal flint. This large and symmetrical point was found in the Chipola River, Florida. *Bill Moody collection, Massachusetts.* $4,500.00.

Clovis point, resharpened and with possible graver tip, blue Upper Mercer flint. It is 1½" long and is from Tuscarawas County, Ohio. *Bill Moody collection, Massachusetts.* $250.00.

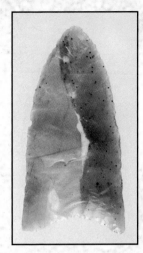

Eastern fluted Clovis point, 2⅜", weathered silicified shale. It has small ears and came from near Hunting Creek in northern Iredell County, North Carolina. *Collection of and photograph by Ron Harris, North Carolina.* $650.00.

Eastern fluted Clovis point, 2⅝", light green high-grade rhyolite. Well fluted, this point was picked up in Stokes County, North Carolina. *Collection of and photograph by Ron Harris, North Carolina.* $1,200.00.

Fluted point, 1" x 2", highly translucent unidentified flint in three colors, 1" x 2". An excellent, thin, and well-made point, provenance is unknown. *Private collection.* $1,000.00 plus.

Fluted point, ¾" x 2½". This is a gem, one of the more attractive Early Paleo points. It is made of glossy swirled translucent green and yellow flint, and is ex-collections Tilton and Jack Hooks. Kansas. *Private collection.* $2,500.00.

Fluted Paleo knife, 3½" long, gray hornstone. Quite wide for size, it came from Franklin County, Indiana. *Frank Meyer collection.* $400.00.

Fluted point, 1" x 2⅜", translucent gray unknown flint with brown and green bull's-eye. Quite thin, this beautiful point has matching overlapped (stair-stepped) flutes on each face. It is ex-collection Pinkston and was found in Grayson County, Kentucky. *Private collection.* $2,500.00.

Fluted point, 3¹⁄₁₆", yellowish-orange and red patina. A break in the patina shows that the flint is a white chalcedony. Scioto County, Ohio. *Frank Meyer collection.* Museum grade.

Fluted point, pale gray unknown flint, 3⅝", overlapped obverse flutes. It is ex-collections Shipley and Copeland, and was found in Seneca County, Ohio. *Frank Meyer collection.* $750.00.

Fluted point, black Zaleski (Upper Mercer) flint, 3¹¹⁄₁₆". The obverse flute is wide and short on this well-finished point. It has a Perino COA and is from Coshocton County, Ohio. *Earthworks Artifacts.* $3,400.00.

Clovis point, broken across flute hinge, dark Upper Mercer flint with a meandering lightning line. Ex-collections Pipes and Larson, it is 2½" long. Perry County, Ohio. *Bill Moody collection, Massachusetts.* $450.00.

Clovis point, hornstone with lighter inclusions, 3½" long. The fluted point is ex-collections Morgan, Atkins, and Larson. The Clovis came from Kentucky. *Bill Moody collection, Massachusetts.* $2,500.00.

Clovis point, fairly short flutes on both faces, 3³⁄₁₆". Quite symmetrical, the point is light Harrodsburg chert and it has a Davis COA. Only a minority of fluted points were made from this material. Kentucky. *Earthworks Artifacts.* $3,300.00.

Clovis point, fluted both faces, mottled Tyrone flint, 3¼" long. Nicely fluted, it has a Perino COA. Whitley County, Kentucky. *Earthworks Artifacts.* $2,200.00.

Fluted point, obverse, deep blue Upper Mercer flint, 3¼". This fine point is ex-collection Kramer, from Ohio. *Frank Meyer collection.* Museum grade.

Fluted point, reverse, basal edges ground, solid blue Upper Mercer. At 3¼", both faces are fluted for about two-fifths of point length. Ohio. *Frank Meyer collection.* Museum grade.

Fluted point, burnt amber unknown translucent flint, 3⅜", a very attractive piece. Unidentified but very high-grade material that is typical of many fluted points. This piece has a Perino COA and it came from Christian County, Kentucky. *Gilbert Cooper collection.* Museum grade.

Fluted point, unknown type, translucent Knife River flint. The point with slightly flared base is ex-collection Wilkins and has a Perino COA. It is 4" long and very fine in size, workstyle, and overall configuration. Washington County, Arkansas. *Gilbert Cooper collection.* Museum grade.

Eastern fluted Clovis point, 3½" long, jasper-like material. This large point has a long flute on the obverse lower face and was found in Allegheny County, North Carolina. *Collection of and photograph by Ron Harris, North Carolina.* $2,200.00.

Eastern Clovis fluted point, 2" long, clear crystal quartz. This rare regional material adds greatly to the appeal and value of a fluted point, especially one like this that has such pleasing lines. Alexander County, North Carolina. *Collection of and photograph by Ron Harris, North Carolina.* $2,000.00.

Fluted point, highly translucent off-white Kentucky agate, 2⅝". This point has a Perino COA and was found in Christian County, Kentucky. *Earthworks Artifacts*. $2,200.00.

Fluted point, brown and tan hornstone with partial bullseye, 4⅜". This large example has both Earthworks and Jackson COAs and was found in Meade County, Kentucky. *Earthworks Artifacts*. $3,700.00.

Clovis point, dark mixed maroon Carter Cave flint, 3" long. This fluted point has a Perino COA and was found in Bath County, Kentucky. *Christopher Smith collection, New York*. $2,200.00.

Clovis point, mottled light gray Upper Mercer flint, 3⅛". Fluted for over half of obverse length, this excellent Clovis has a Perino COA. Clermont County, Ohio. *Christopher Smith collection, New York*. $3,000.00.

Clovis point, wide obverse flute, Onondaga chert in shades of grayish brown. It is 2" long and is from Seneca County, New York. *Christopher Smith collection, New York*. $650.00.

Clovis point, obverse flute, "Ohio Blue" Coshocton (Upper Mercer) flint. Upper Mercer is the typical flint for Ohio fluted points, and this excellent specimen is 3½" long. Ohio. *Christopher Smith collection, New York*. $2,750.00.

Clovis point, resharpened size at 2⅛", ex-collection Col. Vietzen. Made of translucent Flint Ridge, it came from the Orient area, Ohio. *Bill Moody collection, Massachusetts.* $600.00.

Fluted point, high-grade brown Kentucky translucent flint, 2¾". The obverse has two flutes on this piece, found in Kentucky. *Frank Meyer collection.* $600.00.

Ross County type fluted point or knife, 3½" long, probably glossy and patinated Carter Cave flint. Ross County, Ohio. *Frank Meyer collection.* $600.00.

Fluted point, Carter Cave flint, 2⁹⁄₁₆". It has a deeply incurvate baseline and was found in Bath County, Kentucky. *Frank Meyer collection.* $350.00.

Fluted point group, all Early Paleo period and shown elsewhere in book. The fluted point at bottom left is 4⅝" long. *Dr. David R. Thrasher collection, Alabama.*

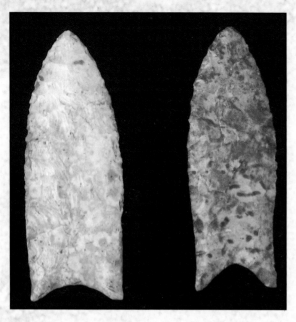

Clovis points, colorful materials. Left, has Jackson COA. Unlisted. Right, ⅞" x 2¾", unidentified flint, Jackson COA #WFJ-4297, ex-collection Fannin, Stewart County, Tennessee. $2,500.00. *Dr. David R. Thrasher collection, Alabama.*

Clovis points, very superior examples. Left, 1⅛" x 3", white Burlington, Davis COA #9044, found after a flood near Huntsdale, Boone Co., Missouri. $4,000.00. Right, 1⅛" x 3⅝", Jackson COA #WFJ-4299, Kansas blue flint, Sumner County, Kansas. $4,500.00. *Dr. David R. Thrasher collection, Alabama.*

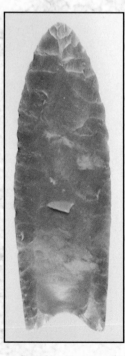

Plainview point, brown translucent flint with lighter spotting, 2⅝". It has a Rogers COA and was found in Gaines County, Texas. *Earthworks Artifacts.* $450.00.

Fluted point, glossy cream Burlington with a pinkish tip, 4½". A fine and large point, it has a Perino COA. Franklin County, Ilinois. *Earthworks Artifacts.* $5,500.00.

Fluted point, unidentified mixed chert, 3¾", Perino COA. The obverse flute is 2⅜" long and the point was found in Franklin County, Illinois. *Gilbert Cooper collection.* Museum grade.

Clovis fluted point, translucent honey and cream Carter Cave flint, 3¹⁵⁄₁₆". This superb point is ex-collection Copeland and has a Perino COA. Licking County, Ohio. *Gilbert Cooper collection.* Museum grade.

Clovis(?) fluted point, 2³/₁₆", translucent amber flint. It has tip and one corner restoration, and was picked up in a nearby creek by the owner in the first year of living at a new home. Jersey County, Illinois. *Collection of and photograph by Kevin Calvin, Illinois.* $250.00.

Fluted point, Ross County or Hazel, short flutes and slight serrations, dark Upper Mercer with a faint diagonal lightning line. Ex-collection Jack Hooks, it is 3½" long. Allen County, Ohio. *Private collection.* $3,000.00.

Holcombe(?) fluted point, thin and almost delicate, 2" long. Both faces are fluted and the obverse flute runs nearly to the tip. Cream and blue Upper Mercer, the point is ex-collection Jack Hooks. Richland County, Ohio. *Doug Hooks collection.* $500.00.

Clovis fluted point, Early Paleo, ⅞" x 2⅜". Made of glossy hornstone, it was found by B. Troke in a load of peat brought from a bog near Warsaw. Kosciusko County, Indiana. *B. Troke and M. Watkins collection, Indiana; Steve Weisser photograph.* $950.00.

Clovis point, 3¼", pale orange-tan unknown flint. The obverse has a short and wide flute and the artifact came from Ohio. *Frank Meyer collection.* Unlisted.

Eastern Clovis point, light yellow jasper-like material, ex-collection Enck. Beautifully worked and with a graceful shape, it is from Wicomico County, Maryland. *Fogelman collection.* $9,000.00.

Barnes fluted point, orange mottled jasper, narrow for length. It came from Lycoming County, Pennsylvania. *Fogelman collection.* $2,000.00.

Clovis point or blade, St. Louis type, light gray-green chert. With typical V-shaped baseline, it is well-fluted. The Clovis came from Somerset County, Pennsylvania. *Fogelman collection.* $2,500.00.

Clovis point, banded Warsaw chert, 3½" long. Well made and in about original size, it was found by D. Jenkins in a creek. This fine point, which has a Perino COA, came from Lee County, Iowa. *Collection of and photograph by A. D. Savage, Iowa.* $2,000.00.

Clovis point, Early Paleo, 2⅜". Wapsipinicon chert was used for this piece, which is reduced in length due to prehistoric impact. It was found by David Savage on the family farm in 2002. Henry County, Iowa. *Collection of and photograph by A. D. Savage, Iowa.* Unlisted.

Clovis point, Early Paleo, 3¼", white chert with darker inclusions. This Clovis was found in Jennings County, Indiana. *Collection of and photograph by A. D. Savage, Iowa.* $550.00.

Clovis point, a large and beautifully chipped example, 4" long. Brown glossy flint was used for the Clovis, which is fluted one-fourth of the obverse base. Ohio River region. *Collection of and photograph by A. D. Savage, Iowa.* $2,500.00.

Fluted point, obverse flute 2½", overall length 3⅝". The material is probably dark Kentucky flint. The point is ex-collection Lewis. Ohio. *Frank Meyer collection.* Unlisted.

Clovis point, small and narrow obverse flute, Edwards flint. It is 2½" long, from Wilson County, Texas. *John and Susan Mellyn collection, Texas.* $500.00.

58

Clovis point or blade, 1⅜" x 3¼", quite thin for size. Made of Indian Creek chert, this artifact was found in Monroe County, Indiana, by the owner. *Collection of and photograph by Jon Hunsberger, Indiana.* $200.00.

Fluted point, probably brown Dover flint, 3⅞". This is one of the Early Paleo points that indeed looks at least twelve thousand years old. It is heavily patinated and has surface deposits. It has a Perino COA and it is from Sevier County, Tennessee. *Gilbert Cooper collection.* $4,000.00.

Crowfield point, 3¹⁵⁄₁₆", blue Upper Mercer in several shades. It has excurvate edges, a tapered base, and a Perino COA. Darke County, Ohio. *Gilbert Cooper collection.* $3,500.00.

Clovis point, 2⅝", three-quarter length flute on obverse, blue and gray Sonora flint. This well-made piece has both Davis and Perino COAs and came from Monroe County, Kentucky. *Christopher Smith collection, New York.* $1,800.00.

Redstone point, brown Flint Ridge material, obverse fluted. It is 2½" long and has the typical widest-at-base configuration. The Redstone has both Davis and Perino COAs and came from Clermont County, Ohio. *Christopher Smith collection, New York.* $1,200.00.

Clovis point, highest-grade Flint Ridge translucent gem material in white and orange-tan, 2⅞". Not a large number of fluted points were made of Flint Ridge. Ohio. *Christopher Smith collection, New York.* $2,500.00.

Clovis fluted point, blue Upper Mercer with white, 2¾". Heavily ground on basal edges, it has a Davis COA. Ohio. *Christopher Smith collection, New York.* $1,300.00.

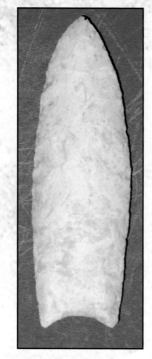

Clovis fluted point, Early Paleo, 3½". High-grade semi-glossy flint or chert, it has good size and form. Ex-collection Vinzant, it was picked up in Mercer County, Missouri. *Collection of and photograph by A. D. Savage, Iowa.* $2,200.00.

Clovis point, 3" long, made of very unusual material, limestone. It has a Perino COA and was found on the Savage family farm in 1997. Henry County, Iowa. *Collection of and photograph by A. D. Savage, Iowa.* Unlisted.

Clovis point, probably a St. Louis variety due to large size, 5¼". White (now patinated) Burlington chert was used for this piece, ex-collection Vinzant. Mercer County, Missouri. *Collection of and photograph by A. D. Savage, Iowa.* Museum grade.

Fluted point, gray striped Upper Mercer flint, 2½". It is ex-collection Dick Johnson and was found in May of 1915. Indiana. *Frank Meyer collection.* Museum grade.

Clovis point, Kentucky dark flint, 3⅞". With large ears, this example was found in Butler County, Ohio. *Frank Meyer collection.* $1,200.00.

Fluted point, triangular, 3¾", reverse flute about 2" long. Dark mixed Upper Mercer blue, it is ex-collections Copeland and Ramsey. Scioto County, Ohio. *Frank Meyer collection.* Museum grade.

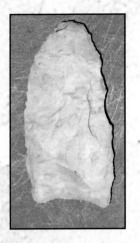

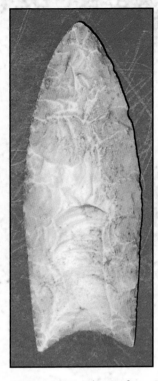

Fluted point, resharpened size, 2¼". Made of Upper Mercer mottled gray, it is ex-collection Smith. Highland County, Ohio. *Frank Meyer collection.* Unlisted.

Clovis point, 2¼", gray-brown flint. It was found by D. Humphrey near Murfreesboro, Tennessee. *Collection of and photograph by A. D. Savage, Iowa.* $125.00.

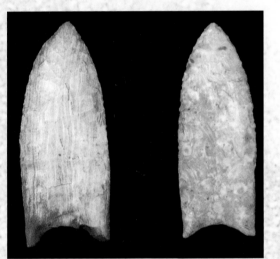

Clovis point, classic form, large flute on obverse, 4" long. The material for this exceptional piece is highly patinated Burlington, and the point came from Pike County, Illinois. *Collection of and photograph by A. D. Savage, Iowa.* $3,000.00.

Fluted point, Paoli (Carter Cave) flint from Kentucky, 5⅜". This quite exceptional piece in near-gem material has multiple flutes on the obverse. It is known as the Russell Spear and has a Perino COA. Jackson County, Kentucky. *Gilbert Cooper collection.* Museum grade.

Paleo points, colorful materials. Left, 1¼" x 3", Jackson COA #7103, ex-collection Elam, petrified wood. It is from Montezuma County, Colorado. $5,000.00. Right, pinkish-purple chert. Unlisted. *Dr. David R. Thrasher collection, Alabama.*

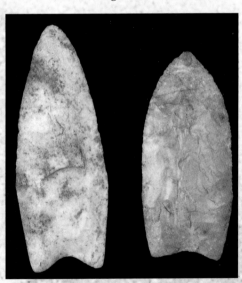

Clovis points, left example about 4" long. Left, mottled chert, ground basal edges. Right, Jackson COA #7142, pink chert, 1⅜" x 3", Grant County, Wisconsin. *Dr. David R. Thrasher collection, Alabama.* Each, $3,000.00.

Clovis point, mottled blue Upper Mercer, ex-collection Shipley. It is 3⅞" long, from Greenup County, Kentucky. *Frank Meyer collection.* $1,200.00.

Fluted point, mixed blue Upper Mercer, 2¹⁵⁄₁₆". Ex-collection Kramer, it came from Ross County, Ohio. *Frank Meyer collection.* $900.00

Clovis point, reverse. The flute shown is 1⅝" long, and narrow, while the obverse flute is the same length, but wide. High-grade Georgia jasper, it has a Perino COA. Dawson County, Georgia. *Earthworks Artifacts.* Museum grade.

Clovis point, obverse, This point measures 1½" x 6⅝" and has a Perino COA. Simply one of the finest North American points, the material is glossy brown Georgia jasper. Dawson County, Georgia. *Earthworks Artifacts.* Museum grade.

Redstone point, crinoid quartz, 1¼" x 4". This well-shaped point with a large flute has a graceful outline, plus Jackson COA #7124. It was found in Lee County, Kentucky. *Dr. David R. Thrasher collection, Alabama.* $15,000.00.

Suwannee, 1¼" x 3⅛", basic gray chalcedony with other colors. Ex-collection Claytor, this is a fine early point that has Davis COA #9096. Origin unlisted. *Dr. David R. Thrasher collection, Alabama.* $2,000.00.

Clovis points, both with Jackson COAs. Left, 1⅛" x 3½", Coshocton flint with diagonal lightning line, Muskingum County, Ohio. Right, 1⅛" x 3⅜", Coshocton mixed flint, Delaware County, Ohio. *Dr. David R. Thrasher collection, Alabama.* Each, $4,000.00.

Clovis point, mixed Upper Mercer blue flint with white clouding, 3⅞" long. The obverse flute is 2¼" long. The point has a Perino COA. Ohio. *Earthworks Artifacts.* $4,000.00.

Clovis point, ice-blue Kentucky quartzite, 2⁵⁄₁₆". It is very thin, ¹⁹⁄₁₀₀" and is fluted to the tip on the face shown. This gem-quality point is from Barron County, Kentucky. *Earthworks Artifacts.* $1,000.00.

Clovis point, white patinated flint, 3⅜" long. The obverse flute is two-fifths length and the point is ex-collection Wilkins. It has an Earthworks COA and came from Highland County, Ohio. *Earthworks Artifacts.* $2,450.00.

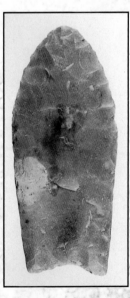

Fluted point, greenish semi-translucent unknown flint, 2⅝". Well-shaped, it has a Perino COA. Scioto County, Ohio. *Gilbert Cooper collection.* $1,100.00.

Fluted point, colorful translucent mixed Flint Ridge, 3⅛". This is a fine point in style and material, with a Perino COA. The reverse flute is 1⅝" long. Bath County, Kentucky. *Gilbert Cooper collection.* $2,200.00.

Fluted point, Flint Ridge multicolor, 2¾". Ex-collection Mueller, it is from Darke County, Ohio. *Frank Meyer collection*. Unlisted.

Fluted point, 2⅛", jewel Flint Ridge material. This piece has tip restoration and was found in Union County, Ohio. *Frank Meyer collection*. Unlisted.

Fluted point, 2¼", almost fully fluted on obverse. The unknown material is near-purple with yellow-tan. The point was found in the Lynchburg area, Highland County, Ohio. *Frank Meyer collection*. Unlisted.

Clovis point, mottled translucent obsidian, 1¼" x 4¼". This very fine point was found by A. Gonzales in the 1920s and is ex-collection Little. It has Jackson COA #7123 and came from Clark County, Nevada. *Dr. David R. Thrasher collection, Alabama.* $15,000.00.

Fluted point, obverse view with flute 2½" long, overall length 5¼". This is a superb point in glossy Edwards Plateau flint, and it has a Perino COA. Mills County, Texas. *Earthworks Artifacts*. Museum grade.

Clovis point, glossy Burlington chert, 3¼". It has had one tip repointing that barely shortened the length. This Clovis has a Perino COA and was found in Adams County, Illinois. *Collection of and photograph by A. D. Savage, Iowa.* $900.00.

Fluted point, reverse view, point length 5¼". The flute on this face is 4" long. Made of Edwards Plateau, there is a Perino COA. Mills County, Texas. *Earthworks Artifacts*. Museum grade.

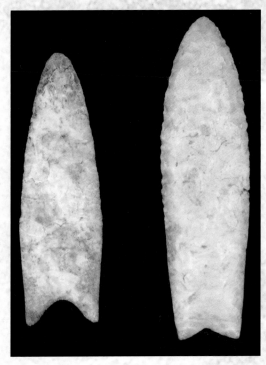

Clovis points, both with Jackson COAs. Left, 1¼" x 3¼", dark unidentified flint, ex-collection Reynolds Thrasher, Indiana. Right, 1¼" x 3", unidentified dark flint, ex-collection Reynolds Thrasher, Indiana. *Dr. David R. Thrasher collection, Alabama.* Each, $3,000.00.

Clovis points, high-grade flints, both with Jackson COAs. Left, 1⅜" x 4⅜", Missouri flint, ex-collections Dodge and Bergman Museum, Montgomery County, Missouri. $7,000.00. Right, 1½" x 5⅛", purple Boyle, ex-collection Kappeler, Walhonding Valley, Coshocton County, Ohio. $10,000.00. *Dr. David R. Thrasher collection, Alabama.*

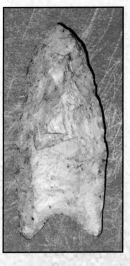

Fluted point, glossy multicolored flint, two flutes on the obverse face, 3³⁄₁₆". An exceptional point in shape and material, it is ex-collection Driskill and has a Perino COA. The reverse flute on this piece is 2⅝" long. Hamilton County, Ohio. *Gilbert Cooper collection.* Museum grade.

Clovis fluted point, small ears, multicolor patinated Flint Ridge. It has a Perino COA and is 2⅝" long. County unknown, Ohio. *Gilbert Cooper collection.* $400.00.

Fluted point, probably a Crowfield, thin and with three flutes on the obverse. The bottom left corner has burin flaking and the point itself is 2⅝" long. It has a Perino COA, is made of reddish unknown flint, and came from Brown County, Ohio. *Gilbert Cooper collection.* $1,000.00.

Clovis point, fluted, 2½". Tan mixed chert was used for this piece, which has had several resharpenings. It has a Perino COA and is from Mississippi County, Missouri. *Collection of and photograph by A. D. Savage, Iowa.* $700.00.

Clovis point, 2¼", glossy Burlington chert. It was found by Alfred Savage on the family farm in 1995. The Clovis has a Perino COA and is from Henry County, Iowa. *Collection of and photograph by A. D. Savage, Iowa.* Unlisted.

Clovis fluted point, gray on gray unknown flint with maroon tip markings, 2⅞". It has a Perino COA and was found in Fleming County, Kentucky. *Gilbert Cooper collection.* $1,200.00.

Fluted point, resharpened size, mixed blue Upper Mercer flint. This point is ex-collecion Wilkins and has a Perino COA. Size is 2⅜" and it came from Fairfield County, Ohio. *Gilbert Cooper collection.* $700.00.

Redstone fluted point, Carter Cave glossy red, Perino COA, 2½" long. The reverse flute is 1½" and the point is ex-collection Bowers. Carter County, Kentucky. *Gilbert Cooper collection.* $2,000.00.

Crowfield point, wide and thin with damaged tip, 1⅛" long. Upper Mercer blue, the point has a Jackson COA and it was found in Ohio. *Earthworks Artifacts.* Unlisted.

Fluted point, patinated creamy Flint Ridge, 3⅜". This is a very superior example, and obverse flute is 1¾" long. Ex-collection Townsend, the point came from Meigs County, Ohio. *Earthworks Artifacts.* $3,200.00.

Clovis fluted point, mixed blue Upper Mercer, 3½". The basal edges are heavily ground and the point has a long history. It is ex-collections Dr. Kramer, Schmitz, and Baranski. Ohio. *Jim Miller collection.* $2,500.00.

Clovis point, high-shouldered and with very good overall lines, mixed Upper Mercer flint. The point is 3½" long and has a Perino COA. Coshocton County, Ohio. *Earthworks Artifacts.* $3,000.00.

Clovis point, missing ear, Fort Payne flint. It has been in several important collections and has an Earthworks COA. The point is 3¾" long, from Nicholas County, Kentucky. *Earthworks Artifacts.* $750.00.

Fluted point, Early Paleo, Upper Mercer blue and cream flint, 2¾" long. It was found near Fresno in 1968. Coshocton County, Ohio. *Stan Hershberger collection.* $1,100.00.

Clovis point, 1⅞", patinated Burlington. This point has had several resharpenings and was assigned a Perino COA. Pike County, Illinois. *Collection of and photograph by A. D. Savage, Iowa.* $250.00.

Clovis point, Early Paleo ca. 9500 BC, 2½". Medium-sized, this fluted point in Burlington was resharpened and was once over an inch longer. It has a Perino COA. Brown County, Illinois. *Collection of and photograph by A. D. Savage, Iowa.* $700.00.

Clovis point, Early Paleo, 1½". Made of dark chert, it has had several resharpenings and was originally over twice as long. The projectile point has a Perino COA and came from Pike County, Illinois. *Collection of and photograph by A. D. Savage, Iowa.* $300.00.

Clovis point, Indiana hornstone (Harrison County flint), 3" long. It has a Perino COA and was picked up in Highland County, Ohio. *Collection of and photograph by A. D. Savage, Iowa.* $600.00.

Fluted Clovis point, mixed blue Upper Mercer flint, 2½". The curved blade end suggests knife use. Fluted on both faces, the Clovis was found by the owner in Knox County, Ohio. *Carl Harruff collection.* $600.00.

Fluted Clovis point, 2⅛", dark Indiana hornstone. Nicely chipped, it is fluted on both faces and was a personal find of the owner. Knox County, Ohio. *Paula Harruff collection.* Unlisted.

Fluted point, pale blue Upper Mercer, pronounced flute termination flake depression. It is 3³⁄₁₆", from Fairfield County, Ohio. *Dr. John Winsch collection.* Museum grade.

Fluted point, ex-collection Copeland, 3⅞". Tan Delaware County flint was used for this very fine piece, found in Scioto County, Ohio. *Dr. John Winsch collection.* Museum grade.

Ross County fluted point, dark honey-colored translucent material that is probably Flint Ridge, 3¾". It is ex-collection Jack Hooks, from Ohio. *Doug Hooks collection.* Museum grade.

Redstone-like point, fluted one face, rhyolite. This was found by the owner, on a spring-fed site near Duxbury Marsh. Plymouth County, Massachusetts. *Bill Moody collection, Massachusetts.* Unlisted.

Fluted point, mixed brown Dover flint, 4¼". The point has differing patination on the two faces and has an Earthworks COA. Hardin County, Tennessee. *Earthworks Artifacts.* $3,800.00.

Clovis point, 3½" long, high-grade mixed tan chert or flint. It is ex-collection Townsend, from southwestern Indiana. *Frank Meyer collection.* Museum grade.

Clovis point, glossy blue-gray Upper Mercer, double-fluted on reverse face. A fine point, it is 3⅜" long. Ohio. *Frank Meyer collection.* Museum grade.

Clovis, Eastern fluted type, 2¾". Made of green rhyolite, this Early Paleo piece was found in Randolph County, North Carolina. *Collection of and photograph by Ron Harris, North Carolina.* $450.00.

Eastern Clovis fluted point, silicified shale, 2¾". It is number 619 in the North Carolina fluted point survey. The owner found this example during dam construction for Jordan Lake in northeastern Chatham County, North Carolina. *Collection of and photograph by Ron Harris, North Carolina.* $450.00.

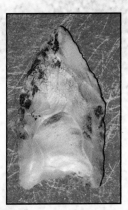

Clovis point, fluted, Early Paleo, 2" long. Carter Cave flint, it is ex-collection Williams and from the Ashland area, Kentucky. *Collection of and photograph by A. D. Savage, Iowa.* $300.00.

Fluted point, Early Paleo, Dover flint patinated white, obverse flute 2⅝". This very large point, 6½", has a Perino COA and is ex-collection Coomer. One of the best points from the state, it came from Muhlenberg County, Kentucky. *Gilbert Cooper collection.* Museum grade.

Clovis point, large size at 5" long, gray hornstone. It has a fluted base and is very well chipped. Clovis points of this size and top condition are very scarce. Ex-collection Friesen, it is from the Corydon area, Indiana. *Collection of and photograph by A. D. Savage, Iowa.* Museum grade.

Fluted point, of creamy, banded, and spotted Flint Ridge, 3" long. This fine glossy point was found in 1974. Clark Township, Holmes County, Ohio. *Stan Hershberger collection.* $3,000.00.

Fluted point, light mottled tan flint or chert, 3¼". It is ex-collection Richter and has a Perino COA. Very symmetrical, it is from Wayne County, Ohio. *Gilbert Cooper collection.* $2,000.00.

Fluted point, Boyle flint from Kentucky, 2⅝" long. It has a Perino COA and is a nicely balanced point. Fleming County, Kentucky. *Gilbert Cooper collection.* $1,500.00.

Clovis point, high-grade Upper Mercer or Flint Ridge material, 3¼". Nicely fluted, it has a Perino COA. Crawford County, Ohio. *Earthworks Artifacts.* $2,800.00.

Fluted point, 4¾", Perino COA. This large point is made of glossy flint and the strong obverse flute is 2½". This superior point was found in Morgan County, Kentucky. *Earthworks Artifacts.* $4,600.00.

Clovis points, both with Jackson COAs. Left, 1⅜" x 4⅝", sugar quartz, ex-collection Cotton, West Virginia. $7,500.00. Right, 1¼" x 4⅝", Carter Cave flint, ex-collection Florence Family, Harrison County, Kentucky. $6,000.00. *Dr. David R. Thrasher collection, Alabama.*

Clovis points, superior examples. Left, 1" x 2¾", colorful Sonora, Davis COA #10003, Indiana. Right, ⅞" x 3", blue and tan hornstone, ex-collection Fannin, Scioto County, Ohio. *Dr. David R. Thrasher collection, Alabama.* Each, $3,000.00.

Fluted point, patinated Fort Payne flint with differing patination on the faces, 5¾". This long and graceful point has a Perino COA and came from Perry County, Tennessee. *Earthworks Artifacts.* $8,000.00.

Fluted point, slender for the length of 5³⁄₁₆", swirled blue Upper Mercer with white veining. Well chipped, it has a Perino COA and was picked up in Wayne County, Ohio. *Gilbert Cooper collection.* Museum grade.

Fluted point, short and wide flute, 3¹⁄₁₆". Brush Creek chert was the material used for this very fine Paleo point, found in Delaware County, Ohio. *Len and Janie Weidner collection.* Museum grade.

Fluted point, Flint Ridge, pale tan with green and red, 2½". Yet another fluted point with the angled baseline indentation, it was found near Baltimore, Fairfield County, Ohio. *Len and Janie Weidner collection.* $800.00.

Fluted point, 3⅝", Enterline-like obverse fluting, mixed Carter Cave flint. This example also has a small flute at the tip. Butler County, Ohio. *Frank Meyer collection.* Unlisted.

Fluted point, classic Clovis form, rectangular flute channel with strong termination ledge. It is 3⁹⁄₁₆" and is made of medium blue Upper Mercer. Henry County, Ohio. *Len and Janie Weidner collection.* Museum grade.

71

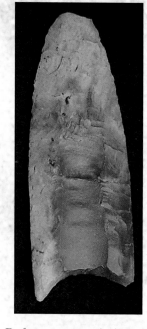

Clovis point, overlap-fluted for nearly one-half of obverse length, 1¼" x 4". A top-grade example, it has a Dickey COA and was found by B. Darnell. Stewart County, Tennessee. *Doug Goodrum collection, Kentucky; Art Gerber photograph.* Museum grade.

Redstone point, tip impact fracture, 1⅜" x 3⅝". Widest at the base, this point was found by M. Gould along the Barren River, Lincoln County, Kentucky. *Doug Goodrum collection, Kentucky.* $1,000.00 – 1,500.00.

Fluted point, wide and full-length reverse flute, 3⅛". Made of unknown patinated material, it has a Perino COA. Cross County, Arkansas. *Gilbert Cooper collection.* $2,500.00.

Fluted point, glossy Kentucky hornstone, nicely fluted and with overall clean lines. It has a Perino COA and is 3½" long. Hardin County, Kentucky. *Gilbert Cooper collection.* $2,750.00.

Clovis point, unidentified mottled dark flint, 1¼" x 2¾". It has Jackson COA #DT-8 and is ex-collection Waters. The Clovis was found in Montana. *Dr. David R. Thrasher collection, Alabama.* $2,500.00.

Clovis point, nicely fluted, Fort Payne chert. It measures 1³⁄₁₆" x 3¾" and was found by J. Craine in Barren County, Kentucky. *Doug Goodrum collection, Kentucky.* $1,200.00 – 1,500.00.

Redstone-like fluted point, translucent white Hixton quartzite, 3¹¹⁄₁₆". An unusual type in scarce material, it is from Eau Claire County, Wisconsin. *Dwight Wolfe collection.* Museum grade.

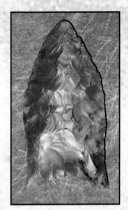

Clovis point, gray and white chert, 3⅜". This fluted point is ex-collections Hodges and Lilljedahl, from Brown County, Texas. *Dr. Guy Gross collection, Texas.* $3,000.00.

Cumberland point, two-thirds flute on obverse, restored tip. It is 2¼" long, made of Ft. Payne chert, and ex-collection Weinstein. Madison County, Alabama. *Bill Moody collection, Massachusetts.* $250.00.

Clovis point, resharpened in prehistoric times, gray glossy flint. It is 2" long and has an Anderson COA. McCracken County, Kentucky. *Collection of and photograph by A. D. Savage, Iowa.* $450.00.

Fluted point, recurved baseline, dark blue Upper Mercer flint. This example is 3¾", from Wyandot County, Ohio. *Frank Meyer collection.* $1,200.00.

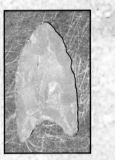

Clovis point, deeply indented baseline, 1½" long. Ex-collection Cross, it is made of quartzite and was found in the Raleigh area, North Carolina. *Collection of and photograph by A. D. Savage, Iowa.* $500.00.

Clovis point, Early Paleo, 4" long. Well shaped, the piece is made of multicolored chert and has a high degree of patination. It was found in the Worland area, Wyoming. *Collection of and photograph by A. D. Savage, Iowa.* $1,300.00.

Ross County type Clovis point, creamy-tan chert or flint, a large and fine example. Ex-collection Lilljedahl, it was found in Wood County, Texas. *Dr. Guy Gross collection, Texas.* $4,200.00.

Fluted point, unusual overall shape, 3⅛". Dark blue Upper Mercer was used for this piece, widest at the base. Delaware County, Ohio. *Frank Meyer collection.* Unlisted.

73

Clovis point, Early Paleo, 1¾". Probably resharpened, it is Alibates flint, ex-collection Lilljedahl. Collingsworth County, Texas. *Dr. Guy Gross collection, Texas.* $500.00.

Clovis fluted point, 2¾", dark Upper Mercer flint. It was found just south of Burbank, Wayne County, Ohio. *Jim Miller collection.* $1,000.00.

Fluted point, patinated yellow Flint Ridge, 3½". This large and fine point is ex-collection Vietzen and was found near Cascade Park, Lorain County, Ohio. *Jim Miller collection.* $4,000.00.

Fluted point, unknown blue material with a frosty patina, 1⁵⁄₁₆" x 4³⁄₁₆". The obverse flute is 2¾" and the point has a Perino COA. Adams County, Ohio. *Gilbert Cooper collection.* $4,000.00.

Fluted point, blue Upper Mercer, 3½". Broken and glued, it is ex-collection Burdette and Sedlin. It was used by Dr. Prufer in a fluted point study. Ohio. *Jim Miller collection.* $1,000.00.

Crowfield fluted point, wide for length and with shallow multiple fluting, 2⁷⁄₁₆" long. Ex-collection Smith, it was found near Barnesville, Belmont County, Ohio. *Jim Miller collection.* $1,000.00.

Fluted point, yellowish-white Flint Ridge, 2⅞". It has pointed basal corners and is ex-collection Buehl. The point was found outside Painesville, Lake County, Ohio. *Jim Miller collection.* $2,000.00.

Clovis fluted point, 3¼" long, deeply incurvate baseline. Made of dark Upper Mercer, it is ex-collection Driskill and is pictured in *Who's Who in Indian Relics #2*, page 62. Defiance County, Ohio. *Jim Miller collection.* $4,000.00.

Clovis fluted point, obverse, mottled dark Upper Mercer flint with lightning lines, multiple flutes, 4⅛" long. Known as the "Harruff Clovis," it is undoubtedly one of the finest Early Paleo points to come from the state of origin. It was found by the owner in June of 1993, in Knox County, Ohio. *Collection of and photograph by Carl Harruff.* Museum grade.

Fluted point, the Harruff Clovis is one of the few Early Paleo points that is equally attractive on each face, and does not have a "better side up." Only the highest-grade and most valuable chipped artifacts have this characteristic. It was pictured in *Ohio Archaeologist*, Vol. 47 No. 3, Summer 1997, on the back cover. The point was also featured on the front cover of *Preshistoric Antiquities Quarterly*, Vol. 11 No. 3, August 2001, and in *Prehistoric American*, Vol. 37 No. 2, 2003, page 22. Knox County, Ohio. *Collection of and photograph by Carl Harruff.* Museum grade.

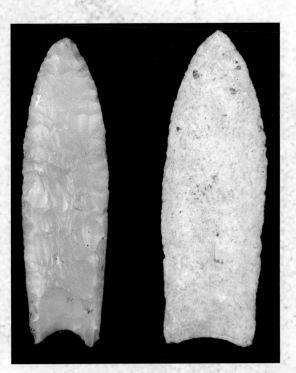

Clovis points, both with Davis COAs. Left, gray glossy hornstone, 1⅜" x 4⅝", Carroll County, Kentucky. $7,000.00. Right, unfluted, 1⅝" x 4⅝", unknown tan chert, from southern Indiana. $5,500.00. *Dr. David R. Thrasher collection, Alabama.*

Clovis points, both with Jackson COAs. Left, 1" x 3", Edwards Plateau flint, ex-collection Highfill, central Texas. Right, ⅞" x 2⅞", Coshocton blue, Delaware County, Ohio. *Dr. David R. Thrasher collection, Alabama.* Each, $3,000.00.

Fluted point, 3½" long, obverse flute 2¼". The Early Paleo artifact is made of Bloomville chert and has a Perino COA. Holmes County, Ohio. *Gilbert Cooper collection.* Museum grade.

Clovis points, both with Jackson COAs. Left, 1" x 2⅞", Sonora flint, ex-collection Dyer, Barren County, Kentucky. $2,500.00. Right, ⅞" x 2½", moss agate, ex-collection Redwine, Culberson County, Texas. $3,000.00. *Dr. David R. Thrasher collection, Alabama.*

Fluted point, Boyle chert with occasional inclusions, 3½". Carefully chipped, the point has a Perino COA. Mason County, Kentucky. *Gilbert Cooper collection.* Museum grade.

Fluted point, 3⅜", unknown black and gray chert or flint with maroon toward the tip. It has a Perino COA and came from Warren County, Ohio. *Gilbert Cooper collection.* Museum grade.

Fluted point, dark blue Upper Mercer with lighter inclusions, 4¹⁄₁₆" long. It has an Earthworks COA and was picked up in Adams County, Ohio. *Earthworks Artifacts.* $3,300.00.

Fluted point, attractive light purple flint of unknown origin, 2¹¹⁄₁₆". Well made, it has a Perino COA. Trigg County, Kentucky. *Gilbert Cooper collection.* Museum grade.

Fluted point, black Zaleski (Upper Mercer) flint, 5¹⁄₁₆" long. It has both Jackson and Earthworks COAs and came from Athens County, Ohio. *Earthworks Artifacts.* $3,300.00.

Fluted point, brownish-gray Sonora (Kentucky) flint with lighter inclusions surrounded with maroon, 3 1/16". It has both Jackson and Motley COAs and came from Hart County, Kentucky. *Gilbert Cooper collection.* $1,300.00.

Fluted point, blue and gray Indiana hornstone (Harrison County flint), 4 1/8". This striking and symmetrical point has equal flutes on both faces and the obverse flute is bold and clean. This has a Perino COA and came from Meade County, Kentucky. *Earthworks Artifacts.* Museum grade.

Fluted point, reverse flute 2" long, 3 3/4". Made of blue Upper Mercer, it is from Lucas County, Ohio. *Frank Meyer collection.* Unlisted.

Fluted point, finely chipped and with a wide tip, reddish-orange Carter Cave flint. There is a possible graver tip on one base corner. The example is 3 5/8" and came from Allen County, Ohio. *Frank Meyer collection.* $450.00.

Fluted point, tapered outline, Upper Mercer mixed flint. This fine point is 4 1/4" long and the obverse flute (shown) is 2" long. The point has a Perino COA and came from Lake County, Ohio. *Earthworks Artifacts.* $4,900.00.

Clovis point, Knife River translucent flint, 2 11/16". The obverse is fluted and the reverse has the frosty patination seen on some Knife River examples. This point has a Perino COA and was found in Lincoln County, Wisconsin. *Earthworks Artifacts.* $2,500.00.

Fluted point, Fort Payne chert, equal-length flutes on both faces. It is 3 15/16" long, and the point has a Davis COA. Hardin County, Tennessee. *Earthworks Artifacts.* $4,200.00.

Clovis fluted point, large size at 4⁵⁄₁₆", dark olive and black Onondaga(?) flint. This exceptional piece is pictured in *Survey of Ohio Fluted Points No. 2*, 1960, page 13. It was found about 1900 in Kirtland Township, Lake County, Ohio. *Len and Janie Weidner collection.* Museum grade.

Clovis point, Early Paleo, creamy Burlington, 3³⁄₁₆". This fluted point is ex-collections Keeley and Anderson, and was found in the Jerseyville area, Illinois. *Len and Janie Weidner collection.* $1,150.00.

Fluted point, pale blue Upper Mercer, 2⁵⁄₈". The rectangular flute runs for two-fifths of obverse length. Pickaway County, Ohio. *Len and Janie Weidner collection.* $650.00.

Clovis points, Early Paleo, midwestern. Left, brown Dover, 1" x 3½", Davis COA #11045, Benton County, Tennessee. Right, streaked Carter Cave, 1⅛" x 3⅜", Jackson COA #WFJ-4280, ex-collection West, Carter County, Kentucky. *Dr. David R. Thrasher collection, Alabama.* Each, $6,000.00.

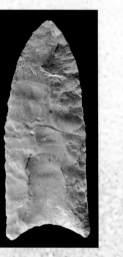

Eastern Clovis fluted point, yellow jasper, 2½". The example has restoration on one ear and was picked up in Ashe County, North Carolina. *Collection of and photograph by Ron Harris, North Carolina.* $450.00.

Eastern fluted Clovis point, 3¼" long, slight ear restoration. The material is speckled green rhyolite and the point was found in Randolph County, North Carolina. *Collection of and photograph by Ron Harris, North Carolina.* $450.00.

Eastern fluted Clovis point, 2½", milky white quartz. It has a distinct flute termination ledge, and the obverse face has a graceful overall configuration. Alexander County, North Carolina. *Collection of and photograph by Ron Harris, North Carolina.* $1,300.00.

Eastern fluted Clovis point, 2¼", speckled green rhyolite. With an obverse flute, the example came from Randolph County, North Carolina. *Collection of and photograph by Ron Harris, North Carolina.* $300.00.

Eastern fluted Clovis point, 2⅜", speckled green rhyolite with faint streaks in the material. This fluted point came from Randolph County, North Carolina. *Collection of and photograph by Ron Harris, North Carolina.* $450.00.

Clovis points, both superior examples with Jackson COAs. Left, 1⅛" x 4⅛", hornstone, ex-collection Planck, Mason County, Kentucky. $6,000.00. Right, 1⅛" x 3⅝", Carter Cave, ex-collection Maynard, Greenup County, Kentucky. $4,000.00. *Dr. David R. Thrasher collection, Alabama.*

Fluted point, Sonora flint from Kentucky, 3⅛". The point has a short obverse flute and an arc of lighter-colored material. With a Perino COA, it came from Warrick County, Indiana. *Gilbert Cooper collection.* $2,500.00.

Fluted point, creamy gray mixed Flint Ridge, 3" long. Double-fluted on the reverse and with dark edge patina, it was found in Seneca County, Ohio. *Frank Meyer collection.* $450.00.

Fluted point, Logan County speckled chert, 3½" long. This large point in a local material came from Logan County, Ohio. *Frank Meyer collection.* $950.00.

Fluted point or blade, 3⅛", ex-collection Sims. Edge damage suggests knife use for this piece, found in Butler County, Ohio. *Frank Meyer collection.* $300.00.

79

Fluted point, broken at the flute termination ledge, 4" long. It is made of burnt orange Carter Cave flint, and both pieces were found in a rock shelter. Kentucky. *Frank Meyer collection.* $750.00.

Clovis points, unusual materials, both with Jackson COAs. Left, Flint Ridge translucent moss agate, 1¼" x 4½", ex-collection, Weick, Licking County, Ohio. $10,000.00. Right, Ogallala chert, 1⅜" x 3⅜", ex-collection Elam, Baca County, Colorado. $6,000.00. *Dr. David R. Thrasher collection, Alabama.*

Fluted point, pale mixed blue Upper Mercer, 2³⁄₁₆". The size of the base indicates that this was a resharpened (shortened) point. Scioto County, Ohio. *Len and Janie Weidner collection.* $750.00.

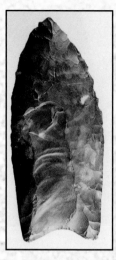

Fluted point, dark glossy undetermined flint with lighter spotting, 2½" long. It is fluted for nearly two-thirds of obverse length. Franklin County, Ohio. *Len and Janie Weidner collection.* $600.00.

Fluted point, glossy gray-brown unknown flint. This example, ex-collection Copeland, has an excellent tip flute. It is 3⅝", from Henry County, Ohio. *Frank Meyer collection.* Museum grade.

Fluted point, 3¹⁄₁₆", reverse flute half of point length. Made of dark Kentucky flint, it was found in Highland County, Ohio. *Frank Meyer collection.* Unlisted.

Fluted point, gray Harrison County (Indiana hornstone) material, 2⁹⁄₁₆". The point has a Perino COA and is ex-collection Brandenburg. Clemont County, Ohio. *Gilbert Cooper collection.* $1,200.00.

80

Clovis point, Early Paleo, made of gray flint. It is 2½" long, thin, and well chipped. Ex-collection Beading, it is from Louisa County, Iowa. *Collection of and photograph by A. D. Savage, Iowa.* $600.00.

Clovis point, glossy cream Missouri flint, 3⅜". With a short and wide flute, it is ex-collection Vinzant. Mercer County, Missouri. *Collection of and photograph by A. D. Savage, Iowa.* $1,800.00.

Fluted point, Debert-like deeply concave baseline, unknown blackish-blue and gray flint. It is 4½" long and has a Perino COA. This is a fine point in all respects. Adams County, Ohio. *Gilbert Cooper collection.* Museum grade.

Fluted point, unknown chert in shades of grayish brown, 4¹⁵⁄₁₆". It has a Perino COA and good overall form. Franklin County, Virginia. *Gilbert Cooper collection.* Museum grade.

Fluted point, blue glossy Upper Mercer, 2⅞". The obverse is double-fluted with narrow channels, and the artifact is ex-collection Weick. Pickaway County, Ohio. *Len and Janie Weidner collection.* $900.00.

Fluted point, extremely long and slender for a Clovis, double-fluted on the obverse. It is 6⅜", ex-collection Roland, and has a Perino COA. This superb example was picked up in Geauga County, Ohio. *Gilbert Cooper collection.* Museum grade.

Fluted point, Early Paleo, 2⅞" long. The material is a beautiful unknown flint, translucent milky flint with reddish-purple spotting. It was picked up in Athens County, Ohio. *Len and Janie Weidner collection.* Museum grade.

Fluted point, multiple shallow flutes on the obverse, 4⅜", unidentified flint. It was found by R. Ford in the 1930s, and has differing patination on the two faces. Tishomingo County, Mississippi. *Len and Janie Weidner collection.* Museum grade.

Fluted point, unidentified orange flint, 3⅜" long. Very well chipped, the point came from Highland County, Ohio. *Len and Janie Weidner collection.* $1,250.00.

Fluted point, unknown flint in shades of gray, 2⅝". Fluted almost full length, the example was found in Indiana. *Len and Janie Weidner collection.* $900.00.

Clovis point, fluted for two-thirds length on the obverse, 3" long. Tan glossy flint, this is a superior point in pristine condition. Jasper region, Alabama. *Collection of and photograph by A. D. Savage, Iowa.* $1,700.00.

Clovis point, Early Paleo, 3¼" long. Carter Cave flint from Kentucky, both lower faces of the Clovis are fluted. A fine example, it was found in Kentucky. *Collection of and photograph by A. D. Savage, Iowa.* $1,500.00.

Fluted point, intermixed blue and gray-tan Harrison County (Indiana) flint, 3⅛". The large obverse flute runs for two-thirds of length, and the artifact came from Morgan County, Ohio. *Len and Janie Weidner collection.* $650.00.

Fluted point, gray Indiana or Kentucky hornstone, 2⅞". The basal flute is crisp and distinct, with a pronounced termination ledge. The fluted point came from Pickaway County, Ohio. *Len and Janie Weidner collection.* $900.00.

Fluted point, mixed blue Upper Mercer with darker blue and near-yellow, 2⅞". It was found in Licking County, Ohio. *Frank Meyer collection.* Unlisted.

Clovis point, Indiana or Kentucky hornstone, 3¼". Well chipped, it was found in Pickaway County, Ohio. *Frank Meyer collection.* $400.00.

Fluted point, Carter Cave amber-brown, ex-collection Bussel. The point is 2⅜" and has a Davis COA. Fleming County, Kentucky. *Gilbert Cooper collection.* $500.00.

Holcombe point, ultra thin and 2¼" long, three flutes on the obverse. Made of mixed Upper Mercer, the lower left corner has burin flaking. This piece has a Perino COA and came from Ross County, Ohio. *Gilbert Cooper collection.* Unlisted.

Fluted point, 3¹⁵⁄₁₆" long, pale blue Upper Mercer with lighter and darker inclusions. The point has a recurved baseline and is ex-collection Ritchie. Franklin County, Ohio. *Jim Miller collection.* $3,000.00.

Simpson point, brown river-stained Coastal Plains chert, 1½" x 3¼". It has Davis COA #10011 and is ex-collection Claytor. It was found in Florida. *Dr. David R. Thrasher collection, Alabama.* $4,000.00.

Fluted point, Carter Cave flint in three colors, 2⅞" long. Not all Paleo points need large size to be highly desirable. It has a Perino COA and was picked up in Fleming County, Kentucky. *Gilbert Cooper collection.* $2,500.00.

83

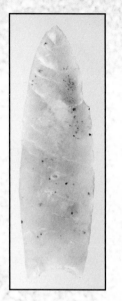

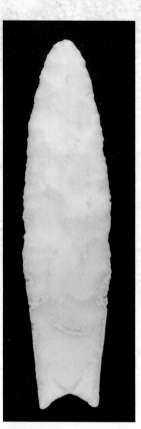

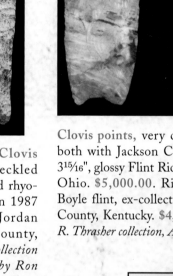

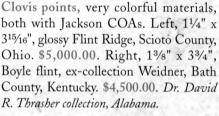

Clovis point, highly translucent agate with small inclusions, 2⅞". The obverse flute is ⅝" long, and the point is ex-collection Mullins. It has a Davis COA, and the Clovis is from New Mexico. *Earthworks Artifacts.* $2,800.00.

Clovis point, fluted on both lower faces, 6⅞". This very long point or blade is made of novaculite and has a Perino COA. It is a very superior piece in terms of size and workstyle, from Woodruff County, Arkansas. *Earthworks Artifacts.* Museum grade.

Eastern fluted Clovis point, 3" long, speckled green and weathered rhyolite. It was found in 1987 by a farmer near Jordan Lake. Chatham County, North Carolina. *Collection of and photograph by Ron Harris, North Carolina.* $450.00.

Clovis points, very colorful materials, both with Jackson COAs. Left, 1¼" x 3¹⁵⁄₁₆", glossy Flint Ridge, Scioto County, Ohio. $5,000.00. Right, 1⅜" x 3¾", Boyle flint, ex-collection Weidner, Bath County, Kentucky. $4,500.00. *Dr. David R. Thrasher collection, Alabama.*

Fluted point, high-grade Flint Ridge in patinated colors and with quartz veins, 3½" long. It has a small tip flute and fine workstyle. Marion County, Ohio. *Len and Janie Weidner collection.* $950.00.

Fluted point, cream and gray Upper Mercer, ex-collection Wertz. This point is 2½" and has a Perino COA. Point Pleasant area, West Virginia. *Gilbert Cooper collection.* $450.00.

Clovis point, Early Paleo, double flutes on reverse, 2⅝". Made of dark Upper Mercer, this point is ex-collection Bob Champion and was depicted on his business card. Also ex-collection Hyatt, the Clovis was found in the town of Mount Vernon, Knox County, Ohio. *Jim Miller collection.* $1,500.00.

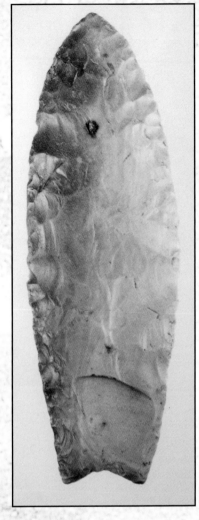

Fluted point, Sonora (Kentucky) flint in two basic colors, 4" long. The reverse flute on the specimen is 2¼" long. It has a Perino COA and was picked up in Fleming County, Kentucky. *Gilbert Cooper collection*. Museum grade.

Clovis point, classic form with deep V-shaped baseline, ex-collection Townsend. This point has a Perino COA, and the material is Upper Mercer in several shades of blue. This very fine point is 4⅜" long and has all attributes of size, condition, material, and workstyle. Stark County, Ohio. *Gilbert Cooper collection*. Museum grade.

Fluted point, glossy Indiana hornstone in several shades, 5¼". This piece has good size, workstyle, and condition, plus a Perino COA. Jay County, Indiana. *Earthworks Artifacts*. $8,500.00.

Clovis points, both with Jackson COAs. Left, 1⁵/₁₆" x 4⅝", Knife River flint, ex-collection Sourgarten. It came from near Alliance in Box Butte County, Nebraska. $7,000.00. Right, Ross County variety, 1⁷/₁₆" x 3¹⁵/₁₆", ex-collection Simms. Carter Cave flint, it was found in the 1950s in Dickenson County, Virginia. $4,500.00. *Dr. David R. Thrasher collection, Alabama*.

Holcombe point, both faces with multiple flutes, 3⅝", mixed blue Upper Mercer flint. A very fine example, it is ex-collection Copeland. Franklin County, Ohio. *Frank Meyer collection.* $1,800.00.

Fluted point, translucent Boyle flint, 4" long. (Boyle has so many color variations it is sometimes mistaken for Flint Ridge.) This point has a Perino COA and came from Fleming County, Kentucky. *Gilbert Cooper collection.* Museum grade.

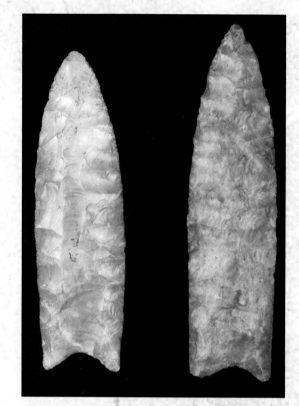

Clovis points, high-grade specimens with Jackson COAs. Left, 1⅛" x 4", ex-collection Ritter, pink Missouri flint, Stoddard County, Missouri. $4,500.00. Right, 1⅛" x 4½", gray-brown Coshocton, ex-collection Shipley. Pictured in *Artifacts*, and *CSAJ* in January 1991, it is from Perry County, Ohio. $6,000.00. *Dr. David R. Thrasher collection, Alabama.*

Clovis point, translucent Carter Cave flint in two shades, reverse with double flutes. Attractive and in high-grade material, the point is 3⅞" and has a Perino COA. Jackson County, Kentucky. *Earthworks Artifacts.* Museum grade.

Clovis fluted point, 3¹¹⁄₁₆" long, gold-colored quartzite. With a long obverse flute, this fine point has a Perino COA. It is from near Berea, Kentucky. *Tony Putty collection, Indiana.* $2,800.00.

Clovis fluted point, 3³⁄₁₆", black and off-white Upper Mercer (Coshocton) flint. It has an overlapping obverse flute and a Perino COA. Scioto County, Ohio. *Tony Putty collection, Indiana.* $2,200.00.

Cumberland fluted point, 3¼", dark gray hornstone with strong fluting on both faces. This scarce point type has a Perino COA and was found in Christian County, Kentucky. *Tony Putty collection, Indiana.* $2,600.00.

Clovis point, Early Paleo, 2" long, translucent honey agate. The base is double-fluted on this example. Ex-collections Lilljedahl and Easterwood, it is from West Texas. *Dr. Guy H. Gross collection, Texas.* $750.00.

Clovis fluted point, 2⅞". It is finely made in a glossy bluish-beige flint and has a Perino COA. The point was found along the Ohio River in Spencer County, Indiana. *Tony Putty collection, Indiana.* $1,200.00.

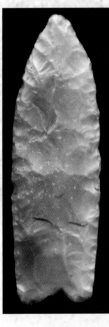

Clovis fluted point, Early Paleo, 3½" long, gray high-grade flint. It has two flutes on the obverse face and is ex-collection German. The Clovis was found on Long King Creek, Polk County, Texas. *Dr. Guy H. Gross collection, Texas.* $2,700.00.

Clovis fluted point, Early Paleo, translucent cream and gold Alibates flint, 2³⁄₁₆" long. It is ex-collection Knowlton and was found in Lincoln County, Nebraska. *Dr. Guy H. Gross collection, Texas.* $1,300.00.

Allen point or blade, 2³⁄₁₆", river-polished Florence chert. It is ex-collections Merriam, Peter, and Richardson, from Osage County, Oklahoma. *Dr. Guy H. Gross collection, Texas.* $450.00.

87

FLUTED POINTS — VARIETIES

East or West, there are many fluted points that are not exact copies of named points. In the East, there are points with characteristics of several fluted point types. If a particular piece looks somewhat like a Clovis, but has differences such as width or baseline, it may be called Clovis-like. Or a more technical term may be used, and *Clovis afinis* (meaning "Clovis-related") may be employed.

Fluting itself ranges from full-length on a point to quite short, and from wide to narrow. Fluting may be on just one face, and single to multiple in terms of flute numbers on a face. One type of fluting, Enterline, has preliminary guide flutes on the left and right, and a final, larger flute between the two.

The ancient experts who did fluting were quite skilled, and usually the flute is fairly well centered on the blade face. However, directional and depth problems sometimes arose, as modern knappers know; sometimes the flint or obsidian seems to have a mind of its own. The flute may angle across the face, and go to and off the edge. Or, the flute may drive part way at a normal depth and then fracture through the flint, breaking the point. Not only are most fluted points demonstrations of fine skill, but they are survivors of the fluting process itself.

Apparently a North American invention, fluted points are mostly signposts of the Early Paleo period, though in the East and West there are Late Paleo fluted points as well. It was not so much that the knowledge of how to make fluted points died out, it was simply that the need for fluted points died away with the eventual disappearance of the large animals (megafauna) that the points had been designed to kill. If mammoths and mastodons had thrived for another few thousand years, the fluted point tradition might have continued as well. It may be that large game animals lived in the watered East longer than in the more arid West, or that cultural chipping fashions continued longer in some regions.

In some places vestiges of fluting survived, almost a lithic echo or memory. Even during fluted point times, other points were made that were nearly identical but lacked the flutes. Some later points retained the lance-like shape. Basal thinning (to aid hafting, not for deep penetration) was at times so bold that the thinning scars mimic fluting.

Folsom point, 1¹⁄₁₆", translucent Knife River flint, well fluted. Found by the owner in 2000, it came from Brookings County, South Dakota. *Harlan Olson collection, South Dakota.* $750.00.

Folsom point, resharpened to a rounded tip, fully fluted. Made of Knife River flint, it was found by the owner in 2001. Brookings County, South Dakota. *Harlan Olson collection, South Dakota.* $100.00.

Cumberland point, 2¾", found in the fall of 2002 by G. Witt. It is fully fluted on the obverse and fluted nearly to the tip on the reverse. The Cumberland's right ear has been restored, and the basal edges are heavily ground. Clark County, Kentucky. *Jeff Schumacher collection, Kentucky.* $1,200.00 – 1,500.00.

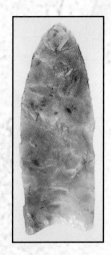

Fluted point, glossy red and milky translucent flint, 2⅜". The tip has some restoration. This piece was found by the owner in 1973. Knox County, Ohio. *Sam Speck collection.* Unlisted.

Fluted point, ex-collection Charles C. Smith, 3⅜". The obverse has multiple flutes and the point was found in 1942. Made of unknown glossy black flint with orange, it is from Jay County, Indiana. *Private collection.* Museum grade.

Fluted point, 2⅛" long, ex-collection Charles C. Smith. Indiana Green flint, there is slight restoration to one ear. Wabash River area, Indiana. *Private collection.* Unlisted.

Fluted point, glossy gray Harrison County (Indiana hornstone) flint, 4⅝" long. The point is ex-collection Mills, and the tip has restoration. Knox County, Ohio. *Sam Speck collection.* Unlisted.

Fluted point, patinated Upper Mercer in four colors, ex-collection Wengard. Very thin, it is 3¼" long. Stark County, Ohio. *Allen Selders collection.* Unlisted.

Fluted point, dark blue Upper Mercer, ex-collections Hyatt and Champion. The point is 2⅝" long and is from Knox County, Ohio. *Allen Selders collection.* Unlisted.

Fluted point, resharpened form, 2¼". Material is gray and cream Upper Mercer, and the point is ex-collection Kiefer. It has a Perino COA and was found in Union County, Ohio. *Gilbert Cooper collection.* $500.00.

Fluted point, Cumberland family, 3" long. The material is probably a glossy variety of Upper Mercer and the point is double fluted on the obverse. Ex-collections Copeland and Wilkins, it has a Perino COA. Licking County, Ohio. *Gilbert Cooper collection.* Museum grade.

89

Fluted point, Early Paleo, tan mixed flint, 1⅝". It is ex-collection Sims, from Clinton County, Ohio. *Private collection.* $300.00.

Fluted point, mottled blue and green Flint Ridge, ex-collection Max Shipley. The example is 1⅝" and was found in Pickaway County, Ohio. *Private collection.* $200.00.

Cumberland point, Bloomville chert, 3⅝". It has multiple COAs and was pictured in *Prehistoric Antiquities Quarterly*, May 2003. The Cumberland was found in Warrick County, Indiana. *Earthworks Artifacts*; *Ed Rowe photograph.* $3,500.00.

Folsom point, translucent Montana dendritic agate. It was found by Norvil Evans, ca. 1948 – 1955. Hooker County, Nebraska. *Jim Horst collection, Nebraska.* $2,500.00.

Fluted point, patinated blue, green, and tan Flint Ridge, 2⅜" long. A well-made point in near-jewel material, it came from Delaware County, Ohio. *Private collection.* $1,500.00.

Cumberland point, fine specimen, Late Paleo, 1" x 4⅜". The material is blue-black flint and the point has balanced ears and is fluted on both lower faces. Ex-collection Lyerla, it came from Alabama. *Tom Fouts collection, Kansas.* $3,500.00.

Folsom point, fully fluted, high-grade pinkish tan mottled flint, ⅞" x 1⅞". It was found in northeastern Alabama. *Tom Fouts collection, Kansas.* $2,500.00.

Clovis point, Attica chert (Indiana Green), tip reworked. This example was found by the owner in Rush County, Indiana. *Jeff Anderson collection, Indiana.* $150.00.

Fluted point, resharpened size, 2¹⁄₁₆". It is made of weathered silicified shale and is ex-collection Mabe. The point was found near Cameron in Moore County, North Carolina. *Collection of and photograph by Ron Harris, North Carolina.* $350.00.

Paleo point, with shallow flute, slight restoration, 2⅜" long. The material is weatherized silicified shale and the point is ex-collection Mabe. Randolph County, North Carolina. *Collection of and photograph by Ron Harris, North Carolina.* $350.00.

Fluted point, resharpened size, lower blade edges ground. It is 1½" long, and the material is Flint Ridge or high-grade Upper Mercer. Morrow County, Ohio. *Jesse Weber collection; photograph by Norman's Photo, Newcomerstown, Ohio.* $450.00.

Fluted point, slight restoration, 5¼" long. This large and fine point is ex-collection Mabe and was found in Randolph County, North Carolina. *Collection of and photograph by Ron Harris, North Carolina.* $850.00.

Fluted point, blue Upper Mercer or Harrison County (Indiana), flint, 1⅘". Ex-collection Fisher, it is from Fairfield County, Ohio. *Mike Diano collection, Florida.* $300.00.

Fluted point, with two small flutes on the obverse, 2¾". Made of glossy Coshocton gray flint, it came from Morgan County, Ohio. *Jesse Weber collection; photograph by Norman's Photo, Newcomerstown, Ohio.* $250.00.

Cumberland point, fluted to tip on obverse and serrated edges, 1³⁄₁₆" x 3⅜". The material is nodular chert and it has a Burgess/Mabry COA. It was found by J. Caudell in Simpson County, Kentucky. *Doug Goodrum collection, Kentucky.* Museum grade.

Fluted point, resharpened size and needle tip, Delaware County chert. It has Enterline multiple fluting and is 2" long. Found by the owner, the point is from Fairfield County, Ohio. *Mike Diano collection, Florida.* $200.00.

Folsom point, 1⅛", Edwards Plateau chert, ex-collection Clauss. It has a large obverse flute and was found in Angelina County, Texas. *Dr. Guy Gross collection, Texas.* $1,200.00.

Folsom point, Late Paleo, 1¼", Alibates flint. This point, with part of the fluting protrusion still present, is ex-collections Hough and Selmer. Gaines County, Texas. *Dr. Guy Gross collection, Texas.* $1,800.00.

Cumberland point, fluted full-length on obverse, 3³⁄₁₆". The material is Fort Payne chert and it is ex-collections Ross and Rowe. Perry County, Kentucky. *Bill Moody collection, Massachusetts.* $2,500.00.

Clovis-related point, shallow flute on one face, 2" long. It is made of Felsite and was found along a brook that flows into North River. Plymouth County, Massachusetts. *Bill Moody collection, Massachusetts.* $250.00.

Fluted point, multiple obverse flutes, 2¼". This piece is fluted on both faces, and the right ear was restored. Fairfield County, Ohio. *Don Casto collection.* Unlisted.

Clovis point or small blade, Burlington chert, 2⅛" long. With a flute about two-fifths length, it came from the Western Bluff area, Jersey County, Illinois. *Gregory L. Perdun collection, Illinois.* $325.00.

Cumberland fluted point, fluted to the tip on both faces, 3⅕" long, ⁹⁄₁₀" wide. It has a Granger COA, and its material is chocolate brown Dover flint. With patination and water stain, it was river found in 1994, by a clam diver. Florence area, Alabama. *Mike Trekell collection, Minnesota.* $3,500.00.

92

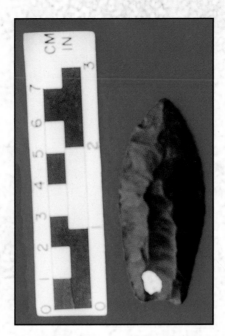

Paleo point, obverse with long flute and reverse unfluted, 2⁵⁄₁₆". The material is patinated Upper Mercer and the point is probably from Ohio. *Private collection.* Unlisted.

Northumberland fluted point or blade, obverse with wide full-length flute, black chert. The example is also fluted on the reverse. Berks County, Pennsylvania. *Fogelman collection.* $400.00.

Northumberland fluted point or blade, reverse with narrow flute for three-fifths overall length, black chert. Berks County, Pennsylvania. *Fogelman collection.* $400.00.

Fluted point, blue Upper Mercer flint, 1¾" long. Many Ohio fluted points are made of dark Upper Mercer material. Marion County, Ohio. *Terry Elleman collection, Ohio.* $500.00.

Fluted point, flutes wide and flat on both faces, translucent creamy tan material that may be Flint Ridge. For size, fluted points are the most valuable chipped artifacts in North America. It is 1½" long. Ohio county unknown. *Terry Elleman collection, Ohio.* $750.00.

Fluted point, blue Upper Mercer flint, 2⅜". It is ex-collection Ayres and was found in the Zanesville area, Muskingum County, Ohio. *Sam Speck collection.* Unlisted.

Fluted point, Flint Ridge translucent gray, 1¾" long, well made. It is probably from Hardin County, Ohio. *Frank Otto collection.* $500.00.

Fluted point, 2¾", translucent yellow-brown flint. Ex-collection Robinson, it came from Darke County, Ohio. *Frank Meyer collection.* $150.00.

Unfluted-fluted point, dark Kentucky flint, 2¼" long. It was found in Ohio. *Frank Meyer collection.* Unlisted.

Folsom point, tan and brown flint, 1⅝". This rare point is ex-collection Barnett and was found in Colorado. *Private collection.* Museum grade.

Fluted point, large flute termination hinge, dark Onondaga(?) flint. It is 2" long, from Portage County, Ohio. *Frank Meyer collection.* Unlisted.

Fluted point, creamy tan Burlington flint, ex-collection Townsend. The point is 3⅛" long, from Fulton County, Illinois. *Private collection.* Museum grade.

Fluted point, chipped into a lanceolate form, with flutes near center of both faces. This would be a combination Early Paleo — Late Paleo piece. An unusual example, it is 3¼" and made of black Upper Mercer flint. Wood County, Ohio. *Frank Meyer collection.* $300.00.

Fluted point, waxy Boyle chert from Kentucky, 3⅝". The reverse flute is 2¾" and runs to the edge. The point has a Perino COA and is from Nicholas County, Kentucky. *Gilbert Cooper collection.* $1,500.00.

Fluted point, glossy butterscotch that may be a patinated Flint Ridge, 2¼". Found in the 1930s, it has a Perino COA and the reverse flute is full length. Ross County, Ohio. *Gilbert Cooper collection.* $600.00.

Fluted point or blade, very rounded tip, ex-collection Wertz. It is made of Brush Creek or Brassfield chert and carries both Earthworks and Perino COAs. The size is 2⅝" and the point came from Brown County, Ohio. *Gilbert Cooper collection.* $750.00.

Folsom point, Late Paleo, 1¹⁄₁₆" x 2¾". Found in recently broken condition and now glued, it is the owner's best find (year 2002) in over fifty years of surface hunting. Made of a form of High Plains agate, the Folsom is fluted to the tip on both faces. It is considered the best type find from the state, and has been pictured in *Indian Artifact Magazine*. The Folsom came from Brookings County, South Dakota. *Harlan Olson collection, South Dakota.* Museum grade.

Northumberland point, obverse with nearly full-length flute, base slightly concave. It is from New Castle County, Delaware. *Fogelman collection.* $1,000.00.

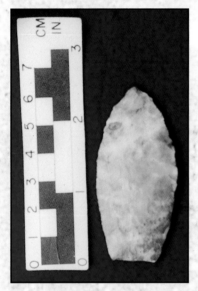

Fluted point, fully fluted on both faces, 1⅞" long. The material is highly translucent cream and white Flint Ridge. Ohio county unknown. *Terry Elleman collection, Ohio.* $900.00.

Cumberland point, found in two halves and now reassembled. Normanskill chert. Well formed, it was found near Saginaw, York County, Pennsylvania. *Fogelman collection.* $2,000.00.

Northumberland point, unfluted reverse face, pale variegated jasper. The artifact was found in New Castle County, Delaware. *Fogelman collection.* $1,000.00.

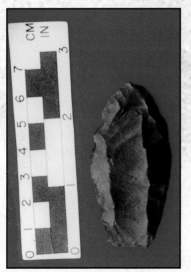

Northumberland fluted point or blade, obverse with nearly full-length flute, reverse unfluted, black chert. This rare Paleo artifact form came from Berks County, Pennsylvania. *Fogelman collection.* $400.00.

Debert point, Late Paleo period, medium-colored jasper. With typical, very deeply incurvate baseline, it is ex-collection Savidge. Lycoming County, Pennsylvania. *Fogelman collection.* $4,000.00.

Fluted point, rounded tip often seen on Clovis-related points. Onondaga chert. It was found by P. Frey and came from a major site in Pennsylvania. *Fogelman collection.* $500.00.

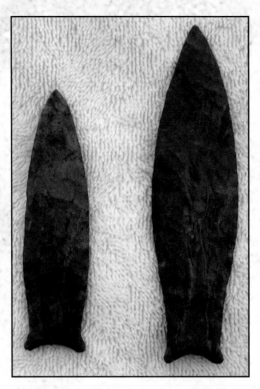

Cumberland points, dark chert, Late Paleo. Both are ex-collection Snyder, from Humphreys County, Tennessee. Left, 1" x 3¾", short flute. $2,000.00. Right, 1¼" x 4¾", short flute, classic shape. $5,000.00. *Collection of and photograph by Gary Henry, North Carolina.*

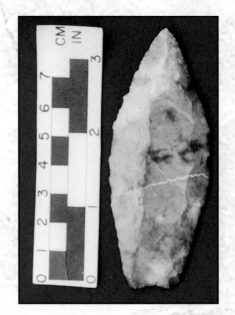

Northumberland point, obverse with large flute for three-fourths of length, variegated jasper. This example came from Indiana County, Pennsylvania. *Fogelman collection.* $1,500.00.

Folsom point, full-length obverse flute, glossy white flint with darker inclusions. It is 1⅝" long. New Mexico. *John and Susan Mellyn collection, Texas.* $1,800.00.

Folsom points, Late Paleo, both from Illinois. Left, mixed flint, 1¼". Right, white flint, 1½". *John and Susan Mellyn collection, Texas.* Each, $1,250.00.

Northumberland point, reverse unfluted, variegated jasper with white clouding. This is a classic example of a rare Paleo point or blade type. Indiana County, Pennsylvania. *Fogelman collection.* $1,500.00.

Fluted point, obverse face fluted nearly to tip, reverse fluted about one-half of length. The point is 2½" long, thin, and made of mixed Upper Mercer flint. Crawford County, Ohio. *Dwight Wolfe collection.* Museum grade.

Fluted point, short obverse flute, dark Upper Mercer flint. This slender point is 3⅛" and is from the Oak Harbor area, Ohio. *Dwight Wolfe collection.* $350.00.

Fluted knife, Indiana Green flint, 2⅝". The obverse flute is 1¾" long, and the artifact came from Lake County, Indiana. *Dwight Wolfe collection.* $50.00.

Fluted point, nearly full-length flute on obverse, brown jasper. This piece is ¾" x 1¹⁵⁄₁₆" and was found by the owner in Hunterdon County, New Jersey. *Bob Bronish collection, New Jersey.* Unlisted.

Paleo point, fluted both faces, Indiana Green flint. It is probably from the eastern Midwest. *Dwight Wolfe collection.* $400.00.

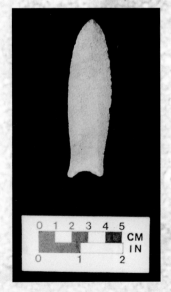

Cumberland point, Late Paleo, brown and gray chert. With extended ears, the point came from the Mammoth Cave area, Kentucky. *Rodney M. Peck collection, North Carolina.* $5,000.00.

Cumberland point, Late Paleo fluted point, slender example made of brown Dover chert. It came from Wayne County, Kentucky. *Rodney M. Peck collection, North Carolina.* $3,000.00.

Quad(?) point, fluted obverse base, glossy tan jasper, 1" x 2⅝". This piece with narrowed ears has a Davis COA and came from Indiana. *Keith and Rhonda Dodge collection, Michigan.* $800.00.

97

Fluted point, gray and cream Onondaga or Upper Mercer, fully fluted on both faces. The obverse fluting was done from the tip. This point, 1⅞" long, was obtained from the finder about 1952 and was the first fluted point in the author's collection. Coshocton County, Ohio. *Lar Hothem collection.* $300.00

Fluted points, Early Paleo, white flint example on right with wide flute is 2¹³⁄₁₆" and was found in 1987. The river-stained point on left has two flutes and was found by A. Armstrong in 1993. Both points are from Van Buren County, Iowa. *Dale and Betty Roberts collection, Iowa.* Each, $900.00.

Folsom point, rare type, pink and gray chert. It has a full flute on the obverse, a one-third flute on the reverse face, and retains the fluting protrusion near the baseline center. Holt County, Missouri. *Mike George collection, Missouri; Terry Price photograph.* Museum grade.

Folsom point, rare type, gray chert, ⅞" x 1¼". Faces are both fluted from one-half of point length and there are remnants of the basal fluting nipple. The Folsom was found following terrace construction. Holt County, Missouri. *Mike George collection, Missouri; Terry Price photograph.* Museum grade.

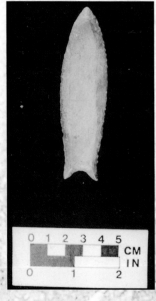

Cumberland point, light brown Dover chert, fluted to tip on obverse face. A very fine example of a scarce type, it was found in Taylor County, Kentucky. *Rodney M. Peck collection, North Carolina.* $7,000.00.

Cumberland point, gray and white Fort Payne chert, ¹⁵⁄₁₆" x 2⁹⁄₁₆". This Late Paleo point, fully fluted, has a Davis COA. Bath County, Kentucky. *Keith and Rhonda Dodge collection, Michigan.* $750.00.

Cumberland point, Late Paleo, gray mottled hornstone, ¹⁵⁄₁₆" x 2¹⁵⁄₁₆". It has a Davis COA and was found in Crawford County, Indiana. *Keith and Rhonda Dodge collection, Michigan.* $1,000.00.

Cumberland point, off-white Brassfield chert, 13/16" x 2½". With a Davis COA, it is from Clark County, Kentucky. *Keith and Rhonda Dodge collection, Michigan.* $900.00.

Cumberland point, Late Paleo, tan and white Fort Payne chert, 7/8" x 2⅛". It has a Davis COA and came from Logan County, Kentucky. *Keith and Rhonda Dodge collection, Michigan.* $600.00.

Cumberland point, Dover gray with black chert, 21mm x 71mm. It was found by Steve Ham and has a Perino COA. Benton County, Tennessee. *Keith and Rhonda Dodge collection, Michigan.* $500.00.

Folsom points, lengths range from 1¼" to 1 15/16". Made of various high-grade regional materials, they are from the states of Colorado, Oklahoma, Texas, and New Mexico. *Michael Hough collection, California.* Each, $2,000.00 – 4,000.00.

Crowfield point, gray flint, with typical shallow multiple fluting. This example is 1" x 2" long and was found in Pennsylvania. *Collection of and photograph by H. B. Greene II, Florida.* $175.00.

Paleo fluted point, black mixed flint, obverse face fully fluted. It measures 1" x 2" and was found near Duncannon, Pennsylvania. *Collection of and photograph by H. B. Greene II, Florida.* $175.00.

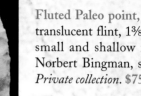

Fluted Paleo point, light and dark gray translucent flint, 1⅜". The obverse has a small and shallow flute. Ex-collection Norbert Bingman, southeastern Illinois. *Private collection.* $75.00.

Fluted point, with flared base, 1⅞" long, black flint with gray stripes. The obverse flute is 1" long on this point, found in Delaware County, Ohio. *Private collection.* $125.00.

Paleo point, rectangular baseline, creamy tan quartzite. It is 2⁵⁄₁₆" and has a short and narrow flute on the obverse base. Ex-collection Norbert Bingman, southeastern Illinois. *Private collection.* $100.00.

Fluted point, retipped and shortened, 1¾". Dark blue Upper Mercer, it is ex-collection Driskill and Jack Hooks. Ohio. *Doug Hooks collection.* $500.00.

Fluted knife blade, St. Louis variety, patinated brownish-gray flint. This scarce type example measures 1⅝" x 4½" and is ex-collection Norbert Bingman. It has wide and short flutes on each face. Southeastern Illinois. *Private collection.* Museum grade.

Fluted point, non-glossy Upper Mercer blue, 3⅜" long. This point is ex-collection Copeland and was found in Delaware County, Ohio. *Len and Janie Weidner collection.* $575.00.

Fluted point, greenish-gray Upper Mercer, both faces fluted. This fine and slender piece is ex-collections Beer and Jack Hooks. Richland County, Ohio. *Private collection.* $2,500.00.

Fluted point, blue flint in two shades with specks, 2¾". Wide for size, and sturdy, it came from Fairfield County, Ohio. *Len and Janie Weidner collection.* $650.00.

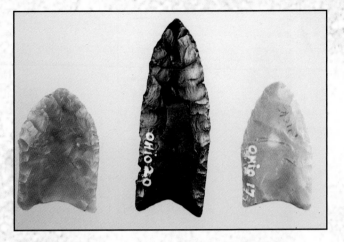

Fluted point, narrowed flute for more than two-thirds of obverse length, blue Upper Mercer flint. It is 2⅜" long, ex-collection Copeland. Highland County, Ohio. *Len and Janie Weidner collection.* $550.00.

Three Ohio fluted points, all ex-collection Copeland, center example 2⅜". Left, Flint Ridge gem material. Center, glossy Upper Mercer. Right, Flint Ridge multicolored. *Len and Janie Weidner collection.* Each, $275.00 – 500.00.

Cumberland fluted point, Late Paleo period, fluted full length on both faces, Fort Payne chert. It is 3⅛" long and has a Granger COA. This is a rare piece in undamaged condition and was found in Limestone County, Alabama. *Back to Earth.* Musuem grade.

Paleo points, sold May 4, 2002, bid amounts included 10% buyers' premiums. Left, lot 183, 1¹⁄₁₆" x 2⁵⁄₁₆", Folsom, Howard COA, southeastern Iowa. $495.00. Right, lot 184, ¾" x 2¹³⁄₃₂", Barnes Clovis, Perino and Howard COAs, Madison County, Illinois. $2,750.00. The two thin Folsom sections at right, lot 185, have Perino COAs and are from Cheyenne County, Colorado. $357.50. *Rainbow Traders, Illinois.*

Fluted Paleo points, bid amounts included 10% buyers' premiums. Left, Hixton sugar quartz Clovis, 1" x 3¾", lot 163, with Howard COA. Green Lake County, Wisconsin. $4,675.00. Right, lot 158, Perino and Howard COAs, high-grade mixed flint. At 1" x 2⅞", it is from Union County, Ohio. $1,540.00. *Rainbow Traders, Illinois.*

Fluted Paleo point (on right), pictured with a Cache River from the Early Archaic period. Lot 7, sold August 24, 2002, has a 10% buyers' premium reflected in the final figure. It is 1⅜" long and has a Howard COA. *Rainbow Traders, Illinois.* $742.50.

Paleo point, lot 110, shown with Archaic bottleneck on left, auction date August 24, 2002. Number 110 displays top chipping, and bid figure included a 10% buyers' premium. The point is 1⁵⁄₁₆" x 3⁵⁄₁₆" and has both Howard and Perino COAs. Craighead County, Arkansas. *Rainbow Traders, Illinois.* $770.00.

Paleo point, well fluted, lot 92 of auction date August 24, 2002. Bid figure reflected the 10% buyers' premium for this piece, which has both Howard and Motley COAs. The piece is 1" x 3" and was picked up in Fayette County, Illinois. *Rainbow Traders, Illinois.* $880.00.

Cumberland point, with nearly two-thirds flute, Fort Payne chert, tip reworked into a tool shape. It was found in Barren County, Kentucky. *Craig Ferrell collection.* $200.00.

Fluted point (in group picture elsewhere), large flute for point size, Hughes River chert. This piece came from Mason County, West Virginia. *Craig Ferrell collection.* $125.00.

Ross County(?) subtype Clovis point, fluted, Hughes River (Crookville?) chert. Probably resharpened, it came from Putnam County, West Virginia. *Craig Ferrell collection.* $275.00.

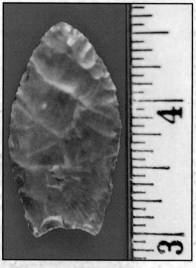

Crowfield (in group picture elsewhere), typical smaller size, very excurvate edges and pointed basal corners. It is chipped in Hillsdale chert and came from near Ripley, Jackson County, West Virginia. *Craig Ferrell collection.* $350.00.

Crowfield (left three) fluted points, all from West Virginia. Left, Hillsdale chert, Jackson County. Next, Coshocton flint, Mason County. Finally, Hughes River flint, Mason County. On the right is a Hughes River from Putnam County. *Craig Ferrell collection.* Each, $60.00 – 350.00.

Fluted points, made of dark gray (left) and light gray (right) Coshocton flints. They came from a well-known Paleo site in Stark County, Ohio. *Rodney M. Peck collection, North Carolina.* Each, $2,000.00.

Clovis and related points, Little River Clovis complex. The three largest are made of Hopkinsville chert and the small point is red Harrodsburg chert. Christian County, Kentucky. *Rodney M. Peck collection, North Carolina.* All, $700.00.

Fluted point, 4½" long, yellow jasper. This large Early Paleo artifact is strongly fluted on the obverse and was found in northern Pennsylvania. *Private collection.* $2,500.00 plus.

Fluted point, triple-fluted on the obverse, 2⅞" long. The material is black flint and the point was found in Cumberland County, Pennsylvania. *Private collection.* $800.00 plus.

Paleo point, 2" long, gray and white striped flint. Fluted on one face, it was found by the owner in Macoupin County, Illinois. *Dortha Milligan collection, Illinois; Kevin Calvin photograph.* Unlisted.

Northumberland(?) fluted lanceolate, a rare combination of characteristics, 3⅞". The material is patinated Upper Mercer and the point is ex-collections Shipley and Tolliver. Pickaway County, Ohio. *Private collection.* $1,500.00.

Folsom point, lot 146 of auction date September 22, 2001, bid figure included 10% buyers' premium. Late Paleo Folsoms are rare fluted points, and this example is ⅞" x 2⅛". It has a Perino COA, is made of petrified wood, and came from Yuma County, Colorado. *Rainbow Traders, Illinois.* $2,117.00.

Northumberland(?) fluted lanceolate, multiple shallow flutes, 3¾". It is Upper Mercer flint patinated to blue-gray, with a small section of the original flint surface in maroon. Ex-collection Jack Hooks, it was found in Richland County, Ohio. *Doug Hooks collection.* $1,500.00.

Paleo point, Perino auction date August 24, 2002, lot 168. This finely chipped piece was one of Mr. Perino's best, measuring 4½" long. The bid figure included a 10% buyers' premium. Jersey County, Illinois. *Rainbow Traders, Illinois.* $8,250.00.

Cumberland points, each with Jackson COAs. Left, Carter Cave flint, 4" long, Fleming County, Kentucky. $5,000.00. Center, unidentified flint, 3¼", Tennessee. $4,000.00. Right, Indiana hornstone, 3¾", Daviess County, Kentucky. $5,000.00. *Dr. David R. Thrasher collection, Alabama.*

Paleo points, all left to right, each value figure has 10% buyers' premium added to bid figure. These were all sold February 9, 2002, in the first Filbrandt auction. Quad, lot 164, 3⅛", Perino COA, Bangor chert, Tennessee. $990.00. Cumberland, lot 161, 3 1/16", Perino COA, Fort Payne flint. $2,420.00. Clovis, lot 167, wide with bull's-eye, Cobden chert, 3 3/16", Howard and Dickey COAs, Stewart County, Tennessee. $4,785.00. Clovis, lot 166, 2⅜", Dover chert, Davis COA, Henry County, Tennessee. $412.50. *Rainbow Traders, Illinois.*

Folsom point, translucent Edwards Plateau flint, ¾" x 1½". This very scarce point is ex-collections Anthony and Jones, and has Jackson COA #7025. It was found along the Leon River, Bexar County, Texas. *Dr. David R. Thrasher collection, Alabama.* $7,000.00.

Paleo points, both with Jackson COAs. Left, 1¼" x 2½", unidentified flint, ex-collection Waters, Nebraska. $2,500.00. Right, white quartzite. Unlisted. *Dr. David R. Thrasher collection, Alabama.*

Fluted point group, most Early Paleo and shown elsewhere in book. The bottom right Clovis is 3⅜" long. *Dr. David R. Thrasher collection, Alabama.*

Holcombe point, multiple flutes, 2¾". Made of brownish gray Upper Mercer, it is ex-collection Johanson, from Ottawa County, Ohio. *Jim Miller collection.* $2,000.00.

Fluted point, fluted for more than two-thirds obverse length, 2⅞". It is made of blue Upper Mercer and is ex-collection Copeland. Knox County, Ohio. *Len and Janie Weidner collection.* $575.00.

Fluted point, 3" long, patinated light tan flint with a bold and angled flute termination. It was picked up in the Baltimore locality, Fairfield County, Ohio. *Len and Janie Weidner collection.* $700.00.

Fluted points from Ohio, left example 2¼" long. Left, Upper Mercer flint. Center, Delaware County flint. Right, Flint Ridge. *Len and Janie Weidner collection.* Each, $400.00 – 600.00.

Cumberland point, double flutes on obverse, black Kentucky flint. Size is ¾" x 2¹³⁄₁₆", and the point has a Davis COA. It was found in Kentucky. *Keith and Rhonda Dodge collection, Michigan.* $600.00.

Cumberland point, ⅞" x 3⅛", Fort Payne chert in tan and white. This point has a Davis COA and was found in Tennessee. *Keith and Rhonda Dodge collection, Michigan.* $1,500.00.

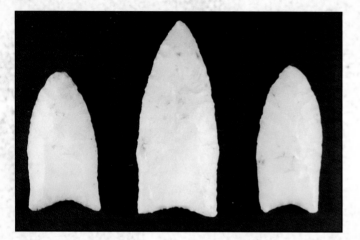

Fluted points, all pale glossy Flint Ridge and from Ohio. Left, ex-collections Vietzen and Wolfe, Lorain County. $800.00. Center, 2¾", found east of North Lewisburg. $1,000.00. Right, ex-collection Hiles, found near Mason, Warren County. $1,000.00. *Jim Miller collection.*

Fluted point, Early Paleo, Flint Ridge with red and orange spotting. It is 1½" long and the obverse face has multiple flutes. It was found by the owner in Knox County, Ohio. *Carl Harruff collection.* $300.00.

Fluted point, mottled opaque Upper Mercer patinated in several colors, bottom corner tip restored. It is 2½", from Licking County, Ohio. *Dr. John Winsch collection.* Unlisted.

Fluted point, 3½" long, yellow jasper shading to red at the tip. It has a shallow basal concavity and was found in Franklin County, Pennsylvania. *Private collection.* $1,500.00 plus.

Fluted point, 2⅞", several shades of yellow jasper. It has ground basal edges and was found in northeastern Pennsylvania. *Private collection.* $800.00 plus.

Fluted point, brown and tan flint, 1¼" x 2⅞". There are double short flutes on the reverse, and a shaft-scraper was chipped in the left edge. With tip rounded from use, it is ex-collection Norbert Bingman. Southeastern Illinois. *Private collection.* $175.00.

Fluted Paleo point, translucent gray with tan granular flint, 2¹⁄₁₆". With casual shouldering, it is ex-collection Norbert Bingman, from southeastern Illinois. *Private collection.* $100.00.

Fluted point, Early Paleo period, colorful Flint Ridge that is very translucent in parts, 2¹⁵⁄₁₆". It came from Pickaway County, Ohio. *Dr. John Winsch collection.* Unlisted.

Fluted point, glossy mixed Upper Mercer, 2⁵⁄₁₆". The obverse has both a wide and a narrow flute, and the baseline is deeply incurvate. It has an Earthworks COA and was found in Ohio. *Earthworks Artifacts.* $650.00.

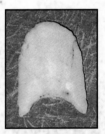

Folsom point, Late Paleo, 1⅛" long. High-grade Burlington was used for this rare piece, which has a Motley COA. Adams County, Illinois. *Collection of and photograph by A. D. Savage, Iowa.* $500.00.

Fluted point, dark brown flint that is translucent on the edges, 2½". The point has a Rogers COA and was found in Sutton County, Texas. *Earthworks Artifacts.* $400.00.

Fluted point, patinated Carter Cave flint, 2½". It has Davis and Perino COAs and was found in Lincoln County, Kentucky. *Earthworks Artifacts.* $1,100.00.

Fluted point, Boyle chert (Kentucky), 2⅝". Nicely shaped, this point is ex-collection West. With a Perino COA, it is from Breathitt County, Kentucky. *Earthworks Artifacts.* $1,100.00.

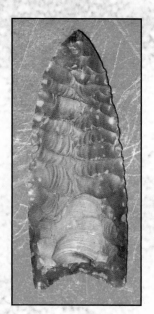

Fluted point, Paleo period, gray and tan flint with a medium gloss. The point is 3" long and has transverse flaking. It came from Tennessee. *Collection of and photograph by A. D. Savage, Iowa.* $1,300.00.

Fluted Paleo point, obsidian, 2¼". This well-made point was found in 1953 by M. Powell in the Sandhills region of New Mexico. *Collection of and photograph by A.D. Savage, Iowa.* $900.00.

Fluted point, barbed ears, 2" long. The material is Burlington chert and the artifact is ex-collection Johnson. Ouachita County, Arkansas. *Collection of and photograph by A. D. Savage, Iowa.* $500.00.

Paleo point, multiple flutes on obverse, unidentified glossy flint in two colors. Carefully fluted, the example is 2⁷/₁₆". Union County, Ohio. *Len and Janie Weidner collection.* $750.00.

Fluted point, blue flint streaked with lighter and darker colors, 2½" long. The Early Paleo point was found in Franklin County, Ohio. *Len and Janie Weidner collection.* $500.00.

Fluted point, 2⅝", resharpened to hafting area. The material is Kentucky Elkhorn and the point or blade came from Hopkins County, Kentucky. *Len and Janie Weidner collection.* $650.00.

Fluted point, light tan flint, 3⅝". This material is from southern Illinois, and the artifact has an ex-Stephens sticker. The point is also ex-collection Rivers Anderson. Jackson County, Illinois. *Len and Janie Weidner collection.* $1,750.00.

Fluted point, high-grade Upper Mercer or Flint Ridge in four colors, ex-collection Werk, with multiple obverse fluting. It is 2½" long and was found in Allen County, Ohio. *Len and Janie Weidner collection.* $675.00.

Fluted point, overlapped flutes on obverse, dark Upper Mercer or Onondaga, 2³⁄₁₆". It is perhaps in resharpened size, and it is ex-collections Saunders and Potter. Brown County, Ohio. *Jim Miller collection.* $1,000.00.

Fluted point, lightly shouldered (which provides a broad stem), three side-by-side flutes. It is 2¹⁵⁄₁₆" and is made of dark Upper Mercer flint. Coshocton County, Ohio. *Jim Miller collection.* $1,200.00.

Fluted point, reddish-brown chert or jasper, 2³⁄₈". It has an Earthworks COA and was found in Pulaski County, Kentucky. *Earthworks Artifacts.* $725.00.

Fluted point, brown opaque Dover flint, 3³⁄₁₆" long. This sturdy point has an Earthworks COA and came from Montgomery County, Tennessee. *Earthworks Artifacts.* $1,600.00.

Fluted point, resharpened length, 2⅛". Made of Indiana hornstone, it was found in Harrison County, Indiana. *Earthworks Artifacts.* $525.00.

Fluted point, unknown subtype, expanded blade, fluted for nearly two-fifths of length. It is fluted on both faces and is made of dark blue Upper Mercer. Ex-collection K. Saunders, it is 2¼" long. Hancock County, Ohio. *Lar Hothem collection.* $450.00.

With changes in lifeways, lanceolate (lance-like) points became the main hunting tools in Late Paleo times. These were suitable for both medium-large game (bison, elk, caribou) and smaller game (black bears, deer), and larger points could and did serve as knives.

While the East has more fluted point types than the West, the West has more lanceolate types than the East. In the West, Scotts-bluff squared-stem points were widely used, and also the related Alberta farther north. Hell Gap (shouldered) and Agate Basin (pure lanceolate, also in the East) and Angostura (serrated edges) developed, plus half a dozen others. Between the East and the West, Daltons came into being. This was a very successful point or blade design, and regional varieties or subtypes branched off.

The East also had Agate Basins and many forms of stemmed lances, some almost mirroring those that were in use far to the west. In general, the eastern classes are either unstemmed or have at least some degree of stemming that creates shouldering.

Most lanceolate forms anywhere in North America are long compared to their width, at least when first made and before breakage or resharpening. (The extensive resharpening on many types is the sign that they were used for knives at least part of the time.) Lanceolates, like the fluted points before them, tend to have edge grinding on lower blade edges and on the baseline so that the lashing sinew or cord was not cut.

Midwestern Daltons (ca. 8500 BC), whose length and width echo their lanceolate ancestors, began to have shallow side-notches and edge serrations. The latter suggests that Daltons may have served more as knives than projectile points.

Milnesand or Plainview point, resharpened to a triangular configuration, 3" long. Ex-collection Wilkins, the material is a highly translucent agate in four colors. Western United States. *Gilbert Cooper collection.* $750.00.

Beaver Lake point, ground basal edges, cream and pink flint. It is 3" long and was found in Hamilton County, Tennessee. *John and Susan Mellyn collection, Texas.* $450.00.

Agate Basin point, banded translucent obsidian, 3⅞". This beautiful gem-quality point was found at Baker Dry Lake in eastern Oregon. *John and Susan Mellyn collection, Texas.* Museum grade.

Zella point, Angostura related, excurvate edges and tapered lower blade. The example is 3⅛", from Wilson County, Texas. *John and Susan Mellyn collection, Texas.* $600.00.

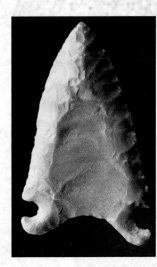

Stemmed Paleo point or blade, mixed pinkish tan glossy flint or chert, 2⁵⁄₁₆", extra-long stem. It was found in Missouri. *John and Susan Mellyn collection, Texas.* $350.00.

Hardaway fluted side-notch point, 2½", high-grade light green rhyolite. This is an exceptional point or blade, and has been pictured in *Central States Archaeological Journal, Carolina Country Magazine, Who's Who in Indian Relics #10,* and *Indian Artifact Magazine.* Stokes County, North Carolina. *Collection of and photograph by Ron Harris, North Carolina.* $975.00.

Dalton point, fluted, 2⅛" long. While the material appears to be Indiana Green flint, it was found in Missouri. *Dwight Wolfe collection.* $300.00.

Dalton points and drills, various grades of chert, longest specimen 2³⁄₁₆". These are ex-collections Snyder and Williams, and their origin is unknown. *Collection of and photograph by Gary Henry, North Carolina.* All, $2,000.00.

Dalton point, Late Paleo, quartzite with darker inclusions. It is ¾" x 1¹⁵⁄₁₆" and was found by the owner. Buncombe County, North Carolina. *Gary Henry collection, North Carolina; Nick Lanier photograph.* $150.00.

Dalton points, resharpened sizes, all from Tennessee. Left, ⅞" x 1¹³⁄₁₆". $30.00. Center, 1³⁄₁₆" x 1½". $40.00. Right, 1⁵⁄₁₆" x 2". $40.00. *Collection of and photograph by Gary Henry, North Carolina.*

Dalton point, mixed chert, ⅞" x 2⁹⁄₁₆". Ex-collection Lantz, it was found in Tunica County, Mississippi. *Collection of and photograph by Gary Henry, North Carolina.* $60.00.

Dalton point, resharpened size, large serrations, 1¾" long. The obverse face has a flute or basal thinning scar that is one-third point length. The Dalton was made of pink flint and came from Missouri. *Brenda Rivers collection, Ohio.* $75.00.

Hardaway Dalton point, greatly resharpened to a triangular form, 2½". The extended ears add much to the artistic appeal of the artifact. Made of banded rhyolite, it came from Alexander County, North Carolina. *Collection of and photograph by Ron Harris, North Carolina.* $275.00.

Alamance point, Late Paleo, 2" long. It is made of weathered rhyolite, and the basal edges are ground. Moore County, North Carolina. *Collection of and photograph by Ron Harris, North Carolina.* $225.00.

Stringtown lance, black Upper Mercer flint, 2⁷⁄₁₆". There are two graver spurs on the base's bottom corners. Perry County, Ohio. *Private collection.* $60.00.

Stringtown lance, Late Paleo, pale gray and maroon unknown flint. The lance is 2⁷⁄₁₆" long, and there are graver spurs (one worn) at base's bottom corners. Perry County, Ohio. *Private collection.* $40.00.

Stringtown lance, gray with cream Upper Mercer, 2⅝". It has worn graver spurs on both of base's bottom corners. Perry County, Ohio. *Private collection.* $50.00.

Beaver Lake point, Late Paleo, two-tone gray flint. The example is 1⅞" long, ex-collection Norbert Bingman. Southeastern Illinois. *Private collection.* $100.00.

Dalton point or blade, creamy chert, 2¾". This piece has resharpened edges and is ex-collection Norbert Bingman. Southeastern Illinois. *Private collection.* $100.00.

Dalton point, Late Paleo, brown and black chert. The example has extended ears and worn serrations. Ex-collection Norbert Bingman, it is 2¾" long. Southeastern Illinois. *Private collection.* $125.00.

Dalton family point or blade, unusual and large serrations, Late Paleo. It is 2⅝" long, milky chert, and ex-collection Norbert Bingman. Southeastern Illinois. *Private collection.* $100.00.

Dalton blade, 5¼", strongly beveled edges from hafting area to tip, which is screwdriver shaped. The material is light tan with purple, orange, and black. Ex-collection Norbert Bingman, southeastern Illinois. *Private collection.* Museum grade.

Dalton point, blue-gray mixed and patinated flint, 3¼". Purchased at a 1989 auction, the Dalton is from the eastern Midwest. *Private collection.* $350.00.

Plainview point, yellow-tan flint, 2" long. It came from the Colorado River area, Colorado County, Texas. *John and Susan Mellyn collection, Texas.* $325.00.

Plainview-related point or blade, pink and white sugar quartz, 1⅞" long. It was picked up in Wilson County, Texas. *John and Susan Mellyn collection, Texas.* $250.00.

Angostura point, rootbeer translucent flint, 2¹⁵⁄₁₆". This is a well-shaped and graceful point, found in Wilson County, Texas. *John and Susan Mellyn collection, Texas.* $600.00.

Beaver Lake point, Late Paleo, tan chert, lower side edges heavily ground. This piece is 2¼" long and was found in Scioto County, Ohio. *Private collection.* $125.00.

Late Paleo lanceolate point, Stringtown variety with worn single graver spur on stem bottom corner, 2⅜". Mixed blue Upper Mercer was used for this point, found in Fairfield County, Ohio. *Private collection.* $45.00.

Holland point or blade, mixed chert, 5⅛" long. This late Paleo artifact came from Worth County, Iowa. *John and Susan Mellyn collection, Texas.* $650.00.

Plainview point, a fine example, 2" long. With ground basal edges, it was found in South Texas. *John and Susan Mellyn collection, Texas.* $450.00.

Milnesand point, a nicely balanced piece, 1⅞". It came from the Grants area, New Mexico. *John and Susan Mellyn collection, Texas.* $250.00.

Plainview or Meserve point, Edwards flint, symmetrical base. This example is 3⅛" long, from Travis County, Texas. *John and Susan Mellyn collection, Texas.* $500.00.

Milnesand point or blade, Late Paleo, small flute on one face. It is 1¹⁵⁄₁₆", from Hood County, Texas. *John and Susan Mellyn collection, Texas.* $200.00.

Stringtown stemmed lance, unknown reddish chert, 2⅜". A personal find of the owner, it came from Delaware County, Ohio. *Mike Barron collection, Ohio.* $150.00.

Paleo lancolate blade, 4" long, expertly knapped, rounded base. Found by the grandfather of Walter Sims (who was a major collector), the lance came from Jackson County, Ohio. *Mike Barron collection, Ohio.* $850.00.

Stringtown stemmed lance, with graver spur on base corner, 5¾" long. The material may be Onondaga flint, and the point or knife came from Pennsylvania. *Doug Hooks collection.* $2,500.00.

Stemmed lance, red and near-orange Carter Cave flint, 4⅞". An outstanding point or blade, it is ex-collections Ewing, Hill, Wehrle, and Jack Hooks. Provenance unlisted. *Doug Hooks collection.* $3,500.00.

Paleo points and blades, left to right. Hell Gap, 3⁷⁄₁₆", Spanish Diggings chert, Pueblo County, Colorado. $1,400.00. Plainview, 2¹⁵⁄₁₆", Spanish Diggings chert, ex-collection Glasscock, Morgan County, Colorado. $650.00. Goshen, 2¾", petrified wood, Elbert County, Colorado. $450.00. Plainview, 2¼", orange moss agate, ex-collection Woods, Coconino County, Arizona. $650.00. *Michael Hough collection, California.*

Agate Basin point, Late Paleo, blue Upper Mercer with touches of white. This is a superior artifact in every way — size, workstyle, material, and condition. It is 4½" long, ex-collections Townsend and Jack Hooks. Ohio. *Doug Hooks collection.* $3,500.00.

Lanceolate point or blade, very large at 7¼". It is made of what may be highly patinated Flint Ridge, and this extraordinary example is ex-collections Carroll and Jack Hooks. Champaign County, Ohio. *Doug Hooks collection.* Museum grade.

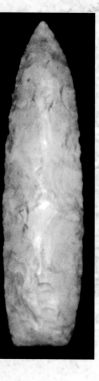

Agate Basin point, Late Paleo, mixed glossy off-white flint. This very fine example is 3¹⁵⁄₁₆", from Missouri. *John and Susan Mellyn collection, Texas.* Museum grade.

Angostura(?) point, chipped or resharpened to a pentagonal outline, 2½". It is made of Edwards flint, and its base edges are ground. Wilson County, Texas. *John and Susan Mellyn collection, Texas.* $275.00.

Stemmed points and blades, some examples shown elsewhere in book. Scale, middle row far right is 2¼" long. Midwestern and western United States. *John and Susan Mellyn collection, Texas.* Unlisted.

Agate Basin point, Late Paleo, white speckled flint. The bottom edges are ground for about one-third of length, and the point has a Davis COA. Indiana. *Pete Timoch collection, Ohio.* $500.00.

Angostura point, base sides smoothed and sides serrated, light-colored jasper. It measures ½" x 2½" and was collected by the owner's father in the early 1940s. U.S. Southwest. *Collection of and photograph by H. B. Greene II, Florida.* $650.00.

Eden point, Late Paleo period, translucent banded jasper. With slanted shoulders, this example is ⁹⁄₁₆" x 2½". It was obtained in the early 1940s by the owner's father in the American Southwest. *Collection of and photograph by H. B. Greene II, Florida.* $800.00.

Plainview point, Late Paleo, 2⅛" long. Edwards Plateau flint was used for this piece, which is creamy light tan with tan inclusions. It has three basal thinning flutes and oblique transverse flaking. Lampasas County, Texas. *Pete Timoch collection, Ohio.* $300.00.

Angostura point, basal edge grinding for one-third of length, tan chert. Late Paleo, it is 2⅞" long and came from Austin County, Texas. *Pete Timoch collection, Ohio.* $250.00.

Dalton points or blades, colored (left to right) gray, black, and tan flint, longest 1⅝". Tan and black Daltons were resharpened to beveled edges, while the gray point was bifacially resharpened into a drill cross section. Yell County, Arkansas. *Tony Napier collection.* Each, $30.00 – 60.00.

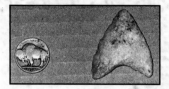

Dalton point, fishtail base, high-grade banded flint, 2" long. Late Paleo, this artifact was found in Arkansas. *Private collection.* $150.00.

Beaver Lake point, Late Paleo, small flute or large basal thinning flake scar. It is made of pinkish-orange flint or chert and is 2⅝" long. Kentucky. *John and Susan Mellyn collection, Texas.* $400.00.

Alamance point, Late Paleo triangular with indented baseline, size as indicated. The only type example of an Alamance found in the state; the usual distribution range for Alamances is in the U.S. Southeast. This was found by the owner in 1999 and is made of Swan River chert from Canada. Brookings County, South Dakota. *Harlan Olson collection, South Dakota.* Unlisted.

Milnesand point, milky flint, 1¹³⁄₁₆". This Late Paleo point came from Wilson County, Texas. *John and Susan Mellyn collection, Texas.* $500.00.

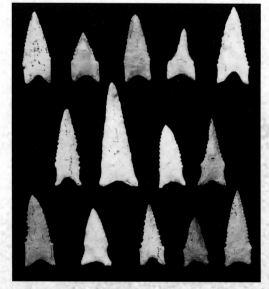

Plainview-related point, incurvate baseline, agate-like translucent flint. The point is 1⅞" long and was found in Midland County, Texas. *John and Susan Mellyn collection, Texas.* $550.00.

Dalton points and one drill, **various flints and cherts,** largest 1¼" x 3⅛". Ex-collection Snyder, the origin of these is unknown but is probably Tennessee. There are some fine examples in the group, several in the $400.00 range. *Collection of and photograph by Gary Henry, North Carolina.* All, $3,500.00.

San Patrice(?) point, Late Paleo, petrified wood, 1⁵⁄₁₆" x 1⅝". Ex-collection Cordeiro, it came from Vernon Parish, Louisiana. *Collection of and photograph by Gary Henry, North Carolina.* $30.00.

Cougar Mountain or Haskett knife, 10" long, gray "mouse" obsidian, no use wear. Ex-collection Rhoades, this is a superb and rare piece. Found near Denio, Nevada. *Michael Hough collection, California.* $8,000.00 plus.

Hardaway Dalton points, both found by Harwood and from North Carolina. Left, 1" x 1⅜", quartz. $50.00. Right, 1" x 1¼", fine-grained quartzite or chalcedony. $20.00. *Collection of and photograph by Gary Henry, North Carolina.*

Hardway side-notch points or blades, from two different sites in Buncombe County, North Carolina. Left, ¹³⁄₁₆" x 1¹⁄₁₆". $20.00. Right, ¹³⁄₁₆" x ¹³⁄₁₆". $10.00. *Collection of and photograph by Gary Henry, North Carolina.*

Hardaway Dalton point, 3¼", well-weathered silicified shale. It was featured in a 1987 *Charlotte Observer* newspaper story about the Baucom-Hardaway site along the Rocky River. Union County, North Carolina. *Collection of and photograph by Ron Harris, North Carolina. $375.00.*

Paleo points and blades, left to right. Holland, 3¹³⁄₁₆", Jefferson City chert, ex-collection L. L. "Val" Valdivia, Osage County, Missouri. $1,200.00. Holland, 3¾", found by R. Nickle, Pike County, Illinois. $1,000.00. Beaver Lake, 3⅛", Fort Payne chert, Macon County, Tennessee. $850.00. Eden Eared, 2¾", Hixton quartzite, Vernon County, Wisconsin. $650.00. *Michael Hough collection, California.*

Lanceolate point, mixed Upper Mercer flint with mineral deposits, 3⅛" long. It was found in Ohio, county unknown. *Mike Barron collection, Ohio.* $250.00.

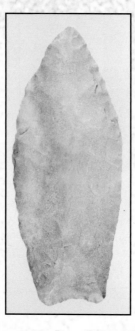

Stringtown lance, patinated Flint Ridge, 3¼". With basal spurs, this artifact was heated at one time and has three small "fire pops." Ex-collection Seeley, Franklin County, Ohio. *Mike Barron collection, Ohio.* $950.00.

Lanceolate, Late Paleo, 3⅛". Made of Delaware County flint in two shades of tan, it has an indented baseline and high shoulders. Ex-collection Mel Wilkins, Ohio county unknown. *Mike Barron collection, Ohio.* $400.00.

Agate Basin point, mottled blue Upper Mercer, 3⅞". This fine piece is ex-collections Townsend and Jack Hooks. Ohio. *Doug Hooks collection.* $2,500.00.

Western Paleo points and blades, left to right. Scottsbluff, 2⅝", ex-collection Rhoton, Lincoln County, Colorado. $1,200.00. Hell Gap (shown elsewhere), Hell Gap, 2⅞", petrified wood, ex-collection Rhoton, Morgan County, Colorado. $850.00. Goshen, 2⁹⁄₁₆", yellow petrified wood, ex-collection Glasscock, El Paso County, Colorado. $550.00. *Michael Hough collection, California.*

Western Paleo points and blades, left to right. Eden, 3⅜", ex-collection Glasscock, Gaines County, Texas. $4,000.00. Firstview, fluted, 3", western Texas. $1,500.00. Eden, 3⅛", Spanish Diggings chert, Carbon County, Wyoming. $1,000.00. *Michael Hough collection, California.*

120

Western Paleo points and blades, left to right. Allen, 2¹¹⁄₁₆", yellow Hartville Uplift chert, ex-collections Dean and Glasscock, Morgan County, Colorado. $850.00. Allen, 2½", Alibates flint, ex-collection L. L. "Val" Valdivia, De Baca County, New Mexico. $850.00. Plainview, 2¹³⁄₁₆", heavily patinated Edwards Plateau, found by R. Milam in the early 1950s, Coryell County, Texas. $300.00. *Michael Hough collection, California.*

Agate Basin point, translucent striped obsidian, 3¾". This long and narrow specimen came from northern California. *John and Susan Mellyn collection, Texas.* Museum grade.

Western points or blades, all left to right. Early stemmed, 3¼", obsidian, ex-collection Geinger, ground base edges, Lake County, Oregon. $400.00. Early stemmed, 3³⁄₁₆", obsidian, found by C. Howe at Silver Lake, Lake County, Oregon. $200.00. Eden variant, 3⅝", clear banded obsidian, found by L. L. "Val" Valdivia, Churchill County, Nevada. $400.00. Pinto Basin, 3⁷⁄₁₆", recurvate blade edges, ex-collection Valdivia, Inyo County, California. $450.00. Windust, 2", found by C. Howe at Silver Lake, Lake County, Oregon. $250.00. *Michael Hough collection, California.*

Western Paleo points or blades, left to right. Eden, 3⁹⁄₁₆", clear banded obsidian, Crump Lake, Lake County, Oregon. $1,200.00. Eden, 4¹¹⁄₁₆", banded obsidian, found by L. L. "Val" Valdivia, Churchill County, Nevada. $1,000.00. Eden, 2¹¹⁄₁₆", red jasper, ex-collection Miner, Benton County, Washington. $500.00. *Michael Hough collection, California.*

Western Paleo points, left to right. Windust, 3⅛", obsidian, Lake County, Oregon. $750.00. Windust, 3", found by C. Howe at Silver Lake, Lake County, Oregon. $500.00. Windust, 3" long, found by C. Howe, Lake County, Oregon. $1,000.00. *Michael Hough collection, California.*

Hardway Dalton point, extended ears, 2¼". This resharpened example is made of green weathered rhyolite and was picked up in Randolph County, North Carolina. *Collection of and photograph by Ron Harris, North Carolina.* $650.00.

Hardaway Dalton point or blade, first stage, 3¼". Weathered rhyolite was used for this, and it came from Davidson County, North Carolina. *Collection of and photograph by Ron Harris, North Carolina.* $350.00.

Angostura point, tapered lower blade and incurvate baseline, white mixed flint. It is 2⅜" long, from Wilson County, Texas. *John and Susan Mellyn collection, Texas.* $700.00.

Hardaway Dalton point, green rhyolite, 2¼". With bold basal extensions, this resharpened example came from Montgomery County, North Carolina. *Collection of and photograph by Ron Harris, North Carolina.* $375.00.

Milnesand point, glossy two-color flint, 2⅛". This piece was picked up in Austin County, Texas. *John and Susan Mellyn collection, Texas.* $700.00.

Gypsum Cave points or blades, 1¾" x 2³⁄₁₆" long, basalt and chert materials. They were found by O. G. Spencer Sr. in Clark County, Nevada. *Michael Hough collection, California.* Each, $75.00 – 200.00.

122

Western points and blades, all found by Keith Glasscock, left to right. Hell Gap, 3⁷⁄₁₆", Alibates flint, Mora County, New Mexico. $1,500.00. Goshen, 3", Mora County, New Mexico. $1,000.00. Firstview, Midland County, Texas. $1,600.00. Hell Gap, 2⅜", Alibates flint, Lipscomb County, Texas. $1,200.00. *Michael Hough collection, California.*

Plainview point salvaged as a scraper, 1⅜" long. It was found in Midland County, Texas. *John and Susan Mellyn collection, Texas.* $350.00.

Angostura point, upper sides resharpened and narrowed, 3¼". It came from Wilson County, Texas. *John and Susan Mellyn collection, Texas.* $600.00.

Northwestern U.S. Paleo points or blades, left to right. Parman, stemmed, 5¼", ex-collection Geinger, Lake County, Oregon. $650.00. Haskett, 6³⁄₁₆", ex-collection Geinger, Lake County, Oregon. $1,500.00. *Michael Hough collection, California.*

Western Paleo points or blades, all from California, first three found by P. Roehr, left to right. Silver Lake, 2⁹⁄₁₆", red-orange jasper, Kings County. $400.00. Silver Lake, 1¹¹⁄₁₆", heavily patinated Franciscan chert, Kings County. $250.00. Clovis, 2¹⁄₁₆", heavily patinated Franciscan chert, Kings County, $200.00. Clovis, 1½", white quartzite, Mono County. $200.00. *Michael Hough collection, California.*

Angostura point, tapered lower blade, large percussion flake scars on face, Foraker flint. Provenance unlisted. *Jim Horst collection, Nebraska.* $200.00.

Angostura point, Late Paleo, oblique flaking, Foraker permian flint. This is a well-made point, provenance unlisted. *Jim Horst collection, Nebraska.* $500.00.

Angostura point, upper blade area resharpened, about 2⅜" long. It is from Nuckolls County, Nebraska. *Jim Horst collection, Nebraska.* $175.00.

Agate Basin point, Late Paleo, light tan quartzite. It measures ¹⁵⁄₁₆" x 4⅛" and came from Eastern Weber County, northern Utah. *Mark Stuart collection, Utah.* $275.00.

Haskett point or blade, black obsidian, 1⅛" x 3⅞". The base on this example was broken off and was picked up nearby; the two pieces are now glued together. Western Box Elder County, northern Utah. *Dann Russell collection, Utah.* $400.00.

Exact cast, made by Lithics Casting Lab, of Haskett point. The original was picked up by a boy on U.S. Forestry Service land. This fine specimen is 1½" x 5⅞" and the original (now property of the U.S. Forestry Service) is made of tan quartzite. Eastern Weber County, northern Utah. *Dann Russell photograph, Utah.* Unlisted.

Alberta point, Late Paleo, creamy tan chert, 1" x 3¾". Stem edges are ground; the artifact was broken when found and is now glued. Central Box Elder County, northern Utah. *Mark Stuart collection, Utah.* $125.00.

Browns Valley point, Late Paleo, 1⅛" x 2⅝". Made of Prairie du Chien chert, it was found in 1995 by the owner's grandfather, Orville Reysen, while working on the family farm. Sheboygan County, Wisconsin. *Rob Reysen collection, Wisconsin; Tom Davis photograph.* Unlisted.

Milnesand point, 3¼", Perino COA, Smokey Hills silicified chert, Niobrara or Republican Jasper. Provenance unlisted. *Jim Horst collection, Nebraska.* $300.00.

Agate Basin point, Late Paleo, 1⅛" x 4½". Pale Burlington chert was used for the point, and the basal edges are ground. Grundy County, Illinois. *Paul Weisser collection, Indiana.* $550.00.

Scottsbluff type 1 point or blade, 3½" long, oblique chipping. The material is a medium dark fossiliferous chert, and the artifact came from Washington County, Kansas. *Jim Horst collection, Nebraska.* $350.00.

Midland point, Late Paleo, resharpened size at 1½". Made of Hartville Uplift flint, it was found in Wyoming. *Jim Horst collection, Nebraska.* $150.00.

Eden point, Perino COA, parallel oblique flaking. The base has an angled chipping platform, and the material itself is Spanish Diggings. *Jim Horst collection, Nebraska.* Unlisted.

Scottsbluff point, glossy brown marbled chert, ¾" x 1¹¹⁄₁₆". Stem edges are ground on this tapered example, picked up in western Box Elder County, northern Utah. *Dann Russell collection, Utah.* $225.00.

Lovell constricted point or blade, gray and olive green chert, ⅞" x 3³⁄₁₆". Basal edges are ground, and the piece was found in eastern Cache County, northern Utah. *Mark Stuart collection, Utah.* $125.00.

Dalton point, classic form, found by the owner, 1" x 3½". Made of creamy flint, it came from Jasper County, Missouri. *Tom Fouts collection, Kansas.* $125.00.

Dalton point, classic type, 1" x 4¾". With strong ears, it is glossy white flint with red streaks. Ex-collections Allen and Lyerla, it was found in Christian County, Missouri. *Tom Fouts collection, Kansas.* $700.00.

Agate Basin point, 1⅛" x 3¾", ex-collections Triplett and Lyerla. Pink and white fossiliferous chert, it came from Bourbon County, Kansas. *Tom Fouts collection, Kansas.* $300.00.

Agate Basin point, 1⁵⁄₁₆" x 5", glossy creamy white flint. This exceptional piece is ex-collection Triplett and was found in St. Charles County, Missouri. *Tom Fouts collection, Kansas.* $850.00.

Dalton point or blade, classic form, 1¼" x 3". Made of glossy high-grade creamy white chert, the owner found this specimen near Carthage, Jasper County, Missouri. *Tom Fouts collection, Kansas.* $350.00.

Plainview or unfluted Clovis point, ⅞" x 3⅛", creamy flint or chert with pink streaks. The owner found this example near Cato, Crawford County, Kansas. *Tom Fouts collection, Kansas.* $250.00.

Greenbrier Dalton point, 1³⁄16" x 3", creamy white fossiliferous chert. It was found by the owner near Carthage, Jasper County, Missouri. *Tom Fouts collection, Kansas.* $150.00.

Holland point or blade, 1¼" x 5¼", ex-collection Triplett. Made of a quality white chert, this fine piece came from St. Charles County, Missouri. *Tom Fouts collection, Kansas.* $900.00.

Dalton point, classic type, gray-white flint, worn serrations. Measuring 1¹⁄16" x 3", it was found on the banks of Village Creek near Chanute, Neosho County, Kansas. *Tom Fouts collection, Kansas.* $350.00.

Pelican(?) point, found by the owner, white flint. This piece is 1¹⁄16" x 2", from Cherokee County, Kansas. *Tom Fouts collection, Kansas.* $150.00.

Scottsbluff point, 1⅜" x 2⅞", found by the owner. Off-white flint with tan spots, it came from the Neosho River near Oswego, Labette County, Kansas. *Tom Fouts collection, Kansas.* $175.00.

127

Dalton point, classic form, found by the owner. Of glossy black flint, it is ¾" x 1⅛" and came from near Seneca, McDonald County, Missouri. *Tom Fouts collection, Kansas.* $75.00.

Milnesand point, ¹¹⁄₁₆" x 1¹¹⁄₁₆", gray chert. A scarce point type from the Late Paleo, it came from eastern Arkansas. *Bybee collection, Kentucky; Tom Davis photograph.* $65.00.

Dalton point or blade, ⅞" x 2½", serrated edges. Provenance unlisted. *Jeff Anderson collection, Indiana.* $230.00.

Agate Basin point, symmetrical lines and lower blade edge grinding, 1⅛" x 3⅞". It was found in Illinois. *Jeff Anderson collection, Indiana.* $800.00.

Agate Basin point, 1" x 3¼". Nicely banded, it is quite thin and has good basal grinding. Illinois. *Jeff Anderson collection, Indiana.* $750.00.

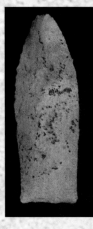

Dalton point, Late Paleo, ¹⁵⁄₁₆" x 1¾". It has worn serrations and is made of Crowley's Ridge chert. Greene County, Arkansas. *Bybee collection, Kentucky; Tom Davis photograph.* $65.00.

Dalton point or blade, 1" x 2⅞". It has serrated edges and some use wear. Provenance unlisted. *Jeff Anderson collection, Indiana.* $175.00.

Agate Basin point, Late Paleo, 2½" long. It was found by the owner in 1982. St. Louis County, Missouri. *Jeff Anderson collection, Indiana.* $100.00.

Agate Basin point, 2" long, grinding on lower blade edges and base. The owner found this example in Rush County, Indiana. *Jeff Anderson collection, Indiana.* $125.00.

Wheeler or Barber point, ⅝" x 1½", deeply incurvate baseline. Made of near-black flint, it is from southwestern Missouri. *Tom Fouts collection, Kansas.* $50.00.

Dalton point, classic type, found by the owner. Of glossy white chert with gray streaks, it is ⅞" x 3⅛". The Dalton came from the Carthage-Alba area, Jasper County, Missouri. *Tom Fouts collection, Kansas.* $350.00.

Hardaway side-notch point, green rhyolite, first stage, 3¼" long. Found by a nine-year-old boy in 1986 while playing with his dog in a cornfield on his grandparents' farm, this is considered one of the finest Hardaways from the state. Jackson Springs area, Moore County, North Carolina. *Collection of and photograph by Ron Harris, North Carolina.* $1,200.00.

Dalton point, classic form, gray-white flint. The size is 1¼" x 4¼", and the artifact was found near Seneca, McDonald County, Missouri. *Tom Fouts collection, Kansas.* $350.00.

Stringtown stemmed lance, with graver spur, 2⅝". Nellie chert, the artifact was obtained at auction in 2000. Ohio. *Jesse Weber collection; photograph by Norman's Photo, Newcomerstown, Ohio.* $90.00.

Stemmed lance, Stringtown type, 3" long. The material is Delaware chert and the artifact was found near Belle Center, Ohio. *Jesse Weber collection; photograph by Norman's Photo, Newcomerstown, Ohio.* $150.00.

Early triangluar point, bluish flint, 1⁹⁄₁₆". It was picked up in Wilson County, Texas. *John and Susan Mellyn collection, Texas.* $125.00.

Golondrina point, Late Paleo, salvaged as a scraper. This example in pinkish flint is 2¹⁄₁₆". Wilson County, Texas. *John and Susan Mellyn collection, Texas.* $400.00.

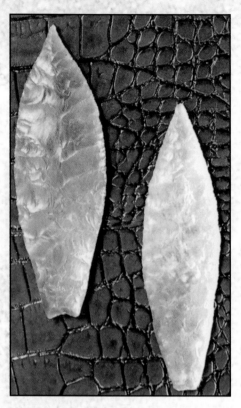

Angostura points, both from Texas. Left, 1⁷⁄₁₆" x 4³⁄₈", tapered tip, translucent brown flint with black specks. A superb example, it came from Mill Creek, Austin County. Right, translucent gray patinated flint, 1¼" x 4¼", found by Bruce Thompson in Lake Creek. Montogmery County. *William M. German collection, Texas; photograph by DWC Photography.* Both museum grade.

Scottsbluff points or blades, all found in Texas. Left, 1⅜" x 5⁷⁄₁₆", broad stem, found by Willie Fields and ex-collection Dana Harper. Cass County. Center, 1½" x 5⅜", beautifully tapered, ex-collection Doug Weeks. Polk County. Right, 1³⁄₁₆" x 5", short flared stem, ex-collection Ted Nemec Jr., Cherokee County. *William M. German collection, Texas.* All museum grade.

Birch Creek point or blade, reddish-brown jasper with basal color line, ground basal edges. It measures ½" x 2³⁄₁₆" and came from central Box Elder County, northern Utah. *Mark Stuart collection, Utah.* $225.00.

Dalton points or blades, found on the same site on the same day. Left example is 1" x 3⅛" and right is 1⅛" x 3¼". Both are made of creamy white chert. Webster County, Missouri. *Tom Fouts collection, Kansas.* Each, $300.00.

Alamance point, ⅞" x 1½", found by LTC Floyd Lyerla. Made of orange flint or chert, it came from Georgia. *Tom Fouts collection, Kansas.* $35.00.

Plainview point, white flint turned cherry-yellowish with age, 1" x 3". Found by M. Ralls, it is ex-collection Lyerla. Pettis County, Missouri. *Tom Fouts collection, Kansas.* $250.00.

Alberta point, translucent yellowish red agate, ¾" x 1¹³⁄₁₆". The basal edges are ground on this fine example, found in central Box Elder County, northern Utah. *Mark Stuart collection, Utah.* $275.00.

Santa Fe point, quartzite, 1" x 2", ex-collections Snyder and Williams. It was found in Roane County, Tennessee. *Collection of and photograph by Gary Henry, North Carolina.* $40.00.

Hardaway side-notch point, chert, ⁹⁄₁₆" x ¾". It came from Buncombe County, North Carolina. *Collection of and photograph by Gary Henry, North Carolina.* $20.00.

Dalton point, classic form, creamy flint with fossil inclusions, 1¼" x 4". Ex-collection Triplett, it is one point from a cache of twelve. Seneca area, McDonald County, Missouri. *Tom Fouts collection, Kansas.* $700.00.

Greenbrier Dalton point, dark chert, ⅞" x 1⅛". Ex-collection Price, it is from Washington County, Tennessee. *Collection of and photograph by Gary Henry, North Carolina.* $30.00.

Beaver Lake point, ¾" x 1⅜", tan chert. In resharpened size, it came from Fayette County, Kentucky. *Bybee collection, Kentucky; Tom Davis photograph.* $40.00.

Scottsbluff points or blades, Late Paleo. Left, 1¼" x 6⅛", ex-collection Sam Dickinson, found in the 1920s. This is a large and fine piece. Nevada County, Arkansas. Right, 1⅛" x 5⅝", very symmetrical. It has a long collecting history: Jack Hooks, Owen Davis, Floyd Ritter, Dwain Rogers, and Bob Galvin. Northeastern Texas. *William M. German collection, Texas.* Both museum grade.

Paleo points, both Texas. Left, Zella, the best example yet found, 1¼" x 5⅜", translucent gray flint with bleach patina on each face. Kerr County. Right, Plainview, 1⅛" x 4⅞", gray flint. It is ex-collection Fred Eiserman, and it came from northcentral Texas. *Williams M. German collection, Texas; photograpy by DWC Photography.* Both museum grade.

131

Dalton point, fluted, 1" x 1⅝". Blue and tan chert, this blade has large serrations for size. Greene County, Arkansas. *Bybee collection, Kentucky; Tom Davis photograph.* $100.00.

Dalton point, resharpened and serrated, ¾" x 1¹³⁄₁₆". Tan chert, it is ex-collections Smith and Thomas. Greene County, Arkansas. *Bybee collection, Kentucky; Tom Davis photograph.* $150.00.

Stringtown lance, 2⅝", black Upper Mercer flint. The point or blade was found in Stark County, Ohio. *Jesse Weber collection; photograph by Norman's Photo, Newcomerstown, Ohio.* $25.00.

Stringtown lance, resharpened to triangular shape, 2⁷⁄₁₆". Nellie gray flint was used for this piece, from Coshocton County, Ohio. *Jesse Weber collection; photograph by Norman's Photo, Newcomerstown, Ohio.* $75.00.

Hardaway point, dark chert, ⅞" x 1⅛". Greatly resharpened, it was a personal find of Harwood. Bunbombe County, North Carolina. *Collection of and photograph by Gary Henry, North Carolina.* $30.00.

Greenbrier Dalton point, Late Paleo, silicified shale, 1" x 1⁵⁄₁₆". Found by the owner, it came from Morgan County, West Virginia. *Collection of and photograph by Gary Henry, North Carolina.* $40.00.

Hardaway blade remnant, quartz, 1⅛" x 1¼". A personal find of Harwood, it is from Buncombe County, North Carolina. *Collection of and photograph by Gary Henry, North Carolina.* $50.00.

Golondrina point, obverse flute, resharpened size. This example is 2¹⁄₁₆" and is from Bexar County, Texas. *John and Susan Mellyn collection, Texas.* $450.00.

Golondrina point, translucent white flint, 2¼". The Late Paleo artifact came from Wilson County, Texas. *John and Susan Mellyn collection, Texas.* $475.00.

Point, probably early Dalton, near-clear chalcedony, ¾" x 2". This point was a personal find by the owner in Madison County, North Carolina. *Collection of and photograph by Gary Henry, North Carolina.* $150.00.

Agate Basin points, Late Paleo, mixed unidentified cherts, ex-collection Lantz. Left, 15/16" x 3¾", Union County, New Mexico. $350.00. Right, 1¹/16" x 3¹/16", Morton County, North Dakota. $400.00. *Collection of and photograph by Gary Henry, North Carolina.*

Colbert Dalton point, Late Paleo, quartzite, ⅞" x 1¾". A personal find by Harwood, it probably came from North Carolina. *Collection of and photograph by Gary Henry, North Carolina.* $50.00.

Dalton point, resharpened size, medium-light chert, 1¼" x 2¼". This piece is ex-collection Snyder and probably came from Tennessee. *Collection of and photograph by Gary Henry, North Carolina.* $50.00.

Dalton point or blade, classic form, 1⅜" x 4⅛". A large and fine specimen with serrations, it has a Dickey COA. Greene County, Arkansas. *Doug Goodrum collection, Kentucky.* $1,000.00 – 1,500.00.

Greenbriar Dalton point, beveled edges, 1⅜" x 4¼". This sturdy and well-made example was found by M. Harris in Livingston County, Kentucky. *Doug Goodrum collection, Kentucky.* $1,200.00 – 1,500.00.

Greenbrier Dalton point, 1" x 2", Late Paleo. From Goodflint.com, it was found by O. Randsford in Montgomery County, Tennessee. *Doug Goodrum collection, Kentucky.* $175.00.

Beaver Lake point, Late Paleo, 1⅛" x 1⁹/16". Boyle chert was used for this piece from Goodflint.com. It was found by P. Qualls in Hart County, Kentucky. *Doug Goodrum collection, Kentucky.* $75.00.

Wheeler triangular point, chert, 1" x 1⅝". Ex-collections Snyder and Williams, it is from Roane County, Tennessee. *Collection of and photograph by Gary Henry, North Carolina.* $40.00.

Dalton point, classic form, 1" x 2¹/₁₆". This example has unusual fluting to the tip on both faces. Cream-colored chert, it came from southeastern Missouri. *Bybee collection, Kentucky; Tom Davis photograph.* $200.00.

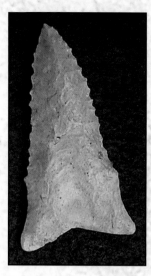

Greenbrier Dalton point, 1³/₁₆" x 2⅝". This Late Paleo artifact was found by A. Baggett in Stewart County, Tennessee. *Doug Goodrum collection, Kentucky.* $300.00 – 400.00.

Harpeth River point, a stemmed lance-like form that is Late Paleo – Early Archaic, 1" x 3¾". It was found in western Kentucky. *Doug Goodrum collection, Kentucky.* $250.00.

Dalton point, serrated edges, tan translucent fossiliferous chert. The size is ¾" x 1¹⁵/₁₆", and the piece came from Greene County, Arkansas. *Bybee collection, Kentucky; Tom Davis photograph.* $50.00.

Hardaway Dalton points, quartz, left two found by owner. Left, 1¹/₁₆" x 1¹³/₁₆", Buncombe County, North Carolina. $50.00. Center, ¹³/₁₆" x 1½", Buncombe County, North Carolina. $40.00. Right, 1" x 1¾", western North Carolina. $60.00. *Collection of and photograph by Gary Henry, North Carolina.*

Greenbrier Dalton point, 1" x 1¹⁵/₁₆", tan and brown chert. It has a broken tip and was picked up in Greene County, Arkansas. *Bybee collection, Kentucky; Tom Davis photograph.* $35.00.

Hardaway Dalton point or blade, chert, ¹³/₁₆" x 1¼". This resharpened piece is ex-collection Snyder, probably from Tennessee. *Collection of and photograph by Gary Henry, North Carolina.* $50.00.

Beaver Lake point, Late Paleo, 13/16" x 2⅜". The example, with typical ears, is ex-collection Gamble and was found in Christian County, Kentucky. *Doug Goodrum collection, Kentucky.* $500.00 – 700.00.

Harpeth River point, 1" x 2⅞". It is from Goodflint.com and was found in Montgomery County, Tennessee. *Doug Goodrum collection, Kentucky.* $85.00.

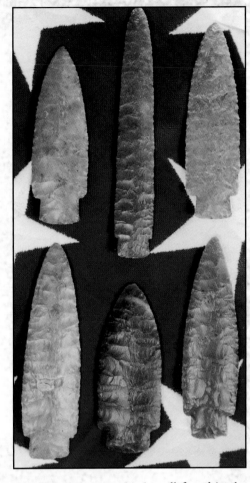

Scottsbluff points or blades, all found in the west fork of the San Jacinto River, Montgomery County, Texas. Top row, left, 1³⁄₁₆" x 3¾", pinkish tan flint with rust spotting, found by Troy Ayers. Top row, center, Eden(?), ¾" x 5¼", found by Curtis Gorney, brown flint. Top row, right, 1¼" x 4¼", light brown conglomerate chert, found by Troy Ayers. Bottom row, left, 1¼" x 4⁹⁄₁₆", found by Kenneth Nelson, tan flint with quartz eye. Bottom row, center, dark brown translucent flint, 1⅜" x 3⅝", found by Bill Carpenter. Bottom row, right, 1¼" x 4⅜", ex-collections Mark Mullins and Dana Harper, translucent medium-brown flint. *William M. German collection, Texas; photograph by DWC Photography.* All museum grade.

Beaver Lake or Cumberland-related point, Late Paleo, ground stem sides, ⅞" x 3¼". It is made of Boyle chert and has a Dickey COA. This point was found by C. Gentry in Barren County, Kentucky. *Doug Goodrum collection, Kentucky.* $700.00 – 1,000.00.

Quad point, Late Paleo, 1½" x 3¾". This superb example is made of hornstone and has a Burgess/Mabry COA. Ex-collection Snyder, it is from western Kentucky. *Doug Goodrum collection, Kentucky.* Museum grade.

Sloan Dalton point, 1¼" x 4", Burlington chert. It has a Davis COA and was found in Greene County, Arkansas. *Bybee collection, Kentucky; Tom Davis photograph.* $1,200.00.

Hardaway point or blade, Late Paleo, quartzite, 1 1/16" x 1 13/16". The owner found this piece in 2003 and it came from Buncombe County, North Carolina. *Collection of and photograph by Gary Henry, North Carolina.* $40.00.

Scottsbluff points or blades, superb examples. Left, 1 1/16" x 5¼", ex-collection Wallace Culpepper and Ted Nemec Jr. Robertson County, Texas. Right, 1⅛" x 4⅞", ex-collections Dwain Rogers, Dana Harper, and Mike Speer. Kaufman County, Texas. *William M. German collection, Texas.* Both museum grade.

Hardaway Dalton point, Late Paleo, chert, 13/16" x 1 3/16". Resharpened, it was found by the owner in Monroe County, Tennessee. *Collection of and photograph by Gary Henry, North Carolina.* $50.00.

Dalton points, Late Paleo, chert, both ex-collection Snyder and origin unknown. Left, 1⅛" x 2 3/16". Right, 1 3/16" x 2". *Collection of and photograph by Gary Henry, North Carolina.* Each, $40.00.

Nansemond Dalton point, Late Paleo, chert, ⅞" x 1½". The example is tip-fluted and was found by the owner. Stewart County, North Carolina. *Collection of and photograph by Gary Henry, North Carolina.* $40.00.

Allen point, deeply incurvate baseline, Alibates flint. Ex-collections Roland and Rowe, it is 2 5/16" long. Cass County, Texas. *Dr. Guy Gross collection, Texas.* $1,200.00.

San Patrice point, Late Paleo, chert, ¾" x 1". It is ex-collection Snyder, and its origin is unknown. *Collection of and photograph by Gary Henry, North Carolina.* $40.00.

Dalton point, tan chert, serrated edges, ⅞" x 2⅛". It came from Greene County, Arkansas. *Bybee collection, Kentucky; Tom Davis photograph.* $125.00.

Scottsbluff point, creamy flint, shoulder remnants, excurvate baseline. It is 1⅞" and was found in Texas. *John and Susan Mellyn collection, Texas.* $450.00.

Alamance point, 1¾", silicified shale. This material was somewhat difficult to chip, which attests to the skill of the ancient maker. Iredell County, North Carolina. *Collection of and photograph by Ron Harris, North Carolina.* $175.00.

Hardaway side-notch point, 1½", silicified shale. This artifact was found in the early 1960s during dam construction for Lake Norman. Catawba County, North Carolina. *Collection of and photograph by Ron Harris, North Carolina.* $300.00.

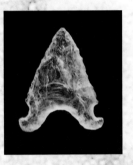

Suwannee point, serrated edges, slightly fluted, basal edge grinding. It is 1⁷⁄₁₆" and the material is an unknown translucent chert. Found in the 1960s, it came from the Carolina Piedmont region. *Collection of and photograph by Ron Harris, North Carolina.* $225.00.

Hardaway side-notch point, Late Paleo, 1½". The material is highly desirable and scarce native clear quartz crystal. Iredell County, North Carolina. *Collection of and photograph by Ron Harris, North Carolina.* $750.00.

Hardway Dalton point, resharpened to shoulder protrusions, 2¾". It is made of well-weathered speckled rhyolite and was found near Cameron in Moore County, North Carolina. *Collection of and photograph by Ron Harris, North Carolina.* $375.00.

Hardaway Dalton point, 3" long, weathered and speckled rhyolite. The specimen was picked up in Iredell County, North Carolina. *Collection of and photograph by Ron Harris, North Carolina.* $550.00.

Hardaway Dalton point, banded slicified shale, 2⅝". The point or blade came from Alamance County, North Carolina. *Collection of and photograph by Ron Harris, North Carolina.* $350.00.

137

Lanceolate point or blade, blue-black Upper Mercer, 3" long. This specimen is from Ohio. *John and Susan Mellyn collection, Texas.* $200.00.

Lanceolate point or blade, shallow side notches, corner with ears. It is 2¼" long and made of white chert. McDonald County, Missouri. *John and Susan Mellyn collection, Texas.* $125.00.

Early stemmed point, possibly Scottsbluff related, 2⁹⁄₁₆". This piece was picked up in Wilson County, Texas. *John and Susan Mellyn collection, Texas.* $700.00.

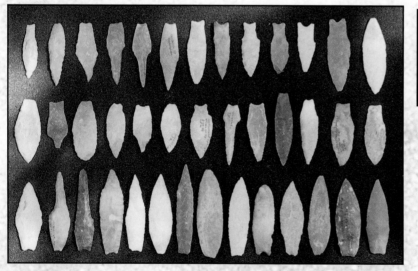

Hardaway side-notch point, 1" long, rhyolite. Resharpened size, this example has nicely balanced notches and ears. Davie County, North Carolina. *Collection of and photograph by Ron Harris, North Carolina.* $225.00.

Lanceolate points, Angostura and others, various Texas materials. This is a good example of the wide range of western points from Late Paleo times. Scale: Third from left, bottom row, 3¼". All are from Wilson County, Texas. Values for some are listed with individual specimens elsewhere in the book. *John and Susan Mellyn collection, Texas.*

Hardaway side-notch point, 1⁵⁄₁₆", rhyolite material. Resharpened (rechipped) from a larger artifact, the point or blade came from Wake County, North Carolina. *Collection of and photograph by Ron Harris, North Carolina.* $190.00.

Hardaway Dalton point, 3" long, light tan rhyolite. With deeply incurvate baseline, it is from Rowan County, North Carolina. *Collection of and photograph by Ron Harris, North Carolina.* $550.00.

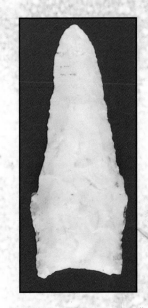

Dalton point, Burlington chert, 3¼". The basal edges are heavily ground on this example, from the Midwest. *Dwight Wolfe collection.* $100.00.

Dalton point, resharpened to hafting region, serrated knife edges. Made of creamy chert, it is 2¹³⁄₁₆" long. Missouri. *Dwight Wolfe collection.* $75.00.

Dalton point or blade, thin and well made, 2⅞". The material is mixed gray Elco with tiny sparkles. Southern Illinois. *Dwight Wolfe collection.* $125.00.

Sloan Dalton point, 2⅞", tan and cream Burlington. Resharpened to the hafting area. It is from Salina County, Illinois. *Dwight Wolfe collection.* $75.00.

Agate Basin point, patinated very colorful Upper Mercer, basal grinding, 3¾". It was found in Morrow County, Ohio. *Doug Hooks collection.* $1,500.00.

Dalton point or blade, large worn serrations, 3⅛". Probably Burlington chert, it is from the Midwest. *Dwight Wolfe collection.* $100.00.

Stemmed lance, patinated tan Delaware chert, graver tip on base corner. The point or blade is 3¹³⁄₁₆" long and was found in Medina County, Ohio. *Dwight Wolfe collection.* $250.00.

139

Lanceolate, Late Paleo, blue Upper Mercer flint, lower blade edges ground, 4¼". This exceptional example is ex-collections Dunn and Jack Hooks. Ohio. *Private collection.* $3,500.00.

Sloan Dalton point, thin, gray and tan Burlington, serrated edges and basal edge grinding. It is 1⅛" x 2½" and has been extensively resharpened. With a Perino COA, it is ex-collection Harvey. Illinois. *Collection of and photograph by Jim Frederick, Utah.* $400.00.

Early triangular point, Edwards flint, 2⅜". This example was picked up in Wilson County, Texas. *John and Susan Mellyn collection, Texas.* $300.00.

Early triangular point, two-fifths fluted on obverse, Edwards flint. The point is 2⅞" long, from Wilson County, Texas. *John and Susan Mellyn collection, Texas.* $450.00.

Dalton point, of tan, gray, and cream Burlington chert, 1" x 3⅜". Fluted on one face, it has very good basal grinding and nice overall flaking. Ex-collection Tom Davis, it has a Perino COA. Missouri. *Collection of and photograph by Jim Frederick, Utah.* $500.00.

Early triangular point, Edwards flint, small flute on obverse, serrated edges. At 1¾", it is from Wilson County, Texas. *John and Susan Mellyn collection, Texas.* $250.00.

Dalton point or blade, tan and white Burlington chert, 1⅛" x 2⅝", Davis COA #1139. It is serrated and has a strong bevel and very pointed tip. St. Charles County, Missouri. *Collection of and photograph by Jim Frederick, Utah.* $150.00.

Hardaway Dalton point, resharpened size, 15/16" x 17/16". The owner found this piece in 1998. Buncombe County, North Carolina. *Collection of and photograph by Gary Henry, North Carolina.* $50.00.

Hardaway Dalton blade, dark mixed chert, 5/8" x 17/16". Found by the owner in 1989, it is from Madison County, North Carolina. $40.00. *Collection of and photograph by Gary Henry, North Carolina.*

Dalton point, Late Paleo, white Burlington, 1¼" x 4¼". Ex-collection Dr. Neil, the artifact is thin and has good size. This classic form has Davis COA #7021. Warren County, Missouri. *Collection of and photograph by Jim Frederick, Utah.* $1,500.00.

Dalton point, Late Paleo, 1⅛" x 3¾", white Burlington chert. The collecting history includes Ed Buel, Jim Cox, and Dave Harvey, and the point has Davis COA #979. This slender artifact has good basal grinding and strong serrations. Saline County, Missouri. *Collection of and photograph by Jim Frederick, Utah.* $950.00.

Dalton point, bull's-eye red and tan jasper, 1⅜" x 3¾". Ex-collections Jenny Dixon and David Menz, it has Davis COA #17002. It is thin and well flaked, and the colors are striking on this piece from Lincoln County, Missouri. *Collection of and photograph by Jim Frederick, Utah.* $850.00.

Dalton point or blade, an exceptionally fine piece in speckled chert, 1⅛" x 6³/₁₆". It is ex-collection Snyder and was found in St. Louis County, Missouri. *Collection of and photograph by Gary Henry, North Carolina.* $2,750.00.

141

Nuckolls Dalton point, tan and brown Burlington chert, 1½" x 3". Once in a fire, it has good color and patina. The Dalton is ex-collection Harold Carr and has a Perino COA. Midwestern. *Collection of and photograph by Jim Frederick, Utah.* $450.00.

Scottsbluff point, blue-gray flint, 2¼". It has resharpened edges and was found in Henry County, Missouri. *John and Susan Mellyn collection, Texas.* $350.00.

Beaver Lake point, Late Paleo, light gray quartzite, 1" x 2½". The owner found this example, fluted on one face and with good patina, in 1962 along the Buffalo River. Searcy County, Arkansas. *Collection of and photograph by Jim Frederick, Utah.* $200.00.

Agate Basin point, Late Paleo, Burlington chert in tan, brown, cream, and red. The size is 1¼" x 4⅛", and the point has a Perino COA. Thin and colorful, it is ex-collections Randy Foster and Dennis DeRosear. This is a fine and classic example. St. Charles County, Missouri. *Collection of and photograph by Jim Frederick, Utah.* $1,200.00.

Hell Gap and related points or blades, some shown elsewhere in the book. Scale, top row on right example is 1¹³⁄₁₆". Western United States. *John and Susan Mellyn collection, Texas.* Unlisted.

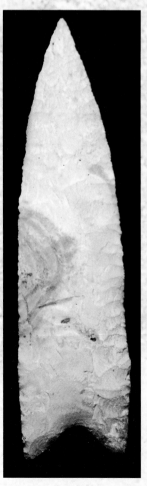

Dalton blade, Late Paleo period, 4⅞". Patinated hornstone with a partial bull's-eye was used for this piece, found in Alexander County, Illinois. *Len and Janie Weidner collection.* $1,000.00.

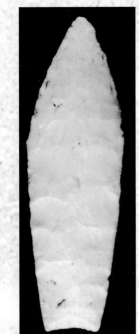

Scottsbluff point or blade, Late Paleo, 3⅛". This piece has slight shouldering and ground stem edges and is made of Burlington chert. Henry County, Iowa. *Len and Janie Weidner collection.* $475.00.

Agate Basin point or blade, Late Paleo period, with collateral flaking. It is 3½" long and made of Burlington flint. The artifact is ex-collections Keeley and Anderson, and is from the Jerseyville area, Illinois. *Len and Janie Weidner collection.* $800.00.

Hell Gap point, brownish purple chert, high shoulders. The artifact is 1¹³⁄₁₆" long and from western Canada. *John and Susan Mellyn collection, Texas.* $300.00.

Eden points or blades, translucent dark amber Knife River flint. The left example is unlisted. Right, slightly shouldered, 2¼" long, from Nebraska. *John and Susan Mellyn collection, Texas.* $1,000.00.

Dalton point, variegated Burlington (minority material) chert, collateral flaking and ground basal edges. It has good patination and measures 1⅛" x 4⅝". This point or blade was found by the owner, and it has a Berner COA. St. Clair County, Illinois. *Collection of and photograph by Jon Boyes, Illinois.* $1,500.00.

Lance point, blue-gray chalcedony from Flint Ridge, 3¹⁄₁₆". This Late Paleo artifact is from Licking County, Ohio. *Len and Janie Weidner collection.* $350.00.

Agate Basin point, Late Paleo, lenticular cross section, heavily ground lower blade edges. Mottled blue Upper Mercer was used for the point, which is 1³⁄₁₆" x 3". Ex-collection Hawkes, it is from Marion County, Ohio. *Lar Hothem collection.* $200.00.

Wheeler point, Paleo, red jasper, ¾" x 2¼". It has a deeply incurvate baseline and slight edge serrations. Hardin County, Tennessee. *George and Elizabeth Williamson collection, Kentucky; Tom Davis photograph.* Unlisted.

Dalton point or blade, white Burlington chert, 1" x 3½". A long and slender Dalton, it is well balanced and has good patina. Ex-collection Ben Thompson, it has a Perino COA. Adams County, Illinois. *Collection of and photograph by Jim Frederick, Utah.* $750.00.

Dalton-like fluted point, resharpened length at 2⅛", jasper. It is ex-collection Casterline, from Pennsylvania. *Bill Moody collection, Massachusetts.* $350.00.

Dalton blade, fine form, glossy and milky chert, ex-collection Palmer. The blade is 4½" long, from Boone County, Missouri. *Bill Moody collection, Massachusetts.* $900.00.

Dalton point, resharpened from wider point or blade, serrated edges, 2¾". Of light-colored chert, it is ex-collection Garvin, from Greene County, Arkansas. *Bill Moody collection, Massachusetts.* $150.00.

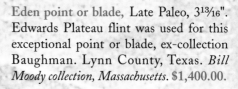

Plainview point, 2⁹⁄₁₆", water-polished flint. Ex-collection Nickel, it came from the Arkansas River, Osage County, Oklahoma. *Bill Moody collection, Massachusetts.* $125.00.

Eden point or blade, Late Paleo, 3¹³⁄₁₆". Edwards Plateau flint was used for this exceptional point or blade, ex-collection Baughman. Lynn County, Texas. *Bill Moody collection, Massachusetts.* $1,400.00.

Dalton point, 2½", Crowley's Ridge chert, ex-collection Johnson. Serrated, it was found in Clay County, Arkansas. *Bill Moody collection, Massachusetts.* $150.00.

Quad point, 2", Late Paleo, gray hornstone, base sides ground. Probably resharpened length, it has a Davis COA. Marion County, Kentucky. *Christopher Smith collection, New York.* $400.00.

Quad point or blade, lower edges ground, gray Fort Payne flint. It is 3¼" long and has a Davis COA. Marion County, Kentucky. *Christopher Smith collection, New York.* $750.00.

Dalton point or blade, white Burlington flint, 1¹⁄₁₆" x 2¼". The artifact is balanced, has uniform thickness, and has matching ears. It has Davis COA #1138 and is from Arkansas. *Collection of and photograph by Jim Frederick, Utah.* $250.00.

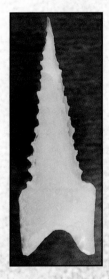

Dalton point, 2", resharpened to hafting region, basal edges ground, deeply indented baseline. It has large serrations and is made of tan flint. Arkansas. *Christopher Smith collection, New York.* $250.00.

Dalton point, Late Paleo, pale Burlington, 2⅝". The example has been heavily resharpened and has large serrations. Pike County, Illinois. *Christopher Smith collection, New York.* $375.00.

Dalton point or blade, white Burlington, 1¼" x 3¾". Ex-collection Tom Davis, it has a Perino COA and is a fine example, with classic shape, good color, and fine workstyle. Warren County, Missouri. *Collection of and photograph by Jim Frederick, Utah.* $1,000.00.

Dalton point or blade, Burlington chert, serrated edges, resharpened to hafting region. This fine artifact is 3⅞" and came from Calhoun County, Illinois. *Christopher Smith collection, New York.* $750.00.

Midland point, shallow flute on reverse face, white flint, 1⅝". It has heavy partial patina and was found in New Mexico. *John and Susan Mellyn collection, Texas.* $750.00.

Scottsbluff point, resharpened and with small portions of shoulders remaining, 2¼". Of high-grade mixed Edwards flint, it is from Wilson County, Texas. *John and Susan Mellyn collection, Texas.* $500.00.

Sloan Dalton(?) point, very similar to the Holland that is found farther to the west, gray Dover flint, 3³⁄₁₆". This blade has worn serrations, and the shoulders have been nearly resharpened away. A top piece, it is from Tennessee. *Christopher Smith collection, New York.* $700.00.

Dalton blade, made of black flint, V-shaped baseline with ground basal edges. This serrated blade is 2¾" long, ex-collection Wilkins. Brown County, Illinois. *Christopher Smith collection, New York.* $450.00.

Scottsbluff point, Late Paleo, tip damage, shoulders resharpened off, high-grade pale mixed Edwards flint. It is 2" long, from Wilson County, Texas. *John and Susan Mellyn collection, Texas.* $200.00.

Dalton point or blade, worn serrations on one edge, 2½". The material is Burlington chert, and the piece was found in Pike County, Missouri. *Christopher Smith collection, New York.* $175.00.

Agate Basin point, chert in two colors, flute-like basal thinning, 3¹³⁄₁₆". It was found in Logan County, Illinois. *Christopher Smith collection, New York.* $450.00.

Western Paleo points or blades, obsidian, left to right. Scotts-bluff, 2½", ex-collection Geinger, Klamath County, Oregon. $350.00. Alberta, 2½", found by D. Cummings, Klamath County, Oregon. $500.00. Black Rock Concave base, 2¾", ex-collections Wolff and Geinger, broken and glued, Lake County, Oregon. $350.00. *Michael Hough collection, California.*

Hardaway Dalton points, both ¹⁵⁄₁₆" x 1¾", found by the owner on the same site in Buncombe County, North Carolina. Left, quartzite, found in 1998. $40.00. Right, jasper, found in 2002. $30.00. *Collection of and photograph by Gary Henry, North Carolina.*

Hardaway Dalton point, Late Paleo, mixed chert, ¹⁵⁄₁₆" x 1¼". Found by the owner in 1998, it is from Buncombe County, North Carolina. *Collection of and photograph by Gary Henry, North Carolina.* $30.00.

Hardaway side-notch point, chert, ¹¹⁄₁₆" x ⅞". The owner found this point, which has slight basal damage, in 1985. Buncombe County, North Carolina. *Collection of and photograph by Gary Henry, North Carolina.* $20.00.

Hardaway Dalton point, resharpened and with needle tip, ⅞" x 1⅜". It is made of quartzite, and the owner found this example in 1995. Buncombe County, North Carolina. *Collection of and photograph by Gary Henry, North Carolina.* $50.00.

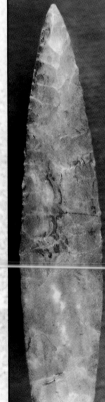

Agate Basin point, two small flute-like basal thinning scars, 4⅝". Made of high-grade patinated flint, this fine piece came from Illinois. *Christopher Smith collection, New York.* $800.00.

Dalton point or blade, Late Paleo, ground basal edges, recurved baseline. Made of Burlington chert, it is 3¼", from Illinois. *Christopher Smith collection, New York.* $350.00.

Agate Basin point, Late Paleo, 2¾", Burlington chert. Resharpened, this point was found in the 1980s. Henderson County, Illinois. *Fred Smith collection, Illinois.* $75.00 – 100.00.

Agate Basin point or blade, 3" long, Moline chert. It was found by I. Kneer and was purchased by the owner at a farm sale in 1992. Resharpened, this colorful piece came from Knox County, Illinois. *Fred Smith collection, Illinois.* $150.00 – 175.00.

Greenbrier Dalton point or blade, 2⅞" x 4", found on a mainly Mississippian site by Richard Windish in the 1960s. It is made of Avon chert, a material not often used by Paleo people in the area. Very thin, the point or blade came from Fulton County, Illinois. *Fred Smith collection, Illinois.* $300.00 – 350.00.

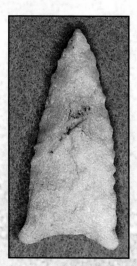

Dalton point or blade, Hixton sugar quartzite, an unusual material for area where found, 2½". Warren County, Illinois. *Fred Smith collection, Illinois.* $100.00 – 150.00.

Tallahassee Dalton point, 2¼", tapered tip. Made of river-stained flint, it was found in the Santa Fe River, Florida. *Bill Moody collection, Massachusetts.* $100.00.

Beaver Lake point, 2¾", light-colored flint. This is a symmetrical and artistic point, from northern Florida. *Bill Moody collection, Massachusetts.* $400.00.

Tallahassee Dalton point, 2¼", ex-collection Fuller. It is made of river-stained flint and came from the Suwannee River, Florida. *Bill Moody collection, Massachusetts.* $125.00.

Dalton point, 2¼", patinated Felsite, found by the owner along Taunton River. Plymouth County, Massachusetts. *Bill Moody collection, Massachusetts.* $75.00.

Hardaway Dalton point, 1¾" long, heavily patinated Felsite. The owner found this example near Pudding Brook, Plymouth County, Massachusetts. *Bill Moody collection, Massachusetts.* $85.00.

Lance point, Late Paleo, blue Upper Mercer flint with lighter inclusions. The tip is burin flaked on one side, and the point is 5¼" long. Hardin County, Ohio. *Jeff Schumacher collection, Kentucky.* $600.00.

Paleo lance, patinated Flint Ridge in light gray plus faint tan and purple, 3⅞". Found in 1974, it came from Brown Township, Delaware County, Ohio. *Frank Otto collection.* $450.00.

Quad point, Late Paleo period, Fort Payne flint. It is 2⅜" long, from Marion County, Kentucky. *Jim Beckman collection, Ohio.* $200.00.

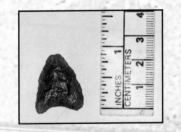

Allen or Dalton family point or blade, resharpened many times to smaller size, amber agate from the Wyoming-Montana region. Found by the owner in 2003, it is from Brookings County, South Dakota. *Harlan Olson collection, South Dakota.* $75.00.

Hell Gap point, 2¹⁄₁₆", found by the owner in 1992. It was pictured in *Indian Artifact Magazine* and the material is a Burlington-like flint or chert. Brookings County, South Dakota. *Harlan Olson collection, South Dakota.* $125.00.

Midland point, Knife River flint, 1" long. Late Paleo, this small point was found by the owner in 1998. Brookings County, South Dakota. *Harlan Olson collection, South Dakota.* $125.00.

149

Plainview point, 1³⁄₁₆", translucent agate from the Wyoming-Montana area. It was found by the owner in 2002 and came from Brookings County, South Dakota. *Harlan Olson collection, South Dakota.* $150.00.

Beaver Lake variant, 2⁷⁄₈", Carter Cave flint in tan and grays. The artifact is quite thin and the flaking is well done. Found by M. Amos in the fall of 2001, it has a Davis COA. It has basal grinding and is from Clark County, Kentucky. *Jeff Schumacher collection, Kentucky.* $1,500.00 plus.

Stringtown stemmed lance, blue Upper Mercer, worn graver spur on stem corner. It measures 2⁵⁄₁₆" and was picked up in Coshocton County, Ohio. *Lar Hothem collection.* $18.00.

Quad, black Kanawha flint, basal grinding, 1¼" x 2³⁄₈". The example has resharpened edges, and was found by the owner's father-in-law, Sam Jenkins. Ohio River Valley, West Virginia. *Private collection, Rodney Roberts photograph.* $45.00.

Paleo artifact group from Kentucky, each pictured separately elsewhere in book. For scale, the large bipointed artifact is 5⅜" long. The range of materials, forms, and sizes is instructive for authentic artifacts from one region. *Jeff Schumacher collection, Kentucky.*

Dalton family point or blade, patinated Knife River flint, 1½". It was found by the owner in 1999 and was pictured in *Indian Artifact Magazine*, Brookings County, South Dakota. *Harlan Olson collection, South Dakota.* $75.00.

Plainview point, Late Paleo, 2³⁄₁₆". Made of Hixton quartzite, it has been pictured in *Indian Artifact Magazine*. The owner found the point in 1999. Brookings County, South Dakota. *Harlan Olson collection, South Dakota.* $225.00.

Agate Basin point, 2³⁄₁₆", Knife River flint. Pictured in *Indian Artifact Magazine*, it was found by the owner in 1998. Brookings County, South Dakota. *Harlan Olson collection, South Dakota.* $150.00.

Agate Basin point, Late Paleo, translucent agate from the Wyoming area. It was found by the owner in 1997. Brookings County, South Dakota. *Harlan Olson collection, South Dakota.* $100.00.

Agate Basin point, 1¾", Swan River chert from Canada, found by the owner in 2001. It came from Brookings County, South Dakota. *Harlan Olson collection, South Dakota.* $75.00.

Alamance point, weathered silicified shale, 2½". With a deeply incurvate baseline, this Late Paleo artifact came from Chatham County, North Carolina. *Collection of and photograph by Ron Harris, North Carolina.* $275.00.

Hardaway Dalton point or blade, large and well shaped, 3⅛". An unknown porous lithic material was used for the point or blade, found in the north-central Piedmont region of North Carolina. *Collection of and photograph by Ron Harris, North Carolina.* $800.00.

Hardaway Dalton point or blade, concave ground base, 3" long. The material is weathered rhyolite, and the artifact was found in Randolph County, North Carolina. *Collection of and photograph by Ron Harris, North Carolina.* $325.00.

Hardaway corner notch point, 3¼", resharpened one time. It is large for type and the material is unknown. Northcentral Piedmont, North Carolina. *Collection of and photograph by Ron Harris, North Carolina.* $850.00.

San Patrice point, 1¼" x 1¹³⁄₁₆", mottled flint in shades of bluish gray. The owner found this example in Wayne County, North Carolina. *Michael Womble collection, North Carolina.* $90.00 – 175.00.

Western Paleo points, left to right. Cougar Mountain, 3¹⁵⁄₁₆", ex-collection Geinger, Lake County, Oregon. $750.00. Unknown type, 3⁹⁄₁₆", Cody-style flaking, fluted one face, ex-collection L. L. "Val" Valdivia, obsidian hydration tested to ca. 8500 – 7500 BC, Bass Lake, Madera County, California. $800.00. Clovis, 2⅞", found by Leroy Geinger, Klamath County, Oregon. $1,500.00. *Michael Hough collection, California.*

Greenbrier point, ⅞" x 1⅞", light tan chert. The owner picked up this example in Wilson County, North Carolina. *Michael Womble collection, North Carolina.* $35.00 – 60.00.

Hardaway point, 1⅛" x 1¼", quartz crystal. White with some translucency, it was found by the owner in Wayne County, North Carolina. *Michael Womble collection, North Carolina.* $125.00 – 200.00.

San Patrice point or blade, 1⅛" x 1⅞", bluish gray chert with dark blue specks. This point or blade was found by the owner in Wilson County, North Carolina. *Michael Womble collection, North Carolina.* $90.00 – 175.00.

Hardaway point, Late Paleo, 1³⁄₁₆" x 1⅜". Light tan chert with shades of gray, it was found by the owner in Wilson County, North Carolina. *Michael Womble collection, North Carolina.* $125.00 – 200.00.

Midland or Milnesand point, Knife River flint, resharpened size. This material is dark amber, usually translucent, and was a favorite of Paleo Indians on the High Plains. McLean County, North Dakota. *Collection of and scan by Larry Bumann, North Dakota.* $175.00.

152

Colby point or blade, indented baseline, heavily patinated Knife River flint. This artifact came from Emmons County, North Dakota. *Collection of and scan by Larry Bumann, North Dakota.* $250.00.

Agate Basin point, Knife River flint with patination, good type example. It came from Emmons County, North Dakota. *Collection of and scan by Larry Bumann, North Dakota.* $400.00.

Hell Gap variant, shorter stem than usual, Late Paleo period. This superb example is made of Knife River flint and has excellent size, chipping, material, and condition. A rare artifact. Emmons County, North Dakota. *Collection of and scan by Larry Bumann, North Dakota.* $8,000.00 plus.

Midland point, Late Paleo, Alibates flint, 1⁵⁄₁₆". It is ex-collections Clauss and Ellison. West Texas. *Dr. Guy Gross collection, Texas.* $700.00.

Allen point, good form, Florence chert, 2½" long. With short serrations, it was found along the Arkansas River in Osage County, Oklahoma. *Dr. Guy Gross collection, Texas.* $700.00.

Allen point or blade, Florence chert, 4¼". This slender artifact was found on the Kaw River near Leavenworth, Kansas. *Dr. Guy Gross collection, Texas.* $2,000.00.

Golondrina point, gray chert, 3³⁄₁₆". It has lower blade taper and a recurved baseline. West Texas. *Dr. Guy Gross collection, Texas.* $750.00.

Dalton point, serrated edges, 2¾", novaculite. This piece is ex-collection Cordeiro and was found in Arkansas. *Bill Moody collection, Massachusetts.* $200.00.

Dalton point or blade, Boone chert, 2¾". It was found by M. Holloway and is ex-collection Steven. McIntosh County, Oklahoma. *Bill Moody collection, Massachusetts.* $100.00.

Dalton point or blade, 3⅝", good size and form, light chert with inclusions. Ex-collection Stevens, it came from the Springfield area, Missouri. *Bill Moody collection, Massachusetts.* $350.00.

Sloan Dalton point, 2¾", light mixed flint, ex-collection Bushey. It came from Lawrence County, Arkansas. *Bill Moody collection, Massachusetts.* $100.00.

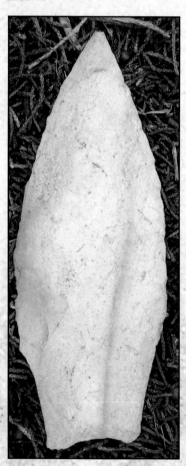

Dalton blade, glossy Crescent Quarry flint, 145mm x 39mm. This large knife was an inch or more longer before resharpenings that reduced the size. It has been pictured in several publications and is ex-collections Golden, Dougherty, and Roberts. With a Perino COA, it was found near Rector, Clay County, Arkansas. *Mike Trekell collection, Minnesota.* $3,500.00.

Stemmed lance, Late Paleo, basal edges ground, 4⅝". This large point or blade is made of chert in four colors, and came from Missouri. *John and Susan Mellyn collection, Texas.* $450.00.

154

Scottsbluff point, Edwards flint in three colors. Shoulders are resharpened off on this example, 2¾" long. Wilson County, Texas. *John and Susan Mellyn collection, Texas.* $350.00.

Agate Basin point, resharpened to hafting region, 2½". The material is Edwards flint, and the piece came from Wilson County, Texas. *John and Susan Mellyn collection, Texas.* $225.00.

Early triangular point, large flute on obverse face, 2½". It is made of Edwards flint and came from Wilson County, Texas. *John and Susan Mellyn collection, Texas.* $400.00.

Early triangular point, Edwards flint, 2⅛". It has a large flute on the obverse and was found in Wilson County, Texas. *John and Susan Mellyn collection, Texas.* $300.00.

Lovell point, 1⁷⁄₁₆", found by the owner in 1998. Pictured in *Indian Artifact Magazine*, it is made of Knife River flint. Brookings County, South Dakota. *Harlan Olson collection, South Dakota.* $175.00.

Hell Gap point, 1⅝", pictured in *Indian Artifact Magazine.* Gray chert was used for this piece, found by the owner in 1998. Brookings County, South Dakota. *Harlan Olson collection, South Dakota.* $100.00.

Dalton point, fluted on one face and beveled, 1¾", Onondaga flint. The owner found this piece on a rise bordering a stream that flows into North River. Plymouth County, Massachusetts. *Bill Moody collection, Massachusetts.* $75.00.

Agate Basin point, gray hornstone, 3¹⁵⁄₁₆". The basal edges are heavily ground and the piece has good overall form. It is pictured in *Overstreet #8*, page 364, and was found in Clark County, Kentucky. *Jeff Schumacher collection, Kentucky.* $350.00 – 500.00.

Hardaway Dalton point, 1½", well-patinated Felsite. It was found by the owner near Herring Brook in Plymouth County, Massachusetts. *Bill Moody collection, Massachusetts.* $85.00.

Greenbrier Dalton point, 2¼", Felsite, found by the owner on a hilltop site with a spring at the base of the hill. Plymouth County, Massachusetts. *Bill Moody collection, Massachusetts.* $50.00.

Greenbrier Dalton point, 2½", Felsite, found by the owner near the Taunton River. Plymouth County, Massachusetts. *Bill Moody collection, Massachusetts.* $65.00.

Dalton point, 2½", Felsite, found by Mark Swinney near a coastal pond adjacent to Narragansett Bay. Newport County, Rhode Island. *Bill Moody collection, Massachusetts.* $75.00.

Midland point, made on a flake of brown and orange chert, 1⅜". Ex-collection Ray, it is from Angelina County, Texas. *Dr. Guy Gross collection, Texas.* $1,000.00.

Agate Basin–like point, late Paleo, Upper Mercer flint with a quartz line down the centerline, 3¹⁵⁄₁₆". A fine example of an eastern Agate Basin, it came from the Pickerington area, Fairfield County, Ohio. *Don Casto collection.* $800.00.

Milnesand point, cream-colored chert, 2⅝". It is ex-collection Forshage and was found in Wilson County, Texas. *Dr. Guy Gross collection, Texas.* $600.00.

Stringtown stemmed lance, 2⁷⁄₁₆", patinated Walhonding Valley flint. It has two basal spurs and came from the Clear Creek area, Fairfield County, Ohio. *Don Casto collection.* $50.00.

Stringtown lance, graver extension on base corner, streaked Flint Ridge, 2⅜". Sometime in the past this point was fire damaged, and it now has potlid blowouts and fire breaks. Coshocton County, Ohio. *Private collection.* $10.00.

Dalton point, resharpened size, tan and gray Delaware County flint. It is 1⅞" long and ex-collection Bob Champion. The find site is considerably east of the usual distribution area. Knox County, Ohio. *Lar Hothem collection*. $35.00.

Beaver Lake point, Late Paleo, Kentucky or Indiana gray hornstone. This artifact is 2⅜" long, ex-collections Dick Johnson and Copeland. Adams County, Ohio. *Frank Meyer collection*. $250.00.

Beaver Lake point, Late Paleo, 2⅜", Burlington or Crescent Quarry flint. It was found in Jersey County, Illinois. *Gregory L. Perdun collection, Illinois*. $65.00.

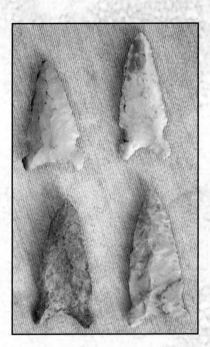

Beaver Lake points or blades, with top two showing some traits of later Graham Cave artifacts types. All are made of Burlington except the bottom left example, which is of unknown chert. The longest example is 2¼". Jersey County, Illinois. *Gregory L. Perdun collection, Illinois*. Each, $65.00 – 100.00.

Meserve Dalton point, Late Paleo, 1½", Burlington chert. It has extended ears and was found in Jersey County, Illinois. *Gregory L. Perdun collection, Illinois*. $40.00.

Sloan Dalton point or blade, heat-treated Burlington, 1⁵⁄₁₆" x 4¾". The artifact was found during basement excavation in Holt County, Missouri. *Mike George collection, Missouri; Terry Price photograph*. $500.00.

Dalton point, resharpened probably to exhaustion and discarded, 1⅛" x 1⁵⁄₁₆". It is made of Foraker flint and the basal edges are ground. Holt County, Missouri. *Mike George collection, Missouri; Terry Price photograph*. $25.00.

Agate Basin knife, resharpened and angled blade, gray chert. This blade measures ⅝" x 2¼" and has a beveled edge. It came from Holt County, Missouri. *Mike George collection, Missouri; Terry Price photograph*. $50.00.

157

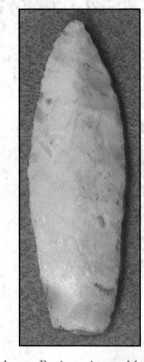

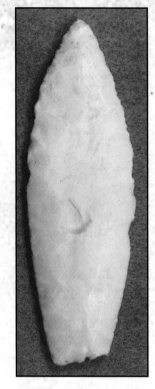

Agate Basin point, Late Paleo, very thin and well made of Burlington chert. The point is 3⅞" long and was found by the owner in 1996. Warren County, Illinois. *Fred Smith collection, Illinois.* $300.00 – 350.00.

Agate Basin point or blade, Burlington chert, 3½" long. It was found by J. Proctor in the 1950s and was obtained by the owner at the Windish estate sale. Peoria County, Illinois. *Fred Smith collection, Illinois.* $200.00 – 250.00.

Scottsbluff point, mixed pale Edwards flint, resharpened and shoulders partially removed, 2⁹⁄₁₆". Wilson County, Texas. *John and Susan Mellyn collection, Texas.* $550.00.

Sloan Dalton point or blade, Late Paleo, high-grade Burlington, 1⅝" x 5¼". This fine artifact was found during the excavation of a basement. Holt County, Missouri. *Mike George collection, Missouri; Terry Price photograph.* $600.00.

Early triangular point, fluted on obverse, Edwards flint. The point is 2" long, from Wilson County, Texas. *John and Susan Mellyn collection, Texas.* $250.00.

Agate Basin point, 3¼", Burlington chert, slight damage near base. This was found by the owner in 1988. Knox County, Illinois. *Fred Smith collection, Illinois.* $100.00 – 150.00.

Dalton point, greatly resharpened and with beveled edges, 2¹⁵⁄₁₆". It was found by B. McIntire near Quincy, and the owner obtained the artifact at an estate sale. Adams County, Illinois. *Fred Smith collection, Illinois.* $125.00 – 150.00.

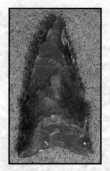

Dalton point or blade, resharpened size, 1⅝" long. The material is an unknown translucent red agate with patination. This piece is from the Hendricks estate auction, but the find location is unknown. *Fred Smith collection, Illinois.* $50.00 – 60.00.

Agate Basin point, 3" long, Burlington chert. This was found by J. Norris, and the owner obtained the point directly from him. The angled base is not damaged, since the point was made that way. Fulton County, Illinois. *Fred Smith collection, Illinois.* $100.00 – 125.00.

Dalton point, resharpened condition, 2¾", mottled Burlington chert. Ex-collection Crum, it is from southern Warren County, Illinois. *Fred Smith collection, Illinois.* $100.00 – 125.00.

Greenbrier Dalton point, Late Paleo, chert, ⅞" x 1¾". With one shoulder resharpened off, it came from Franklin County, Tennessee. *Collection of and photograph by Gary Henry, North Carolina.* $60.00.

Dalton point or blade, distal end damage, mottled chert, 1" x 2⅝". The owner found this piece in 1999. Buncombe County, North Carolina. *Collection of and photograph by Gary Henry, North Carolina.* $40.00.

Lovell point, Late Paleo, Niobrara chert, 1⅟₁₆". Found by the owner in 2001, it has been pictured in *Indian Artifact Magazine* and *Overstreet #8.* Brookings County, South Dakota. *Harlan Olson collection, South Dakota.* $75.00.

Browns Valley point, Late Paleo, Niobrara chert, 1⅞", found by the owner in 1997. Brookings County, South Dakota. *Harlan Olson collection, South Dakota.* $75.00.

Stemmed lance, possibly a Hell Gap, rounded tip, ¹⁵⁄₁₆". It is Knife River flint and was pictured in *Indian Artifact Magazine.* The owner found this artifact in 1998. Brookings County, South Dakota. *Harlan Olson collection, South Dakota.* $75.00.

Dalton point or blade, obverse, Perino COA, 96mm x 29mm. The large dart or knife form has had a resharpening that produced serrations and shortened the width only slightly. The material is Crowley's Ridge chert. Greene County, Arkansas. *Mike Trekell collection, Minnesota.* $2,500.00.

Dalton point or blade, reverse, Perino COA, ex-collections Morast and Roberts. The owner comments, "This is the closest to a perfect point that I have yet seen. It is wafer thin and without a blemish." Greene County, Arkansas. *Mike Trekell collection, Minnesota.* $2,500.00.

Holland point or blade, with at least one resharpening that only slightly reduced blade size. The material is oolithic chert and the size is 98mm x 36mm. It has a Perino COA, and the material sparkles under light. It was found in Camden County, Missouri. *Mike Trekell collection, Minnesota.* $1,500.00 – 2,000.00.

Plainview point, Late Paleo, Burlington chert. It is 2⅝" long and the chipping is excellent. Quite thin, this artifact came from the Western Buff area, Jersey County, Illinois. *Gregory L. Perdun collection, Illinois.* $1,200.00.

Barber point, Edwards flint, 2¾". It has a deeply incurvate baseline and a needle tip, and it came from Jackson County, Texas. *John and Susan Mellyn collection, Texas.* $275.00.

Lerma point, possibly Paleo, rootbeer flint with heavy patina. It is 2½" long, from Wilson County, Texas. *John and Susan Mellyn collection, Texas.* $250.00.

Fluted point, Redstone-like, 2" long. It is made of red Payson chert and is scarce both in style and material. Pike County, Illinois. *Gregory L. Perdun collection, Illinois.* $650.00.

Lanceolate point, Burlington chert, 3" long. The point was picked up in Jersey County, Illinois. *Gregory L. Perdun collection, Illinois.* $65.00.

Agate Basin(?) point or blade, light Edwards flint, 2⅞". The artifact has a rounded tip indicative of knife use, and came from Wilson County, Texas. *John and Susan Mellyn collection, Texas.* $150.00.

Arkabutla point, Late Paleo, 1⅜", pale chert. It has obverse fluting or basal thinning and came from California. *John and Susan Mellyn collection, Texas.* $150.00.

Agate Basin blade, 1¼" x 3¼", Late Paleo period. It is made of very unusual material, hematite (natural iron ore), and was found in an erosion ditch. Holt County, Missouri. *Mike George collection, Missouri; Terry Price photograph.* Unlisted.

Dalton variant, Burlington chert, 1½" x 3". Found by J. Worth, this triangular artifact came from Buchanan County, Missouri. *Mike George collection, Missouri; Terry Price photograph.* $75.00.

Scottsbluff blade, Florence chert, ⅞" x 2½". This stemmed blade, found by L. Hinton, came from Buchanan County, Missouri. *Mike George collection, Missouri; Terry Price photograph.* $125.00.

Dalton point, resharpened size, 1" x 1¾". Glossy Burlington was used for the point, found in Doniphan County, Kansas. *Mike George collection, Missouri; Terry Price photograph.* $75.00.

Scottsbluff point, glossy tan Edwards flint, rounded tip and wide base, 2⅜". Some shouldering remains on this piece, found in Harris County, Texas. *John and Susan Mellyn collection, Texas.* $700.00.

Scottsbluff point, white flint with inclusions, tapered tip, 2⅞". Made of Edwards flint, it was found in Wilson County, Texas. *John and Susan Mellyn collection, Texas.* $700.00.

Agate Basin point, lower two-fifths of edges ground, 2¹¹⁄₁₆". Ex-collection Johnson, the piece is of tan-blue Upper Mercer with inclusions. Morrow County, Ohio. *Lar Hothem collection.* $100.00.

Agate Basin point, dark patinated agate, 1" x 4½". Ex-collection Waters, this is a long and well-made point in high-grade material. It has Jackson COA #DT-4. Nebraska. *Dr. David R. Thrasher collection, Alabama.* $2,500.00.

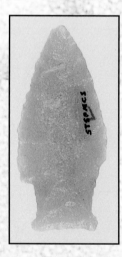

Agate Basin point, gray Onondaga (NY) or Upper Mercer (OH), 2¾". There is a chipped thinning platform at the base and both lower side edges are heavily ground. Ex-collection Bob Champion, Knox County, Ohio. *Lar Hothem collection.* $125.00.

Stemmed lanceolate, Stringtown variety with two graver spurs, 3⁹⁄₁₆". The material is Nellie chert in shades of brownish gray. Stark County, Ohio. *Lar Hothem collection.* $100.00.

Eden earred point, Hixton quartzite, 2⅜". An unusual point type, it has an Earthworks COA and came from Wisconsin. *Earthworks Artifacts.* $1,100.00.

162

Dalton point, Late Paleo, obverse with basal thinning scars. The point or blade is 3⅜", and the material is Bloomville chert. This Dalton has an Earthworks COA and was found in Indiana. *Earthworks Artifacts*. $650.00.

Early triangular point, Edwards flint in white and off-white, 2⁹⁄₁₆". It is from Wilson County, Texas. *John and Susan Mellyn collection, Texas*. $400.00.

Angostura point, Late Paleo, 3½". Edwards Plateau flint was used for this piece, ex-collection Pohler, that has a Jackson COA. Texas. *Earthworks Artifacts*. $650.00.

Lance point, Flint Ridge multicolor, 3¹⁄₁₆". Ex-collection Richie, it is pictured in *First Hunters*, page 70. The majority of lanceolates from the state are made of dark Upper Mercer. Coshocton County, Ohio. *Earthworks Artifacts*. $675.00.

Beaver Lake point, flared base, 3⅛". The material is Coastal Plains chert and the point has an Earthworks COA. Georgia. *Earthworks Artifacts*. $400.00.

Agate Basin point, Late Paleo, orange jasper of unknown origin. The point is 3⅜" long and has an Earthworks COA. Decatur County, Indiana. *Earthworks Artifacts*. $750.00.

Scottsbluff point, Late Paleo period, 2½". Ex-collection Schinstock, it was picked up in Henry County, Iowa. *Collection of and photograph by A. D. Savage, Iowa*. $175.00.

163

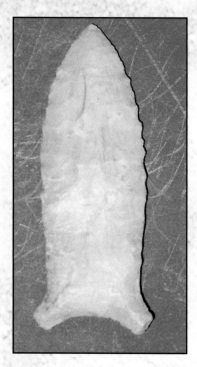

Quad point, Late Paleo, 3½", in a good grade of light-colored Dover chert. Well chipped, it came from the area of Louisville, Kentucky. *Collection of and photograph by A. D. Savage, Iowa.* $550.00.

Stemmed lance, McConnell type, blue and gray Coshocton. Ex-collection Weidner, it is 2⅖" and from Medina County, Ohio. *Dave Summers collection, New York.* $100.00.

Stemmed lance, Stringtown subtype, unknown chert. It measures 1⅛" x 2¼" and came from the Newton Falls area, Trumbull County, Ohio. *Pat Layshock collection; Thomas R. Pigott image.* $50.00.

Cumberland point, Brassfield chert colored cream to light yellow, ¹⁵⁄₁₆" x 3⅝". This is a fine artifact, with a short and wide flute on one face only. The Late Paleo point was found in Madison County, Kentucky. *George and Elizabeth Williamson collection, Kentucky; Tom Davis photograph.* Museum grade.

Dalton family point or blade, 2¼". Made of glacial flint, it was found near Thornport, southcentral Ohio. *Fred Winegardner collection.* $200.00.

Agate Basin point or blade, 1" x 5¼", light-colored flint. The lower blade edges are ground, with the remainder left sharp. This fine piece was found by the owner in Osage County, Missouri. *Jim McKinney collection, Missouri; Mary Jane Wieberg photograph.* $700.00 – 800.00.

Greenbrier Dalton point or blade, fluted obverse, resharpened size. The artifact is made of mottled white flint and is 1⅜". Colbert County, Alabama. *Christopher Smith collection, New York.* $100.00.

Dalton point or blade, 2⅛", ex-collection Claytor. It is water polished and river stained and is from Florida. *Christopher Smith collection, New York.* $225.00.

Agate Basin point or blade, Late Paleo, Onondaga mottled gray, tan, black, and blue. It is 3¹¹/₂₀" and was found in Wayne County, New York. *Dave Summers collection, New York.* $300.00.

Agate Basin lance, superb example with incurvate baseline, 4¼". This streamlined Late Paleo lance was found in Callaway County, Missouri. *Christopher Smith collection, New York.* Museum grade.

Stemmed lance point or knife, Stringtown variety, 1⅝" x 4⅛". One of the larger type examples, it is made of Carter Cave (KY) flint with lighter inclusions. It has Davis and Jackson COAs and was found in Ohio. *Earthworks Artifacts.* $1,500.00.

Late Paleo stemmed lance, Stringtown variety, 3⅝". The striped dark blue is probably Upper Mercer flint, the base corner has a graver spur, and the lance has an Earthworks COA. Ohio. *Earthworks Artifacts.* $350.00.

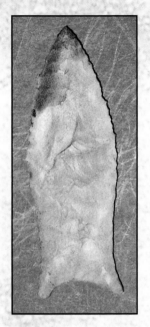

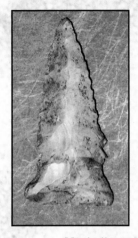

Dalton point, Nucholls variety, Late Paleo. Brown and gray chert, the Dalton is 2¼". Ex-collection Stevens, it came from Greene County, Arkansas. *Collection of and photograph by A. D. Savage, Iowa.* $150.00.

Beaver Lake point or blade, Late Paleo, nicely earred, 3⅛". It is made of brown Dover chert and has a Davis COA. Pike County, Illinois. *Collection of and photograph by A. D. Savage, Iowa.* $600.00.

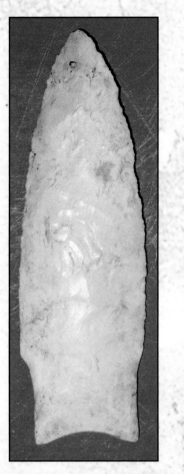

Holland point or blade, Late Paleo period, 4⅝". This large artifact has had one resharpening and is made of Burlington. The Holland has a Perino COA, and it is from St. Louis County, Missouri. *Collection of and photograph by A. D. Savage, Iowa.* $1,700.00.

Holland-point or blade, Late Paleo, tan Burlington, 4¾" long. Resharpening shortened the length and eliminated most of shoulders. It has a Perino COA and was found in Jersey County, Illinois. *Collection of and photograph by A. D. Savage, Iowa.* $800.00.

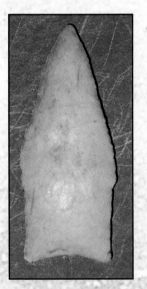

Quad point, 2¾", extended ears, mixed chert. The example came from Nevada County, Arkansas. *Collection of and photograph by Duane Treest, Illinois.* $300.00 – 500.00.

Holland point, Late Paleo, lightly stemmed, 2¾" long. Made of glossy Burlington, it was a 2002 find by Andria Savage on the family farm. Henry County, Iowa. *Collection of and photograph by A. D. Savage, Iowa.* Unlisted.

Dalton point, fluted obverse, 2", mixed chert. It came from Nevada County, Arkansas. *Collection of and photograph by Duane Treest, Illinois.* $100.00 – 150.00.

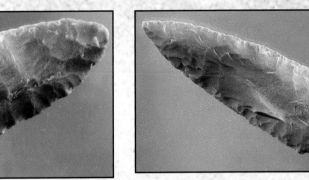

Clovis fluted point, double flute on obverse and single flute on reverse. Kentucky gray hornstone was used for this piece, 1" x 2¹¹⁄₁₆". It has a Davis COA and came from Boone County, Kentucky. *George and Elizabeth Williamson collection, Kentucky; Tom Davis photograph.* Museum grade.

Dalton-Hemphill point or blade, Late Paleo period, red jasper. It has a Davis COA, measures ⅞" x 2½", and was found in Graves County, Kentucky. *George and Elizabeth Williamson collection, Kentucky; Tom Davis photograph.* $250.00.

Agate Basin point or blade, 2⁵⁄₁₆", found by D. Neushwander in 1962. It came from Will County, Illinois. *Collection of and photograph by Duane Treest, Illinois.* $65.00 – 125.00.

Scottsbluff point, pink Missouri flint with other colors, 1⁵⁄₁₆" x 2⅜". This piece, ex-collection Nault, has Jackson COA #7092. Stoddard County, Missouri. *Dr. David R. Thrasher collection, Alabama.* $1,000.00.

Scottsbluff point or blade, Late Paleo, reddish purple jasper. Resharpened by percussion flaking, it is 3½" long and has a Perino COA. Shelby County, Texas. *Earthworks Artifacts.* $775.00.

Unfluted Cumberland point, mottled Kentucky hornstone, 5¹⁄₃₂". A dramatic and artistic Late Paleo point, it has a Perino COA. Laurel County, Kentucky. *Earthworks Artifacts.* Museum grade.

Scottsbluff(?) variant, heavy stem grinding, patinated Edwards flint. This point or blade is 2⅜" and came from the Salado area, Texas. *John and Susan Mellyn collection, Texas.* $275.00.

Lerma point or blade, rounded-base form, possibly Paleo, Edwards flint. The example measures 3⅜" long. Wilson County, Texas. *John and Susan Mellyn collection, Texas.* $350.00.

Dalton(?) variant, Edwards flint, 2¼". This artifact with delicate ears has overall water polish and came from the San Bernard River. Colorado County, Texas. *John and Susan Mellyn collection, Texas.* $225.00.

Quad points, Late Paleo period, each 2⅛" long. Made of Burlington chert, these were found in Jersey County, Illinois. *Gregory L. Perdun collection, Illinois.* Each, $350.00 – 450.00.

Holland point or blade, Late Paleo, slightly shouldered, two-tone Burlington chert. A scarce artifact type, it is 3⅜" long. Western Bluff area, Jersey County, Illinois. *Gregory L. Perdun collection, Illinois.* $1,200.00.

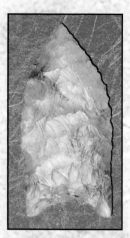

Holland point, shortened due to resharpening, Crowley Ridge chert. It has a Perino COA and is 2¼" long. Clay County, Arkansas. *Collection of and photograph by A. D. Savage, Iowa.* $400.00.

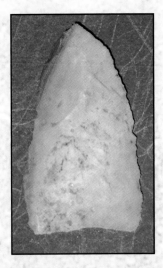

Dalton blade, Sloan variety, 2½". This is a small flake knife made from Burlington, and it has a Perino COA. LaSalle County, Illinois. *Collection of and photograph by A. D. Savage, Iowa.* $200.00.

Dalton point or blade, Late Paleo ca. 8500 BC, 3½" long. Made of white Burlington, it has a Davis COA. Cooper County, Missouri. *Collection of and photograph by A. D. Savage, Iowa.* $400.00.

Hardaway "Cowhead" corner-notch point, 1⅜", green rhyolite. It was found at the Yadkin River Narrows near Badin, Stanley County, North Carolina. *Collection of and photograph by Ron Harris, North Carolina.* $325.00.

Hardaway Dalton point, 2" long, weathered "snowflake" rhyolite. The resharpened example came from the Yadkin River Narrows, Stanley County, North Carolina. *Collection of and photograph by Ron Harris, North Carolina.* $225.00.

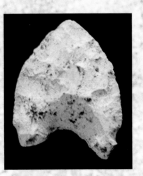

Hardaway blade, resharpened to exhaustion, 1⅝". Of heavily weathered rhyolite, it was found at the Yadkin River Narrows, Stanley County, North Carolina. *Collection of and photograph by Ron Harris, North Carolina.* $75.00.

Hardaway blade, exceptionally long for type, oblique Paleo flaking. It is 5½" and was found, broken, in a logging track during land-clearing operations. Ex-collection Richardson, it is from southwestern Randolph County, North Carolina. *Collection of and photograph by Ron Harris.* $500.00.

Hardaway Dalton point, 2¾", heavily weathered rhyolite. It was found near the Yadkin River Narrows near Badin, Stanley County, North Carolina. *Collection of and photograph by Ron Harris, North Carolina.* $375.00.

Dalton point or blade, dark Harrison County (Indiana) hornstone, 2¾". It was found in Marion County, Ohio. *Joel Embrey collection.* $175.00.

Stringtown lance, Walhonding Valley mixed gray flint, 2¼". Ex-collection Farley, it came from Licking County, Ohio. *Private collection.* $25.00.

Lanceolate point, one of a cache of nine Late Paleo artifacts. The material is translucent mixed moss agate from Flint Ridge, and the point is ex-collection Copeland. It is 5" long and one of the best pieces in the cache. Licking County, Ohio. *Joel Embrey collection.* $3,000.00.

Stemmed lance, Stringtown type, Nellie gray and black fossiliferous flint. This is typical material for Late Paleo artifacts in Ohio, and the unusually long lance is 4⅝". Adams County, Ohio. *Joel Embrey collection.* $550.00.

Dalton family point or blade, gray Harrison County flint, 1⅞" long. It was found in southern Illinois. *Private collection.* $10.00.

Dalton family blade, large at 5¼", tan patinated Burlington. It was found in Illinois. *Private collection.* $225.00.

Agate Basin lance point, blue Upper Mercer with a bold quartzite lightning line. This attractive and well-made piece is 3¼", and was reportedly found in Van Buren County, Iowa. *Larry Garvin collection.* $300.00.

170

Dalton point, 1½", resharpened to hafting area. Made of chert, it is from Nevada County, Arkansas. *Collection of and photograph by Duane Treest, Illinois.* $25.00 – 35.00.

Dalton point or blade, Late Paleo, 2⅜". The base with extended ears is heavily ground on edges, and the material is blue and tan flint. Logan County, Kentucky. *Back to Earth.* $125.00.

Greenbrier Dalton blade, mixed gray-tan chert, 2⅜". This resharpened knife form is Late Paleo and came from Fentress County, Tennessee. *Back to Earth.* $90.00.

Dalton point or blade, resharpened but with small shoulders retained, 2½". Golden brown glossy flint was used for this piece, which has a nicely balanced form. *Back to Earth.* $80.00.

Points, left to right. Left, Dovetail, Early Archaic, 2⅛" x 6", Howard COA, Knox County, Illinois. Right, Beaver Lake/Pike County, Late Paleo. Both were sold December 7, 2002, and value relects a 10% buyers' premium. The Beaver Lake/Pike County (lot 132, Howard COA) is a well-known point and has been in several important collections. It is 1⅛" x 4¹⁵⁄₁₆", from Pike County, Illinois. *Rainbow Traders, Illinois.* Lot #132, $6,600.00.

Scottsbluff(?) variant, heavy stem edge grinding, 2¾". It is made of mottled Edwards flint and came from Wilson County, Texas. *John and Susan Mellyn collection, Texas.* $325.00.

Zella point, pale Edwards flint with a few white spots, 2¾", Iron from Wilson County, Texas. *John and Susan Mellyn collection, Texas.* $350.00.

Dalton point, serrated edges, white chert or flint, 3⅞". Ex-collection Squire, it was found in Grant County, Wisconsin. *Collection of and photograph by Duane Treest, Illinois.* $200.00 – 250.00.

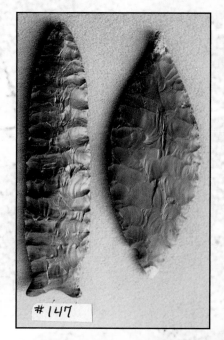

Agate Basin point or blade, 3½", colorful flint or chert. The well-chipped example is ex-collection Squire of Wisconsin. It is from Illinois. *Collection of and photograph by Duane Treest, Illinois.* $350.00 plus.

Dalton point, Late Paleo, edges resharpened to hafting area, 2⅞". Made of multi-colored chert, it came from Nevada County, Arkansas. *Collection of and photograph by Duane Treest, Illinois.* $150.00 – 250.00.

Dalton point or blade, large serrations for size, 3¼". It is made of white flint and is ex-collection Squire. Boone County, Missouri. *Collection of and photograph by Duane Treest, Illinois.* $200.00 – 250.00.

Greenbrier Dalton (on left) and Turkeytail (on right, Early Woodland) pieces. The Greenbrier (lot 147) was sold March 15, 2003, and the high bid included the 10% buyers' premium. It is 1½" x 5¹⁵⁄₁₆" and is made of Fort Payne chert or flint. The Greenbrier, which has outstanding flaking, has a Howard COA and came from near Memphis, Tennessee. *Rainbow Traders, Illinois.* Lot #147, $3,410.00.

Quad point, Late Paleo, auctioned March 15, 2003. Price included the added 10% buyers' premium. The point measures 1⅛" x 2½" and was lot 330. The Quad has a Howard COA and came from Alexander County, Illinois. *Rainbow Traders, Illinois.* $330.00.

Sloan Dalton point or blade, Late Paleo, sold May 4, 2002, as lot 83. Made of strawberry chert, it is thin and has a Perino COA. The Sloan is 4½" long, and the value figure includes a 10% buyers' premium. Marin County, Missouri. *Rainbow Traders, Illinois.* $825.00.

Hardaway side-notch point, pale Delaware County flint, probably resharpened. It has a wide shallow flute or basal thinning scar and came from Fairfield County, Ohio. *Craig Ferrell collection*. $40.00.

Greenbrier Dalton point, high-grade Sonora flint, probably resharpened size. It was found in Russell County, Kentucky. *Craig Ferrell collection*. $50.00.

Eden point, Late Paleo, lot 135 of May 24, 2003, auction. The bid figure for this rare artifact included a 10% buyers' premium. Made of highly patinated material, it is ⅞" x 4⅛" and has a Motley COA. Osage River area, Missouri. *Rainbow Traders, Illinois*. $4,070.00.

Dalton point, resharpened and with beveled edges, a nicely balanced piece. It is made of Hillsdale (Greenbrier) chert and came from Putnam County, West Virginia. *Craig Ferrell collection*. $100.00.

Hardaway side-notch point or blade, fine blade chipping and delicate serrations, quality mixed flint. Logan County, West Virginia. *Craig Ferrell collection*. $35.00.

Sloan Dalton point or blade, Late Paleo, Winterset chert, 1⅛" x 4⅞". Found by N. Preschel, it has Jackson COA #7089. Sumner County, Kansas. *Dr. David R. Thrasher collection, Alabama*. $5,000.00.

173

Dalton point, 2", Late Paleo, ex-collection Greg Perino. This example in novaculite was found in Arkansas. *Collection of and photograph by Duane Treest, Illinois.* $35.00 – 50.00.

Dalton point, worn serrations, mixed tan chert, 2½" long. It was found in Nevada County, Arkansas. *Collection of and photograph by Duane Treest, Illinois.* $150.00.

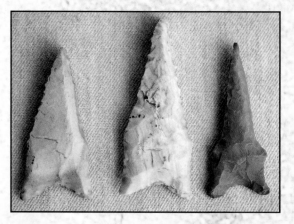

Dalton points or blades, Late Paleo. Left and center, Crescent Quarry flint. Each, $65.00. Other is unknown. $125.00. The largest of these artifacts is 2³⁄₁₆" long. Jersey County, Illinois. *Gregory L. Perdun collection, Illinois.*

Greenbrier Dalton point or blade, 1¼" x 4¾", unidentifed high-grade chert. This piece was found by the owner, and has Jackson COA #DT-9. Madison County, Alabama. *Dr. David R. Thrasher collection, Alabama.* $5,000.00.

Dalton points or blades, resharpened sizes, both 1⅝". Made of Burlington chert, they are from Jersey County, Illinois. Left, $45.00. Right, $25.00. *Gregory L. Perdun collection, Illinois.*

Crowfield point, Late Paleo, reverse with double flutes. Made of brown jasper, this point is 2½" long and was found in southeastern Pennsylvania. *Private collection.* $2,500.00 plus.

Debert fluted point, 2¹⁄₁₆", black chert. Displaying the typical deep and recurved baseline, it was found in York County, Pennsylvania. *Private collection.* $900.00 plus.

Sloan Dalton blade, Late Paleo, 1⅝" x 5¾". This very fine piece has parallel flaking and light basal grinding. It is made of white Burlington and has mineral deposits. Overall patina is present. The blade has a Berner COA and is ex-collection Sulka. Boone County, Missouri. *Jon Boyes collection, Illinois.* Museum grade.

Dalton point or blade, resharpened size, 2¼". It has an Earthworks COA and is made of white chert. Illinois. *Earthworks Artifacts; Ed Rowe photograph.* $125.00.

Stemmed lanceolate, probably Stringtown type, pale quartzite. It is 2¹⁄₁₆" long and has an Earthworks COA. Scioto County, Ohio. *Earthworks Artifacts; Ed Rowe photograph.* Unlisted.

Agate Basin point or blade, 3¼", creek-stained dark brown and red with some orange. It was found by the owner in a creek bed with another Agate Basin in Scott County, Illinois. *Collection of and photograph by Kevin Calvin, Illinois.* $50.00.

Plainview point, light-colored chert, 2⅞". Ex-collection Arnold, it has a Rogers COA. Bell County, Texas. *Earthworks Artifacts; Ed Rowe photograph.* $650.00.

... ety, 2¾". Burlington chert was used for this piece, ex-collection Schinstock. Henry County, Iowa. *Collection of and photograph by A. D. Savage, Iowa.* $125.00.

175

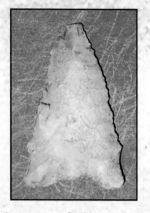

Dalton point, Colbert variety, 2" long. Brown Burlington, it is ex-collection Schinstock. Henry County, Iowa. *Collection of and photograph by A. D. Savage, Iowa.* $100.00.

Dalton point or blade, Late Paleo ca. 8500 BC, 3¼". Glossy white Burlington, the Dalton has a Johnson COA. Yell County, Arkansas. *Collection of and photograph by A. D. Savage, Iowa.* $250.00.

Late Paleo points or blades. Daltons (3" long) on left and in center, and Holland (1⅞") on right. The material is Kentucky gray flint, and all pieces were found by the owner in Pope County, Illinois. *Dortha Milligan collection, Illinois; Kevin Calvin photograph.* Unlisted.

Browns Valley point or blade, 2⅝", in resharpened size, lightly ground basal edges. It is made of Burlington and was found in a creek bed by the owner. Macoupin County, Illinois. *G. Sloan collection; photograph by Kevin Calvin, Illinois.* $50.00 – 60.00.

Holland point or blade, 2⅞", light tan Burlington. With slight tip damage, it was found in a creek bed by Perry Slone. Madison County, Illinois. *Perry Sloan collection; Kevin Calvin photograph, Illinois.* $100.00.

Dalton point or blade, Late Paleo, 1⅜" x 3⅛". Well-chipped and with serrated edges, it has been resharpened to the hafting region. Brownish-white flint, the piece is ex-collections Templeton and Seth Watkins. Cooper County, Missouri. *Collection of and photograph by Steve Weisser, Indiana.* $300.00.

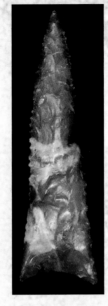

Dalton point or blade, Late Paleo, 1³⁄₁₆" x 3⅞". Made of cream chert and well shaped, it is ex-collection Murray. Lincoln County, Missouri. *Bob Rantz collection, Indiana; Steve Weisser photograph.* $475.00.

Tallahassee point or blade, glossy Coastal Plains chert in tan, cream, and reddish, ⅞" x 3". It has serrated edges and is ex-collection Claytor. The piece has Davis COA #9094, but the origin is unlisted. *Dr. David R. Thrasher collection, Alabama.* $3,500.00.

Gilchrist point or blade, Late Paleo, 1¼" x 3⅛". The example is ex-collection Claytor and is made of tan river-stained multicolored chalcedony. It has Davis COA #9098. Origin unlisted. *Dr. David R. Thrasher collection, Alabama.* $2,500.00.

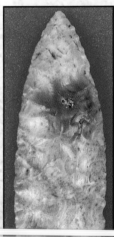

Beaver Lake point or blade, Late Paleo, mottled high-grade Carter Cave. Well designed, it is 1" x 3⅝" and has Jackson COA #4263. Greenup County, Kentucky. *Dr. David R. Thrasher collection, Alabama.* $4,000.00.

Agate Basin blade, Late Paleo, 1¹³⁄₁₆" x 7¹⁄₁₆". It is thin and ⸻⸻⸻⸻⸻ was found in 1969, and the material is orange river-stained chert with patina. Ex-collection Seth Watkins, Atchison County, Missouri. *Collection of and photograph by Steve Weisser, Indiana.* $850.00.

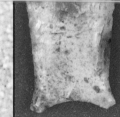

Allen point, light-colored Edwards Plateau flint, ¾" x 2½". It is ex-collection McWilliams and has Jackson COA #7058. Hale County, Texas. *Dr. David R. Thrasher collection, Alabama.* $1,000.00.

Quad point or blade, Knife River material, 2¹⁵⁄₁₆" long and 1⅜" wide at base. It has Jackson COA #4266. The Late Paleo artifact was found in Stewart County, Tennessee. *Dr. David R. Thrasher collection, Alabama.* $1,500.00.

Hell Gap lance, Winterset chert, 1¼" x 3⅞". Found by B. Nutt, this is a well-designed lance with a tapered stem. It has Jackson COA #7214 and came from Wyandotte County, Kansas. *Dr. David R. Thrasher collection, Alabama.* $1,500.00.

Paleo points and blades, left to right. Cumberland, 3¼", Fort Payne chert, Jackson County, Tennessee. $3,800.00. Clovis, 3", Greene County, Illinois. $1,800.00. Clovis, 3", Edwards Plateau flint, ex-collections Rhoton and Fenn, Oldham County, Texas. $2,500.00. Clovis, 2¹¹⁄₁₆", black Georgetown chert, found by Keith Glasscock, Curry County, New Mexico. $800.00. *Michael Hough collection, California.*

Angostura blade, rounded tip, Edwards flint. The knife is 2½" long, from Wilson County, Texas. *John and Susan Mellyn collection, Texas.* $250.00.

Victoria point or blade, Late Paleo, 2¹¹⁄₁₆". It has a narrowed or stemmed lower blade and was found in Wilson County, Texas. *John and Susan Mellyn collection, Texas.* $275.00.

Eden(?) point or blade, parallel oblique flaking, high-grade glossy dark flint. This excellent piece is 3⁹⁄₁₆" and came from Morton County, Kansas. *John and Susan Mellyn collection, Texas.* $1,100.00.

Victoria point or blade, bifurcated stem bottom, Edwards flint. It is 3" long and from Wilson County, Texas. *John and Susan Mellyn collection, Texas.* $325.00.

Dalton point, 3⅜" long and ⅜" thick. Mottled gray flint, this piece was found by the owner. It came from Stone County, Missouri. *Curtis Chisam collection, Missouri.* $20.00.

Angostura point, Edwards flint, tapered lower blade, 2¾". It was found in the Liberty Hill area, Texas. *John and Susan Mellyn collection, Texas.* $300.00.

Dalton point, resharpened size, gray Carter Cave flint. This example is 1½", and was picked up in Scott County, Kentucky. *Jeff Schumacher collection, Kentucky.* $35.00.

Agate Basin point, 2⅝", light gray-brown chert. Some basal grinding is present, and the artifact was pictured in *Prehistoric American* in 2002, page 47. It was found in Nicholas County, Kentucky. *Jeff Schumacher collection, Kentucky.* $75.00.

Dalton point, 2" long, white flint. The owner found this artifact in Stone County, Missouri. *Curtis Chisam collection, Missouri.* $10.00.

Dalton(?) point, 2¼" long, made of white flint and found by the owner. Ozark County, Missouri. *Curtis Chisam collection, Missouri.* $10.00.

Datlon point, resharpened edges, 2¼". It has a ground base and serrated edges, and this Dalton of white flint was found by the owner. Ozark County, Missouri. *Curtis Chisam collection, Missouri.* $20.00.

Dalton family point or blade, white flint, ex-collections Grindell and Cox. It is 3⅛" long and is very symmetrical and well chipped. Union County, Illinois. *Dale and Betty Roberts collection, Iowa.* $900.00.

Angostura point or blade, 3" long, mixed Burlington with a frosty patina. The artifact was a personal find by Mr. Roberts in Van Buren County, Iowa. *Dale and Betty Roberts collection, Iowa.* $650.00.

Dalton point or blade, 4¾", creek-stained Burlington chert. This well-made large artifact was found by M. Hines in Van Buren County, Iowa. *Dale and Betty Roberts collection, Iowa.* $450.00.

Quad point, Indiana hornstone (Harrison County flint), 2¾". This is a classic example, with balanced ears and good overall form. Ex-collections Rose and Ritter, it came from Pope County, Illinois. *Dale and Betty Roberts collection, Iowa.* $700.00.

Dalton point or blade, 3½", found by the owners' daughter, Darla. It is made of high-grade mixed Burlington and was picked up in Scotland County, Missouri. *Dale and Betty Roberts collection, Iowa.* $225.00.

Pike County point, creamy tan Burlington, found by S. Wader. This is a fine example, 4¾", with well-extended ears. Lee County, Iowa. *Dale and Betty Roberts collection, Iowa.* $1,100.00.

Beaver Lake point or blade, Late Paleo, creamy mixed Burlington, 3⁵⁄₁₆". Balanced and with tapered waist, this beautiful piece was found by R. Shaver. Greene County, Illinois. *Dale and Betty Roberts collection, Iowa.* $1,400.00.

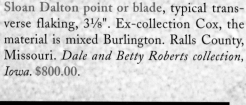

Sloan Dalton point or blade, typical transverse flaking, 3⅛". Ex-collection Cox, the material is mixed Burlington. Ralls County, Missouri. *Dale and Betty Roberts collection, Iowa.* $800.00.

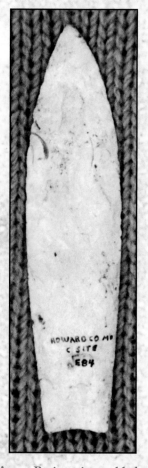

Holland point or blade, Late Paleo, 3¾". The example is in milky Burlington chert and is ex-collection Dr. Kritchel. Finely made, it has the typical base configuration and small edge serrations. A fine piece in all respects. Henry County, Iowa. *Dale and Betty Roberts collection, Iowa.* $1,500.00.

Agate Basin point or blade, Burlington chert in several shades, 1⅛" x 4⅝". It has a short flute measuring ½" long, and its basal edges are ground. This is a very superior artifact, found in Howard County, Missouri. *Bob Rampani collection, Missouri.* Museum grade.

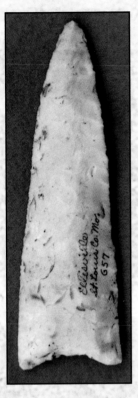

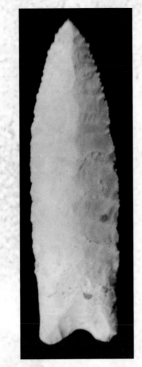

Plainview point or blade, Burlington chert, 1¼" x 3⅞". The base is thinned and the edges are ground. The piece came from St. Louis County, Missouri. *Bob Rampani collection, Missouri.* $400.00.

Dalton blade, fluted form, Burlington chert, 1" x 3⅝". It has parallel flaking and was found by Steve Rampani in 1979. This is a very superior Late Paleo knife form. St. Louis County, Missouri. *Bob Rampani collection, Missouri.* Museum grade.

Dalton blade, white Burlington, 1³⁄₁₆" x 3⁷⁄₁₆". The blade edges are serrated and the baseline is deeply concave. A 1984 find, it came from St. Louis County, Missouri. *Bob Rampani collection, Missouri.* $300.00.

Angostura-like point, glossy tan chert, 1" x 4". It has fine parallel-oblique flaking, and the basal edges are ground. This artistic piece came from Callaway County, Missouri. *Bob Rampani collection, Missouri.* $900.00.

Dalton point or blade, tan Burlington chert, 1³⁄₁₆" x 4¼". The basal edges are ground on this artifact, found in 1988. Montgomery County, Missouri. *Bob Rampani collection, Missouri.* $450.00.

Dalton point or blade, serrated edges, beveled from being resharpened, 7/8" x 2½". White Crescent chert was used for the Dalton, which has heavily ground base edges. A 1987 find by the owner, it came from St. Charles County, Missouri. *Bob Rampani collection, Missouri.* $300.00.

Quad point, Late Paleo, fine-grained gray chert, 1⅜" x 2⅜". Wide and quite thin, it is a good type example. It is from near Badin, Missouri. *Bob Rampani collection, Missouri.* $275.00.

Meserve Dalton point or blade, Late Paleo, Burlington chert, 2⅜". This artifact came from the Western Bluff area, Jersey County, Illinois. *Gregory L. Perdun collection, Illinois.* $35.00 – 45.00.

Dalton blade, 1¼" x 4¾", a torqued blade in Burlington. Stem edges are heavily ground, and baseline is deeply indented. This blade came from Stoddard County, Missouri. *Bob Rampani collection, Missouri.* $550.00.

Pike County Dalton Point, Burlington chert, strongly beveled from resharpening (rechipping), 5 9/16". This is an excellent point, found in Jersey County, Illinois. *Gregory L. Perdun collection, Illinois.* $1,800.00.

Dalton points or blades, Late Paleo, all Burlington chert. The largest is 2⅜" long and all were found in Jersey County, Illinois. Left and center, $155.00. Right, $65.00. *Gregory L. Perdun collection, Illinois.*

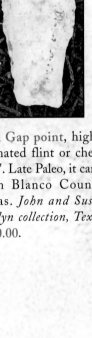

Hell Gap point, highly patinated flint or chert, 2⁷⁄₁₆". Late Paleo, it came from Blanco County, Texas. *John and Susan Mellyn collection, Texas.* $350.00.

Sloan Dalton point or blade, Late Paleo, 4³⁄₈". The artifact has minor base (ear) damage and is made of Burlington chert. It came form the Western Bluff area, Jersey County, Illinois. *Gregory L. Perdun collection, Illinois.* $550.00.

Sloan Dalton point or blade, high-grade glossy Burlington chert, 4⁹⁄₁₆" long. This is a superb piece in all respects — size, chipping, material, and condition. It came from the Western Bluff area, Jersey County, Illinois. *Gregory L. Perdun collection, Illinois.* $3,000.00.

Goshen(?) point or blade, Late Paleo, 4¹⁄₂" long. This is a fine lance point, picked up in Comanche County, Texas. *John and Susan Mellyn collection, Texas.* $750.00.

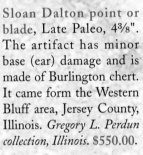

Zella point, mixed Edwards flint, tapered lower portion, 2⁷⁄₈". The artifact was found in Wilson County, Texas. *John and Susan Mellyn collection, Texas.* $350.00.

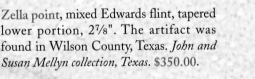

Lerma point or blade, possibly Paleo, dark sugar quartz material. This piece is 3¹⁄₈" long, from Wilson County, Texas. *John and Susan Mellyn collection, Texas.* $350.00.

Dalton point, resharpened size, 1⅞". It is of near-black Upper Mercer or Zaleski flint, and the base sides are heavily ground. The piece is ex-collection Farley, from Knox County, Ohio. *Lar Hothem collection.* $75.00.

Morrow County type lance, stemmed but not shouldered, 3" long. Of mixed gray and cream Upper Mercer, there is an angled basal chipping platform on the reverse stem base. Coshocton County, Ohio. *Lar Hothem collection.* $150.00.

Dalton point or blade, reverse, a fine Late Paleo knife form. St. Louis County, Missouri. *Bob Rampani collection, Missouri.* Museum grade.

Dalton point or blade, obverse, fluted on both lower faces, serrated blade edges and needle tip. A good grade of Burlington was used for this artifact, which measures 1⅛" x 4½". Picked up in 1966, it came from a farm in St. Louis County, Missouri. *Bob Rampani collection, Missouri.* Museum grade.

Dalton point or blade, resharpened probably until discarded, Florence chert. It measures ¾" x 1½" and came from Holt County, Missouri. *Mike George collection, Missouri; Terry Price photograph.* $60.00.

Dalton point or blade, Late Paleo, Burlington chert, size 1¼" x 4¾". This well-made large artifact was found near the town of Fanning, Doniphan County, Kansas. *Mike George collection, Missouri; Terry Price photograph.* $500.00.

Dalton point or blade, Late Paleo, glossy Burlington, ¾" x 2". This well-used artifact was a creek find. Holt County, Missouri. *Mike George collection, Missouri; Terry Price photograph.* $100.00.

Dalton point or blade, Florence chert, 1" x 3⅛". Colored in several shades, it came from the Wolf River area, Doniphan County, Kansas. *Mike George collection, Missouri; Terry Price photograph.* $175.00.

Scottsbluff stemmed point, Late Paleo, 1⅛" x 3". It is made of Florence chert and was found in Holt County, Missouri. *Mike George collection, Missouri: Terry Price photograph.* $300.00.

Agate Basin point or blade, Late Paleo, Niobrara jasper, 1⅛" x 4⅛". This large piece has a classic Agate Basin form and good patina. Richardson County, Nebraska. *Mike George collection, Missouri; Terry Price photograph.* $550.00.

Sloan Dalton point or blade, Late Paleo, 1⅜" x 4½". Of heat-treated Burlington, this blade was picked up in Holt County, Missouri. *Mike George collection, Missouri; Terry Price photograph.* $350.00.

Dalton point or blade, heavily resharpened sides that continue to the hafting area, 1⅛" x 4⁵⁄₁₆". Made of Kay County chert, it was found in Doniphan County, Kansas. *Mike George collection, Missouri; Terry Price photograph.* $450.00.

Dalton point, broken tip, Burlington chert, 1³⁄₁₆" x 2⅝". This piece came from a renovated pasture in June of 2003. Holt County, Missouri. *Mike George collection, Missouri; Terry Price photograph.* Unlisted.

Dalton blade, resharpened size with large serrations on one edge, Burlington chert. It came from a multi-component site and measures ¾" x 1⅛". The Dalton was found by Andrea George in Holt County, Missouri. *Mike George collection, Missouri; Terry Price photograph.* $40.00.

Dalton point or blade, resharpened and serrated edges, Burlington chert. The size is 1⅛" x 2⅝", and it was a creek find. Buchanan County, Missouri. *Mike George collection, Missouri; Terry Price photograph.* $175.00.

Dalton point or blade, gray flint, 1" x 2⅜". Picked up in a farm field, it is from Holt County, Missouri. *Mike George collection, Missouri; Terry Price photograph.* $75.00.

Agate Basin point, a large and well-made point in top condition, Niobrara jasper. The point is 1⅛" x 4¼" and was a personal find of the owner. The piece was found in a plowed field. Holt County, Missouri. *Mike George collection, Missouri; Terry Price photograph.* Museum grade.

Agate Basin point or blade, Late Paleo, mixed Burlington chert. It is 1½" x 4¾" and has excellent flaking. A creek find, it came from Holt County, Missouri. *Mike George collection, Missouri; Terry Price photograph.* $200.00.

Scottsbluff point or blade, Late Paleo, very colorful novaculite. It measures 1⅛" x 3" and was found by Andrea George near Forest City. Holt County, Missouri. *Mike George collection, Missouri; Terry Price photograph.* Unlisted.

Dalton point, edges resharpened to hafting region, flute on obverse base. A creek find, the Dalton is 1⅛" x 2⁹⁄₁₆". Holt County, Missouri. *Mike George collection, Missouri; Terry Price photograph.* $100.00.

San Patrice point, Late Paleo, brown mixed chert, 1" x 2¾". The obverse has a shallow flute or large thinning flake. Holt County, Missouri. *Mike George collection, Missouri; Terry Price photograph.* $100.00.

Plainview point, very translucent pale flint, 2⅜". It was found in Wilson County, Texas. *John and Susan Mellyn collection, Texas.* $700.00.

Early stemmed point, Late Paleo, 2⁵⁄₁₆". Of mixed chert or flint, it came from Wilson County, Texas. *John and Susan Mellyn collection, Texas.* $450.00.

Hell Gap point, Late Paleo but fluted on the obverse nearly full-length, 2³⁄₁₆". Of tri-colored flint, it is from Bexar County, Texas. *John and Susan Mellyn collection, Texas.* $400.00.

Hell Gap point, Late Paleo, heavily patinated Knife River flint. Resharpened, it is ¾" x 1½" and was a creek find in Holt County, Missouri. *Mike George collection, Missouri; Terry Price photograph.* $150.00.

Agate Basin point, brown chert, 1¼ x 4½". The basal edges are ground on this point, found near Forest City. Holt County, Missouri. *Mike George collection, Missouri; Terry Price photograph.* $350.00.

Dalton point or blade, white chert, 2¾" long. The upper left edge just at the tip has been burin fractured, a technique seen on some Paleo points. This Dalton was found in Holt County, Missouri. *Mike George collection, Missouri; Terry Price photograph.* $175.00.

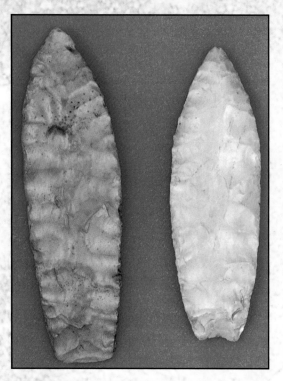

Lance points or blades, Late Paleo. Left, gray hornstone, 5¾", Jackson COA #DT-2, ex-collection Waters, Tennessee. $2,500.00. Right, 5⅛", Perino and Jackson COAs, Ft. Payne chert, Union County, Kentucky. $3,000.00. *Dr. David R. Thrasher collection, Alabama.*

Holland point or blade, Late Paleo, 1⅜" x 4⅞". Mixed pale Burlington was used for this superior example of a rare type. Found by S. Dooley, this piece is ex-collection Redwine and has Jackson COA #WFJ-4295. It came from Clay County, Arkansas. *Dr. David R. Thrasher collection, Alabama.* $10,000.00.

Lanceolate group, Late Paleo, most artifacts shown elsewhere in this book. The longest lance is 6⅞". *Dr. David R. Thrasher collection, Alabama.*

Hell Gap point, resharpened size, 1¾" long. Made of orange-amber flint, it is from Wilson County, Texas. *John and Susan Mellyn collection, Texas.* $250.00.

Lanceolate, resharpened size, blue Upper Mercer. The lance is 2¹¹⁄₁₆" long, ex-collections Cameron and Quimby, from Licking County, Ohio. *Lar Hothem collection.* $45.00.

Meserve point, typical serrated edges from resharpening, a nicely balanced piece. It is of high-grade flint and has basal grinding, and it is 2½" long. Wilson County, Texas. *John and Susan Mellyn collection, Texas.* $1,000.00.

Hell Gap point or blade, mixed flint, 1⅝". It was found in the Grants area, New Mexico. *John and Susan Mellyn collection, Texas.* $150.00.

Golondrina point, salvaged as an end-scraper, 2⅜". One ear is restored on this specimen, found in Wilson County, Texas. *John and Susan Mellyn collection, Texas.* $350.00.

Angostura knife, mixed flint, 3⅛" long. The artifact came from Travis County, Texas. *John and Susan Mellyn collection, Texas.* $500.00.

Dalton point, Breckenridge variety, 1" x 2½". It is made of high-grade white flint, and there is a groove between the notches. This piece was found by the owner in Maries County, Missouri. *Jim McKinney collection, Missouri; Mary Jane Wieberg photograph.* $100.00 – 125.00.

Lerma-like blade, rounded baseline, 1" x 4½". Well chipped, it is made of white flint and has beveled edges from resharpening. It was found by the owner in Maries County, Missouri. *Jim McKinney collection, Missouri; Mary Jane Wieberg photograph.* $300.00 – 350.00.

Lerma point or blade, possibly Paleo, white flint. This artifact measures 1¼" x 4½" and is thin for size. It was found by the owner in Maries County, Missouri. *Jim McKinney collection, Missouri; Mary Jane Wieberg photograph.* $225.00 – 250.00.

189

Dalton point or blade, thick, white flint with sharp edges, 1" x 3¼". The example appears to have had little resharpening, judging from the excurvate edge. It was found by the owner in Maries County, Missouri. *Jim McKinney collection, Missouri; Mary Jane Wieberg photograph.* $150.00 – 200.00.

Lerma or round-base Agate Basin point or blade, white flint with two reddish streaks, 1¼" x 5¾". Thin and well-made, the artifact is from Franklin County, Missouri. *Jim McKinney collection, Missouri; Mary Jane Wieberg photograph.* $200.00 – 300.00.

Dalton point or blade, classic form, 5" long and fluted on both lower faces. It has collateral flaking and is made of white flint. The owner found this fine piece in Osage County, Missouri. *Jim McKinney collection, Missouri; Mary Jane Wieberg photograph.* $750.00 – 800.00.

Dalton point or blade, fluted on both lower faces, 1" x 4½". Made of brown and white flint, the owner found this large specimen in 2002. Osage County, Missouri. *Jim McKinney collection, Missouri; Mary Jane Wieberg photograph.* $650.00 – 750.00.

Sloan Dalton point or blade, white flint with a darker inclusion, fluted on both lower faces. The size is 1" x 3½". It was found by the owner in Maries County, Missouri. *Jim McKinney collection, Missouri; Mary Jane Wieberg photograph.* $600.00 – 700.00.

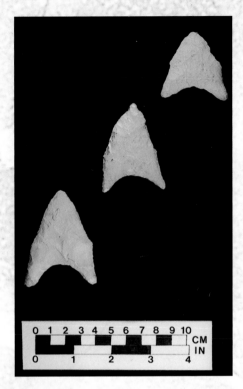

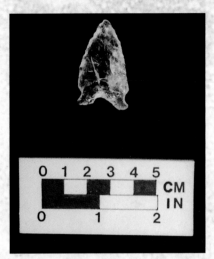

Hardaway side-notch point, transparent crystal quartz. A scarce point of rare material, it is from Moore County, North Carolina. *Rodney M. Peck collection, North Carolina.* $450.00.

Alamance points, green silicified shale, middle example with worn graver tip. The three were found in North Carolina. *Rodney M. Peck collection, North Carolina.* Each, $200.00 – 500.00.

Holland point or blade, Late Paleo, ground base and serrated edges. This is probably a knife, due to the size and edge treatment, and it is 1½" x 5¼". Ex-collection Zimmerman, it is made of white flint. St. Joseph area, Missouri. *Jim McKinney collection, Missouri; Mary Jane Wieberg photograph.* $700.00 – 800.00.

Hardaway Dalton point, light green silicified shale, serrated edges. It was found in Moore County, North Carolina. *Rodney M. Peck collection, North Carolina.* $500.00 – 1,000.00.

Beaver Lake point, Late Paleo, gray hornstone, 1" x 2⅞". With a Davis COA, the Beaver Lake came from Franklin County, Indiana. *Keith and Rhonda Dodge collection, Michigan.* $450.00.

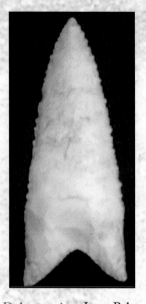

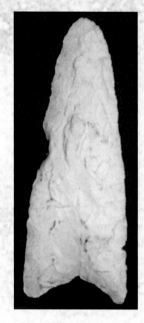

Dalton point, Late Paleo, basal flute and edge serrations. It is of light gray hornstone, has a Davis COA, and measures 1" x 2⅞". Franklin County, Indiana. *Keith and Rhonda Dodge collection, Michigan.* $450.00.

Dalton point or blade, 1¼" x 3¼", white Burlington chert. There is a spoke-shave in one side edge and the artifact has a Davis COA. Jersey County, Illinois. *Keith and Rhonda Dodge collection, Michigan.* $175.00.

Agate Basin point or blade, Late Paleo, highly translucent flint with parallel oblique flaking, 3 1/16". Northern Minnesota. *John and Susan Mellyn collection, Texas.* $800.00.

Plainview point, creamy flint with some yellow, 2 5/16". It was picked up in eastern Texas. *John and Susan Mellyn collection, Texas.* $700.00.

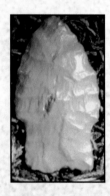

Scottsbluff point, glossy near-orange flint, irregular baseline, 1¾". It came from Morgan County, Oregon. *John and Susan Mellyn collection, Texas.* $500.00.

Paleo points, first three ex-collection Glasscock, left to right. Cody-Scottsbluff, 2⅛", Crowley County, Colorado. $300.00. Firstview, 2", Gaines County, Texas. $500.00. Cody-Scottsbluff, 1⅞", El Paso County, Colorado. $400.00. Firstview, 1½", El Paso County, Colorado. $500.00. *Michael Hough collection, California.*

Beaver Lake, Late Paleo, pink and cream jasper. This point measures 1" x 3⅛" and has a Davis COA. Woodford County, Kentucky. *Keith and Rhonda Dodge collection, Michigan.* $700.00.

Quad point, gray hornstone, 1⅛" x 2½". It is pictured in *Ohio Flint Types* and has a Davis COA. Gallia County, Ohio. *Keith and Rhonda Dodge collection, Michigan.* $350.00.

Midland points, glossy regional materials, ex-collection Glasscock. Rounded tips on some suggest at least secondary knife use. All are from sites in Texas and New Mexico. *Michael Hough collection, California.* Each, $300.00 – 3,500.00.

Milnesand point or blade, translucent white flint, 2¼". The artifact was found in Kerr County, Texas. *John and Susan Mellyn collection, Texas.* $700.00.

Scottsbluff blades, resharpened into rounded-edge tool forms, both Midwest. Left, pinkish flint, 1⅝". $225.00. Right, mixed chert, 1¾". $100.00. *John and Susan Mellyn collection, Texas.*

Plainview point or blade, serrated edges, 4¼". It is made of white flint and came from Wilson County, Texas. *John and Susan Mellyn collec-tion, Texas. $1,200.00.*

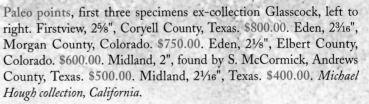

Paleo points, first three specimens ex-collection Glasscock, left to right. Firstview, 2⅝", Coryell County, Texas. $800.00. Eden, 2³⁄₁₆", Morgan County, Colorado. $750.00. Eden, 2⅛", Elbert County, Colorado. $600.00. Midland, 2", found by S. McCormick, Andrews County, Texas. $500.00. Midland, 2¹⁄₁₆", Texas. $400.00. *Michael Hough collection, California.*

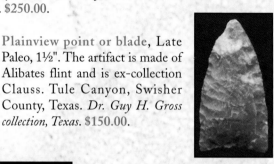

Eden point or blade, 2⅝" long, ex-collections Fenn and Clauss. This slender artifact is made of Tecovas jasper and is from Garza County, Texas. *Dr. Guy H. Gross collection, Texas.* $250.00.

Plainview point or blade, Late Paleo, 1½". The artifact is made of Alibates flint and is ex-collection Clauss. Tule Canyon, Swisher County, Texas. *Dr. Guy H. Gross collection, Texas.* $150.00.

Plainview point or blade, 1¾", Alibates flint. Probably resharpened size, it is ex-collection Clauss. Dallam County, Texas. *Dr. Guy H. Gross collection, Texas.* $250.00.

Firstview or Scottsbluff point or blade, 3" long, dark obsidian. It has Rogers, Motley, Taylor, and Jackson COAs and is ex-collections Jones, Loke, and Moss. It was picked up near Twin Falls, Idaho. *Dr. Guy H. Gross collection, Texas.* $1,400.00.

Eden point or blade, 2¾", dark obsidian. This piece is ex-collections Dickerson, Keith, DeCamp, and Partain, find location unknown. *Dr. Guy H. Gross collection, Texas.* $500.00.

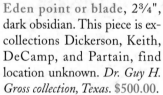

Firstview point, Late Paleo, 1⅞". It has attractive opposed flaking and is made of light gray glossy flint. Found in 1955 near Sweetwater, it is ex-collection Meador. Nolan County, Texas. *Dr. Guy H. Gross collection, Texas.* $850.00.

Firstview(?) point, Late Paleo, mottled Florence chert, 2⅞". It is ex-collection McMichael and was found near Broken Arrow, Oklahoma. *Dr. Guy H. Gross collection, Texas.* $1,200.00.

Firstview point, Late Paleo, red jasper material, 2 1/16". It is ex-collections Keele and Meador, and was found in the Republican River, Kansas. *Dr. Guy H. Gross collection, Texas.* $950.00.

Allen point or blade, 2" long, dark gray chert. The artifact is ex-collection German, from Geary County, Kansas. *Dr. Guy H. Gross collection, Texas.* $300.00.

Allen point or blade, 3 7/16", Niobrara jasper. This piece is ex-collections Meador and Merriam, from Osage County, Oklahoma. *Dr. Guy H. Gross collection, Texas.* $800.00.

As is true of fluted points, lanceolates tend to have an established type or a variety of types. Sometimes groups consist of a few lanceolates of a kind. Many are even only lance-like enough to be placed in the Late Paleo period and can't be solidly placed in any specific type class. That is, the mixture of traits may not always be consistent or there may not be enough examples to form a new class or type. Sometimes, a lanceolate is simply one of a kind.

At some Western kill sites of extinct bison, lance points found together were of several very different forms. This proves that specific (usually named) types do not always or necessarily reflect different cultures or times. Why this is so remains yet another mystery of Paleo times.

An element of confusion is sometimes added as well. The general lanceolate form — a tip and a base connected by a body with excurvate edges — is so simple it was inevitable that somewhat look-alike types would be created in later times. Some Late Archaic Nebo Hills resemble some Late Paleo Agate Basins, though they are separated by perhaps seven thousand years. The main difference is that Agate Basins are more finely chipped, have ground basal edges, and are much more widely distributed.

Other lanceolates, some unnamed, have flattened faces and are either stemmed or unstemmed. The greatest differences are in the stemmed forms, because the extra basal contours allow more scope for variety. The Stringtown, for example, has one or two projections on the base corner(s), which either allowed a more sturdy haft, or the projections served as graver tips, or both.

As with fluted points, Late Paleo lanceolates are usually made of the highest-grade flints and cherts available ten-thousand-plus years ago, though lesser grades of material were sometimes used. Well-chipped lances of superior materials are second only to fluted points in collector popularity.

Stemmed lanceolate, Late Paleo, silicified shale. Found by the owner, the example is 1¹/₁₆" x 2³/₁₆". Morgan County, West Virginia. *Collection of and photographed by Gary Henry, North Carolina.* $50.00.

Stemmed lance, top right blade near tip burin fractured, 3¼". Milky Flint Ridge, it was found in Hardin County, Ohio. *Frank Otto collection.* $250.00.

Lance point, cream and gray translucent Flint Ridge, 3" long. This unstemmed example came from Hardin County, Ohio. *Frank Otto collection.* $300.00.

Lance point, Burlington chert, 4½", one darker inclusion. Well made, the point or blade is ex-collection Crum. Knox County, Illinois. *Fred Smith collection, Illinois.* $400.00 – 450.00.

Stemmed lance, gray Nellie chert with lighter and darker inclusions. It is 2⅞" and has a needle tip. Geauga County, Ohio. *Private collection.* $30.00.

Stemmed lance, gray banded Nellie chert from the Walhonding Valley, 2⅝". The lance point was found in Geauga County, Ohio. *Private collection.* $20.00.

Lance point or blade, 4⅜", creamy tan Flint Ridge. This fine artifact has excellent flaking and good size. Franklin County, Ohio. *Len and Janie Weidner collection.* $800.00.

Stemmed lance, Late Paleo, 5⅝" long. It is pictured in *First Hunters,* page 91, and is ex-collection Shipley. The material is highly translucent pale honey Flint Ridge with lighter and darker inclusions. Fairfield County, Ohio. *Len and Janie Weidner collection.* Museum grade.

Stemmed lance, angled shoulders, 2¹¹⁄₁₆". Made of gray Upper Mercer, this Late Paleo artifact is from Geauga County, Ohio. *Private collection.* $20.00.

Stemmed lance, light brownish gray Upper Mercer, tapered stem. The lance is 2½" long and was picked up in Coshocton County, Ohio. *Private collection.* $15.00.

Lanceolate blade, Late Paleo, collateral flaking, black Zaleski flint. the lance is 3¹¹⁄₁₆" long and was collected in Darke County, Ohio. *Terry Elleman collection, Ohio.* $300.00.

Paleo point, brown and near-yellow unknown flint, shallow side indentations. The point or blade is 2⅜" long. Morrow County, Ohio. *Terry Elleman collection, Ohio.* $150.00.

Paleo point, Harrison County flint with nodule cortex on base ends and bull's-eye in the blade, 2⅜". It was found in Montgomery County, Ohio. *Terry Elleman collection, Ohio.* $275.00.

Lanceolate blade, Late Paleo, Carter Cave cream, tan, and maroon, ex-collection Reeder. This exceptional piece measures 1⅝" x 4¾" and was picked up in Miami County, Ohio. *Terry Elleman collection, Ohio.* $1,250.00.

Paleo lanceolate point or blade, Knife River flint, 2³⁄₁₆". It has been pictured in *Indian Artifact Magazine*, and was picked up by the owner in 1999. Brookings County, South Dakota. *Harlan Olson collection, South Dakota.* $100.00.

Paleo point, unnamed fluted lanceolate form, patinated Knife River flint. It is fluted for about one-half of point length, which is 1⅞". Pictured in *Indian Artifact Magazine*, it was found by the owner in 1998. Brookings County, South Dakota. *Harlan Olson collection, South Dakota.* $450.00.

Lanceolate point, Late Paleo, blue and tan Upper Mercer flint. The projectile point is 2¾" long and was found in Geauga County, Ohio. *Private collection.* $35.00.

197

Keiser stemmed point, light tan Delaware County flint. 1⅝" long. It was found in Delaware County, Ohio. *Private collection*. $20.00.

Stringtown stemmed lance, broken off graver tips on both base corners, 1⅝". Mottled yellow and tan flint, the lance was found in Delaware County, Ohio. *Private collection*. $40.00.

Stemmed lance, with base corner graver tip and small shaft-scraper. Gray Warsaw flint was used for the point, which is 2⅝" long. Geauga County, Ohio. *Private collection*. $50.00.

Lanceolate point or blade, broken and glued, both pieces found the same day in 1978. Gray Warsaw (Coshocton County) flint was used for the artifact, which has partial stemming and an edge shaft-scraper. *Private collection*. Unlisted.

Keiser point, Late Paleo period, mottled dark Upper Mercer. The typical Keiser long stem and short blade can be seen on the example, 1⅞". Coshocton County, Ohio. *Private collection*. $20.00.

Keiser stemmed point or blade, with needle tip, 1¾" long. The example is made of translucent light tan Flint Ridge and came from central Ohio. *Private collection*. $15.00.

Stemmed lance, deep blue Upper Mercer flint, ex-collection Pierce. It is 2⅝" long and from Fairfield County, Ohio. *Lar Hothem collection*. $45.00.

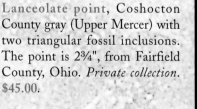

Lanceolate point, Coshocton County gray (Upper Mercer) with two triangular fossil inclusions. The point is 2¾", from Fairfield County, Ohio. *Private collection*. $45.00.

Stemmed lance, dark gray hornstone from Indiana or Kentucky, 2¹¹⁄₁₆". Ex-collections Farley and Saunders, it is from Coshocton County, Ohio. *Lar Hothem collection*. $75.00.

Stemmed lance, gray-tan Upper Mercer, 2⅝" long. It is from Geauga County, Ohio. *Lar Hothem collection*. $20.00.

Lanceolate point, blue and cream Upper Mercer flint with fossils, 3½" long. The lance is ex-collections Cameron and Quimby, from Licking County, Ohio. *Lar Hothem collection*. $175.00.

Stemmed lance, dark blue Upper Mercer, possible broken graver spur on bottom corner. The lance is 2⅜" long. Coshocton County, Ohio. *Private collection*. $15.00.

Stemmed lanceolate point or blade, gray Nellie chert with fossils, 3⅛". Coshocton County, Ohio. *Private collection*. $15.00.

Stemmed lanceolate point or blade, Nellie fossiliferous gray chert, 2⅞". There is a probable broken graver spur on the bottom corner. Coshocton County, Ohio. *Private collection*. $25.00.

Stemmed lance, Nellie mixed blue chert with fossils, probable worn graver spur on corner. The artifact is 2⅝" and from Coshocton County, Ohio. *Private collection*. $20.00.

Stemmed lance, resharp-ened and shortened size, 2⅛" long. Of blue and tan Upper Mercer, the lance was found in Geauga County, Ohio. *Lar Hothem collection*. $20.00.

Stemmed lance, resharp-ened size, gray chert. It is 1⅝" long and at this length was probably discarded in Late Paleo times. Illinois. *Private collection*. $20.00.

199

Lanceolate, red flint with other colors, ¾" x 1⅜". This resharpened example was found by the owner's father-in-law, Sam Jenkins, on an Ohio River site. West Virginia. *Private collection; Rodney Roberts photograph.* $30.00.

Paleo blade, gray Nellie flint, 1⅛" x 2½". It was found by the owner's father-in-law, Sam Jenkins, on a site in the Ohio River Valley. West Virginia. *Private collection; Rodney Roberts photograph.* $45.00.

Late Paleo stemmed blade, unknown banded chert, 2⁷⁄₁₆". It has light basal grinding and came from Montezuma County, Colorado. *John and Susan Mellyn collection, Texas.* $350.00.

Late Paleo points, left to right: Dalton (NC), Hardaway blade (NC), and two Hardaway Daltons (AL and NC, respectively), chert and quartzite. All were found by Harwood except the second from right, which is ex-collection Holland. Far left, ¹⁵⁄₁₆" x 1⅞", $40.00. Near left, ¹³⁄₁₆" x 1³⁄₁₆", $20.00. Near right, 1" x 1¼", $30.00. Far right, 1¹⁄₁₆" x 1¼", $20.00. *Collection of and photograph by Gary Henry, North Carolina.*

Late Paleo lance, dark mixed quartzite, 1¼" x 3½". It was found by the owner in Buncombe County, North Carolina. *Collection of and photograph by Gary Henry, North Carolina.* $75.00.

Paleo lance, brown and gray chert, 1¼" x 2⅝". It was found by the owner in Wilson County, Tennessee. *Collection of and photograph by Gary Henry, North Carolina.* $75.00.

Lanceolate, blue unknown chert, partial thinning platform on base. The lance is 2⅞" long and from Geauga County, Ohio. *Private collection.* $25.00.

Stemmed lance, Late Paleo, gray Upper Mercer. The point is 2⅝" long and has a worn graver spur at the base corner. Coshocton County, Ohio. *Private collection.* $35.00.

Stemmed lance, gray and black Walhonding Valley chert, 2⅜". It was found in Perry County, Ohio. *Private collection.* $35.00.

Late Paleo lance, dark high-grade chert, ⅞" x 2⁷⁄₁₆". It was found by Harwood, location unknown. *Collection of and photograph by Gary Henry, North Carolina.* $100.00.

Late Paleo artifacts, both chert. Left, Colbert Dalton, 11⁄16" x 1⅜", ex-collections Holland and Harwood, Alabama. $30.00. Right, Greenbrier Dalton, ⅜" x 2½", found by Harwood, Limestone County, Alabama. $75.00. *Collection of and photograph by Gary Henry, North Carolina.*

Lanceolate, Late Paleo, chert, 11⁄16" x 1¾". Ex-collection Cordeiro, it came from Logan County, Ohio. *Collection of and photograph by Gary Henry, North Carolina.* $30.00.

Lanceolate, lightly stemmed, 3¾". The unknown flint is red, yellow, and tan, and the artifact was picked up in Cass County, Illinois. *John and Susan Mellyn collection, Texas.* $150.00.

Lanceolate point or blade, blue Upper Mercer flint, 3½" long. It is probably from southeastern Ohio. *Dwight Wolfe collection.* $100.00.

Lanceolate point, shaftscraper near tip, 3⅛". Made of blue-gray Upper Mercer, it is from Ohio. *Dwight Wolfe collection.* $100.00.

Paleo point, very shallow side indentations, gray patinated flint. This piece has some edge rechipping by later Indians, and measures 2½" long. Darke County, Ohio. *Terry Elleman collection, Ohio.* $350.00.

Lanceolate blade, translucent bluish-purple Flint Ridge with some butterscotch coloring, 5½". It is shown in *Ancient Art of Ohio*, page 27. This exceptional piece is from Delaware County, Ohio. *Len and Janie Weidner collection.* Museum grade.

Lance, dark blue Upper Mercer with numerous lightning lines, 3¼". Ex-collection Rankin, this is an impressive specimen from Ross County, Ohio. *Jim Beckman collection, Ohio.* $300.00.

Lanceolate blade, Late Paleo, mixed gray and black Walhonding Valley flint. The lance is 2¾" and is ex-collection Horner. It was found between Shelby and Tiro, Richland County, Ohio. *Jim Beckman collection, Ohio.* $200.00.

Lanceolate point, 1¼" x 3⅛", gray and tan Delaware County flint. It was found where Eastland Shopping Center is now located, in Columbus. Franklin County, Ohio. *Private collection.* $250.00.

Keiser points, Late Paleo perhaps transitional into Early Archaic, left example 1¾". Both are made of Upper Mercer flints and are from Ohio. *Dwight Wolfe collection.* Each, $15.00.

Lanceolate point, probably Late Paleo, white quartzite. It is 2" long and from Putnam County, Ohio. *Dwight Wolfe collection.* $40.00.

Keiser point or blade, 1⅝". It is of gray (possibly Upper Mercer) chert, and the stem sides and the base are heavily ground. It was bid-in by the owner at a farm estate sale. Licking County, Ohio. *Jesse Weber collection; photograph by Norman's Photo, Newcomerstown, Ohio.* $25.00.

Stemmed lance, 1⁵⁄₁₆" x 2⅝", combined Nellie gray and dark Coshocton. The point is ex-collection Swartz, from Ashland County, Ohio. *Jesse Weber collection; photograph by Norman's Photo, Newcomerstown, Ohio.* $50.00.

Lanceolate, Late Paleo, 3¾". It is made of dark Upper Mercer with lighter clouding. Washington County, Ohio. *Jesse Weber collection; photograph by Norman's Photo, Newcomerstown, Ohio.* $100.00.

Lanceolate, fine chipping, glossy dark Upper Mercer, 3¾". Thin and well made, it has collateral flaking, and the lower blade edges are ground. Guernsey County, Ohio. *Jesse Weber collection; photograph by Norman's Photo, Newcomerstown, Ohio.* $700.00.

Stemmed lance, 2¹³⁄₁₆", Nellie chert with fossil inclusions. It was found in Wood County, Ohio. *Jesse Weber collection; photograph by Norman's Photo, Newcomerstown, Ohio.* $50.00.

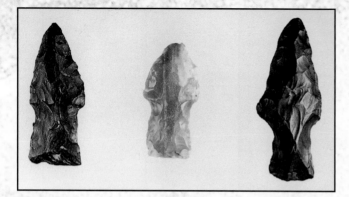

Keiser stemmed points or blades, left example (with probable corner graver spur) 1⅞". These have typical short blades and long stems. Left and right are of dark Upper Mercer, and the center example is made of creek cobble. All are from Ohio. *Lar Hothem collection.* Each, $7.00 – 15.00.

Stemmed lance, Late Paleo, near-black Upper Mercer with lighter inclusions, 2½" long. The chipped thinning platform can be seen at the base bottom. Hardin County, Ohio. *Lar Hothem collection.* $45.00.

Hardaway Dalton point, chert, 1³⁄₁₆" x 1⅜". It was found by the owner in Madison County, North Carolina. *Collection of and photograph by Gary Henry, North Carolina.* $40.00.

Lance, Late Paleo period, probably Boyle flint from Kentucky. It is 3¼" long, and the base has an angled chipping platform that is part of the original surface of the flint core from which the large flake was struck. Ex-collection Champion, Erie County, Ohio. *Lar Hothem collection.* $75.00.

Stemmed lanceolate, mixed dark low-grade chert with fossils and inclusions. The lance is 2¾" and came from Coshocton County, Ohio. *Private collection.* $10.00.

Lanceolate point, unstemmed, 3⅞", dull gray Upper Mercer. Ex-collections Young and Hutchinson, it came from Franklin County, Ohio. *Mike Diano collection, Florida.* $225.00.

Lanceolate point or knife, 2³⁄₅", dull Upper Mercer flint. The owner found this artifact on a site that has also produced a fluted point and a uniface blade. Fairfield County, Ohio. *Mike Diano collection, Florida.* $75.00.

Stemmed point or blade, 2⅕", gray Upper Mercer flint. The indented baseline suggests this may be a transitional piece between the Late Paleo and Early Archaic. Owner found, it is from Ross County, Ohio. *Mike Diano collection, Florida.* $50.00.

Stemmed lance, Late Paleo, 2½" long. Made of Nellie (Walhonding Valley) chert, it was picked up by the owner in Ross County, Ohio. *Mike Diano collection, Florida.* $75.00.

Stemmed lance, 1" x 2⅞", dark blue Upper Mercer with a spot of red near the tip. Ex-collection Fuller, it came from Medina County, Ohio. *Private collection.* $250.00.

Lerma-like point or blade, Transitional Paleo, 1" x 3⅝", 5/16" thick. Made of semi-translucent high-grade gray flint, it has beveled edges and one side of the tip was burin flaked. It was found in Colorado. *Mark Boswell collection, Colorado; photograph by Infocusphotography.com, Colorado.* $225.00.

Lanceolate, Late Paleo, reverse with quality flaking. Made of Plum Run(?) flint, it came from Stark County, Ohio. *Jesse Weber collection; photograph by Norman's Photo, Newcomerstown, Ohio.* $75.00.

Stemmed lance, Upper Mercer flint with thin diagonal lightning line, 3½". Ex-collection Swartz, it came from northcentral Ohio. *Jesse Weber collection; photograph by Norman's Photo, Newcomerstown, Ohio.* $300.00.

Stemmed lance point or blade, 4" long. The material is a combination of Nellie gray and Coshocton (darker) flint. It was obtained at an auction of Vietzen artifacts. Ohio. *Jesse Weber collection; photograph by Norman's Photo, Newcomerstown, Ohio.* $375.00.

Stemmed lance, Nellie gray flint, 1¼" x 2⁹⁄₁₆". The owner's father-in-law, Sam Jenkins, found this on an Ohio River site. West Virginia. *Private collection; Rodney Roberts photograph.* $35.00.

Dalton-like point, flared base, some basal grinding on baseline, pink and gray Flint Ridge. The artifact is ¹⁵⁄₁₆" x 1⅝" and came from an Ohio River site. West Virginia. *Private collection; Rodney Roberts photograph.* $15.00.

Paleo point, undetermined type, translucent blue-gray Flint Ridge with touches of red. This beautiful piece is 3¾" long and ex-collections Dr. Henkler, Ben Thompson, and Floyd Ritter. Originally from Ohio. *Dale and Betty Roberts collection, Iowa.* $2,500.00.

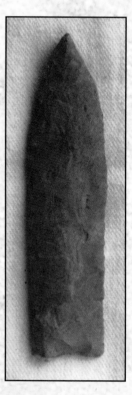

Lanceolate, black Kanawha flint, light basal grinding. It measures ¹³⁄₁₆" x 2⅛" and is from a site in the Ohio River Valley. West Virginia. *Private collection; Rodney Roberts photograph.* $60.00.

Stemmed lance, basal grinding, black Kanawha flint, ⅞" x 2¹⁄₁₆". The point was found in the Ohio River Valley, West Virginia. *Private collection; Rodney Roberts photograph.* $25.00.

Stemmed lanceolate, tan unknown chert, ¹⁵⁄₁₆" x 2⅜". Found on an Ohio River site, it is from West Virginia. *Private collection; Rodney Roberts photograph.* $25.00.

Paleo lanceolate point or blade, ¹⁵⁄₁₆" x 3¾", gray-tan chert. The tip is reworked, the base is thinned, and the basal edges are ground. Jackson County, Missouri. *Bob Rampani collection, Missouri.* $375.00.

Keiser stemmed blade, Late Paleo, 1¾". It is tip fluted, probably to thin that portion of the blade, and material is a pale tan unknown flint. Knox County, Ohio. *Private collection.* $15.00.

Stemmed lance, thin, 2¹⁵⁄₁₆". It has a damaged tip and is of translucent gray Flint Ridge. An angled chipping platform is at the base bottom edge. Delaware County, Ohio. *Lar Hothem collection.* $55.00.

Keiser stemmed blade, creamy gray flint, 1⅜" long. The obverse has a narrow flute or thinning flake ⅞" long. Ohio. *Private collection.* $10.00.

Stemmed lance, gray Nellie chert with a black swirl, 2⅞" long. This late Paleo artifact was found in Geauga County, Ohio. *Lar Hothem collection.* $30.00.

Stemmed lance, Late Paleo, unknown tan and blue flint. It is 2⅝" long, ex-collection Williams. The lance was found near Meeker, Marion County, Ohio. *Lar Hothem collection.* $75.00.

Stemmed lance, Late Paleo, streaked blue chert, probable broken graver spur on one corner. The lance is 2¾" long and from Fairfield County, Ohio. *Lar Hothem collection.* $30.00.

Stemmed blade, Late Paleo, 1¹⁄₁₆" x 3⅛". Of creamy white flint, this well-chipped example came from Holt County, Missouri. *Mike George collection, Missouri; Terry Price photograph.* $300.00.

Paleo point, resharpened to the extent that it was likely thrown away, ¾" x 1⅛". Gray chert was used for this piece, which has a graver tip. Andrew County, Missouri. *Mike George collection, Missouri; Terry Price photograph.* $20.00.

Late Paleo point or blade, light brown flint, ¾" x 2⅝". Finely flaked, it came from a farm field in Doniphan County, Kansas. *Mike George collection, Missouri; Terry Price photograph.* $150.00.

Paleo point or blade, Burlington chert, ¾" x 2⅜". The basal edges are heavily ground on this piece, which is from Holt County, Missouri. *Mike George collection; Missouri; Terry Price photograph.* $60.00.

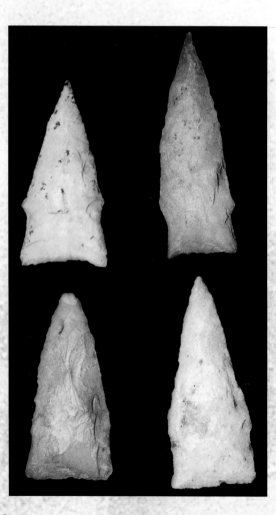

Late Paleo stemmed lance, pink and brown flint, 1⅜" x 4¼". The upper right recessed blade edge was not broken but was rechipped. A well-made piece, this was found by Andrea George in Holt County, Missouri. *Mike George collection, Missouri; Terry Price photograph.* Unlisted.

Stemmed lances, probably Scottsbluff family, 2" x 2½" long. Of various white, brown, and gray cherts, all were found by the owner. Maries County, Missouri. *Jim McKinney collection, Missouri; Mary Jane Wieberg photograph.* Each, $100.00 – 125.00.

Lanceolate point or blade, 1⅛" x 2⅞", light green flint with bands of green. The owner found this example in Wayne County, North Carolina. *Michael Womble collection, North Carolina.* $20.00.

Lanceolate, ⅞" x 2⅛", chert, light gray base and medium gray remainder with dark gray stripes. The owner found this piece in Wayne County, North Carolina. *Michael Womble collection, North Carolina.* $20.00.

Stemmed point, white crystal quartz with clear portions, ¾" x 1⅞". The owner found this example in Wayne County, North Carolina. *Michael Womble collection, North Carolina.* $35.00.

Stemmed lance blade, base well-ground, 1" x 6". The material is chert in white, brown, and gray. The lance was found by the owner along the Gasconade River. Maries County, Missouri. *Jim McKinney collection, Missouri; Mary Jane Wieberg photographs.* $500.00 – 600.00.

Unfluted Clovis or wide lanceolate, probably black Upper Mercer flint from eastern Ohio. It is 1⅛" x 3¼", and its provenance is unknown. *Collection of and photograph by H. B. Green II, Florida.* $400.00.

Lanceolate point or blade, shale-like material, 1⅛" x 3½". Much-weathered, it was found on Cape Cod, Massachusetts. *Collection of and photograph by H. B. Greene II, Florida.* $35.00.

Lanceolate, Late Paleo, patinated tan-cream Flint Ridge. It is 3¼" long and has a narrow basal chipping platform. Perry County, Ohio. *Private collection.* $150.00.

209

Keiser point, Late Paleo, 1⅝", stem area ground. It is made of dark Upper Mercer flint and was found in Tuscarawas County, Ohio. *Jesse Weber collection; photograph by Norman's Photo, Newcomerstown, Ohio.* $20.00.

Lanceolate, Late Paleo period, tan-cream patinated Flint Ridge material. The base bottom has a ground-in chipping platform. The example is 3⅛" and was found in Perry County, Ohio. *Private collection.* $175.00.

Stemmed Late Paleo lance, 3¹⁄₁₆", Nellie chert in three colors. It is ex-collection Swartz, from northcentral Ohio. *Jesse Weber collection; photograph by Norman's Photo, Newcomerstown, Ohio.* $125.00.

Lanceolate, Late Paleo, 2½", dark Upper Mercer with lighter inclusions. It is from Ohio. *Jesse Weber collection; photograph by Norman's Photo, Newcomerstown, Ohio.* $275.00.

Keiser stemmed point, Late Paleo, dark blue Upper Mercer. It is 1⅞" long, from Coshocton County, Ohio. *Private collection.* $20.00.

Salvaged Keiser blade, made into a Late Paleo drill/perforator. Black Upper Mercer was used for this piece, 1½" long. The projecting shoulders were probably used as gravers. Tuscarawas County, Ohio. *Private collection.* $25.00.

Keiser stemmed point, Late Paleo, 1¾" long. Made of dark blue Upper Mercer, it is from Ohio. *Private collection.* $20.00.

Stemmed lance, Late Paleo, unknown tan chert with small white fossils. Thin and well chipped, it is 3⅛". Perry County, Ohio. *Private collection.* $45.00.

Stemmed lance, Late Paleo, Upper Mercer flint in tan, light blue, and dark blue. It is 2⅝" and from Perry County, Ohio. *Private collection.* $45.00.

Lanceolate point, Late Paleo, tan and brown Delaware County flint. This example, 2⅝" long, was found in Perry County, Ohio. *Private collection.* $30.00.

Stemmed lance, Late Paleo, cream and gray highly patinated flint. It has a "can opener" tip, and it is 3" long. Perry County, Ohio. *Private collection.* $35.00.

Stemmed lanceolate, Late Paleo, translucent gray unknown flint with inclusions and tiny solution cavities. The lance is 2¾" and was found at a construction site in Lorain County, Ohio. *Private collection.* $100.00.

Unstemmed lance, Late Paleo, medium blue Upper Mercer flint. It was resharpened to a length of 2⅛". Johnstown area, Licking County, Ohio. *Private collection.* $45.00.

Keiser stemmed point, Late Paleo, gray-green unknown chert. It is 2⅛" long and from Put-nam County, Ohio. *Pri-vate collection.* $25.00.

Lanceolate, 4¼" long, Late Paleo. Made of creamy gray flint, this artifact has a story. The lance itself is old and authentic. However, years ago, someone decided to "improve" it by adding the double set of notches, which greatly damaged the value. Ohio. *Private collection.* Unlisted.

Stemmed lanceolate blade, Late Paleo. Stringtown variety with worn graver spur on one stem corner. This piece is 2⅝" long and of gray and tan Nellie chert. Coshocton County, Ohio. *Private collection.* $35.00.

211

Salvaged lanceolate blade, Late Paleo, with rechipped tip, which gives the artifact a pentagonal outline. It is made from dark blue Upper Mercer flint and is 1⅞" long. Coshocton County, Ohio. *Private collection.* $25.00.

Salvaged lanceolate point, Late Paleo, 2" long. The broken blade was repaired by being slightly stemmed, and the original break area was left untouched at the base. Thin and well-chipped, it is in blue Upper Mercer flint. Richland County, Ohio. *Private collection.* $20.00.

Paleo lance, resharpened size at 2⅛", near-black Upper Mercer flint. The lance was found in Ohio. *Mike Barron collection, Ohio.* $150.00.

Lanceolate, Late Paleo, cream and gray highly patinated Flint Ridge. Stemmed but not shouldered, it is 5½" long. Richland County, Ohio. *Joel Embrey collection.* $750.00.

Lanceolate point or blade, tan-gray unknown flint with darker stripes. the artifact is 5⁷⁄₁₆" and from the Midwest. *Joel Embrey collection.* $350.00.

Lanceolate, Late Paleo, a superb example in dark Upper Mercer with faint green streaks. It is beautifully chipped, 5¼" long, and the lower blade edges are ground for 2¼". It has a median ridge and is in pristine condition. Ex-collection Walls, Delaware County, Ohio. *Joel Embrey collection.* $2,750.00.

Stemmed lance, Wal-honding Valley gray mixed flint, 1⅞". The example has attractive lightning lines in white quartz. Central Ohio. *Private collection.* $20.00.

Stemmed lance, with very slight shouldering, Late Paleo, 2¼" long. Made of yellow-tan chert, it was found in Fentress County, Tennessee. *Back to Earth.* $70.00.

Beaver Lake point or blade, Late Paleo, light-colored chert. It measures 3" long and has a Dickey COA. Perry County, Illinois. *Back to Earth.* $195.00.

Late Paleo points or blades, both with Motley COAs and both auction bid amounts included a 10% buyers' premium. These were sold August 23, 2003. Left, lot 179, Greenbrier Dalton, thin, 3⁹⁄₁₆", Tennessee. $825.00. Right, lot 182, 3⁷⁄₁₆", thin, Tennessee. $550.00. *Rainbow Traders, Illinois.*

Stemmed lance, Late Paleo, 3" long. Nellie chert with dark banding (Walhonding Valley) was used for this piece, ex-collection Swartz. Northcentral Ohio. *Jesse Weber collection; photograph by Norman's Photo, Newcomerstown, Ohio.* $100.00.

Lanceolate point, Late Paleo, mixed Kanawha chert. This piece was found in Putnam County, West Virginia. *Craig Ferrell collection.* $40.00.

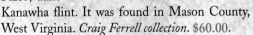

Lanceolate point, Late Paleo, dark Kanawha flint. It was found in Mason County, West Virginia. *Craig Ferrell collection.* $60.00.

Agate Basin(?) point or blade, found with an Agate Basin in a creek bed, 2⅝". Made of translucent light tan flint, it was found by the owner. Scott County, Illinois. *Collection of and photograph by Kevin Calvin, Illinois.* $75.00 – 100.00.

Lanceolate point or blade, good form, 3¼". The lower blade edges are lightly ground, and the material is dark Upper Mercer. Morrow County, Ohio. *Jesse Weber collection; photograph by Norman's Photo, Newcomerstown, Ohio.* $175.00.

Stemmed lance, 3" long, very thin for size. Made of Burlington flint, it was found by Tony Davenport in a creek bed. Jersey County, Illinois. *Collection of and photograph by Kevin Calvin, Illinois.* $150.00.

Lanceolate blade, Late Paleo, 3⅜". Made of mixed Upper Mercer, it was auctioned at a Vietzen sale. Lorain County, Ohio. *Jesse Weber collection; photograph by Norman's Photo, Newcomerstown, Ohio.* $350.00.

Agate Basin(?) point, resharpened size, 1⁹⁄₁₆". Made of peach-colored flint, it has a thinning scar on one face. The artifact was found by the owner in Greene County, Illinois. *Collection of and photograph by Kevin Calvin, Illinois.* $50.00 – 75.00.

Lanceolate point, 3⅝", combined Nellie gray and Coshocton flints. The lance was picked up in Stark County, Ohio. *Jesse Weber collection; photograph by Norman's Photo, Newcomerstown, Ohio.* $75.00.

Stemmed lance, 2½", of yellow, orange, and red flint. The owner found this Late Paleo piece in a creek bed. Scott County, Illinois. *Collection of and photograph by Kevin Calvin, Illinois.* $90.00.

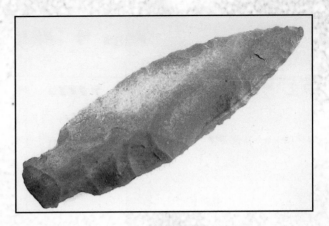

Stemmed lance, creek-stained light brown flint, 2⁹⁄₁₆" long. Found by Tony Davenport, it came from Madison County, Illinois. *Collection of and photograph by Kevin Calvin, Illinois.* $150.00 – 225.00.

Stemmed lance, Late Paleo, 3⅜". Made of water-stained flint in orange, red, and brown, it was found in a creek bed by the owner. Greene County, Illinois. *G. Slone collection; photograph by Kevin Calvin, Illinois.* $125.00 – 150.00.

Dagger-like blade, possibly Late Paleo, 1½" x 6¼". White chert was used for the artifact, which is ex-collection Marko Watkins. Pettis County, Missouri. *Collection of and photograph by Steve Weisser, Indiana.* $450.00.

Stemmed lance, Late Paleo, resharpened size with angled tip. This blade is made of mixed Upper Mercer flint and is 2¼" long. It was found in Stark County, Ohio. *Back to Earth.* $85.00.

Point or blade, Late Paleo, 5⁵⁄₁₆". The material is Burlington chert and the artifact may be in unused condition. It has a Dickey COA and came from Pettis County, Missouri. *Marko Watkins collection, Indiana; Steve Weisser photograph.* $300.00.

Late Paleo blades, both with Jackson COAs. Left, lanceolate, dark Coshocton flint, 6⅞", ex-collection Miller. Pike County, Ohio. Right, knife, green unidentified flint, 5⅞", ex-collection Rice, northern California. *Dr. David R. Thrasher collection, Alabama.* Each, $5,000.00.

Lanceolate point or blade, dark blue Upper Mercer, ex-collections Gobel and Steed. It is 3⁷⁄₁₆", from Guernsey County, Ohio. *Lar Hothem collection.* $45.00.

Lanceolate, gray and tan patinated intermixed Upper Mercer, 3½" long. There is a chipped thinning platform at the base. Coshocton County, Ohio. *Lar Hothem collection.* $125.00.

Stemmed lance, dull black Upper Mercer, 2¹³⁄₂₀". The late Paleo piece came from Medina County, Ohio. *Dave Summers collection, New York.* $70.00.

Tapered lance, glossy tan unidentified material, 4⅖". It was obtained in New York state. *Dave Summers collection, New York.* $170.00.

Lanceolate point or blade, gray with tan material, 3⁹⁄₁₀". Find location is unknown. *Dave Summers collection, New York.* $150.00.

Lanceolate point or blade, Upper Mercer gray flint, 1⅜" x 3". The example came from near Newton Falls, Trumbull County, Ohio. *Pat Layshock collection; Thomas R. Pigott image.* $100.00.

Lanceolate point or blade, Upper Mercer black, 1" x 2⅝". The example was found in the Newton Falls area, Trumbull County, Ohio. *Pat Layshock collection; Thomas R. Pigott image.* $75.00.

Late Paleo lance point, black Upper Mercer flint, 2⅝" long. This specimen was picked up by later prehistoric people and side-notches were put in. The point was found by the owner in Knox County, Ohio. *Carl Harruff collection.* Unlisted.

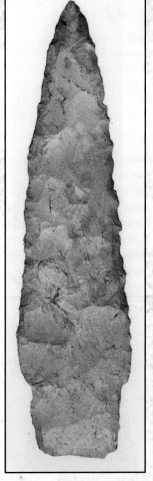

Stemmed lanceolate, patinated Upper Mercer gray flint, 1⅜" x 5". This large point or blade is from Paris Township, Portage County, Ohio. *Pat Layshock collection; Thomas R. Pigott image.* $325.00.

Lanceolate, Late Paleo, ⅞" x 2⅜". It is made of Indiana hornstone and was found in Clark County, Indiana. *Richard B. Lyons collection, Indiana.* $150.00.

Lanceolate, needle tip, 3¼", highly translucent blue-gray Flint Ridge. It is ex-collection Hupp, Brownsville area, Licking County, Ohio. *Fred Winegardner collection.* $325.00.

Lanceolate blade, Late Paleo, Fort Ann(?) flint in light gray. It is 4¹/₂₀" long and came from eastern New York. *Dave Summers collection, New York.* $300.00.

217

OTHER PALEO POINTS AND BLADES

Besides Early and Late Paleo fluted points, and stemmed and unstemmed lances, there are other points or blades that are indeed Paleo. Some do not necessarily look like the usual Paleo artifacts (such as the eastern Midwest Keiser) or are not generally thought of as Paleo (the entire midwestern Dalton family).

While some Daltons (like the 8500 BC Sloan Dalton) are solidly within the Late Paleo period, many examples have features (beveling on two edges, well-developed edge serrations) more common to the Early Archaic period that followed. Daltons are instructive due to both the style and distribution range, and the fact that they tend to be very carefully made. Daltons may have served as projectile points after becoming small and worn out from knife use, but the overall design and size puts them in the knife class.

At the other extreme are regional or even local types, like the small and long-stemmed Keiser that are not always well made or of high-grade material. These are sometimes overlooked because they lack the appeal of fluted points or long lances. Such artifacts are usually not identified until they are repeatedly found with other artifacts that are undeniably Paleo.

Finally, the formation of notches is hinted at with the Hi Lo in the Great Lakes region. Examples of this short lance-like type can range from casually fluted to unfluted and with rudimentary and shallow side notches. Since many Paleo points are isolated surface finds, and are not associated with other Paleo artifacts, it is possible that some true Paleo artifacts will go unrecognized for quite some time.

Unfluted Paleo point or blade, 2⁹⁄₁₆". Of Burlington chert, it was found in 1987. Henderson County, Illinois. *Fred Smith collection, Illinois.* $150.00 – 175.00.

Paleo points, resharpened sizes, both made of Delaware County flint and both from central Ohio. Left, 1½", unfluted-fluted type. $35.00. Right, 1¼", long and narrow basal thinning flakes. $30.00. *Private collection.*

Paleo point, unfluted, pale blue Upper Mercer flint. It is 2¼" and was picked up in Ross County, Ohio. *Terry Elleman collection, Ohio.* $300.00.

Paleo lanceolate point, Late Paleo, Alder Complex, 1¼" long. It is made of Niobrara chert, and the owner found this artifact in 2003. Brookings County, South Dakota. *Harlan Olson collection, South Dakota.* $100.00.

Paleo point, Late Paleo, Alder Complex, red jasper. It is ¹⁵⁄₁₆" x 1" and was found by the owner in 2003. Brookings County, South Dakota. *Harlan Olson collection, South Dakota.* $75.00.

Dalton artifacts, found by Harwood from 1956 through 1965. (Size: largest scraper is 1¹⁄₁₆" x 2³⁄₁₆".) These are from the same site in Morgan County, Alabama. Point, $30.00. Scrapers, $5.00 each. *Collection of and photograph by Gary Henry, North Carolina.*

Unfluted Paleo point, 2³⁄₈", light tan flint with a fossil inclusion. The reverse face has a small flute, and the concave baseline has light grinding. Clark County, Kentucky. *Jeff Schumacher collection, Kentucky.* $100.00.

Unfluted-fluted Paleo point, near-black Upper Mercer, 3¼". Though this piece is unfluted, the county of origin has probably produced more fluted points than any other in the eastern Midwest. Coshocton County, Ohio. *Lar Hothem collection.* $175.00.

Late Paleo artifacts, light and dark quartzites. Haywood County, North Carolina. Left, Hardaway blade, 1¹⁄₈" x 1½". Right, Hardaway Dalton, 1¹⁄₈" x 1½". *Collection of and photograph by Gary Henry, North Carolina.* Each, $50.00.

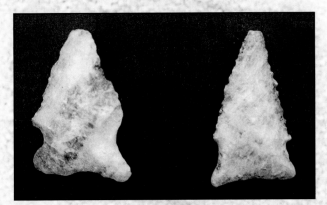

Paleo points or blades, quartz, both ex-collection Pitts and from Fairfield County, South Carolina. Left, Nansemond, ¹⁵⁄₁₆" x 1³⁄₁₆". Right, Colbert Dalton, ¾" x 1¼". *Collection of and photograph by Gary Henry, North Carolina.* Each, $30.00.

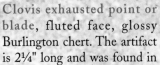

Clovis exhausted point or blade, fluted face, glossy Burlington chert. The artifact is 2¼" long and was found in the Western Bluff area, Jersey County, Illinois. *Gregory L. Perdun collection, Illinois.* $350.00.

Unfluted Clovis point, 1⅞", with Davis COA. It is made from Knox chert and is pictured in *Prehistoric American* 2002, page 47, and in *Overstreet #8* page 406. Clark County, Kentucky. *Jeff Schumacher collection, Kentucky.* $300.00 – 550.00.

Unfluted-fluted point, mixed pale gray and tan patinated Flint Ridge, 2¼". Well chipped and symmetrical, this early point was found in Coshocton County, Ohio. *Lar Hothem collection.* $150.00.

Paleo point, obverse with a natural flute-like depression, unknown multicolored chert. Percussion flaked, it is 2⅛" long and from Delaware County, Ohio. *Private collection.* $20.00.

Paleo point, gray-tan chert, resharpened size, 1⅞". This may have been a much longer lanceolate. Delaware County, Ohio. *Private collection.* $20.00.

Unfluted-fluted point, Flint Ridge in three colors, 2" long. It was picked up near Pigeon Roost Swamp (named in pioneer days for passenger pigeons), Fairfield County, Ohio. *Lar Hothem collection.* $250.00.

Paleo point or blade, Burlington chert with dark specks, 1¾" x 3½". The point has been creek tumbled, and traces of flaking have been removed. It is from Holt County, Missouri. *Mike George collection, Missouri; Terry Price photograph.* Unlisted.

Paleo point, light brown chert, 1" x 2⅛". This was a creek find and has much water stain. Holt County, Missouri. *Mike George collection, Missouri; Terry Price photograph.* $75.00.

Paleo point, brown chert, ¾" x 1¾". Probably resharpened size, the example was found by the owner following terrace construction. Holt County, Missouri. *Mike George collection, Missouri; Terry Price photograph.* $85.00.

Late Paleo point or blade, Burlington chert, 1" x 2¾". This example was found by Otis George in Holt County, Missouri. *Mike George collection, Missouri; Terry Price photograph.* $75.00.

Paleo point, unfluted, gray chert, 1" x 1⅝". The resharpened specimen was found in a plowed field. Buchanan County, Missouri. *Mike George collection, Missouri; Terry Price photograph.* $60.00.

Haw River–like point, similar to points found at the Colby Mammoth Site in Wyoming. The material is an unknown black and blue translucent agate. Alaska. *Rodney M. Peck collection, North Carolina.* $500.00.

Paleo point, unfluted-fluted, tan Fort Payne chert. It has a Davis COA and measures 1" x 2¾". Casey County, Kentucky. *Keith and Rhonda Dodge collection, Michigan.* $400.00.

Holcombe point, glossy red jasper, ⅞" x 2". It has basal thinning, and the provenance is unknown. *Collection of and photograph by H. B. Greene II, Florida.* $200.00.

Paleo point, rock crystal or quartzite, ⅝" x 1⅜". The small artifact was found near South Glastonbury, Connecticut. *Collection of and photograph by H. B. Greene II, Florida.* $125.00.

Paleo point, possibly resharpened size at 1⅛" x 2", black chert with lighter inclusion. Provenance unknown. *Collection of and photograph by H. B. Greene II, Florida.* $30.00.

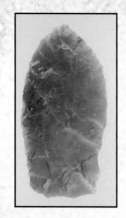

Unfluted Paleo point, dark gray unknown flint, 2¼". It has the characteristics of a fluted point but lacks the flute on either face. Ex-collection Norbert Bingman, southeastern Illinois. *Private collection*. $125.00.

Crowfield point, Paleo period, 2" long. Made of amber Carter Cave flint, it was found in Ohio. *Mike Barron collection, Ohio*. $125.00.

Crowfield point, 2" long, amber-orange Carter Cave (Kentucky) flint. This Paleo point was picked up in Ohio. *Mike Barron collection, Ohio*. $150.00.

Paleo point, unusual cream and red material, 2⅛". It was found by Janie Weidner on the home place near Greenfield, Fayette County, Ohio. *Len and Janie Weidner collection*. Unlisted.

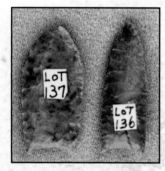

Paleo point, unfluted, Harrison County light gray flint. The base bottom and the lower sides are lightly ground. The piece is 2¹⁄₁₆"and is from Indiana. *Private collection*. $65.00.

Paleo points, auction date May 24, 2003, both figures include 10% buyers' premium. Left to right. Folsom, lot 137, ¹³⁄₁₆" x 1⅝", Holt County, Nebraska. $1,870.00. Late Paleo, lot 136, ⁹⁄₁₆" x 1⅝", Perino COA, Franklin County, Missouri. $660.00. *Rainbow Traders, Illinois*.

Paleo points, all sold at auction February 9, 2002, values each include a 10% buyers' premium. Left to right. Lot 19, Agate Basin, Late Paleo, 3⅞", Howard COA, Greene County, Illinois. $231.00. Lot 20-B, Dalton, 3⅝", Howard COA, Morgan County, Illinois. $440.00. Lot 20-A, Clovis, broken in ancient context, 1⅚" x 2⅝", Morgan County, Illinois. $132.00. *Rainbow Traders, Illinois*.

224

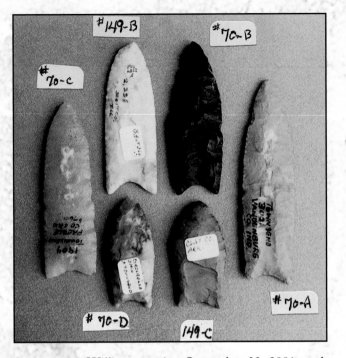

Paleo point, on left, with a Dovetail and a Dalton. The left piece is a rare Folsom, auctioned February 9, 2002, and with a value including the 10% buyers' premium. The Folsom is 1¾" long and has a Motley COA. It was picked up in Missouri. *Rainbow Traders, Illinois.* $605.00.

Paleo group, Williams auction September 22, 2001, each bid amount included a 10% buyers' premium. Counterclockwise, from 3 o'clock: Lot 70-A, Cumberland, 4⅝", Perino COA, Vandenburg County, Indiana. $4,510.00. Lot 149-C, 2⅜", red jasper, Clay County, Arkansas. $550.00. Lot 70-D, Flint Ridge, 2½", Perino COA, Circleville area, Ohio. $1,870.00. Lot 70-C, 3⅞", Hixton sugar quartzite, Perino COA, Preble County, Ohio. $4,950.00. Lot 149-B, Illinois. Unlisted. Lot 70-B, 3½", Perino COA, Licking County, Ohio. $759.00. *Rainbow Traders, Illinois.*

Paleo points left and right, with scarce Early Archaic Hidden Valley at center, auction date March 15, 2003. Listed values include 10% buyers' premiums. Lot 96, Dalton, 2¾", Davis COA, McIntosh County, Oklahoma. $247.50. Lot 84, fluted Clovis, 3¼", Perino COA, St. Charles County, Missouri. $687.50. *Rainbow Traders, Illinois.*

Paleo points, sold February 9, 2002, both with the 10% buyers' premiums included in listed bid amounts. (Left and second from right are Archaic blades.) Second from left, lot 185-C, Plainview, ⅞" x 3⁹⁄₁₆", Perino COA, origin unlisted. $412.50. Right, lot 185, unfluted Clovis, 3⅞". It has a Berner COA and is ex-collection Filbrandt. $632.50. *Rainbow Traders, Illinois.*

Clovis point, resharpened to much shorter length, glossy gray chert. It came from Sumner County, Tennessee. *Craig Ferrell collection.* $125.00.

Clovis fluted point, striped Paoli (Carter Cave) flint. It was found in Clark County, Kentucky. *Craig Ferrell collection.* $200.00.

Clovis point, heavily resharpened and shortened, possibly made of white agatized coral. This material outcrops in Greenbrier County, West Virginia. The point came from Logan County, West Virginia. *Craig Ferrell collection.* Unlisted.

Clovis point, heavily resharpened to shortened length, Paoli (Carter Cave) flint. Very colorful, it is from Adams County, Ohio. *Craig Ferrell collection.* $250.00.

Fluted point, 2¼", possible graver spur at base corner. Provenance is unknown for this piece. *Glenn F. Witchey collection.* $100.00.

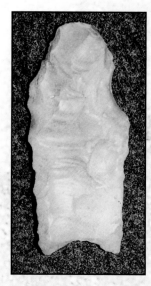

Fluted point, large flute on obverse face and shaft-scraper on top right edge, 2¾" long. It came from Indiana. *Glenn F. Witchey collection.* $100.00.

Fluted point, long flutes on both faces, 2½". It is made of Kentucky hornstone and was found in Kentucky. *Glenn F. Witchey collection.* $100.00.

Paleo point, light-colored flint, 2¼". Flared ears suggest it might be a Beaver Lake. Indiana. *Glenn F. Witchey collection.* $125.00.

Unfluted Clovis point, 11/16" x 15/8", Knox chert. This point was found by the owner in 2003. Fayette County, Kentucky. *Bybee collection, Kentucky; Tom Davis photograph.* $125.00.

Paleo point, lightly fluted, 2" long. In pale-colored striped flint, it has a shaft-scraper on the left side. Kentucky. *Glenn F. Witchey collection.* $100.00.

Fluted points, resharpened sizes, both from Cumberland County, Pennsylvania. Left, 7/8", yellow jasper. $100.00. Right, 11/4", brown jasper. $125.00. *Private collection.*

Paleo blade, patinated preform for a large Clovis, 2" x 53/4". It is made of Burlington chert and is ex-collections Warner, Ryan, and Hap Watkins. It has a Berner COA and was found in the Constantine area, southern Michigan. *Marko Watkins collection, Indiana; Steve Weisser photograph.* $2,000.00.

Paleo point, gray low-grade chert with inclusions, 111/16". It has a smoothly ground baseline. Ohio. *Private collection.* $25.00.

Lanceolate point, needle tip, 23/20". It is made of mixed reddish Flint Ridge, and its find location is unknown. *Dave Summers collection, New York.* $100.00.

Unfluted-fluted point, 23/4", brick red chert. It was found in Delaware County, Ohio. *Dave Summers collection, New York.* $150.00.

Unfluted-fluted type, slightly earred, 15/16" x 21/2". Blue-black Upper Mercer, the point or blade is ex-collection Champion and is pictured in Hothem's *First Hunters.* Knox County, Ohio. *Jim Miller collection.* $1,000.00.

Hi-Lo point, Late Paleo, Upper Mercer gray flint, 1⅜" x 2⅜". It was found in the Newton Falls area, Trumbull County, Ohio. *Pat Layshock collection; Thomas R. Pigott image.* $75.00.

Late Paleo point, possibly Dalton family, 2½" long. Made of dark blue Upper Mercer, it has traces of red ochre present. The point or blade was found by the owner in Knox County, Ohio. *Carl Harruff collection.* $250.00.

Unfluted-fluted point, patinated cream Flint Ridge, nicely chipped and shaped. It is 2⅞" and from Ohio. *Dr. John Winsch collection.* Unlisted.

Fluted point, of white, gray, and tan Lockport flint, 2¼". Fluted on two sides, it is ex-collection Hesse and was found in western New York. *Dave Summers collection, New York.* $500.00.

Paleo point, uncertain type, gray-tan Onondaga flint. The point or blade is 2³⁄₁₀" and from western New York. *Dave Summers collection, New York.* $70.00.

Fluted point, blue-gray Fort Ann flint, 1⅗". It came from western New York. *Dave Summers collection, New York.* $70.00.

Fluted point, unidentified type, black Helderberg flint. The artifact is 1⅘" and from western New York. *Dave Summers collection, New York.* $70.00.

Fluted point, gray-tan Onondaga, 1¹³⁄₂₀". It is ex-collection Whipple, and one face has a full-length flute. Erie County, New York. *Dave Summers collection, New York.* $70.00.

Stemmed lance, speckled white chert, ¾" x 3", ½" thick. This point was found by the owner in Monroe County, Indiana. *Collection of and photograph by Jon Hunsberger, Indiana.* $75.00.

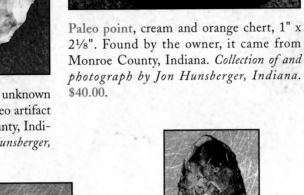

Paleo point, cream and orange chert, 1" x 2⅛". Found by the owner, it came from Monroe County, Indiana. *Collection of and photograph by Jon Hunsberger, Indiana.* $40.00.

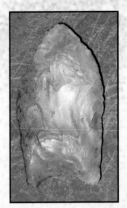

Clovis-like preform(?) biface point or blade, unknown red, cream, and gray flint, 2¾" x 4". This Paleo artifact was picked up by the owner in Monroe County, Indiana. *Collection of and photograph by Jon Hunsberger, Indiana.* $25.00.

Hi-Lo point, Late Paleo, 2" long. Of Spergen chert, this point was resharpened and reduced in length by more than an inch. It has a Perino COA and was found in Des Moines County, Iowa. *Collection of and photograph by A. D. Savage, Iowa.* $300.00.

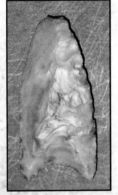

Hi-Lo point, Late Paleo, 1½". The material is cobble chert, and the piece has a Perino COA. Pike County, Illinois. *Collection of and photograph by A. D. Savage, Iowa.* $250.00.

Plainview point, Late Paleo, 2⅜". Delaware chert was the material chipped for this scarce point type, which has a Perino COA. Highland County, Ohio. *Collection of and photograph by A. D. Savage, Iowa.* $300.00.

Plainview point, Paleo, Oneota chert. The point is 2" long and has a Perino COA. Des Moines County, Iowa. *Collection of and photograph by A. D. Savage, Iowa.* $300.00.

Fluted point, local tan chert, 2¹⁄₁₆". The example, which has a Perino COA, was a personal find of the owner. Adams County, Ohio. *Gilbert Cooper collection.* Unlisted.

Unfluted Clovis-like point, 2⅛", ground basal edges. Lake County, Indiana. *John and Susan Mellyn collection, Texas.* $200.00.

Hardaway fluted blade, quartzite, 1³⁄₁₆" x 1⅞". It is No. 701 in Peck's North Carolina fluted point survey and was a personal find by the owner. Buncombe County, North Carolina. *Collection of and photograph by Gary Henry, North Carolina.* $40.00.

229

Dalton point, Hardaway variety on left, both found by owner. Monroe County, Tennessee. Left, ¾" x 1⅝". $75.00. Right, ¾" x 1⅜". $30.00. *Collection of and photograph by Gary Henry, North Carolina.*

Simpson fishtail Paleo point or blade, 3¼", silicified shale. It has a graceful base and was found in Chatham County, North Carolina. *Collection of and photograph by Ron Harris, North Carolina.* $275.00.

Paleo point, Indiana Green flint, ex-collection Kilander. The point is 2¼" and from the Lafayette area, Indiana. *Dwight Wolfe collection.* $150.00.

Paleo point, fluted both faces, 3¼". Of Harrison County flint (Indiana hornstone), it came from Blackford County, Indiana. *Dwight Wolfe collection.* $250.00.

Fluted point or blade, bifurcated base, unidentified type, black obsidian. The basal edges are heavily ground on this example, 1³⁄₁₆" x 2¼". It was picked up in western Box Elder County, northern Utah. *Dann Russell collection, Utah.* $250.00.

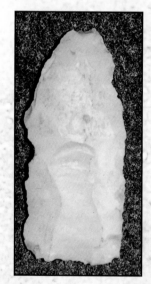

Fluted point, roughly made, 2¾". Made of pale Dover flint, it was found in Tennessee. *Glenn F. Witchey collection.* $50.00.

Fluted point, 2½" long, Indiana Green flint. It is fluted halfway on both faces and was found in Indiana. *Glenn R. Witchey collection.* $100.00.

Fluted point, triangular shape, glossy high-grade flint. The Early Paleo piece is 1¾" long, provenance unknown. *Glenn F. Witchey collection.* Unlisted.

Paleo point, fluted on one face, base damage and possible tip impact fracture. It is 2¾" long and from Kentucky. *Glenn F. Witchey collection.* $100.00.

Paleo point, light-colored flint, 3" long. One basal corner is restored on this piece, and the find location is unknown. *Glenn F. Witchey collection.* Unlisted.

Paleo point, unfluted, gray unknown chert material, 2⅝". It was possibly found in Florida. *Dwight Wolfe collection.* $100.00.

Unfluted Clovis-like point, 1¼" x 4", glossy blue-black flint with tan swirls. Ex-collection Lyerla, it was found by M. Ralls near Sedalia, Missouri. *Tom Fouts collection, Kansas.* $900.00.

Fishtail Paleo point or blade, slight restoration, 2¾". Of attractive banded rhyolite, it is ex-collection Mabe. Randolph County, North Carolina. *Collection of and photograph by Ron Harris, North Carolina.* $350.00.

Paleo variant, unfluted, 2⁷⁄₁₆". High-quality black Upper Mercer was used for the point, which is thin and has fine retouching on both sides edges. Monroe County, Ohio. *Jesse Weber collection; photograph by Norman's Photo, Newcomerstown, Ohio.* $300.00.

Paleo point, deeply concave baseline, 1⅞". The material is Four Mile Creek chert, and the point came from the Belle Center area, Ohio. *Jesse Weber collection; photograph by Norman's Photo, Newcomerstown, Ohio.* $40.00.

Unfluted-fluted point, Paleo, 2⁷⁄₁₆". It is made of Coshocton gray flint and has a needle tip. Stark County, Ohio. *Jesse Weber collection; photograph by Norman's Photo, Newcomerstown, Ohio.* $150.00.

231

Stemmed point with flute, probably Late Paleo, chert, 1³⁄₁₆" x 1¼". Rechipped to exhaustion, the artifact is from Buncombe County, North Carolina. *Collection of and photograph by Gary Henry, North Carolina.* $30.00.

Clovis point and bases, left example ⅞" x 1¾", all from Buncombe County, North Carolina, but from three separate sites. These are pictured as numbers 426, 485, and 534 in Peck's North Carolina fluted point survey. They were all found by the owner. Left, medium dark chert. $500.00. Center, gray quartzite. $50.00. Right, translucent chalcedony. $100.00. *Collection of and photograph by Gary Henry, North Carolina.*

Lanceolate, flute-like basal thinning on obverse, ¾" x 2³⁄₁₆". Made of light green flint, it was found by the owner in Wilson County, North Carolina. *Michael Womble collection, North Carolina.* $60.00 – 85.00.

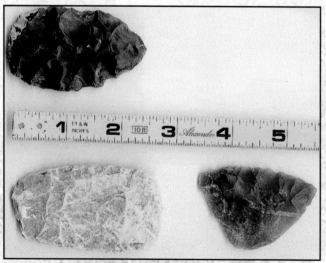

Paleo artifacts, Knife River flint, all from Montrail County, North Dakota. Top left, ovate blade. $60.00. Bottom left, rectangular blade, hightly patinated. $125.00. Bottom right, semi-lunate blade, rounded haft area. $200.00. *Collection of and scan by Larry Bumann, North Dakota.*

Unfluted Clovis point, 2½", pale mixed gray Upper Mercer, ex-collection Col. Vietzen. It was found in Kentucky. *Bill Moody collection, Massachusetts.* $150.00.

Unfluted Clovis point, 2¼", mixed blue Upper Mercer flint with several white spots. Ex-collection Col. Vietzen, it came from Lorain County, Ohio. *Bill Moody collection, Massachusetts.* $300.00.

Holcombe point, 2" long, probably Upper Mercer flint, ex-collection Col. Vietzen. It was recovered from Stark County, Ohio. *Bill Moody collection, Massachusetts.* $500.00.

Suwannee point, 2⅛", river-stained flint. It came from the Aucilla River, Florida. *Bill Moody collection, Massachusetts.* $150.00.

Paleo point, unfluted, unidentified chert, 2⅜". Well shaped, it is from the Midwest. *Don Casto collection.* $85.00.

Unfluted Clovis point, 1" x 2½" and ¼" thick, thinned base, well patinated and with basal edges ground for 1". The left base corner has been burin fractured, and the tip was rechipped in ancient times. Material is gray Fort Payne. The Clovis has a Davis COA, and its origin is unknown. *Mark Boswell collection, Colorado; photograph by Infocusphotography.com, Colorado.* $300.00.

Clovis point, Fern Glen flint, about exhausted size at 2" long. It has an irregular flute and came from the Western Bluff area, Jersey County, Illinois. *Gregory L. Perdun collection, Illinois.* $550.00 – 650.00.

Fluted Paleo point preform or knife, Burlington chert, 3¼". It is fluted only on the obverse and came from the Western Bluff area of Jersey County, Illinois. *Gregory L. Perdun collection, Illinois.* $450.00.

Clovis fluted point preform, broken when the first flute was made, Fern Glen flint. The two piece were found and are now glued together. The preform is 4" long and the remnant of the fluting protrusion is still present. *Gregory L. Perdun collection, Illinois.* $800.00 – 900.00.

233

UNIFACE BLADES

Uniface Paleo blades are easy to recognize when both faces are examined. Most of the edge retouch (chipping) is along the edges of one face, while the opposite retains much of the original smooth surface of the large struck-off blade. At times some edgework is on that face as well, but most of the shaping and edge resharpening work is on only one face.

The outline of uniface blades can best be described as irregular, because the outline or shape is the result of a hard blow to a large core. Depending on the skill of the blade-maker, the form can be haphazard to beautifully controlled and somewhat triangular or rectangular.

Another kind of uniface Paleo artifact is the prismatic bladelet, long and narrow, and with edges usually retouched along one face. Made from carefully formed cores, some of these are delicate and pure works of art. Still another Paleo artifact in the uniface class is the bladelet struck so that it has three faces instead of two. It is triangular in cross section, and so many are found in broken condition they must have received heavy use.

Most of the unifaces tend to be fairly large, so they were capable of extended use and much edge renewal. Excurvate edges could be used for cutting tasks, and some with edge beveling were designed more for scraping. This gave some uniface blades multiple uses, and the basic form could be redone to meet new needs.

There have long been discussions as to whether uniface blades were hafted (had handles) or were finger- or handheld only. Likely, both methods were used. Some unifaces have protrusions shaped for a bone or antler handle, while others have no obvious way they could have been easily hafted. Whatever the shape or size, uniface blades in North America were widely employed by Paleo people.

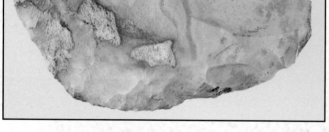

Uniface blade, Buffalo River chert, 3½". The excurvate edge is roughly beveled, suggesting it was resharpened. Tennessee. *Dwight Wolfe collection.* $40.00.

Uniface blade, Indiana Green flint, thin for size. The tool is 3¾" long, ex-collection Cummins. Butler County, Ohio. *Dwight Wolfe collection.* $40.00.

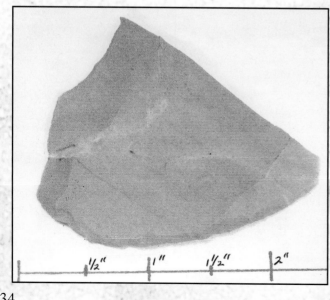

Uniface blade, excurvate scraper/knife edge, brown jasper. the right-angle edge intersection has a small graver tip, and size is as indicated. Found by the owner, it came from Hunterdon County, New Jersey. *Bob Bronish collection, New Jersey.* Unlisted.

Uniface blade, all-purpose tool, both ends retouched. Made of brown flint, it is 2" x 4¼". Ex-collection Rantz, the blade is from Benton County, Tennessee. *Paul Weisser collection, Indiana.* $75.00.

Flake knives, left example 2" long and right example 1¾" long. They are made of light brown flint and both were found by Robert Rantz. Benton County, Tennessee. *Paul Weisser collection, Indiana.* Each, $20.00.

Paleo flake tool, burin tip on wider end, Foraker permian chert, provenance unlisted. *Jim Horst collection, Nebraska.* $25.00.

Paleo uniface blade, large obverse elongated flake scar from previous blade strike-off, Summerset permian flint. The top edge as shown is reworked. Provenance unlisted. *Jim Horst collection, Nebraska.* $75.00.

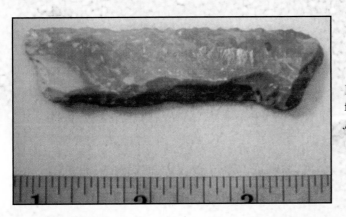

Paleo flake knife, Pennsylvanian rice-grained Nehawka flint. It is worked on all four sides. Provenance unlisted. *Jim Horst collection, Nebraska.* $100.00.

Uniface knife, 1" x 2⅝", cream and purple chert. The curved blade was found in the Pemiscot area, Missouri. *Bybee collection, Kentucky; Tom Davis photograph.* $65.00.

Uniface knife, 1¹³⁄₁₆" x 4¾", Dover chert. It came from the Kentucky Lake area, Calloway County, Kentucky. *Bybee collection, Kentucky; Tom Davis photograph.* $200.00.

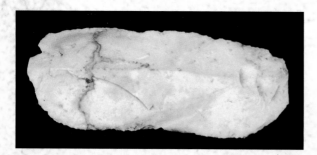

Uniface blade, thin, 3¹⁄₁₆", patinated Flint Ridge colored tan, cream, and brown. It was obtained at a farm auction near West Lafayette, Coshocton County, Ohio. *Jesse Weber collection; photograph by Norman's Photo, Newcomerstown, Ohio.* $150.00.

Uniface tool, ¾" x 3", Flint Ridge material. The example was found by the owner in the 1940s. Liberty Township, Guernsey County, Ohio. *Jesse Weber collection; photograph by Norman's Photo, Newcomerstown, Ohio.* $100.00.

Uniface blade, 1⅜" x 4⅛", graver spur and reamer(?) tip. It is made of Flint Ridge material and was found by the owner in the 1980s. *Jesse Weber collection; photograph by Norman's Photo, Newcomerstown, Ohio.* $150.00.

Uniface blade, thin, 3¾". Made of dark Upper Mercer, the knife was found in Coshocton County, Ohio. *Jesse Weber collection; photograph by Norman's Photo, Newcomerstown, Ohio.* $50.00.

Uniface blade, chert, 1¹⁄₁₆" x 2¹¹⁄₁₆". Ex-collection Cordeiro, the knife is from Mercer County, Ohio. *Collection of and photograph by Gary Henry, North Carolina.* $30.00.

Uniface knives or scrapers, large sizes and good forms, jasper material. Both were found in Pennsylvania. *Fogelman collection.* Each, $200.00 – 300.00.

Uniface knife, gray patinated Walhonding Valley flint in several shades, 5¼". This outstanding blade was found by the owner on a site that had only produced much smaller or incomplete artifacts. Fairfield County, Ohio. *Don Casto collection.* Museum grade.

Uniface blade, 3¾", Coastal Plains chert with a heavy dark amber patina. Partly translucent, the tool came from Lee County, Georgia. *Dwight Wolfe collection.* $150.00.

Uniface tool, Kentucky(?) gray chert, 2⅞". This tool has an end-scraper at the larger end and a possible graver tip at the smaller end. Location unknown. *Dwight Wolfe collection.* $25.00.

Uniface tool, Indiana or Kentucky hornstone, 2⅜". There is an end-scraper at the larger end, with a worn graver spur. Location unknown. *Dwight Wolfe collection.* $25.00.

Uniface blade, 3¹⁵⁄₁₆", patinated Flint Ridge material. Ex-collection Meyer, it came from Mercer County, Ohio. *Dwight Wolfe collection.* $55.00.

Uniface blade, gray Upper Mercer, 3¼". The concave edge has retouch, and there are probable graver tips at each end. Location unknown, probably Ohio. *Dwight Wolfe collection.* $40.00.

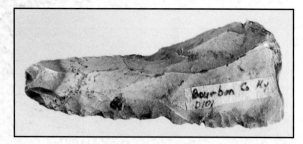

Uniface knife, excurvate edge with retouch, patinated Kentucky flint. It is 3¼" long and from Bourbon County, Kentucky. *Dwight Wolfe collection.* $25.00.

Uniface blade, water stained and water worn, 4" long. The material is probably Coastal Plains chert with a very pleasing patina. It was found in the Lacoochee River, Florida. *Dwight Wolfe collection.* $150.00.

Uniface blade, very thin, 3⅜" long. The material is patinated Sonora translucent flint. Kentucky. *Dwight Wolfe collection.* $35.00.

Uniface blade, long basal flute, 1⁹⁄₁₆" x 4¼", mixed Coshocton gray flint. This piece was found by the owner in the 1940s. Liberty Township, Guernsey County, Ohio. *Jesse Weber collection; photograph by Norman's Photo, Newcomerstown, Ohio.* $150.00.

Uniface blade, serrated edge, 2" x 5½". This large Paleo tool is from Goodflint.com and was found in Stewart County, Tennessee. *Doug Goodrum collection, Kentucky.* $75.00.

Uniface blade, Fort Payne chert, 2¼" x 5⅛". This large knife or tool is from Goodflint.com and was found in Tennessee. *Doug Goodrum collection, Kentucky.* $175.00.

Uniface blade, dark nodular (possibly Kentucky) flint, 3¹⁵⁄₁₆". It was found by the owner on the same site that produced a 2" fluted point. Fairfield County, Ohio. *Mike Diano collection, Florida.* $75.00.

Uniface blade, "Saugus" rhyolite, found by the owner near Herring Brook. It came from Plymouth County, Massachusetts. *Bill Moody collection, Massachusetts.* $50.00.

Uniface blade, 4" long, beveled incurvate edge, patinated unknown glossy flint. A large shaftscraper is on the upper right, and a possible knob-like handle is at the right. Ex-collection Tolliver, Hocking County, Ohio. *Don Casto collection.* $125.00.

Uniface blade, broken and glued, probably a heavily patinated Upper Mercer flint variety. The knife is 4" long and was found by the owner in Fairfield County, Ohio. *Don Casto collection.* $40.00.

239

Uniface crescent blade, patinated translucent Flint Ridge, 2⅞". It is ex-collection Tolliver, from Hocking County, Ohio. *Don Casto collection.* $45.00.

Uniface curved blade, patinated multicolored Flint Ridge, 4⅜". Ex-collection Morehart, it is from Fairfield County, Ohio. *Don Casto collection.* $150.00.

Uniface blade, 3" long, Harrison County (Indiana hornstone) flint. This has a long thin knife edge and was found by the owner in St. Joseph County, Indiana. *Paul Weisser collection, Indiana.* $40.00.

Paleo flake knife, triangular cross section, size as indicated. It has a burin on the side of the wider end. Provenance unlisted. *Jim Horst collection, Nebraska.* $25.00.

Uniface flake blade, straight and excurvate knife edges, provenance unlisted. *Jim Horst collection, Nebraska.* $40.00.

Paleo uniface tool, long knife edge, possible graver tip near shorter bottom edge. Provenance unlisted. *Jim Horst collection, Nebraska.* $30.00.

Uniface blade, Paleo, 1¼" x 2¼". This multi-purpose tool has a worn graver spur and probably has another directly across the blade. The material is tan and purple high-grade agate. It was found by the owner in Morgan County, Colorado. *Mark Boswell collection, Colorado; photograph by Infocusphotography.com, Colorado.* Unlisted.

Uniface scraper, Ellison Creek flint, 3¾" long. The reverse is flat, and the edge chipping is finely done. Henderson County, Illinois. *Fred Smith collection, Illinois.* $25.00 – 40.00.

Uniface blade or large flake knife, 1¾" x 4⅜", 3⁄16" thick. Of gray and white chert, it has a curved blade edge, and the narrower end is heavily polished from use. The knife was found in Colorado. *Mark Boswell collection, Colorado; photograph by Infocus photography.com, Colorado.* $200.00.

Uniface blade, mixed chert, 1¾" x 2¹⁵⁄₁₆". Found by Harwood in 1956, this tool came from Morgan County, Alabama. *Collection of and photograph by Gary Henry, North Carolina.* $15.00.

Uniface blade, Flint Ridge translucent multicolor, ex-collection Lynch. The artifact is 3⅞" long, from Pickaway County, Ohio. *Private collection.* $75.00.

Uniface blade, Kentucky hornstone, 3¹⁄₃₂". The knife has side-scraper edges and is probably from Kentucky. *Dwight Wolfe collection.* $25.00.

Uniface blade, Harrison County flint with cortex remnants, 3½". This Paleo knife was found in Indiana. *Terry Elleman collection, Ohio.* $150.00.

Triangular uniface blade, Paleo, brown and gray flint, 3¼" long. Though the shape is quite basic, not many triangular unifaces exist. Darke County, Ohio. *Terry Elleman collection, Ohio.* $150.00.

Uniface blade, translucent Carter Cave (Kentucky) flint, 4½" long. It has some parallel flaking and is ex-collections Mumaw and Townsend. Eastern Midwest. *Terry Elleman collection, Ohio.* $750.00.

Uniface blade, delicate edge retouch, 3⅛" long. Harrison County flint was used for this piece, which the owner found in Miami County, Ohio. *Terry Elleman collection, Ohio.* Unlisted.

Uniface blade, Paleo, Harrison County (Indiana hornstone) material, 3¾" long. With much edgework, this knife came from Miami County, Ohio. *Terry Elleman collection, Ohio.* $150.00.

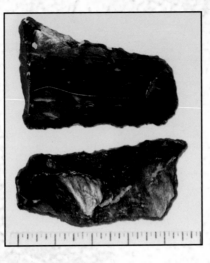

Paleo uniface blades, scraper/knife edges. They are made of Knife River flint. The top example is 2³⁄₁₆" long, and the bottom example is 2⁵⁄₁₆". The owner found both tools, the top in 1999 and the bottom (with worn graver tip) in 2003. Brookings County, South Dakota. *Harlan Olson collection, South Dakota.* Each, $40.00.

Uniface blade, blue and chocolate Upper Mercer, 2³⁄₈". Most of the edges have fine retouch. Fairfield County, Ohio. *Lar Hothem collection.* $20.00.

Uniface blade, light and dark blue Upper Mercer flint, 4½". Made from a long blade struck from a large core, the edges of the knife have secondary retouch. Mercer County, Ohio. *Terry Elleman collection, Ohio.* $225.00.

Uniface knife, made of creamy layer Flint Ridge, 2¾" long, The knife edge is chipped from both faces, and the remainder of the blade has been snapped off to create two-sided working edges. Fairfield County, Ohio. *Private collection.* $15.00.

Paleo prismatic uniface blade, mixed dark Upper Mercer flint. The base terminates with three overlapping flutes. The blade is 3³⁄₈" long, from Fairfield County, Ohio. *Private collection.* $65.00.

Uniface blade, shaft-scraper chipped on lower edge, 4" long. There was an attempt at fluting on the obverse small end. Huron County, Ohio. *Lar Hothem collection.* $75.00.

243

Uniface blade, uniface surface shown with bulb of percussion on right. Two shades of blue Upper Mercer were used for this knife, 4⅜" long. Jefferson County, Ohio. *Lar Hothem collection*. $60.00.

Uniface blade, thin, fluted from larger end, 3⅛". Made of blue Upper Mercer, it has a graver tip at the smaller end. Ohio. *Dwight Wolfe collection*. $45.00.

Uniface blade, with graver tip, 2½". The concave edge has retouch, and the material is blue Upper Mercer. Putnam County, Ohio. *Dwight Wolfe collection*. $20.00.

Uniface blade, flute-like basal flake scars, 2¾". The excurvate edge has delicate retouch on this piece, probably made of translucent high-grade Upper Mercer. Ohio. *Dwight Wolfe collection*. $20.00.

Uniface blade, excurvate scraping/cutting edge, 1¼" x 2¼". It is made of gray and black Nellie flint and was found by the owner's father-in-law, Sam Jenkins, in the Ohio River Valley. West Virginia. *Private collection; Rodney Roberts photograph*. $20.00.

Uniface blade, honey-colored flint, 1⁵⁄₁₆" x 2¾". It was found on a site along the Ohio River. West Virginia. *Private collection; Rodney Roberts photograph*. $30.00.

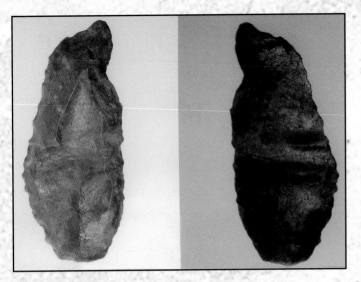

Uniface blade, 1⅛" x 2⅝", gray Upper Mercer with brown clouding. It was found in the Ohio River Valley, West Virginia. *Private collection; Rodney Roberts photograph.* $25.00.

Prismatic blade, with small shaft-scraper and graver tips, honey-colored translucent Flint Ridge. It came from the Ohio River Valley, West Virginia. *Private collection; Rodney Roberts photograph.* $20.00.

Uniface blade, beveled straight edge with graver tip, black flint with tan inclusions. It is $^{13}/_{16}$" x $1^{11}/_{16}$" and came from an Ohio River site. West Virginia. *Private collection; Rodney Roberts photograph.* $15.00.

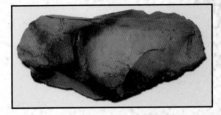

Uniface blade, with knife edges and graver tip, 1" x 2³⁄₁₆". Dark brown and tan flint, it came from the Ohio River Valley. West Virginia. *Private collection; Rodney Roberts photograph.* $15.00.

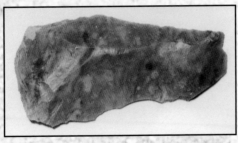

Uniface blade, side-scraper with graver or perforator, 1¼" x 2½". It is made of translucent flint with lighter inclusions. Ohio River Valley, West Virginia. *Private collection; Rodney Roberts photograph.* $20.00.

Uniface blade, with graver tip, knife edge and end-scraper. Amber patinated Carter Cave, it measures 1⅛" x 2⅞". It came from a creek in 2001. Ohio Valley area, West Virginia. *Private collection; Rodney Roberts photograph.* $65.00.

Paleo bipointed uniface blade, of purple, pink, and gray Sonora flint, 5⅜" long. This exceptional blade was found by G. Witt in 2003, and came from Clark County, Kentucky. *Jeff Schumacher collection, Kentucky.* $800.00 – 1,000.00.

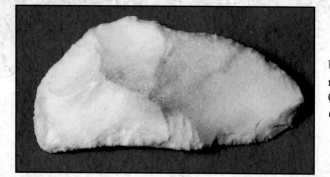

Uniface blade, 3¼", Burlington chert. This tool with edge retouch was found in a creek bed by Jeff Allen. Madison County, Illinois. *Collection of and photograph by Kevin Calvin, Illinois.* $75.00.

Uniface blade, heavily creek-stained brown chert, 4¼". The long edges have retouch and one corner has a large graver tip. Jersey County, Illinois. *Collection of and photograph by Kevin Calvin, Illinois.* $125.00.

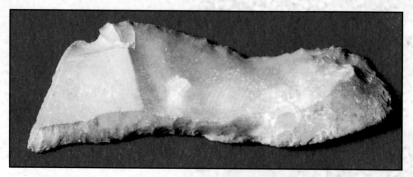

Uniface blade, 4⅜", translucent tan water-stained flint. The fairly straight edge has retouch, and the artifact was found by the owner in a creek bed. Macoupin County, Illinois. *G. Slone collection; photograph by Kevin Calvin, Illinois.* $60.00 – 80.00.

Uniface blade, bulb of percussion at wide end, 3¾". Mottled blue Upper Mercer, both long edges have secondary chipping. It was a personal find of the owner in Greenfield Township, Fairfield County, Ohio. *Lar Hothem collection.* $30.00.

Uniface blade, with hafting extension, near-black Upper Mercer with brown inclusions. Both long edges have secondary retouch. The blade is 4⅝" long and is ex-collection Dutcher. Fairfield County, Ohio. *Lar Hothem collection.* $100.00.

Uniface blade, beveled excurvate edge, 3⅛" long. It is made of Sonora flint and is probably from Kentucky. *Earthworks Artifacts.* $45.00.

Uniface blade, Flint Ridge chalcedony, 1⅜" x 2¾". This colorful example was found by William Platt near Cortland, Trumbull County, Ohio. *Pat Layshock collection; Thomas R. Pigott image.* $75.00.

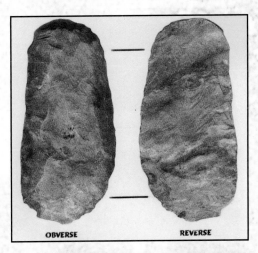

OBVERSE   REVERSE

Uniface knife blade, butterscotch Pennsylvania jasper, 2¹⁹⁄₂₀". It came from the Lower Hudson River Valley, New York. *Dave Summers collection, New York.* $60.00.

Uniface blade, hooked corner, of cream, tan, and red Flint Ridge, 4¼". It is from Licking County, Ohio. *Terry Elleman collection.* $225.00.

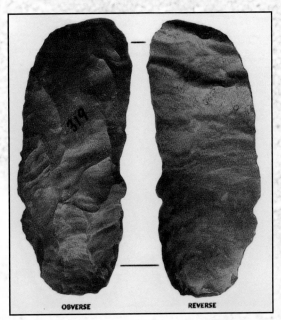

OBVERSE   REVERSE

256

Uniface blade, gray mixed Upper Mercer flint, 1⅞" x 4¼". It was found by William Platt near Cortland, Trumbull County, Ohio. *Pat Layshock collection; Thomas R. Pigott image.* $125.00.

247

Uniface blade, with knife edge, mottled gray Onondaga, 2¹⁄₁₀". It is from Delaware County, New York. *Dave Summers collection, New York.* $30.00.

Uniface blade, mottled dark green-tan Coxsackie flint, 3⅘" long. It is from the Sacandaga River area, Hamilton County, New York. *Dave Summers collection, New York.* $60.00.

Triangular uniface blade, brown Pennsylvania jasper, 2¼". Ex-collection Whipple, it came from western New York. *Dave Summers collection, New York.* $80.00.

Triangular uniface blade fragment, 1¹⁹⁄₂₀". Dull gray Glenerie flint was used for the tool, from eastern New York. *Dave Summers collection, New York.* $2.00.

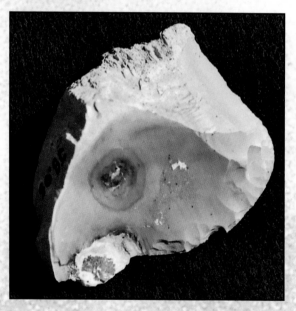

Uniface blade, Indian Creek chert, 1⅛" x 2½". Thin, this tool was found by the owner in Monroe County, Indiana. *Collection of and photograph by Jon Hunsberger, Indiana.* $35.00.

Uniface tool, with sharp excurvate edge for knife use, Harrison County nodular flint. The artifact is 2⅝" x 3" and was found by the owner. Monroe County, Indiana. *Collection of and photograph by Jon Hunsberger, Indiana.* $30.00.

Uniface curved knife, gray and red Harrison County flint, 2¼" long. It was found by the owner in Monroe County, Indiana. *Collection of and photograph by Jon Hunsberger, Indiana.* $20.00.

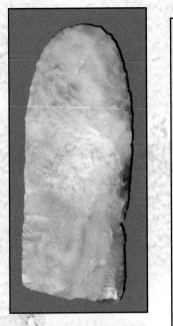

OBVERSE   REVERSE

Uniface blade, Paleo, glossy tan-brown flint. This blade is 3⅛" long and has a small flute at the base. The type is sometimes referred to as "square back." Mississippi County, Missouri. *Collection of and photograph by A. D. Savage, Iowa.* $325.00.

Uniface blade, black Upper Mercer with brownish inclusions, 1½" x 4¼". Fluted at the obverse base and with a graver tip at the opposite end, the knife was found by William Platt near Cortland. Trumbull County, Ohio. *Pat Layshock collection; Thomas R. Pigott image.* $125.00.

Uniface Paleo blade, lightly ground on basal edges, 3¾" long. Made of unknown dark glossy flint, it came from Bath County, Kentucky. *Jeff Schumacher collection, Kentucky.* $50.00 – 100.00.

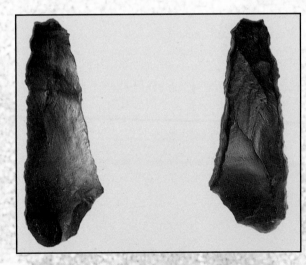

Uniface knives, longest 3¾", both personal finds of the owners. They are made of Burlington chert and came from VanBuren County, Iowa. *Dale and Betty Roberts collection, Iowa.* Each, $50.00.

Uniface blade, black flint, 1⅛" x 3" long. With two probable graver spurs, it came from an Ohio River Valley site. West Virginia. *Private collection; Rodney Roberts photograph.* $50.00.

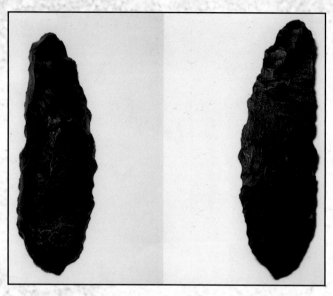

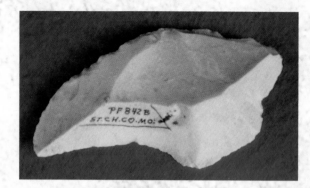

Flake knife, Burlington chert, 1½" x 3". Uniface, it has sharp blade edges. The blade was found by the owner in St. Charles County, Missouri. *Bob Rampani collection, Missouri.* $20.00.

Uniface blade, curved, steeply beveled edges. Black Kanawha flint was used for this piece, 1" x 3 1/16". It came from an Ohio River site. West Virginia. *Private collection; Rodney Roberts photograph.* $30.00.

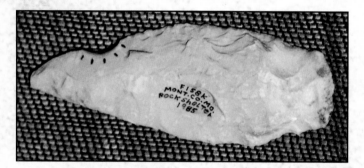

Uniface blade, green flint with light tan spots, 1 1/16" x 2 7/16". Found on an Ohio River site by Sam Jenkins, the owner's father-in-law, it is from West Virginia. *Private collection; Rodney Roberts photograph.* $25.00.

Uniface blade, with spokeshave near the tip, 1⅜" x 3⅝". The base and opposite face have signs of having been in a fire. The tool came from a rock shelter in 1985. Montgomery County, Missouri. *Bob Rampani collection, Missouri.* $40.00.

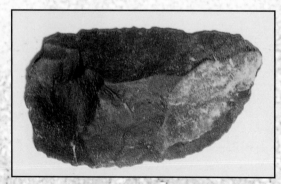

Paleo uniface blade, excurvate edge with retouch, 1 5/16" x 2⅜". It is made of black Kanawha flint and came from an Ohio River site. West Virginia. *Private collection; Rodney Roberts photograph.* $20.00.

Triangular uniface blade, Flint Ridge tan, red, and gray, 1 13/16" x 3". The owner's father-in-law, Sam Jenkins, found this fine specimen on an Ohio River Valley site. West Virginia. *Private collection; Rodney Roberts photograph.* $100.00.

Uniface blade, side edges and graver tips. The material is brown flint with a red bull's-eye, and the tool is 1¾" x 2½". It was picked up by the owner's father-in-law, Sam Jenkins, on an Ohio River site. West Virginia. *Private collection; Rodney Roberts photograph.* $20.00.

Uniface knife, made from vein or layer flint, 2⅝". Translucent Flint Ridge, the knife is from Ohio. *Lar Hothem collection.* $12.00.

Uniface blade, pear shaped, creamy tan Flint Ridge, 2⅞". The excurvate edge has secondary retouch, and the opposite edge is about two-thirds retouched. Ohio. *Lar Hothem collection.* $30.00.

Uniface flake blade, thin for size, dark blue Upper Mercer, 2¾". It was picked up in Fairfield County, Ohio. *Lar Hothem collection.* $10.00.

Uniface tool, gray and tan Harrison County flint, 1" x 2¾". It was found by the owner in Monroe County, Indiana. *Collection of and photograph by Jon Hunsberger, Indiana.* $45.00.

Uniface tool, Harrison County flint, 1" x 3¼". A classic Paleo form, it was found by the owner in Monroe County, Indiana. *Collection of and photograph by Jon Hunsberger, Indiana.* $75.00.

Uniface blade, striped yellowish tan unknown flint, 4¼" long. It has a weak flute at the base, and the bulb of percussion is on the same end. Coshocton County, Ohio. *Lar Hothem collection*. $65.00.

Uniface tool, scraper edge, 1½" across. An unknown white flint was used for this artifact, found by the owner. Monroe County, Indiana. *Collection of and photograph by Jon Hunsberger, Indiana*. $10.00.

Uniface blade, blue and cream Upper Mercer, 3⁵⁄₁₆". It has secondary chipping on all edges and came from Fairfield County, Ohio. *Private collection*. $15.00.

Uniface Paleo knife, 1" x 3⅛", brown Knife River flint. The blade has a Davis COA and came from South Dakota. *Keith and Rhonda Dodge collection, Michigan*. $125.00.

Hafted uniface blade, with small shaft-scraper, angled end-scraper, and knife-edge sides. The flint is blue Upper Mercer with lighter inclusions. Ex-collection Dutcher, the blade is 3⅝" long. Fairfield County, Ohio. *Lar Hothem collection*. $100.00.

Uniface Paleo knives, longest 4¼", possible graver tips at smaller ends. They were found in San Bernardino County, California. *Michael Hough collection, California*. Each, $50.00 – 100.00.

Uniface blade, Paleo, 1⅞" x 3", light green flint. It was found by the owner in Wilson County, North Carolina. *Michael Womble collection, North Carolina.* $15.00.

Paleo uniface blade, Upper Mercer flint, 3⅜" long. The reverse face has fine edge retouch, and there are ripple marks from being struck off the parent core. Medina County, Ohio. *James Timoch collection, Ohio.* $75.00.

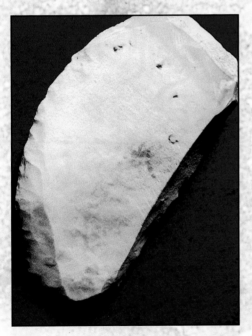

Uniface tool, scraper/knife excurvate edge, light tan and white Burlington. It measures 1¾" x 3⅛" and was a creek find by the owner. Jersey County, Illinois. *Collection of and photograph by Kevin Calvin, Illinois.* $40.00.

Uniface blade, excurvate edge and perforator tip, 1⅜" x 2³⁄₁₆", gray chert with tan specks. The owner found this artifact in Wilson County, North Carolina. *Michael Womble collection, North Carolina.* $15.00.

Uniface blade, 3" long, Burlington flint in several colors. It was found by the owner in a creek bed. Greene County, Illinois. *G. Slone collection; photograph by Kevin Calvin, Illinois.* $25.00.

Uniface flake knife, 1⅞" x 6½". This is a large and well-made blade, a classic Paleo artifact. The long dorsal flake scar indicates other blades were struck from the same original core. Of striped chert in gray, white, and tan, it was found by Duane Neal in a creek bed. Madison County, Illinois. *Collection of and photograph by Kevin Calvin, Illinois.* $300.00 – 400.00.

253

Uniface blade, 3" long, blue Upper Mercer flint. The long straight edge is beveled, the other edges have some retouch, and the base has a wide flute-like flake scar. Fairfield County, Ohio. *Lar Hothem collection*. $15.00.

Uniface blade, mixed Sonora flint, all edges worked. The knife is 3⅛" long and is from Kentucky. *Earthworks Artifacts*. $40.00.

Paleo uniface blades, gray nodular flint, longest 5½". These were found by Col. Raymond Vietzen during his exploration of Glover's Cave in Christian County, Kentucky. *Pete Timoch collection, Ohio*. Each, $100.00 – 200.00.

Paleo uniface flake knives, gray nodular flint, longest 5½". The ten were all found by Col. Vietzen when he excavated at Glover's Cave in Christian County, Kentucky. *Pete Timoch collection, Ohio*. Each, $100.00 – 200.00.

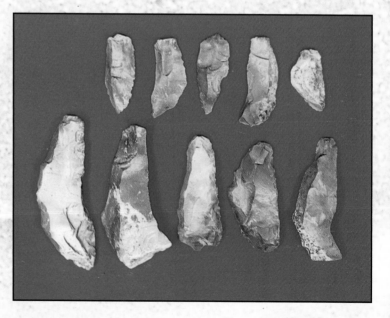

Paleo uniface knife, gray nodular flint, 4¾" long. The long beveled portion was the working edge. This piece was found in Glover's Cave by Col. Vietzen during his extensive explorations there. Christian County, Kentucky. *Pete Timoch collection, Ohio.* $200.00.

Paleo rectangular uniface blade, 4⅛" long, gray nodular flint. The bottom side edge was resharpened from the obverse face only. This piece was found by Col. Vietzen at Glover's Cave in Christian County, Kentucky. *Pete Timoch collection, Ohio.* $70.00.

Paleo flake knives, fluted, longest 2¾". The examples came from Glover's Cave, where they were excavated by Col. Vietzen. The left example has three flutes while the others have only one. Christian County, Kentucky. *Pete Timoch collection, Ohio.* Each, $100.00.

Uniface Paleo knives, slightly stemmed, longest 2⅞". Gray nodular Kentucky flint was used for these pieces, found by Col. Vietzen at Glover's Cave. Christian County, Kentucky. *Pete Timoch collection, Ohio.* Each, $100.00.

255

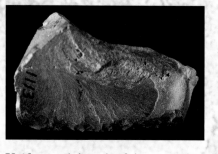

Paleo uniface blades, all made of nodular Kentucky flint. These were found by Col. Raymond C. Vietzen during his excavations at Glover's Cave. Christian County, Kentucky. Left, 5½", resharpening on top face only. $200.00. Center, top face resharpened only. $200.00. Right, large flake uniface. $150.00. *Pete Timoch collection, Ohio.*

Uniface tool, long knife/scraper edge, gray-tan chert, 2⅛" long. This sturdy Paleo artifact was found in Massachusetts. *Private collection.* $10.00.

Uniface tool, 1⅝" high, blue-black Upper Mercer flint. It has a scraper edge and two shaft-scrapers at the smaller end with graver tips on the corners. Coshocton County, Ohio. *Private collection.* $5.00.

Uniface tool, knife/scraper edge on longer side, U-shaped shaft-scraper at top left. This tool is 2" long and from Fairfield County, Ohio. *Private collection.* $8.00.

Paleo triangular biface, translucent Flint Ridge in shades of gray, 3⅜". The longest edge is carefully retouched from both faces. Ex-collection Champion, it is from Knox County, Ohio. *Private collection.* $125.00.

Uniface blade, mixed cream and gray Upper Mercer or Flint Ridge, 1⅝" x 3⅝". It has knife edges on the two long sides, and it was found in Fairfield County, Ohio. *Private collection.* $20.00.

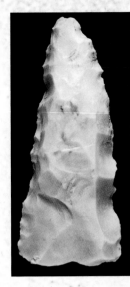

Uniface blade, gray Harrison County (Indiana) flint, 3¹⁄₁₆". Later Indians (see patina disturbance) did some rechipping on this piece and formed a shaft-scraper on the side edge. Ohio. *Private collection.* $20.00.

Triangular uniface blade, knife/scraper sides, milky Flint Ridge. It is 2¾" long, ex-collection Cooperrider, Perry County, Ohio. *Private collection.* $15.00.

Uniface blade, pale blue Upper Mercer, 3¼" long. The elongated flake was struck from a large core and has only minor edge retouch. Fairfield County, Ohio. *Lar Hothem collection.* $25.00.

Uniface blade, Paleo, made of layered Flint Ridge. A translucent light tan, the knife is 3¾". The bottom long working edge is chipped from both faces. Franklin County, Ohio. *Lar Hothem collection.* $30.00.

Uniface blade, translucent Flint Ridge, 2¹⁵⁄₁₆" long. The more rounded edge has careful retouch and probably served as a knife edge. Shelby County, Ohio. *Private collection.* $65.00.

Uniface knife, Flint Ridge mottled in two colors, 3¼" long. It has a flute on the obverse lower blade that is 1¼" long. (While this somewhat resembles a Woodland cache blade, only the outline is similar.) Bob Champion auction, 1985. Knox County, Ohio. *Lar Hothem collection*. $60.00.

Uniface stemmed blade, streaked dark Upper Mercer, 2⅜" long. This piece probably once had a handle, and the needle tip would have made it an effective knife. Mansfield area, Ohio. *Private collection*. $40.00.

Paleo uniface spokeshave, Harrison County (Indiana hornstone) flint. It is 3¼" long, from Spencer County, Indiana. *Private collection*. $40.00.

Uniface blade, deep blue Upper Mercer flint, 3¾" long. There is a triangular flute-like flake scar at one end of the top face. Pickaway County, Ohio. *Private collection*. $50.00.

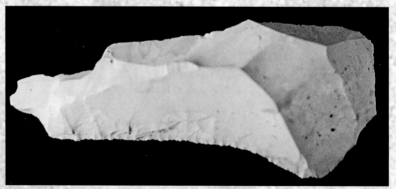

Uniface blade, long scraper or knife concave edge, patinated Flint Ridge. It is 4⅛" long and has several small shaft-scrapers on the wide end. Knox County, Ohio. *Private collection*. $35.00.

Uniface blade, creamy gray Upper Mercer flint, 3⅞". Both long dimensions have been chipped to form knife edges, and the wide end may have a sturdy graver tip. Knox County, Ohio. *Private collection*. $20.00.

Uniface blade, mixed Coshocton (Upper Mercer) flint, 4¼" long. It was found in Ohio, county unknown. *Mike Barron collection, Ohio.* $180.00.

Paleo flake tools, largest 5¼". All are made of glossy and high-grade flints, with top and bottom from Kentucky and middle example from Alabama. *Private collection, Kentucky.* Each, $50.00 – 150.00.

Paleo uniface blade, of blue, tan, and cream Upper Mercer, irregular shape that conforms to the original large flake struck from a core. It is 4½" long and from Fairfield County, Ohio. *Private collection.* $25.00.

Uniface blade, 3¼", blue Upper Mercer flint. This piece has knife edges and a graver tip, and hafting stem to right. It was found by Col. Vietzen in Lorain County, Ohio. *Joel Embrey collection.* $50.00.

Paleo uniface blade tools, largest 4" long. They are made of different shades of glossy Kentucky hornstone, and all have good edgework. They are personal finds of the owner in Kentucky. *Private collection, Kentucky.* Each, $100.00 – 175.00.

259

Uniface tool, Upper Mercer in cream tan, and gray, 2⅛" long. Possibly used as a scraper, it is ex-collection Vietzen, from Ashland County, Ohio. *Joel Embrey collection*. $20.00.

Flake knife, Flint Ridge pale translucent material, 2¼". The long straight edge has delicate retouch and a graver tip, while the opposite short straight edge has almost microscopic retouch. Central Ohio. *Private collection*. $10.00.

Multipurpose uniface blade, 2¾". It has a knife edge, scraper side and scraper base, plus a graver tip. Probably Delaware County flint, it is from Ohio. *Private collection*. $20.00.

Uniface blade, gray flint patinated to tan, double overlapping flutes on obverse base. It is 3⅜" long, from Fairfield County, Ohio. *Joel Embrey collection*. $25.00.

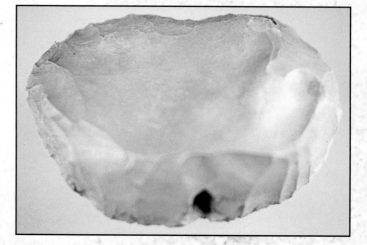

Paleo bladelet, with retouched edges, dorsal ridge, 4¾", unknown flint or chert. This example was found in Ohio. *Private collection*. $100.00 plus.

Uniface scraper/chopper, light tan chert, with one side edge beveled and the other chipped from both faces. One of the larger Paleo tools known, it is 5⅜" long. Dougherty County, Georgia. *Larry Garvin collection*. Unlisted.

Uniface blade, jewel translucent Flint Ridge, 2⅝" long. The excurvate edge has been broken and ground off. Licking County, Ohio. *Private collection*. $10.00.

Uniface blade, high-grade mixed cream, tan, and blue Flint Ridge, fine edgework. It is 2¾" long and was found in Knox County, Ohio. *Private collection*. $40.00.

MULTIPURPOSE ARTIFACTS

There are three main reasons why multipurpose tools were widely employed in Paleo times. One reason could hold true throughout all of North American prehistory, and that is the handiness or convenience factor. After all, if one tool serves two or more purposes, there was no need to make, keep, or search for two or more tools.

Despite evidence that in the Late Paleo more settled living styles developed, much of the Paleo lifeway was probably mobile — not constant travel, but periodic moves in search of food and firewood and shelter. With multipurpose artifacts, fewer tools needed to be stored or carried.

High-grade chert and flint sources were not always immediately available, so the use of already at-hand materials made very good sense. That is, the better the material, the better the tool and the more efficiently it could be used. Good grades were needed for most Paleo tools, and multipurpose tools in these materials chipped easily and held edges. When existence itself depended on material selection, one selected well.

Multipurpose tools (sometimes called combination tools) often have one or two long edges that were retouched. Acute edges may have been used as knives and steeply angled edges may have served as scrapers. Elongated tools may terminate in an end-scraper or graver tip.

Any multipurpose tool with a tip longer than about ⅛ to ¼ inch was probably a perforator for skins or leather. Anything shorter was probably a graver for incising bone or antler to make other tools. Burins are sometimes small and separate flake artifacts, but spokeshaves of several kinds may be on a multipurpose tool.

Combination tool, with graver tip and two knife or scraper edges. Made of Normanskill chert, it came from Massachusetts. *Fogelman collection.* $35.00.

Combination tool, end-scraper with side-scraper or knife edges, reddish jasper. The Paleo artifact was found in Pennsylvania. *Fogelman collection.* $55.00.

Combination Paleo tool, flake knife with two excurvate edges and a spokeshave. Made of jasper, it is from Lehigh County, Pennsylvania. *Fogelman collection.* $25.00.

261

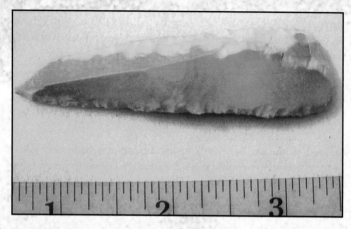

Multipurpose tool, with end-scraper, scraper/knife has long edges and graver tip at small end. This classic Paleo artifact is made of Pennsylvania age chert, provenance unlisted. *Jim Horst collection, Nebraska.* $75.00.

Uniface multipurpose tool, blue Upper Mercer, 2⅛". It has a graver tip at bottom and shaft-scrapers on both sides. Coshocton County, Ohio. *Private collection.* $10.00.

Paleo multipurpose tool, blue and cream Upper Mercer, 2¼". It has an end-scraper at bottom and staggered shaft-scrapers on both sides. Coshocton County, Ohio. *Private collection.* $20.00.

Combination tool, tan and cream Flint Ridge, 3¾". It is an end-scraper and a perforator, and the right side has an edge. It is ex-collection McClelland, from Licking County, Ohio. *Private collection.* $75.00.

Multipurpose tool, 2⅜" long. It has a graver tip, scraper (steeply angled) side, and chipped shallow shaft-scraper. Of blue-streaked Upper Mercer, it is from Fairfield County, Ohio. *Private collection.* $10.00.

Multipurpose Paleo tool, possible shaft-scraper in one edge and graver tip at end. Provenance unlisted. *Jim Horst collection, Nebraska.* $20.00.

Paleo knife/scraper combination, Boone flint, ex-collection Lee Adams. It came from the Springfield area, Missouri. *Jim Horst collection, Nebraska.* $100.00.

Combination tool, end-scraper and side-scraper edges, Normanskill chert. This multipurpose tool was found in Massachusetts. *Fogelman collection.* $50.00.

Paleo scraper and knife combination, duckbill type, blue Carter Cave flint. Size is 1¾" x 2⅞", and the artifact came from southern Kentucky. *Bybee collection, Kenucky; Tom Davis photograph.* $45.00.

Multipurpose tool, end-scraper and perforator/reamer, sides with knife or scraper edges. It is 4⁹⁄₁₆" long and of tan, cream, and brown patinated Flint Ridge. The Paleo tool was obtained at a farm auction in 2002. Coshocton County, Ohio. *Jesse Weber collection; photograph by Norman's Photo, Newcomerstown, Ohio.* $150.00.

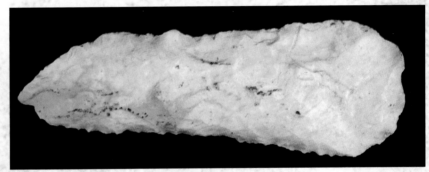

Paleo multipurpose tools, largest 1½" x 2⅛". All were found by Harwood in 1956. Morgan County, Alabama. *Collection of and photograph by Gary Henry, North Carolina.* Each, $3.00 – 10.00.

Multipurpose tool, excurvate edge and spokeshave, banded white and tan flint that is probably Carter Cave. It is 1⅜" x 1⅞" and came from an Ohio River site. West Virginia. *Private collection; Rodney Roberts photograph.* $20.00.

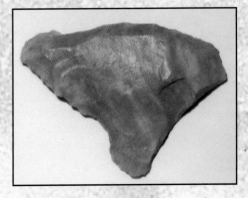

263

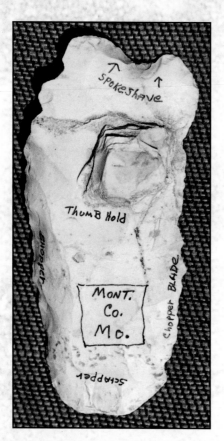

Spokeshave

Thumb Hold

Chopper

Chopper Blade

Mont. Co. Mo.

Scraper

Multipurpose tool, Paleo, 2" x 4¼". Left and right edges are worked, and the bottom is an end-scraper. The top has a spokeshave. The piece was found in Montgomery County, Missouri. *Bob Rampani collection, Missouri.* $40.00.

Uniface blade, with well-defined spokeshave, 2⅝" x 2⅞". Burlington in red, brown, and tan was used for this tool, found in a rock shelter. Montgomery County, Missouri. *Bob Rampani collection, Missouri.* $45.00.

Multipurpose tool, end-scraper, side-scrapers, spokeshave, graver tip. Made of light tan Flint Ridge, it measures ⅞" x 1¾" and came from an Ohio River site. West Virginia. *Private collection; Rodney Roberts photograph.* $20.00.

Paleo tool, blue and white flint with basal grinding, 1½" x 2½". This piece has a needle tip, a shaft-scraper, and a graver tip at the base corner. It was found by the owner in Missouri. *Jim McKinney collection, Missouri; Mary Jane Wieberg photograph.* Unlisted.

Multipurpose tool, with gravers and spokeshaves, 1⅛" x 1¼". Light green flint with darker inclusions was used for this tool, which is from an Ohio River site. West Virginia. *Private collection; Rodney Roberts photograph.* $15.00.

Multipurpose tool, with three gravers and several scraper edges. The material is an unknown light green flint with tan spots. This artifact is 1⅛" x 1⅜" and came from an Ohio River Valley site. West Virginia. *Private collection; Rodney Roberts photograph.* $15.00.

Uniface Paleo multipurpose tools, longest 2¾". Upper Mercer and Flint Ridge materials were used for these artifacts, which have thick bases and perforator tips. These came from central Ohio. *Pete Timoch collection, Ohio.* Each, $40.00.

Paleo uniface multipurpose tool, Dover flint, 2⅞" long. In addition to delicate edge retouch for the sides and tip, the artifact has a small graver and a concave spokeshave. Eastern Tennessee. *Pete Timoch collection, Ohio.* $100.00.

Paleo multipurpose tool, Kentucky hornstone, 2⅝" long. The top face is finely chipped on both long edges, and a short burin tip is present. Western Kentucky. *Pete Timoch collection, Ohio.* $100.00.

Uniface blade, with end-scraper and side shaft-scraper, 3⅜". Made of creamy Flint Ridge, it was found in Fairfield County, Ohio. *Private collection.* $40.00.

Uniface multipurpose tool, reverse, Foraker chert. As is typical for uniface tools, very little edgework was done on the reverse. *Jim Horst collection, Nebraska.* $75.00.

Uniface multipurpose tool, obverse, Foraker permian chert. It has an end-scraper, two long working edges, and a graver tip. Provenance unlisted. *Jim Horst collection, Nebraska.* $75.00.

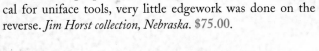

Uniface multipurpose tool, with end-scraper, graver tip, and two sizes of shaft-scrapers. Of translucent Flint Ridge, it is 1⅞" long. Central Ohio. *Private collection.* $10.00.

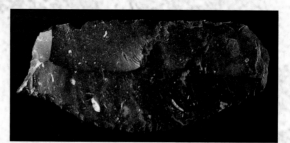

Paleo multipurpose tool, straight and excurvate knife edges, prominent graver tip. Made of black Upper Mercer, it is 2⅞" long and from Fairfield County, Ohio. *Private collection*. $75.00.

Multipurpose tool, perforator(?) with tip ground flat, 4½" long. The base side has graver tip at two levels. Gray and brown Upper Mercer, the tool came from Holmes County, Ohio. *Private collection*. $50.00.

Uniface multipurpose tool, knife or scraper edges and shaft-scraper at larger end, 2⅛" long. The material is local, Fairfield County orange, which may be bog-patinated Upper Mercer. Fairfield County, Ohio. *Private collection*. $15.00.

Uniface tool, end-scraper and knife edge with graver tip, 1½" x 2¹⁄₁₆". The tool is of tan Burlington, and the owner found this example in a creek. Jersey County, Illinois. *Collection of and photograph by Kevin Calvin, Illinois.* $25.00.

Multipurpose tool, with long graver or perforator, end-scraper, and spokeshave. Made of amber Flint Ridge, it is 1" x 1⅜". It came from an Ohio River Valley site. West Virginia. *Private collection; Rodney Roberts photograph.* $25.00.

Uniface tool, blue mottled Upper Mercer, 2⅝". It has a knife edge and chipped-in shaft-scraper on the same side. Coshocton County, Ohio. *Private collection*. $12.00.

Uniface tool, excurvate scraper edge with shaft-scraper, 2¹⁵⁄₁₆". Light brown Delaware County flint was used for this piece, found in Coshocton County, Ohio. *Private collection*. $30.00.

Uniface flake tool, with possible graver tip, mixed Onondaga grays, 1½". It was found in Schoharie County, New York. *Dave Summers collection, New York*. $25.00.

Multipurpose tool, consisting of a cutter, side-scraper, and graver tip. The artifact is 2" long and of Pennsylvania butterscotch jasper. Made from a radial flake, it came from the Sacandaga River area, Hamilton County, New York. *Dave Summers collection, New York*. $50.00.

Multipurpose tool, crescent shaped, blue-gray Whitehall flint. It is 1¾" long and of uniface construction. The inner edge is worked and steep. Schoharie County, New York. *Dave Summers collection, New York*. $60.00.

Multipurpose tool, end-scraper and graver tip, 1¾" x 2⅞". Of Upper Mercer gray flint, it came from the Cortland area, Trumbull County, Ohio. *Pat Layshock collection; Thomas R. Pigott image*. $50.00.

Combination tool, fossiliferous chert, 1" x 3½". It has knife edges, a shaft-scraper end, and a graver tip. The tool was found by the owner in Monroe County, Indiana. *Collection of and photograph by Jon Hunsberger, Indiana*. $40.00.

Combination tool, side-scraper and graver tip, mixed gray Onondaga. It is 1¾" and the fluted top may indicate that previous blades were taken from the core. Orleans County, New York. *Dave Summers collection, New York*. $25.00.

Uniface tool, colorful unknown flint, 1½" x 2½". It has two scraper edges and two probable graver tips. Found by the owner, it came from Monroe County, Indiana. *Collection of and photograph by Jon Hunsberger, Indiana*. $15.00.

Uniface tool, blue-gray Harrison County flint, ¾" x 3½". It has a concave scraper edge and probable worn graver tip. The owner found the artifact in Monroe County, Indiana. *Collection of and photograph by Jon Hunsberger, Indiana*. $100.00.

Uniface blade, unknown greenish with red chert, 1¼" x 2½". The owner found this Paleo artifact in Monroe County, Indiana. *Collection of and photograph by Jon Hunsberger, Indiana*. $35.00.

Uniface blade, Harrison County flint with cortex at smaller end, 1½" x 3". It has at least one graver tip at the corner of the wide end. A personal find by the owner, it came from Monroe County, Indiana. *Collection of and photograph by Jon Hunsberger, Indiana*. $45.00.

PALEO TOOLS

Not surprisingly, and with a single exception, Paleo tools tell us much about their purposes, reflecting certain aspects of Paleo life. The exception is drills, and their purpose is largely unknown. These were not used for drilling stone or slate, as in the later Archaic, and most examples do not have heavy use wear. Suggestions include use as hairpins and clothing toggles, but other objects would have served as well or better.

Perforators — drill-like, but shorter and sometimes with asymmetrical bases, were likely used as awls for holing leather and furs. Gravers are short, sturdy tips that probably scored bone and antler so they could be broken apart for points and needles. A flake or artifact may have from one to several graver tips. Shaft-scrapers (semi-circular depressions) are often seen on flaked or multipurpose tools. These were shaped either by chipping or (partially) by edge-snapping.

End-scrapers are quite common on Paleo sites, and they each have a rounded and beveled working edge. Some also have graver spurs on one or both corners of the edge. Both types probably worked hides before they were tanned, though close examination indicates some end-scraper edges have polish from working wood. Side-scrapers are also common, and they may have served the same purpose.

Hafted shapers were made from broken Paleo points, and the break area was sometimes smoothed to form two strong edges, perhaps used for woodworking. Burin tips were sometimes shaped on the break-area corners. Wedges, made from thick flakes or split end-scrapers, were probably used for wedging antler or bone. Each break-snapped flake provided fresh and sharp working edges, while the tips served as perforators or gravers.

Though smaller tools lack the visual impact of many other Paleo artifacts, they are well worth collecting. They explain (or at least hint at) what took place around the campfires ten thousand and more years ago.

Paleo uniface tool, 2³⁄₁₆" long, concave scraper/knife edge and two graver tips. Made of light tan striped flint, it was found in a creek bed by Duane Neal. Jersey County, Illinois. *Collection of and photograph by Kevin Calvin, Illinois.* $30.00.

Paleo scraper, 1³⁄₈" x 1⁷⁄₈", white Burlington flint. The owner found this tool in a creek bed. Jersey County, Illinois. *Collection of and photograph by Kevin Calvin, Illinois.* $30.00.

Paleo uniface scraper, 1¹¹⁄₁₆" x 1⁷⁄₈", light gray and white banded flint. Nicely made, it was found by the owner in a creek bed. Jersey County, Illinois. *Collection of and photograph by Kevin Calvin, Illinois.* $30.00.

Uniface tool, scraper end with graver tip, 1⅜" x 2½". Tan Burlington was used for this piece, found by the owner in a creek bed. Jersey County, Illinois. *Collection of and photograph by Kevin Calvin, Illinois.* $40.00.

Hand celt, probably Paleo, 2⅝" x 3¾". Made of Dover flint, it was found by J. D. Strain in 2003. Benton County, Tennessee. *Bob Rantz collection, Indiana; Steve Weisser photograph.* $50.00.

Flute spall (shown elsewhere in book), placed on Clovis preform base. While the spall is not from this particular preform, the positioning illustrates the place of removal. The base is 2½" long, and both base and spall are of Burlington. Western Bluff area, Jersey County, Illinois. *Gregory L. Perdun collection, Illinois.* Each, $10.00 – 20.00.

Tools made of flute spalls from Clovis preforms, largest and smallest unifaced. The two largest (left, 2¼") are of Burlington, the smallest of Fern Glen flint. Western Bluff area, Jersey County, Illinois. *Gregory L. Perdun collection, Illinois.* Each, $10.00 – 20.00.

End-scrapers, with graver spurs, Burlington chert, largest 1½". Graver spurs on end-scrapers were only made in Paleo times. Western Bluff area, Jersey County, Illinois. *Gregory L. Perdun collection, Illinois.* Each, $15.00.

Paleo tools, scrapers, gravers, and spokeshaves. All were found in Henderson County, Illinois. *Fred Smith collection, Illinois.* All, $30.00 – 50.00.

Adzes, probably Dalton and Late Paleo, Cedar Creek flint, largest 2½" x 4¼". These were found as a cache in Warren County, Illinois. *Fred Smith collection, Illinois.* Each, $75.00 – 100.00.

Lanceolate section, with scraper edge, mixed gray, blue, and tan Onondaga flint. Ex-collection Whipple, it is 1⁹⁄₁₀" long. Niagara County, New York. *Dave Summers collection, New York.* $25.00.

End-scraper, thumbnail type, Onondaga in light grays, 1½". It was found in New York state. *Dave Summers collection, New York.* $20.00.

Drill or perforator, with use wear, 3¹³⁄₁₆", purchased by the owner at an estate sale. Tazewell County, Illinois. *Fred Smith collection, Illinois.* $150.00 – 175.00.

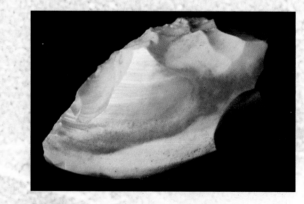

Rounded core for blade strike-offs, specked light gray Onondaga, greatest dimension 2¹⁄₂₀". It is from east-central New York. *Dave Summers collection, New York.* $60.00.

Scraper, nodular Harrison County flint with some remaining cortex, 1" x 2¼". Found by the owner, it came from Monroe County, Indiana. *Collection of and photograph by Jon Hunsberger, Indiana.* $7.00.

Scraper, unknown colorful flint, 1¼" across. It is ⅜" thick and was found by the owner. Monroe County, Indiana. *Collection of and photograph by Jon Huns-berger, Indiana.* $7.00.

Drills, probably Paleo, longest 3¼". Top, tan fossiliferous chert; bottom, Harrison County flint. They were found by the owner in Monroe County, Indiana. *Collection of and photograph by Jon Hunsberger, Indiana.* Each, $50.00.

Paleo tools, with graver tips, longest 2". Top, Indian Creek flint; others are fossiliferous cherts. These were personal finds by the owner in Monroe County, Indiana. *Collection of and photograph by Jon Hunsberger, Indiana.* Unlisted.

Drills, probably Paleo, fossiliferous cherts. Some drills like these were made from lanceolate blades. Both drills are 3" long and were found by the owner. Monroe County, Indiana. *Collection of and photograph by Jon Hunsberger, Indiana.* Each, $75.00.

Drills, probably Paleo, largest ½" x 3⅜". The top example is chert with fossils, while the bottom is Harrison County flint. They were found by the owner in Monroe County, Indiana. *Collection of and photograph by Jon Hunsberger, Indiana.* Each, $75.00.

Drill, probably Paleo, tan and light green fossiliferous chert. It is 3" long and was picked up by the owner in Monroe County, Indiana. *Collection of and photograph by Jon Hunsberger, Indiana.* $75.00.

271

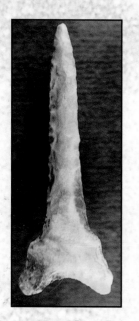

Dalton drill, Late Paleo, Burlington chert. This tool measures 3" long and was found in Missouri. *Christopher Smith collection, New York.* $175.00.

Dalton blade, heavily resharpened, serrated edges. This Dalton is 2¼" long and from Arkansas. *Christopher Smith collection, New York.* $150.00.

Dalton drill, Late Paleo, Flint Ridge in mixed colors. It is 2⅛" long and from Ohio. *Christopher Smith collection, New York.* $175.00.

Drill, Holland or Dalton family, 2⅝". The drill was probably made from a larger blade and still retains the shouldering. Chipped in Burlington, it is from Missouri. *Christopher Smith collection, New York.* $200.00.

Paleo borer tool, mixed blue and gray Helderberg, 1¾". It came from Albany County, New York. *Dave Summers collection, New York.* $25.00.

Drill, probably Late Paleo, mixed chert or flint. It is 4¼" long and has ground basal edges. Mason County, Kentucky. *Christopher Smith collection, New York.* $400.00.

Paleo tool, borer or graver tip, black Lockport flint. It is 1⅘" and from the Erie/Genesee counties area, New York. *Dave Summers collection, New York.* $25.00.

Paleo drill, Burlington chert, 2" long. The example came from Missouri. *Christopher Smith collection, New York.* $125.00.

Paleo artifacts, both from southern Illinois. Left, end-scraper with chipped-in graver spur, translucent cream and maroon flint, 1⅜". $12.00. Right, stemmed lance with two graver spurs, Indiana hornstone. $15.00. *Private collection.*

272

Fluted Paleo drill, Upper Mercer mixed black flint, 1" x 3⅛". Fluted drills are quite scarce, and this example is from near Newton Falls, Trumbull County, Ohio. *Pat Layshock collection; Thomas R. Pigott image.* $250.00.

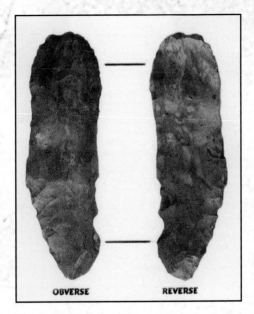

OBVERSE   REVERSE

Tri-faced bladelet, Upper Mercer mottled gray flint, ⅞" x 3". Such blades often are not found complete, as they are quite fragile. This example was found by William Platt near Cortland, Trumbull County, Ohio. *Pat Layshock collection; Thomas R. Pigott image.* $50.00.

Cache lanceolate or preform, butterscotch Pennsylvania jasper, 4" long. This large artifact came from eastern New York. *Dave Summers collection, New York.* $85.00.

Paleo flake tool, retouched edges, 2½". Made of mixed gray Onondaga, it came from Ontario County, New York. *Dave Summers collection, New York.* $10.00.

End-scraper, 2⁵⁄₁₆" long, glossy Flint Ridge. The size, fine material, and find location suggest a Paleo origin. Coshocton County, Ohio. *Private collection.* $25.00.

Paleo bladelet, irregular and nearly serrated edges, tan Delaware County flint. The bladelet is triangular in cross section and is 2¹³⁄₁₆" long. Perry County, Ohio. *Lar Hothem collection.* $25.00.

Paleo drill/perforator, salvaged Keiser blade, 1⅜". One or both shoulders were chipped into graver tips. Tuscarawas County, Ohio. *Private collection.* $20.00.

End-scraper, on a true blade (previous blade strike-off scars can be seen on the obverse face), Paleo, 1⅝". This scraper also has a worn graver tip on the scraper edge corner. Fairfield County, Ohio. *Private collection.* $10.00.

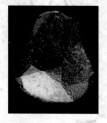

End-scraper, with graver at side, near-black speckled Upper Mercer. It is 1⅛", from central Ohio. *Private collection.* $7.00.

End-scraper, with graver tip and side shaft-scraper, 1⅝". The base is fluted on this Flint Ridge piece, found in central Ohio. *Private collection.* $7.00.

End-scraper, with graver tip, translucent high-grade Upper Mercer or Flint Ridge, 1⅝" long. It was found in Tuscarawas County, Ohio. *Private collection.* $10.00.

End-scraper, glossy black Zaleski flint, 1⅛" wide. There is a rounded graver tip on the right side, and the steep beveled scraper edge suggests this artifact was much-used and resharpened. Ohio. *Private collection.* $5.00.

Biface tool, Flint Ridge mixed caramel, 3¾" long. A large shaft-scraper was chipped on the lower edge. Ohio. *Private collection.* $20.00.

End-scraper, with fluted top at base, brown jasper-like flint. This Paleo tool is 2⁷⁄₁₆" long and is probably from Coshocton County, Ohio. *Private collection.* $25.00.

Drill or perforator, on a uniface flake, pinkish unknown chert with solution cavities. It is 2" long and from Ohio. *Private collection.* $8.00.

End-scraper, with small graver tips, mixed tan Flint Ridge. This artifact is 1¼" high and was picked up in Coshocton County, Ohio. *Lar Hothem collection.* $12.00.

End-scraper, with side graver, tan flint or chert, ¹⁵⁄₁₆" x 1¾". The example was found on a site along the Ohio River. West Virginia. *Private collection; Rodney Roberts photograph.* $15.00.

End-scraper, with graver spurs, tan flint, 1⅛" x 1⅛". Found on an Ohio River site, it is from West Virginia. *Private collection; Rodney Roberts photograph.* $10.00.

End-scraper, with two graver spurs, angular form, red jasper, 1¼" x 1⅜". From a site along the Ohio River, it is from West Virginia. *Private collection; Rodney Roberts photograph.* $15.00.

Paleo end-scraper, with hooked graver and scraper edges on sides, dorsal flute, 1⁵⁄₁₆" x 2⁷⁄₁₆". Made of black flint, it came from along the Ohio River. West Virginia. *Private collection; Rodney Roberts photograph.* $20.00.

Paleo tool, of gray, blue, and black Onondaga, ⅘" long. This is a *piece esquillee*, probably used as a wedge for splitting wood or bone. It is from Yates County, New York. *Dave Summers collection, New York.* $15.00.

End-scraper, on flake, gray and tan Onondaga, 1¹⁹⁄₂₀". Retouched along one edge, it is from Erie County, New York. *Dave Summers collection, New York.* $15.00.

Drill or perforator, possibly on a lanceolate base, two flutes on obverse, pink flint with fossils. The artifact is ¾" x 1⅞" and was found in Ohio. *Private collection; Rodney Roberts photograph.* $25.00.

Beak or lancet, honey Flint Ridge with dark inclusions, ¹⁵⁄₁₆" x 1⁷⁄₁₆". It was found on a site along the Ohio River. West Virginia. *Private collection; Rodney Roberts photograph.* $10.00.

End-scraper, double spurs, Flint Ridge near-maroon, 1¼" x 1⁵⁄₁₆". It is from the Ohio River Valley, West Virginia. *Private collection; Rodney Roberts photograph.* $15.00.

End-scraper, double spurs, Flint Ridge honey with red, 1⁵⁄₁₆" x 1⁵⁄₁₆". It was found in the Ohio River area. West Virginia. *Private collection; Rodney Roberts photograph.* $15.00.

End-scraper, with graver spur, black Kanawha flint, 1¼" x 1⅜". It was picked up on an Ohio River site. West Virginia. *Private collection; Rodney Roberts photograph.* $15.00.

End-scraper, with perforator or graver, Carter County flint, 1¹⁄₁₆" x 1¹⁄₁₆". The Paleo tool came from an Ohio River site. West Virginia. *Private collection; Rodney Roberts photograph.* $15.00.

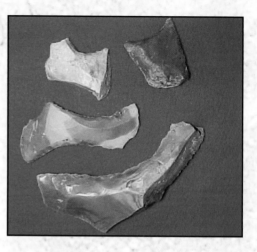

Spokeshaves, longest example 3½". These were all found by the same person, on one site and over several years of surface hunting. Clark County, Kentucky. *Jeff Schumacher collection, Kentucky.* Each, $8.00 – 40.00.

Blade, with shaft-scraper, 2" long and ¼" thick, white flint. It was found by the owner in Stone County, Missouri. *Curtis Chisam collection, Missouri.* $10.00.

Paleo blade or preform, 2⅞" long and ¼" thick. Found by the owner, it is made of white flint. Stone County, Missouri. *Curtis Chisam collection, Missouri.* $20.00.

Fluted preform(?), Paleo, 2⅛". Tan flint was used for this piece, found by the owner in Ozark County, Missouri. *Curtis Chisam collection, Missouri.* Unlisted.

Drill, Dalton family, 4¾", of high-grade milky and yellow Burlington with a red band. Mr. Roberts reports, "Best piece of flint I've ever found." It was picked up in Clark County, Missouri. *Dale and Betty Roberts collection, Iowa.* Museum grade.

End-scraper, with large and rounded spur, black flint, 1" x 1⅜". The tool was found on an Ohio River site. West Virginia. *Private collection; Rodney Roberts photograph.* $12.00.

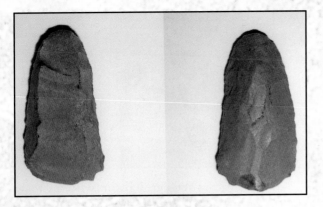

End-scraper, fluted on one face, tan flint. The tool is ⅞" x 1¹¹⁄₁₆" and came from an Ohio River site. West Virginia. *Private collection; Rodney Roberts photograph.* $20.00.

End-scraper, milky Burlington chert, 2⅜" long. It came from the Western Bluff area, Jersey County, Illinois. *Gregory L. Perdun collection, Illinois.* $10.00 – 20.00.

Paleo drill or perforator, uncertain material but similar to Chouteau flint, 2¹⁄₁₆". It came from Jersey County, Illinois. *Gregory L. Perdun collection, Illinois.* $85.00.

Stemmed tool, chisel-like opposite edge, ⅝" x 1⅝". Pink Flint Ridge was used for the artifact, found in the Ohio River Valley. West Virginia. *Private collection; Rodney Roberts photograph.* $45.00.

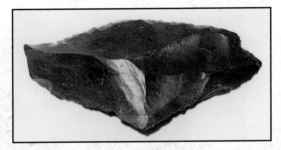

Uniface tool, with three graver tips, black flint, 1⁷⁄₁₆" x 2¹³⁄₁₆" It came from a site along the Ohio River. West Virginia. *Private collection; Rodney Roberts photograph.* $25.00.

Paleo end-scraper, with graver spurs, 1³⁄₁₆" x 2¾", green flint. It was found by the owner's father-in-law, Sam Jenkins, on an Ohio River Valley site. *Private collection; Rodney Roberts photograph.* $30.00.

Lanceolate, salvaged to become a large scraper with spokeshave, gray Deepkill flint. It is 2⅘" and from Schoharie County, New York. *Dave Summers collection, New York.* $50.00.

Beaked tool, on prismatic blade, cream fossil coral, 3¹⁄₂₀". It has use signs and is from Florida. *Dave Summers collection, New York.* $20.00.

Multiple graver, one tip missing, 1¹⁄₁₀". Made of gray Upper Mercer, it may be from Ohio. *Dave Summers collection, New York.* $20.00.

End-scraper made from broken lanceolate, black Leray flint, 1⁹⁄₁₀". Hudson Valley, New York. *Dave Summers collection, New York.* $10.00.

End-scraper, maroon New England jasper, 1²⁄₅" long. One side is almost vertical on this piece, from Albany County, New York. *Dave Summers collection, New York.* $15.00.

Uniface flake knife, Little Falls light gray flint, 2⁴⁄₅". It may have come from eastern New York state. *Dave Summers collection, New York.* $15.00.

End-scraper with snapped base, of gray, tan, and red Onondaga, 1⁹⁄₂₀". This tool was found in the Hudson Valley, New York. *Dave Summers collection, New York.* $15.00.

Paleo scraper, end and side edges, 1¹⁷⁄₂₀". It is of layered gray material, and its provenance is unknown. *Dave Summers collection, New York.* $10.00.

End-scraper, white Flint Ridge, 1¹⁹⁄₂₀". Paleo origin is indicated by size and high-quality material. It was found in western New York. *Dave Summers collection, New York.* $50.00.

Fluted side-scraper, mixed gray-tan Onondaga, 1¹⁷⁄₂₀". Ex-collection Whipple, it shows much wear. Genesee County, New York. *Dave Summers collection, New York.* $35.00.

Uniface scraper, light mixed Onondaga, 2³⁄₅". It was found in Muskingum County, Ohio. *Dave Summers collection, New York.* $25.00.

End-scraper, keeled or dorsal ridge, mottled gray Onondaga, 1³⁄₂₀". It possibly came from western New York. *Dave Summers collection, New York.* $10.00.

Flake tool, multiple graver tips and spokeshaves, 1³⁄₁₀". Of mottled gray and tan Onondaga, it is from western New York. *Dave Summers collection, New York.* $15.00.

Scraper, unusual fossiferous flint or chert, 1" across. A personal find by the owner, it is from Monroe County, Indiana. *Collection of and photograph by Jon Hunsberger, Indiana.* $7.00.

Paleo bladelet, blue-tan fossiliferous chert, 15/16" x 3". It was picked up by the owner in Monroe County, Indiana. *Collection of and photograph by Jon Hunsberger, Indiana.* $20.00.

Paleo bladelet, Indiana hornstone, 15/16" x 25/8". This tool was found by the owner in Monroe County, Indiana. *Collection of and photograph by Jon Hunsberger, Indiana.* $20.00.

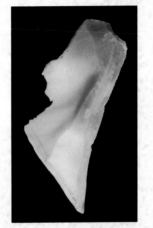

Scraper or knife, nodular Harrison County flint, 1½" across, 3/8" thick. This tool, with tan cortex, was found by the owner in Monroe County, Indiana. *Collection of and photograph by Jon Hunsberger, Indiana.* $15.00.

Paleo lancet or beaked blade, uniface, chipped on both excurvate and straight edges. Made of Flint Ridge, it is 1 15/16" long. Fairfield County, Ohio. *Lar Hothem collection.* $20.00.

Paleo tool, perforator on uniface blade, tip chipped on the short straight edge. Translucent Flint Ridge was used for this example, 2¼" long. Licking County, Ohio. *Lar Hothem collection.* $10.00.

Flake tool, with two graver tips, of artifact Ridge, 1¼" long. This type is sometimes called a coronet because of the crown-like shape of the graver portion. Fairfield County, Ohio. *Private collection.* $10.00.

Flake tool, creamy Flint Ridge, 1¼" long. The artifact has two graver or perforator tips, and the artifact was found in Ohio. *Private collection.* $8.00.

Late Paleo stemmed tool, small flute on obverse is 11/16" long, overall length is 2 7/8". Of gray and white Flint Ridge, it was found in Fairfield County, Ohio. *Private collection.* $40.00.

End-scraper, from Paleo site, greenish-black Upper Mercer. The scraper is 1 7/8" long and nearly ½" thick. Tuscarawas County, Ohio. *Lar Hothem collection.* $7.00.

Paleo bladelet, triangular cross section, dark blue Upper Mercer. The bladelet is 2⁷⁄₁₆" and from Coshocton County, Ohio. *Lar Hothem collection.* $20.00.

Dalton drill, Late Paleo, Burlington chert, ½" x 1¾". The drill came from a plowed field in Holt County, Missouri. *Mike George collection, Missouri; Terry Price photograph.* $50.00.

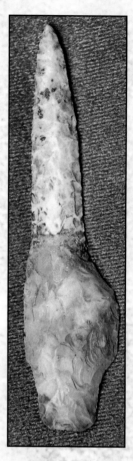

Clovis preforms, Cattail Creek chalcedony. The top row (with color) was heat-treated, while the bottom row was not. These are from Dinwiddie County, Virginia. *Rodney M. Peck collection, North Carolina.* Each, $10.00.

Knife or perforator, broken and glued, probably Late Paleo. It is ¾" x 4½" and has a well-ground stem. The artifact was found by the owner in Maries County, Missouri. *Jim McKinney collection, Missouri; Mary Jane Wieberg photograph.* Unlisted.

Paleo lancets or thin knives. These are made of quartzite, oolitic quartzite, and Cattail Creek chalcedony, and are from a Paleo site in Dinwiddie County, Virginia. *Rodney M. Peck collection, North Carolina.* Each, $10.00 – 15.00.

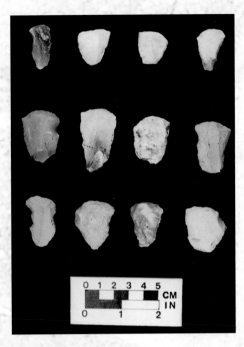

Snubnose end-scrapers, some with graver tips and spokeshaves. All are from a noted Paleo site in Dinwiddie County, Virginia. *Rodney M. Peck collection, North Carolina.* Each, $8.00 – 15.00.

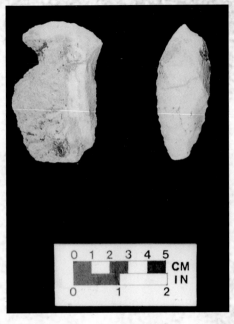

Uniface tools, end-scraper (left) and side-scraper with graver (right). They are made of Cattail Creek chalcedony and came from a Paleo site in Dinwiddie County, Virginia. *Rodney M. Peck collection, North Carolina.* Each, $10.00 – 15.00.

Uniface scraper, white Lockport flint, $2^{17}/_{20}$" long. Ex-collection Whipple, it was found in Orleans County, New York. *Dave Summers collection, New York.* $80.00.

Flake blade, with heavy use polish, gray-tan Onondaga, $1^{19}/_{20}$" long. The tool came from Monroe County, New York. *Dave Summers collection, New York.* $10.00.

Prismatic chisel, of gray, tan, and blue Onondaga, 3" long. The tool is ex-collection Whipple and from Genesee County, New York. *Dave Summers collection, New York.* $60.00.

281

Bladelet, tan Flint Ridge, 1⁹⁄₁₀". Edges show heavy use on this piece, which is from Ontario County, New York. *Dave Summers collection, New York.* $20.00.

Plane, gray-tan Onondaga. The artifact is 4³⁄₂₀" long, ex-collection Whipple. Orleans County, New York. *Dave Summers collection, New York.* $50.00.

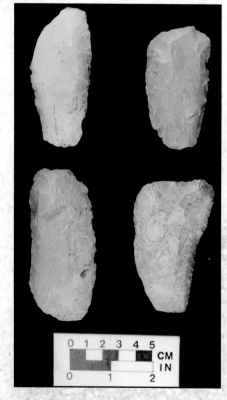

Clovis preforms, both exhibiting reverse hinge fractures that broke the preform. Made of Hopkinsville chert, they are from the Little River Clovis complex. Christian County, Kentucky. *Rodney M. Peck collection, North Carolina.* Each, $10.00 – 20.00.

Clovis drill or perforator, gray flint, point salvaged as a tool. High-grade material was often "recycled" in Paleo times. DeKalb County, Tennessee. *Rodney M. Peck collection, North Carolina.* $200.00.

Paleo side-scrapers, Hopkinsville chert, Little River Clovis complex. All were found in Christian County, Kentucky. *Rodney M. Peck collection, North Carolina.* Each, $25.00 – 35.00.

Uniface Paleo tools, mainly side-scrapers, end-scrapers, and shaft-scrapers. They are made of Cattail Creek chalcedony and were found in Dinwiddie County, Virginia. *Rodney M. Peck collection, North Carolina.* Each, $10.00 – 20.00.

Gravers, on flakes, Cattail Creek chalcedony. All came from an important Paleo site in Dinwiddie County, Virginia. *Rodney M. Peck collection, North Carolina.* Each, $10.00 – 20.00.

Reamer, Cattail Creek chalcedony, angled tip. It was found on a Paleo site in Dinwiddie County, Virginia. *Rodney M. Peck collection; North Carolina.* $50.00 – 150.00.

Paleo cores, Cattail Creek chalcedony. These came from a well-known Paleo site in Dinwiddie County, Virginia. *Rodney M. Peck collection, North Carolina.* Each, $5.00 – 10.00.

Folsom and Midland tools, Late Paleo, found in association with Folsom and Midland type points, largest 2⅝". They have single-direction beveled edges and are ex-collection Glasscock. All are from Gaines County and Ochiltree County, Texas. *Michael Hough collection, California.* Each, $50.00 – 100.00.

Paleo end-scrapers, various Midwestern flints, longest 3⅛". All of these large scrapers were found in Ohio and Kentucky. *John Timoch collection, Ohio.* Each, $20.00 – 50.00.

283

Paleo end-scrapers, various Midwestern flints, longest 2½". These were picked up on sites in Ohio and Kentucky. *James Timoch collection, Ohio.* Each, $10.00 – 20.00.

Paleo uniface chopper, mixed Upper Mercer flint, 2¾" long. This tool was found in Coshocton County, Ohio. *Pete Timoch collection, Ohio.* $100.00.

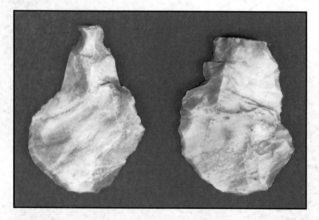

Paleo uniface scrapers, with hafting stems, both made of high-grade tan and gray flint. These are ex-collection Vietzen, and the smaller stem was burin-shaped on both sides. Stemmed Paleo tools are quite unusual, and both of these are from Ohio. *Pete Timoch collection, Ohio.* Each, $75.00 – 100.00.

Paleo tool, a *piece esquillee*, dull black Helderberg flint. It was used for slotting or wedging, is 1⁷⁄₂₀", and was picked up in Clinton County, New York. *Dave Summers collection, New York.* $12.00.

Graver, on rounded flake, tan jasper, 2" long. It came from near Perkinsville, Yavapai County, Arizona. *Dave Summers collection, New York.* $15.00.

End-scraper, keeled, of unidentified orange, gray, and tan material, 2½" long. This is a well-made piece, provenance unknown. *Dave Summers collection, New York.* $25.00.

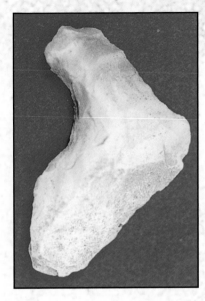

End-scraper, with graver tip on side, gray Warsaw (Upper Mercer) flint, 1⅛" wide. The steeply beveled bottom working edge has been resharpened often. Fairfield County, Ohio. *Private collection.* $5.00.

Uniface Paleo tool, 4" long, gray Georgetown chert. The artifact has the edges resharpened from the top, and the bulb of percussion remains at the small end. Lampasas County, Texas. *Pete Timoch collection, Ohio.* $50.00.

Paleo uniface spokeshave, gray nodular flint, 3½" long. The shorter of the two long measurements has a knife edge, and the concave spokeshave edge is steeply beveled. The tool was excavated by Col. Vietzen at Glover's Cave, Christian County, Kentucky. *Pete Timoch collection, Ohio.* $75.00.

Quartz crystal scrapers, each 1¼". This native North Carolina material was often used by Paleo people in the region. Catawba County, North Carolina. *Collection of and photograph by Ron Harris, North Carolina.* Each, $35.00.

Dalton drill, translucent novaculite, 2¼". This nicely balanced example was found in Arkansas. *Collection of and photograph by Duane Treest, Illinois.* $150.00 – 250.00.

Agate Basin drill, 4" long, fine chipping. The drill came from Macoupin County, Illinois. *Collection of and photograph by Duane Treest, Illinois.* $300.00 – 400.00.

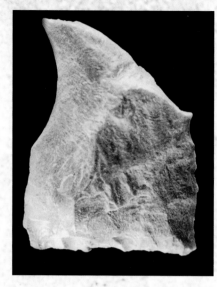

Uniface flake tool, 3¼", weathered rhyolite. It has a straight cutting/scraping edge and is from Wilkes County, North Carolina. *Collection of and photograph by Ron Harris, North Carolina.* $10.00.

Multipurpose tool, with shaft-scraper, burin, and perforator(?). The artifact is 2¾" long and made of weathered rhyolite. Wilkes County, North Carolina. *Collection of and photograph by Ron Harris, North Carolina.* $25.00.

Uniface scraper, large at 2¾", dark rhyolite. It came from a site at the Yadkin River Narrows near Badin, Stanley County, North Carolina. *Collection of and photograph by Ron Harris, North Carolina.* $35.00.

Uniface scrapers with worn graver tips, 2¼"x 1¾" long respectively. They are from the Yadkin River Narrows near Badin, Stanley County, North Carolina. *Collection of and photograph by Ron Harris, North Carolina.* Each, $15.00.

Uniface blade, Paleo plane with graver tips, pale mixed Upper Mercer. The plane or woodworking portion is the angled edge to right. It is 2½" long, from Fairfield County, Ohio. *Joel Embrey collection.* $10.00.

Paleo end-scrapers, both central Ohio. Left, 1½", keeled, graver tips at each blade corner, unknown flint. Right, 1⅜", single graver tip, fluted on obverse. *Private collection.* Each, $10.00.

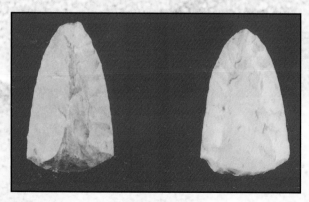

286

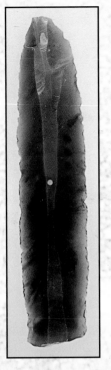

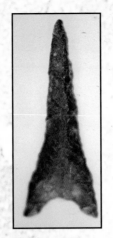

Dalton resharpened blade or perforator, Late Paleo, 2¼" long. Made of dark chert, it is from Conway County, Arkansas. *Back to Earth.* $65.00.

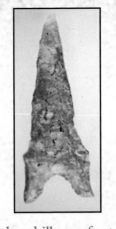

Dalton drill or perforator, mixed tan chert with soil deposits, 2⅛" long. It has a Partain COA and was picked up in Clay County, Arkansas. *Back to Earth.* $100.00.

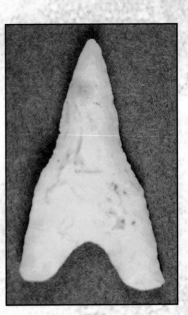

Dalton blade, heavily resharpened from a larger artifact, mixed light-colored chert. It came from Union County, Illinois. *Back to Earth.* $85.00.

Paleo bladelet or flake knife, highest quality moss agate translucent Flint Ridge, yellowish green with darker clouding and several white spots. The classic three dorsal facets indicate other blades were struck off. This superb example is 3¹¹⁄₁₆" and from Franklin County, Ohio. *Joel Embrey collection.* $350.00.

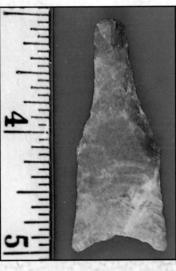

Paleo drill or perforator, Delaware chert, right ear restored. This Paleo tool was found in Mason County, West Virginia. *Craig Ferrell collection.* Unlisted.

Beaver Lake hafted scraper, ¹⁵⁄₁₆" x 1¹⁄₁₆". The salvaged artifact is made of hornstone and was found in Stewart County, Tennessee. *Bybee collection, Kentucky; Tom Davis photograph.* $30.00.

Quad point, Late Paleo, patinated Fort Payne, 1¾". This is a salvaged piece, with the break area chipped into an end-scraper. Probably Kentucky. *Earthworks Artifacts.* $100.00.

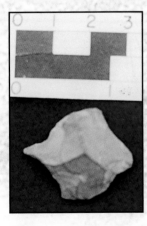

Paleo tool, graver or perforator, Normanskill chert. It was recovered in Massachusetts. *Fogelman collection.* $35.00.

Paleo tool, coronet graver, Normanskill chert. Before wear and damage, this tool had half a dozen working tips. Massachusetts. *Fogelman collection.* $75.00.

287

Paleo tool, coronet graver, originally with three working tips. It was chipped in Normanskill chert and came from Massachusetts. *Fogelman collection.* $35.00.

Flake Paleo tool, narrow-bit chisel with worn tip, reddish jasper. This artifact was found in Lehigh County, Pennsylvania. *Fogelman collection.* $50.00.

Paleo end-scraper, large size and with edges probably trimmed to fit hafting, Normanskill chert. It came from a Paleo site in Massachusetts. *Fogelman collection.* $50.00.

Fluted point base salvaged as an end-scraper, Onondaga (New York) chert. It came from a major Paleo site in Pennsylvania. *Fogelman collection.* $200.00.

Paleo flake knife, thin, Onondaga chert. It was found on a well-known site in Pennsylvania. *Fogelman collection.* $50.00.

Paleo side-scraper, with working edges on two sides, Onondaga chert. The example came from a site in Pennsylvania. *Fogelman collection.* $100.00.

Paleo drill or perforator, base edges ground, 2¾". It is made of Edwards Plateau flint and came from the San Barnard River. Austin County, Texas. *John and Susan Mellyn collection, Texas.* $225.00.

Dalton drill, brown chert, 1⅛" x 2⅜". This is ex-collections Snyder and Williams, and its origin is uncertain but is probably Tennessee. *Collection of and photograph by Gary Henry, North Carolina.* $200.00.

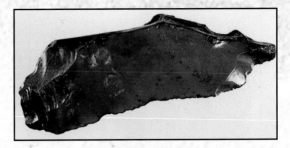

Uniface tool, water stained and river worn, 3" long. Made of Coastal Plains chert, it has a rich red patina with black, and has a graver tip. The tool came from the Suwannee River, Florida. *Dwight Wolfe collection.* $45.00.

Angostura tool, red and yellow flint, 2¹¹⁄₁₆". Resharpened to a drill or perforator form, it is from Wilson County, Texas. *John and Susan Mellyn collection, Texas.* $200.00.

Plainview tool, salvaged to make a rounded scraper edge, very translucent agate-like flint. It is 2" long and from Austin County, Texas. *John and Susan Mellyn collection, Texas.* $350.00.

Angostura tool, Late Paleo, salvaged as a drill or perforator. The example is 2³⁄₁₆" and from Wilson County, Texas. *John and Susan Mellyn collection, Texas.* $400.00.

Paleo salvage tool, point base rechipped to form a scraper end, Dover chert. The artifact is 1¼", and the find location is unknown. *Dwight Wolfe collection.* $35.00.

Uniface tool, fluted top, graver corners on wider end, tan flint. Both sides and the wide end have delicate chipping, and the artifact is 2⅜" long. Midwest. *Dwight Wolfe collection.* $50.00.

Uniface tool, with several shaft-scrapers, knife or scraper edge, one remaining graver, and one end fluted. It is 2¹¹⁄₁₆", probably from Indiana. *Dwight Wolfe collection.* $35.00.

Drill or perforator, obverse base with twin flutes, Indiana Green flint. It is 1¾" and ex-collection Swann, and the find location is unknown. *Dwight Wolfe collection.* $125.00.

Paleo scraper, from a site that contained a Haskett, Haskett pieces, and scrapers. Of olive green glossy chert, it is 1⁵⁄₁₆" x 2⁵⁄₁₆". The straight edge has retouch, and one corner has a possible shaft-scraper. Western Box Elder County, Northern Utah. *Dann Russell collection, Utah.* $30.00.

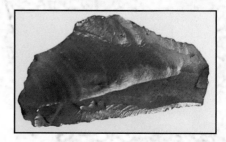

Flake tool, Coastal Plains chert, shaft-scraper in side of excurvate edge, 2⅛". Patinated and water stained a deep orange, it was found in the Suwannee River, Florida. *Dwight Wolfe collection.* $35.00.

Paleo scraper, found on a site that has also produced a Haskett, olive green glossy chert. It is 1¾" x 2½" and has a probable graver tip on the upper left corner. Western Box Elder County, northern Utah. *Dann Russell collection, Utah.* $30.00.

Paleo scraper, found on a site where a Haskett, Haskett pieces, and scrapers were picked up. Made of mottled reddish brown jasper, it is 1½" x 1¹³⁄₁₆". Western Box Elder County, northern Utah. *Dann Russell collection, Utah.* $20.00.

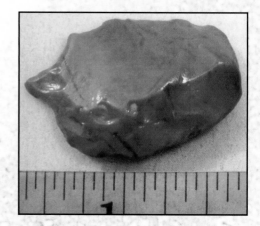

Alamance drill or perforator, 1¼" x 2", base edges ground. It was found by A. Jones in the early 1900s. St. Joseph County, Michigan. *Paul Weisser collection, Indiana.* Unlisted.

Double graver made from a broken triple graver, Nuckolls County, Nebraska. *Jim Horst collection, Nebraska.* $20.00.

Uniface tool, graver on flake, wear or water polished. It came from Nuckolls County, Nebraska. *Jim Horst collection, Nebraska.* $20.00.

Paleo elongated flake knife, sharpened excurvate edge, with white cortex indicating it was one of the first flakes driven from the core. Riley County, Kansas. *Jim Horst collection, Nebraska.* $25.00.

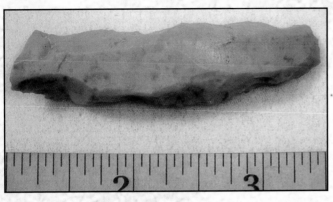

Paleo tool, beveled on all four edges, found by Norvil Evans. It is from Hooker County, Nebraska. *Jim Horst collection, Nebraska.* $20.00.

Paleo flake tool, some retouch on top edge as shown, graver tip to left. It is made of Foraker permian chert, and the provenance is unlisted. *Jim Horst collection, Nebraska.* $15.00.

Paleo flake knife or bladelet, creamy gray patinated Flint Ridge, 2¹⁵⁄₁₆". The owner found this fragile example in 1983. Bloom Township, Fairfield County, Ohio. *Joel Embrey collection.* $75.00.

Perforator, possibly Paleo, ⅞" x 2½". Upper Mercer flint was used for this tool, found in southeastern Indiana. *Bybee collection, Kentucky; Tom Davis photograph.* $25.00.

Graver or perforator, probably Paleo, ¾" x 2³⁄₁₆". Breathitt chert was used for the tool, found in Madison County, Kentucky. *Bybee collection, Kentucky; Tom Davis photograph.* $10.00.

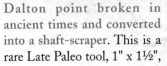

Dalton point broken in ancient times and converted into a shaft-scraper. This is a rare Late Paleo tool, 1" x 1½", and is made of Crowley's Ridge chert. It was found in Greene County, Arkansas. *Bybee collection, Kentucky; Tom Davis photograph.* $75.00.

Paleo blade, Dalton culture, 1½" x 2⅜". Made of tan chert, it came from Alexander County, Illinois. *Bybee collection, Kentucky; Tom Davis photograph.* $35.00.

Paleo end-scraper, with two graver spurs on either side of the bottom scraper edge. Of blue Upper Mercer, it is 1¼" long. Ohio. *Private collection.* $8.00.

Broken sections of Paleo bladelets, left example 1⅛" long. They are made of dark blue Upper Mercer and are triangular in cross section. Central Ohio. *Private collection.* Unlisted.

Paleo end-scrapers, each with graver spurs on the blade corners. Both are made of blue Upper Mercer flint, and the left scraper is 1" wide. Both central Ohio. *Private collection.* Each, $15.00.

Fluted end-scraper, mixed dark blue Upper Mercer, 2⁷⁄₁₆" long. It has a tiny graver spur and was found in Ohio. *Private collection.* $70.00.

Fluted end-scraper, pale gray Harrison County (Indiana) flint, 2⅝" long. It was found in western Ohio. *Private collection.* $65.00.

Graver or perforator, uniface chipping, 2⅛" long. It is made of yellowish red Carter County(?) flint from Kentucky. Paint Creek Valley, Ohio. *Private collection.* $20.00.

Perforator or drill, on a thick uniface flake, mottled Upper Mercer flint. It is 2¼" long, from Fairfield County, Ohio. *Private collection.* $40.00.

Paleo graver-perforator, on a flake, pinkish purple Flint Ridge, 1⅜" wide. The tip at bottom left was chipped on one side, which helped narrow it to a needle tip, and the tip to right was also probably used as a graver. Fairfield County, Ohio. *Private collection.* $10.00.

292

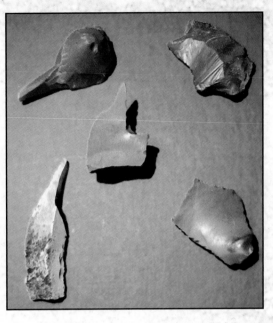

Uniface side-scraper, with end graver tip formed by burin chipping, not by the usual pressure flaking. Heavily patinated, the scraper is 2½" long and made of dark unknown flint in subtle mixed colors. Ohio. *Private collection.* $10.00.

Paleo perforators and gravers, longest 2". All were found by the owner on the same site. Meade County, Kentucky. *Private collection, Kentucky.* Each, $20.00 – 50.00.

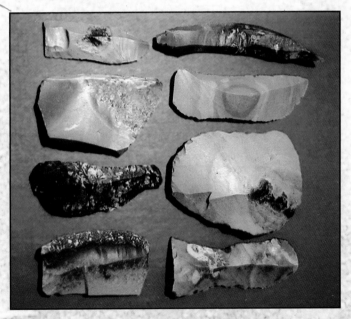

Paleo bladelets, longest example 2½". Triangular in cross section, these sturdy tools were probably mounted in antler, wood, or bone handles. All were personal finds by the owner in Meade County, Kentucky. *Private collection, Kentucky.* Each, $10.00 – 30.00.

Paleo flake tools, all with good edgewear from use. These were recovered from the same site, and the longest is 3¼". Meade County, Kentucky. *Private collection, Kentucky.* Each, $20.00 – 50.00.

Paleo uniface flake tools, fine edge-work on all three, longest 4". These are made of hornstone, and all are from Meade County, Kentucky. *Private collection, Kentucky.* Each, $100.00 – 175.00.

Paleo flake tools, very colorful Kentucky flints and cherts, longest 3¼". These were personal finds by the owner and were found on a Late Paleo site. Far northern Kentucky. *Private collection, Kentucky.* Each, $50.00 – 100.00.

Uniface scraper, with graver tip, Harrison County flint, 1¾". The tool was found by the owner in Rush County, Indiana. *Jeff Anderson collection, Indiana.* $25.00.

Paleo scraper, duckbill form, fossiliferous chert. It measures 2¼" x 3¼" and is from Breckinridge County, Kentucky. *Bybee collection, Kentucky; Tom Davis photograph.* $40.00.

Uniface scraper, 3¼", Harrison County flint. It was found by the owner in 1991. Rush County, Indiana. *Jeff Anderson collection, Indiana.* $45.00.

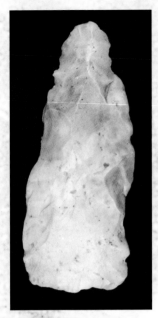

End-scraper, on blade, 3⅛", patinated Flint Ridge colored gray, tan, and cream. The tool came from a farm auction in 2002. West Lafayette area, Coshocton County, Ohio. *Jesse Weber collection; photograph by Norman's Photo, Newcomerstown, Ohio.* $50.00.

Uniface tools, largest 2" x 3⅝". These were personal finds of Harwood and came from Lauderdale, Limestone, and Morgan counties in Alabama, and Buncombe County in North Carolina. *Collection of and photograph by Gary Henry, North Carolina.* All, $400.00.

Uniface tools, largest 1⅜" x 2⁷⁄₁₆". Found by Harwood, these came from Morgan County in Alabama, and Buncombe, Burke, Cherokee, Henderson, Madison, and Transylvania counties in North Carolina. *Collection of and photograph by Gary Henry, North Carolina.* All, $350.00.

End-scraper, on a Cumberland point base, ⅝" x ¾", No. 577 in Peck's North Carolina fluted point survey. It was found by the owner in Buncombe County, North Carolina. *Collection of and photograph by Gary Henry, North Carolina.* $20.00.

End-scraper, on a Clovis fluted base, quartz, ¾" x ¾". Listed as No. 604 in Peck's North Carolina fluted point survey, it was found by the owner in Buncombe County, North Carolina. *Collection of and photograph by Gary Henry, North Carolina.* $20.00.

Wheeler recurvate(?) tool, Late Paleo, chert, 1³⁄₁₆" x 1³⁄₁₆". Found by the owner, it came from Buncombe County, North Carolina. *Collection of and photograph by Gary Henry, North Carolina.* $5.00.

Uniface scraper, from Goodflint.com, 2⅜" x 3¼". It is ex-collection Richardson, and its provenance is unlisted. *Doug Goodrum collection, Kentucky.* $50.00.

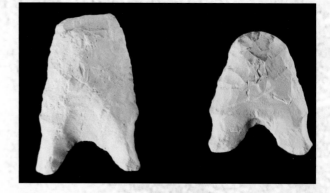

Hardaway Dalton snubnose end-scrapers, weathered silicified shale. Central Piedmont, North Carolina. Left, 2" long. $125.00. Right, 1½". $100.00. *Collection of and photograph by Ron Harris, North Carolina.*

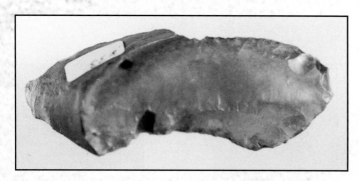

Paleo tool, nodular flint that may be Knox or Lenoir, 3⅛". Both excurvate and incurvate edges have retouch. Tennessee. *Dwight Wolfe collection.* $15.00.

Chopper, probably Paleo period, black shale-like stone. The artifact came from Burleigh County, North Dakota. *Collection of Brian Blotsky and scan by Larry Bumann, both North Dakota.* Unlisted.

Paleo tool, Knife River flint, apparent knife edge and several wide graver tips. It was picked up in Emmons County, North Dakota. *Collection of and scan by Larry Bumann, North Dakota.* Unlisted.

Paleo tool, with excurvate edge and shaft-scraper, patinated Knife River flint. It was picked up in Emmons County, North Dakota. *Collection of Sheila Blotsky and scan by Larry Burmann, both North Dakota.* Unlisted.

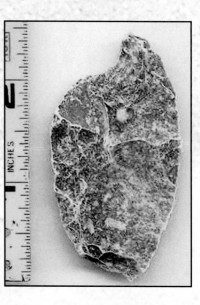

296

Dalton drill, 2⅛", light flint with darker inclusions. This drill is ex-collection Cordeiro and from Clay County, Arkansas. *Bill Moody collection, Massachusetts.* $100.00.

Dalton drill, 2½", light tan flint. The drill was found by J. Bennett along Bear Creek, Pulaski County, Illinois. *Bill Moody collection, Massachusetts.* $125.00.

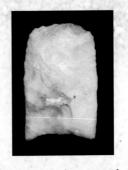

Plainview point reworked as an end-scraper, Late Paleo. The tool is 1½" long, ex-collection McMichael, and was found in Texas. *Bill Moody collection, Massachusetts.* $85.00.

Paleo base reworked as an end-scraper, 1¼" long. Ex-collection Sherman, it is made of flint and is from northern Florida. *Bill Moody collection, Massachusetts.* $50.00.

Paleo fluted scraper, Fort Payne chert, 1⅛" x 1⅝". It came from Christian County, Kentucky. *Bybee collection, Kentucky; Tom Davis photograph.* $25.00.

Round scraper, 1⅞" x 2". It is made of hornstone and was found near Bardstown, Nelson County, Kentucky. *Bybee collection, Kentucky; Tom Davis photograph.* $40.00.

Uniface tool, ⅝" x 1⅜", 1/16" thick. It has a graver tip and two shaft-scraper edges, and was found by the owner in 1996. Douglas County, Colorado. *Mark Boswell collection, Colorado; photograph by Infocusphotography.com, Colorado.* $15.00.

Paleo bladelet, broken about midsection and two pieces found separately, 3¼". The material is typical Upper Mercer, but is patinated orange-tan and black. Found by the owner, the piece came from Fairfield County, Ohio. *Don Casto collection.* $50.00.

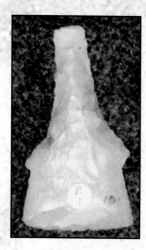

Uniface tool, ⅝" x 1⅝", ⅛" thick. It has a single incurvate cutting edge with delicate flaking, and has graver tips at each end. The material is tan petrified wood with patination. This piece was found by the owner in 1990. Park County, Colorado. *Mark Boswell collection, Colorado; photograph by Infocusphotography.com, Colorado*. $15.00.

Scottsbluff salvaged to become a hafted tool, with blunt tip, Late Paleo, 2⁵⁄₁₆". It is made of Edwards flint, and the basal edges are ground. Travis County, Texas. *John and Susan Mellyn collection, Texas*. $275.00.

Paleo drill or perforator, ground basal edges, 1⅝". The material is Edwards flint, and the artifact was picked up in Bexar County, Texas. *John and Susan Mellyn collection, Texas*. $200.00.

Scottsbluff salvaged to become a drill or perforator, shoulders resharpened away. It is made of Edwards flint and measures 2³⁄₁₆". Wilson County, Texas. *John and Susan Mellyn collection, Texas*. $175.00.

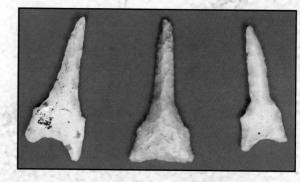

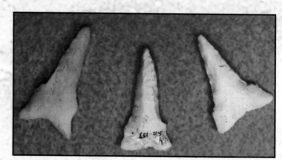

Angostura drill, 1¹³⁄₁₆", high-grade Edwards flint. Finely chipped and symmetrical, it is from Bexar County, Texas. *John and Susan Mellyn collection, Texas*. $225.00.

Golondrina salvaged as an end-scraper, beautiful banded agate with a frosty patina. It is 1⁷⁄₁₆", from Wilson County, Texas. *John and Susan Mellyn collection, Texas*. $350.00.

Dalton drill form, 2½", heavy creek stain. It was found by J. Rahn at Lima Lake, Hancock County, Illinois. *Fred Smith collection, Illinois*. $55.00 – 65.00.

Dalton drills, longest 2½". Made of Burlington chert, all were found between 1970 and 1980. Adams County, Illinois. *Fred Smith collection, Illinois*. All, $125.00 – 150.00.

Dalton drills, longest 1¾", creek-stained Burlington. All were found in the Knox and Warren Counties region, Illinois. *Fred Smith collection, Illinois*. All, $100.00 – 125.00.

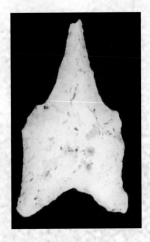

Dalton drill, 2¼", Burlington chert. Probably made from a full-size blade, the drill was found in 1986. Adams County, Illinois. *Fred Smith collection, Illinois.* $40.00 – 50.00.

End-scraper, with graver tips, ¹⁵⁄₁₆" x ¹⁵⁄₁₆", found by Harwood in 1959 or 1960. It is made of chert and came from Limestone County, Alabama. *Collection of and photograph by Gary Henry, North Carolina.* $5.00.

Paleo tool, scraper edge and probable graver tips, 1¼" x 1½". It was found by Harwood in 1954 and came from Limestone County, Alabama. *Collection of and photograph by Gary Henry, North Carolina.* $5.00.

Round scraper, 1⅝" x 1¾", Fort Payne chert. It came from near Bardstown in Nelson County, Kentucky. *Bybee collection, Kentucky; Tom Davis photograph.* $30.00.

Paleo tools and scrapers, chert, center example 1⅞" x 3⁷⁄₁₆". These were found by Harwood in 1956. Limestone County, Alabama. *Collection of and photograph by Gary Henry, North Carolina.* All, $30.00.

Dalton resharpened to a drill-like form, 1" x 2⅛". Cream-colored chert was used for this piece, found in southeastern Missouri. *Bybee collection, Kentucky; Tom Davis photograph.* $100.00.

Paleo tools, six made of chert and middle top row example made of translucent chalcedony. The largest is 1¼" x 1¾". These were found by Harwood between 1955 and 1976 on a site that also produced a Clovis point. Madison County, North Carolina. *Collection of and photograph by Gary Henry, North Carolina.* All, $20.00.

299

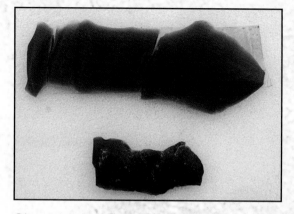

Scrapers and multipurpose tool (upper right), six of quartzite and large upper left example (1¾" x 2¾") made of quartz. They were found by Harwood in 1956 and came from Madison County, North Carolina. *Collection of and photograph by Gary Henry, North Carolina.* All, $20.00.

Channel flakes, Early Paleo, largest is in three pieces. Made of chert, they were found by Harwood. Top, ½" x 1¹⁵⁄₁₆", unknown find site. $15.00. Lower, Buncombe County, North Carolina. $7.00. *Collection of and photograph by Gary Henry, North Carolina.*

Paleo prismatic blades, fifth from left with twist, five (dark) made of chert and two (light) of quartz. The largest is ½" x 1¾". These seven were found by the owner from 1986 to 2003, and they came from seven different sites. Buncombe County, North Carolina. *Collection of and photograph by Gary Henry, North Carolina.* Each, $3.00 – 15.00.

Scrapers, all probably Paleo, chert, largest 2¹⁄₁₆" x 2⅜". These were found by Harwood between the years 1955 and 1958, in Limestone County, Alabama. *Collection of and photograph by Gary Henry, North Carolina.* All, $60.00.

Scrapers, various kinds of chert, largest 1⅞" x 2¾". They were found by Harwood in 1959 and came from Lauderdale County, Alabama. *Collection of and photograph by Gary Henry, North Carolina.* All, $30.00.

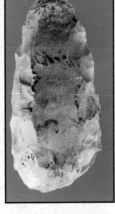

Paleo end-scraper, large at 1½" x 2⅜", gray and tan chert. It is Dalton period and was found on a site in Alexander County, Illinois. *Bybee collection, Kentucky; Tom Davis photograph.* $15.00.

Round scraper, 1⅝" x 1¾", Fort Payne chert. This Paleo tool came from western Kentucky. *Bybee collection, Kentucky; Tom Davis photograph.* $30.00.

Fluted duckbill end-scraper, 1⅛" x 2⅜". Fort Payne chert was used for this piece, found in Christian County, Kentucky. *Bybee collection, Kentucky; Tom Davis photograph.* $15.00.

Paleo scrapers, chert, largest 1⅞" x 2⅞". They were found by Harwood in 1959, and came from Lauderdale County, Alabama. *Collection of and photograph by Gary Henry, North Carolina.* All, $25.00.

Colbert Dalton tool, resharpened, chert, ⅞" x 1¹¹⁄₁₆". It is ex-collection Snyder, and the origin is unknown. *Collection of and photograph by Gary Henry, North Carolina.* $40.00.

Paleo knife, with deep flute, tan-gray Helderberg flint, 2½" long. It came from Schoharie County, New York. *Dave Summers collection, New York.* $40.00.

Triangular bladelet, gray-tan Snake Hill flint, 2⁷⁄₁₀". It was picked up in Schoharie County, New York. *Dave Summers collection, New York.* $45.00.

Paleo bladelet, gray Onondaga flint, 2½⁄₂₀". It was picked up in western New York. *Dave Summers collection, New York.* $10.00.

Uniface blade knife, gray and blue Onondaga, 2¼". Retouched along one edge, it is from Monroe County, New York. *Dave Summers collection, New York.* $30.00.

Uniface double-ended scraper, dull black Oriskany flint, 2¹⁹⁄₂₀" long. It was found in the Taberg area, Oneida County, New York. *Dave Summers collection, New York.* $50.00.

Paleo bladelet, green Normanskill flint, 1¹³⁄₂₀". Triangular in cross section, it is from Greene County, New York. *Dave Summers collection, New York.* $25.00.

301

PALEO KNIVES

Because they lived in a wild land, it is not surprising that Paleo Indians had many kinds of knives. Most were probably employed for skinning and butchering, and for preparing meat for consumption or preservation. Many knives are easy to recognizes as such, but it is also very likely that large fluted points (like the Anzick and the St. Louis) and large lanceolates were also knives.

Known Paleo knives include crescents from the western U.S. and semi-lunate knives that were probably hafted like the northern ulu curved blades. Dagger-like blades are known from Paleo sites, and they may have been used more as weapons than as everyday tools. Rectangular blades, often with short beveled blade edges at one end, seem to have been so helpful that (like a few other Paleo artifact types) they continued into the Early Archaic.

General purpose knives exist in a range of sizes. Most have a relatively small base (sometimes fluted), a long excurvate edge that was retouched, and a tip that may be off center. The opposite or backing edge may be fairly straight or irregular. Large ovate blades are known from Paleo times and a few have small side-notches at one end. Some curved knives, either biface or uniface, have notched ends, and these are among the first notches on tools in American prehistory.

Triangular Paleo blades, often uniface, may be short to long, and have squared or angular bases. Some of these, like many other Paleo knives of various shapes, may be fluted on at least one face and the tips may be quite pointed. Uniface examples are generally quite thin.

Rectangular blade, unknown golden brown flint, 3⅜". It has a Perino COA and came from Adams County, Ohio. *Gilbert Cooper collection.* $400.00.

Paleo rectangular blade, very unusual and unidentified flint or chert. It is 3¾" long and has a Perino COA. A small number of these blades have shallow notches on the sides near one end, perhaps hafting aids. Adams County, Ohio. *Gilbert Cooper collection.* $400.00.

Paleo biface blade, with tiny offset stem, found in 2000, Knife River flint, 3¹⁄₁₆" x 5⅜". Featured in *Indian Artifact Magazine*, it came from near the owner's farm. Kingsbury County, South Dakota. *Harlan Olson collection, South Dakota.* Unlisted.

Preform biface knife, well-shaped, Normanskill chert. It was found in Massachusetts. *Fogelman collection.* $350.00.

Paleo biface knife, crystal quartz, a very unusual and attractive material. It was found in Massachusetts. *Fogelman collection.* $500.00.

Paleo biface core or preform, Normanskill chert. Large Paleo artifacts such as this are extremely scarce. Sunderland area, Massachusetts. *Fogelman collection.* $2,500.00.

Paleo crescent blades, chert, largest 1" x 2⅜". The top two were found by the owner in 1992 and 1993, in the countires of Madison and Buncombe; the other is from Haywood County. All North Carolina. *Collection of and photograph by Gary Henry, North Carolina.* Each, $10.00 – 20.00.

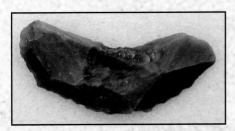

Paleo crescent knife or scraper, high-grade glossy chert, 1" x 2½". Found by Harwood in 1956, it came from Morgan County, Alabama. *Collection of and photograph by Gary Henry, North Carolina.* $10.00.

Red River knife, probably based on a southern Scottsbluff with one shoulder remaining, 2" long. This rare blade is from Angelins County, Texas. *John and Susan Mellyn collection, Texas.* $450.00.

Rectangular blade, thin, 2⅞" long. Ex-collection Katzenberger, it is from Darke County, Ohio. *Dwight Wolfe collection.* $60.00.

Uniface rectangular blade, thin, with graver tip at the left end. One long side edge (at bottom) is beveled, and the knife is 2⅜" x 3⅝". The striped gray and tan material may be patinated Harrison County flint. Darke County, Ohio. *Dwight Wolfe collection.* $125.00.

Stemmed Paleo knife, possibly patinated Carter Cave flint, 2⅜" long. A large thinning flute is near the tip, and the knife is probably midwestern. *Dwight Wolfe collection.* $75.00.

Paleo curved blade, gray and cream translucent Flint Ridge. The knife is 4" long and from Meade County, Kentucky. *Dwight Wolfe collection.* $125.00.

Paleo knife, 4⅛", solution cavity at upper left corner. Made of Coshocton (Upper Mercer) flint, it is ex-collection Jack Hooks. Marion County, Ohio. *Dwight Wolfe collection.* $100.00.

Paleo fluted point or blade, 3" long, blue Upper Mercer flint. It was found in Mercer County, Ohio. *Dwight Wolfe collection.* $75.00.

Paleo knife, angular base with flute-like thinning, 4¼" long. Made of patinated unknown material, it is probably from Indiana. *Dwight Wolfe collection.* $75.00.

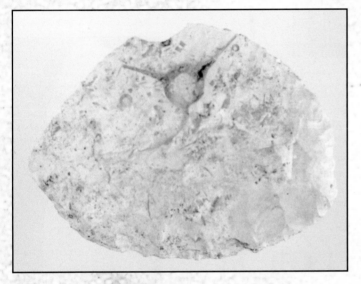

Ovoid knife, small basal stem, 4¼". Burlington chert was used for this very scarce type, ex-collection Ritter. It came from Pike County, Missouri. *Dale and Betty Roberts collection, Iowa.* $700.00.

Ovoid knife, very thin, possible shaft-scraper in upper edge, 2¾". Perhaps made of Ten Mile chert, it is probably from Ohio. *Dwight Wolfe collection.* $35.00.

Semi-lunate knife, less excurvate edge has large percussion flake scars, 4" long. Made of Logan County chert, it is ex-collection Puterbaugh. Darke County, Ohio. *Dwight Wolfe collection.* $60.00.

Paleo knife, patinated creamy tan Burlington, 4¹⁄₃₂". This blade has a flute-like thinning flake taken from the obverse base. Midwest. *Dwight Wolfe collection.* $100.00.

305

Knife, beveled straight edge, 1½" x 2¹³⁄₁₆". It is made of black flint and was found on an Ohio River Valley site. West Virginia. *Private collection; Rodney Roberts photograph.* $25.00.

Knife, lance shape with flute-like thinning flake at base, black flint. The size is ¾" x 2¾", and it came from an Ohio River site. West Virginia. *Private collection; Rodney Roberts photograph.* $40.00.

Crescentic knife, probably Carter Cave chalcedony, ¹³⁄₁₆" x 2¾". The flute-like flake area is from an original blade strike-off from the core. This is a well-made and beautiful piece, and is from an Ohio River site. West Virginia. *Private collection; Rodney Roberts photograph.* $125.00.

Rectangular blade, black flint with tan inclusions, 1⅛" x 3⅜". It was found on a site along the Ohio River. West Virginia. *Private collection; Rodney Roberts photograph.* $150.00.

Uniface blade, heavy thickness, overall water polish. The blade is 3¾" long and came from the Tuscarawas River Valley near West Lafayette. Coshocton County, Ohio. *Lar Hothem collection.* $75.00.

Paleo general-purpose blade, slightly excurvate edge with retouch, 4¾". The material is light tan, probably patinated Flint Ridge, and the knife came from Fairfield County, Ohio. *Lar Hothem collection.* $175.00.

Paleo general-purpose blade, tan chert with medium brown corner, flat chipping platform at base. The excurvate edge has fine secondary chipping, and the knife is 3⅞" long. Fairfield County, Ohio. *Lar Hothem collection.* $150.00.

Paleo knife, faint 1⅜" flute on the obverse, tip broken in ancient times. The knife is 3¼" long, and the material is an unknown brown and gray flint. Delaware County, Ohio. *Private collection.* $15.00.

Paleo blade, cream and gray Flint Ridge, 3" long. Both side edges have secondary flaking, and the piece has a wide basal flute. The blade was chipped into the irregular shape. Ohio. *Private collection.* $25.00.

Paleo knife, Harrison County (Indiana) flint, 3⁹⁄₁₆". The obverse flute is ¹¹⁄₁₆" long, and the knife came from Guernsey County, Ohio. *Private collection.* $65.00.

Paleo knife, chipped-in shaft-scraper on one edge, burin scar at tip on the same edge. The knife is 4⅜" long and has a short basal flute. It is ex-collection Pinney, from Ross County, Ohio. *Lar Hothem collection.* $55.00.

Paleo curved dagger-like knife, base thinned, mixed blue Upper Mercer. The knife is 3½" long, ex-collection Dutcher. Fairfield County, Ohio. *Lar Hothem collection.* $75.00.

Paleo curved blade, uniface, blue Upper Mercer with cream and reddish inclusions. A dorsal flaking scar from previous blade strike-offs runs the length of the artifact. It is 3⁷⁄₁₆" long, ex-collection Dutcher. Fairfield County, Ohio. *Lar Hothem collection*. $75.00.

Paleo knife, gray chert with white, 1¼" x 2½". The knife came from Doniphan County, Kansas. *Mike George collection, Missouri; Terry Price photograph*. $45.00.

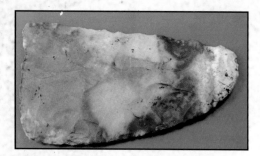

Square-back knife, novaculite in several colors, 1¾" x 4½". It was found in Holt County, Missouri. *Mike George collection, Missouri; Terry Price photograph*. $150.00.

Square-back knife, gray flint, 1⅜" x 3¾". It was found by J. Worth in Andrew County, Missouri. *Mike George collection, Missouri; Terry Price photograph*. $125.00.

Paleo knife, glossy pale Burlington, 2" x 4⅛". It has double basal fluting on the obverse and came from Andrew County, Missouri. *Mike George collection, Missouri; Terry Price photograph*. $500.00.

Paleo triangular blade, Florence chert in several colors, 1½" x 3½". It was found in Richardson County, Nebraska. *Mike George collection, Missouri; Terry Price photograph*. $350.00.

Paleo fluted knife, obverse flute is for more than half of length, 1" x 2¾". Broken, both pieces were found by the owner in Maries County, Missouri. *Jim McKinney collection, Missouri; Mary Jane Wieberg photograph.* Unlisted.

Paleo rectangular blade, thin and made of chert, 1½" x 5¼". It was found in 1979. These large specialized knife forms were made in Paleo times, and continued into the Early Archaic. Henry County, Missouri. *Jim McKinney collection, Missouri; Mary Jane Wieberg photograph.* $200.00 – 300.00.

Ovoid blade, 2¼" x 5", white and brown flint. Probably Paleo, this large knife is well made and was a personal find of the owner. Maries County, Missouri. *Jim McKinney collection, Missouri; Mary Jane Wieberg photograph.* $500.00 – 600.00.

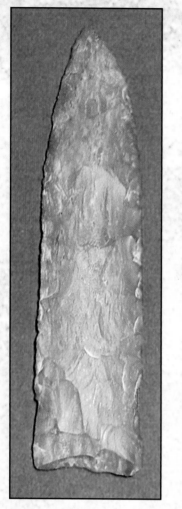

Lake Manix knives, possibly pre-Clovis, longest 4⅜". Made of high-grade and colorful flints, they came from Lake Manix, San Bernardino County, California. *Michael Hough collection, California.* Each, $150.00 – 400.00.

Paleo knife, brown and black Dover chert, 1¹⁵⁄₁₆" x 5⅛". The knife came from Madison County, Kentucky. *Keith and Rhonda Dodge collection, Michigan.* $400.00.

Paleo knife, brown and gray Dover chert, 1⁵⁄₁₆" x 4¾". It was found in Grundy County, Tennessee. *Keith and Rhonda Dodge collection, Michigan.* $350.00.

Paleo knife, bifacial horizontal transverse percussion flaking, 6¼". This rare large blade is ex-collection L. L. "Val" Valdivia and is made of translucent chalcedony. Churchill County, Nevada. *Michael Hough collection, California.* $4,000.00 plus.

Paleo blade, 1⅜" x 3⅝", light green chert with inclusions. This artifact was found by the owner in Wayne County, North Carolina. *Michael Womble collection, North Carolina.* $20.00.

Paleo point or blade, dark brown chert, 1⅛" x 2½". This artifact was acquired in Pennsylvania. *Collection of and photograph by H. B. Greene II, Florida.* $100.00.

Paleo uniface blade, pale Upper Mercer flint, 1¹³⁄₁₆" long. It is uniface, thin at the base and thick at the tip, which has remnants of the percussion bulb from the original blade strike-off. Medina County, Ohio. *Pete Timoch collection, Ohio.* $100.00.

Paleo crescent uniface knife, 3¼" long. Made of gray nodular flint, it was excavated by Col. Vietzen in Glover's Cave, Christian County, Kentucky. *Pete Timoch collection, Ohio.* $50.00.

Unhafted knives, probably Paleo, longest 3½". From left to right, they are of white flint, brown glossy flint, and white chert. All came from western Ohio. *Pete Timoch collection, Ohio.* Each, $150.00 – 200.00.

Rectangular blade, Upper Mercer(?) in mottled blue, brown, and cream. Mainly percussion flaked, there is little edge retouch. The knife is 1⅜" x 4⅛" and was a personal find of the owner. Fairfield County, Ohio. *Lar Hothem collection.* $40.00.

Paleo rectangular blade, gray and tan Upper Mercer, 1⅝" x 3". This is a scarce blade type, and the piece has somewhat irregular edges. Fairfield County, Ohio. *Private collection.* $25.00.

Rectangular blade, translucent blue-gray Flint Ridge, 1½" x 3". The obverse base has three parallel flutes on this early knife, found by the owner in Greenfield Township, Fairfield County, Ohio. *Lar Hothem collection.* $100.00.

Paleo dagger, Delaware County flint, 7⅛" long. It is ex-collection F. B. Hill, a banker who exchanged loans for artifacts in the 1930s. Most long Paleo daggers are found in damaged or broken condition. Delaware County, Ohio. *Mike Barron collection, Ohio.* $1,500.00.

Paleo blade, with wide basal flute that is ⅞" long. Gray and blue Upper Mercer was used for this piece, 3½" long. It is from Fairfield County, Ohio. *Private collection.* $100.00.

Paleo knife, 2¾", mottled dark Upper Mercer flint. It has multiple side-by-side or enterline fluting, and was found in Columbiana County, Ohio. *Mike Barron collection, Ohio.* $200.00.

Paleo knife, unknown reddish-brown striped material, 4" long. Ex-collections Klee and Miller, it was found on a farm in Delaware County, Ohio. *Mike Barron collection, Ohio.* $900.00.

Paleo fluted knife, gray hornstone, 3¾". The wide flute, which nearly reaches the tip, appears to be part of the original flake surface. The knife is ex-collection Copeland and from Ross County, Ohio. *Len and Janie Weidner collection.* $750.00.

Fluted knife, glossy blue Upper Mercer with milky clouding, 3½". This blade is fluted for nearly one-half of length. Ohio. *Len and Janie Weidner collection.* $950.00.

Rectangular blade, blue Coshocton (Upper Mercer) flint. The knife is 4¼" long and came from northern Fairfield County, Ohio. *Joel Embrey collection.* $450.00.

Rectangular blade, resharpened size, 2¼" long. Mixed gray Walhonding Valley flint, it is ex-collection Vietzen. Ohio. *Joel Embrey collection.* $20.00.

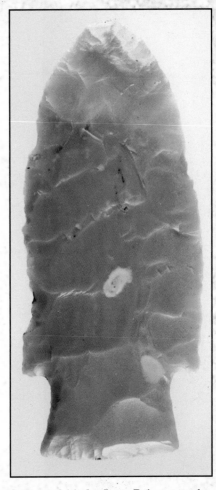

Stemmed blade, Late Paleo, translucent tan Carter Cave flint with cream spotting. This exceptional piece is large for type and is 4⅞" long. Ex-collection Dilley, the knife came from Summit County, Ohio. *Joel Embrey collection.* $2,500.00.

Paleo knife, unknown gray-black chert, 3⅝". The rounded tip suggests this may have been used for skinning purposes. Michigan. *Joel Embrey collection.* $150.00.

Ovoid knife, 3⅞". Patinated cream Burlington, it has a curved dark quartz(?) vein. Part of the edge is beveled for scraper use. Illinois. *Private collection.* $85.00.

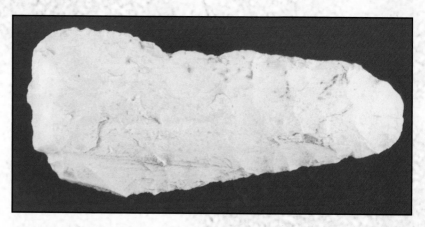

Paleo knife, tan-pink chert, with chisel tip. It is 4⅜" long, ex-collection Champion, and from Knox County, Ohio. *Private collection*. $50.00.

Paleo rectangular blade, 1⅝" x 3⅛", cream and blue Upper Mercer. This early knife was found in Ohio. *Joel Embrey collection*. $200.00.

Late Paleo blade, high-grade gray flint, 4¹⁵/₁₆". It is thin and well chipped, and from Medina County, Ohio. *Joel Embrey collection*. $1,100.00.

Early Paleo blade, large flute at base, mixed blue flint. The site where it was found will shortly be destroyed by strip mining. Logan County, West Virginia. *Craig Ferrell collection*. $100.00.

Clovis point or blade, tip with possible impact fracture, shaft-scraper in right base edge. The material is Kanawha chert, and the Clovis itself came from Putnam County, West Virginia. *Craig Ferrell collection*. $150.00.

Paleo knife, 4⅛", dark Walhonding Valley chert with lighter inclusions. It was found in Coshocton County, Ohio. *Jesse Weber collection; photograph by Norman's Photo, Newcomerstown, Ohio.* $150.00.

Rectangular blade, 3¼" long, light-colored chert. This Paleo knife was found in Indiana. *Glenn F. Witchey collection.* $200.00.

Paleo flake blade, 4" long, unusual camouflage colors of tan, brown, black, light green, and dark green. A fine piece, it was found by the owner in a creek bed. Greene County, Illinois. *G. Sloan collection; photograph by Kevin Calvin, Illinois.* $150.00 – 175.00.

Paleo dagger, 5⅛", of brown, white, and orange chert. It was picked up by the owner, in a creek bed in Macoupin County, Illinois. *G. Slone collection; photograph by Kevin Calvin, Illinois.* $100.00 – 125.00.

Knife, two shallow flutes on obverse base, 3⅜". Coastal Plains chert patinated an orange-red, this was a river find. Albany area, Georgia. *Dwight Wolfe collection.* $85.00.

Paleo fluted knife, pale Upper Mercer, 3⅛". With a long main excurvate edge, there is a possible graver at the tip. Wayne County, Ohio. *Dwight Wolfe collection.* $25.00.

315

Paleo curved blade, long excurvate edge with full retouch, 3⅞" long. The blade was once stored with other materials, and the green color is paint. Coshocton County, Ohio. *Lar Hothem collection.* $65.00.

Rectangular Paleo blade, stained and patinated Flint Ridge, 1¾" x 3¼". This artifact was found along the edge of Buckeye Lake and is ex-collections Smith and Dutcher. Southcentral Ohio. *Lar Hothem collection.* $150.00.

Rectangular Paleo blade, angled end beveled from rechipping, 2¹⁵⁄₁₆". Of mixed translucent Flint Ridge with orange-red, the knife was picked up in Coshocton County, Ohio. *Lar Hothem collection.* $150.00.

Rectangular blade, both long and straight edges have secondary chipping. The slanted end has bevel chipping. The material is blue-gray Upper Mercer. This blade is 3⅝" long, and a fluted point was found on the same site. Fairfield County, Ohio. *Lar Hothem collection.* $75.00.

Rectangular blade, caramel translucent Flint Ridge, both long edges with retouch. The knife is 4½" long and was found in Fairfield County, Ohio. *Lar Hothem collection.* $200.00.

Paleo knife chipped on vein or layer flint, chocolate and blue Upper Mercer, 3¼" long. The excurvate edge has delicate secondary chipping and the tip is in the form of a graver. Richland County, Ohio. *Lar Hothem collection.* $40.00.

Lanceolate tip used as knife, gray and tan Onondaga, 2¹¹⁄₂₀". It is from Erie County, New York. *Dave Summers collection, New York.* $20.00.

Clovis knife, multicolored and translucent Flint Ridge, 4¾". This blade with indented baseline has an Earthworks COA. Warren County, Ohio. *Earthworks Artifacts.* $1,300.00.

Knife or point, Late Paleo, 4¹⁄₂₀". It is made of sandy brown unidentified material, and the find location is unknown. *Dave Summers collection, New York.* $150.00.

Paleo knife, fluted base, Indiana hornstone, 3⅕". It is probably midwestern. *Dave Summers collection, New York.* $160.00.

Paleo knife or point, red and tan chert, 3⅖" long. Provenance unknown. *Dave Summers collection, New York.* $50.00.

Paleo knife, two shallow flutes at one end, gray Whitehall flint. It is 4½", ex-collection Palmer, and from eastern New York. *Dave Summers collection, New York.* $150.00.

Biface knife blade, large basal flutes, dull gray Deepkill flint. Ex-collection Palmer, it is from eastern New York. *Dave Summers collection, New York.* $140.00.

Paleo(?) blade, medium blue-gray Harrison County flint patinated to lighter gray, 4¹⁄₁₆". On the obverse (shown), a large angled flute-like chip is removed from the irregular base. Ex-collection Norbert Bingman, southeastern Illinois. *Private collection.* $125.00.

Paleo rectangular blade, unknown material but probably glacial chert, 2⅜". The smaller end is ground flat, and the larger end has a beveled edge with graver spurs at each corner. Fairfield County, Ohio. *Private collection.* $25.00.

Paleo rectangular blade, with narrow flute on base, uniface reverse. The knife or tool is 3⅝" long and is made of dark blue Upper Mercer flint. Knox County, Ohio. *Private collection.* $75.00.

Knife probably Paleo, blue Upper Mercer, 4⁵⁄₁₆" long. It has a burin-chipped tip and is from Perry County, Ohio. *Private collection.* $65.00.

Paleo knife, fluted from the right for 1⅜", overall length 3⅛". Dark blue Upper Mercer with some inclusions was used for this tool, found in Fairfield County, Ohio. *Private collection.* $15.00.

Paleo knife, fluted from base for 1", overall length 3". Of dark Upper Mercer flint, the knife was found in central Ohio. *Private collection.* $20.00.

Fluted point or blade, dark mixed Upper Mercer flint, 3½". It is ex-collections Johnson and Rhoades, from Crawford County, Ohio. *Jim Miller collection.* $1,500.00.

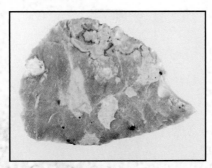

Paleo knife, thin, translucent gray flint with yellow-tan inclusions, 2⅛". The long (at bottom) edge was carefully retouched from both faces. At right, there is a shaft-scraper and a graver tip formed by burin flaking on two sides. Illinois. *Private collection.* $15.00.

Fluted knife, Early Paleo, 5¼" long and very long for an Ohio fluted piece. Probably of a gray-brown Upper Mercer or Onondaga flint, it is ex-collections Platt, Thullen, and Barth. It came from near Berlin Lake Dam, probably from Stark County, Ohio. *Jim Miller collection.* $5,000.00.

Paleo knife, Upper Mercer mixed black flint, 1¼" x 3¾". This blade was found in the Newton Falls area, Trumbull County, Ohio. *Pat Layshock collection; Thomas R. Pigott image.* $100.00.

319

Semi-lunate or Ulu knife, excurvate working edge, black Upper Mercer with lighter inclusions. It measures 2¾" x 3½" and was found by William Platt near Cortland, Trumbull County, Ohio. *Pat Layshock collection; Thomas R. Pigott image.* $125.00.

Paleo blade, Upper Mercer gray mixed flint, 1¼" x 3½". This knife was found near Cortland, Trumbull County, Ohio. *Pat Layshock collection; Thomas R. Pigott image.* $50.00.

Square knife or rectangular blade, Upper Mercer gray flint, 1⅝" x 3¼". It came from the Cortland area, Trumbull County, Ohio. *Pat Layshock collection; Thomas R. Pigott image.* $50.00.

Late Paleo lance or knife, black Upper Mercer with brownish inclusions, 4¼" long. The owner found this artifact in Knox County, Ohio. *Carl Harruff collection.* $450.00.

Rectangular blade, Paleo period, Flint Ridge in blue-gray and cream. The knife is 4¾" long and was picked up by the owner in Knox County, Ohio. *Carl Harruff collection.* $600.00.

Paleo rectangular blade, creamy chert, 3³⁄₁₆" long. Ex-collection Vietzen, the knife was found along the Big Darby in Union County, Ohio. *Private collection.* $200.00.

Paleo rectangular blade, creamy chert with several darker inclusions, 3¼" long. The knife was found in Jefferson County, Missouri. *Private collection.* $200.00.

Paleo rectangular blade, dark blue Upper Mercer flint, 3¾" long. The less-excurvate edge has a slight bevel from resharpening. Delaware County, Ohio. *Private collection.* $200.00.

Fluted knife, Deepkill flint mottled brown and dark green, 2¾". One face has a long and deep flute. Chautauqua County, New York. *Dave Summers collection, New York.* $160.00.

Paleo knife, gray and tan Onondaga, solution or fossil cavity at lower right, 4³⁄₁₀". It is from Chautauqua County, New York. *Dave Summers collection, New York.* $110.00.

Triangular knife, gray and tan Onondaga, 3²⁄₅". The knife is ex-collection Whipple and is from the Genesee/Erie counties area, New York. *Dave Summers collection, New York.* $150.00.

321

Rectangular blade, 1⅝" x 3", thin, and found by the owner. The fossiliferous chert is white, pink, and blue. Monroe County, Indiana. *Collection of and photograph by Jon Hunsberger, Indiana.* $100.00.

Paleo knife, reddish fossiliferous chert, 1" x 5¼". This thin artifact was found by the owner in Monroe County, Indiana. *Collection of and photograph by Jon Hunsberger, Indiana.* $100.00.

Paleo square knife (rectangular blade), black Zaleski flint, 4½" long. It has basal thinning flakes and was found in Ohio. *Christopher Smith collection, New York.* $450.00.

Paleo knife, indented and thinned base, 2¾". It is made of Normanskill flint and came from Dutchess County, New York. *Christopher Smith collection, New York.* $275.00.

Paleo square knife, Onondaga chert, 3½" long. It was picked up in Broome County, New York. *Christopher Smith collection, New York.* $300.00.

Paleo square knife or rectangular blade, 4" long, dark blue Coshocton (Upper Mercer) flint. Ex-collection Wilkins, it came from Monroe County, Ohio. *Christopher Smith collection, New York.* $400.00.

Late Paleo lanceolate-shaped knife, Bloomville chert, ex-collection Townsend. It is 4⅜" long and only ³⁄₁₆" thick. Indiana. *Earthworks Artifacts*. $2,200.00.

Paleo square knife or rectangular blade, high-grade glossy Upper Mercer, 2" x 3½". Found in 1979, it is from Holmes County, Ohio. *Stan Hershberger collection*. $250.00.

Paleo knife, stemmed, mixed blue Upper Mercer flint, 4¾". The example is burin flaked along the top right edge, something occasionally seen on Paleo points or blades. It was found near Killbuck in 1965. Holmes County, Ohio. *Stan Hershberger collection*. $300.00.

Biface blade, small basal flute, 3¾". It is resharpened from both faces on the excurvate edge. Henry County, Ohio. *Dwight Wolfe collection*. $50.00.

Rectangular blade, golden water-stained flint, 1⁹⁄₁₆" x 2¼". It came from a creek in the Ohio River Valley. West Virginia. *Private collection; Rodney Roberts photograph*. $25.00.

323

Knife, straight beveled edge, tan flint. The blade measures 1½" x 2⁹⁄₁₆", and it came from the Ohio River Valley. West Virginia. *Private collection; Rodney Roberts photograph.* $25.00.

Knife, straight beveled edge, 1¼" x 3". The material is golden Carter Cave flint from Kentucky. This piece was a 2002 find in a creek in the Ohio River Valley. West Virginia. *Private collection; Rodney Roberts photograph.* $50.00.

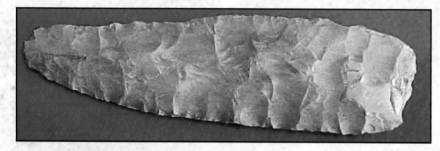

Paleo knife, light brown hornstone, 4½" long. This piece, in the general-purpose shape, is well chipped and has secondary edge retouch. It came from Clark County, Kentucky. *Jeff Schumacher collection, Kentucky.* $125.00 – 150.00.

Paleo crescent uniface blade, multicolored Carter Cave flint, 3" long. Pictured in *Prehistoric American* in 2002, on page 47, it is an excellent type example. Clark County, Kentucky. *Jeff Schumacher collection, Kentucky.* $150.00 – 200.00.

Curved knife or preform, probably Paleo, ⅜" x 4⅛". The owner found this piece, made of white flint, in Stone County, Missouri. *Curtis Chisam collection, Missouri.* $15.00.

Rectangular blade, Paleo, 3¼" long and ⅜" thick. White flint was used for the piece, found by the owner in Stone County, Missouri. *Curtis Chisam collection, Missouri.* $85.00.

Paleo rectangular blade, slightly translucent Indiana or Kentucky hornstone, 2⅝". It came from Barren County, Kentucky. *Dwight Wolfe collection.* $75.00.

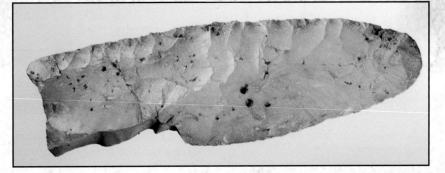

Clovis knife, fluted both faces, 4½" long. It is made of gray-tan unknown flint, and has a large burin flake scar on the base and lower blade edge. Franklin County, Missouri. *Dwight Wolfe collection.* $600.00.

Rectangular Paleo blade, classic form, dark blue Upper Mercer flint. It is 3⅝" long and was picked up in Auglaize County, Ohio. *Dwight Wolfe collection.* $150.00.

Paleo knife, black obsidian, $^{31}/_{32}$" x 2¾", straighter edge with retouch. It came from the same site that produced an obsidian Haskett. Western Box Elder County, northern Utah. *Dann Russell collection, Utah.* $125.00.

Semi-lunate blade, beveled straight edge, 3¼". The excurvate edge has a burin scar ⅞" long, and one end has a graver tip. Wayne County, Ohio. *Dwight Wolfe collection.* $45.00.

Paleo lamellar flake knife, working edge as shown at top, Florence permian flint. This piece was found by the owner in Jefferson County, Nebraska. *Jim Horst collection, Nebraska.* $20.00.

Paleo tool, curved knife form, two long working edges. An excellent example, it is made of Foraker permian flint and has a crushed graver tip. Provenance unlisted. *Jim Horst collection, Nebraska.* $150.00.

Paleo flake knife, long two edges beveled from resharpening, Foraker permian chert. There is also an end-scraper on this artifact. Provenance unlisted. *Jim Horst collection, Nebraska.* $100.00.

Paleo blade, 1⅞" x 6⅜", grayish-white flint with pinkish tip. It is ex-collections Allen and Lyerla, and there is a shaft-scraper on the lower blade edge. Find date is August 22, 1902. Provenance unknown. *Tom Fouts collection, Kansas.* $450.00.

Rectangular blade, 1⅞" x 3¹⁄₁₆". Made of gray hornstone with a large bull's-eye, it was found in Nelson County, Kentucky. *Bybee collection, Kentucky; Tom Davis photograph.* $100.00.

Paleo knife, 1⅝" x 3⅜", hornstone. This blade was found in Marshall County, Kentucky. *Bybee collection, Kentucky; Tom Davis photograph.* $20.00.

Paleo dagger-like blade, with parallel oblique flaking, creamy white flint. The artifact is ⅞" x 5⅜" and is ex-collections Allen and Lyerla. Missouri. *Tom Fouts collection, Kansas.* $650.00.

Paleo square-end knife, 1½" x 3⅛", Dover chert. It came from the Kentucky Lake area, Calloway County, Kentucky. *Bybee collection, Kentucky; Tom Davis photograph.* $20.00.

Rectangular blade or square knife, 2⅝" x 4⅜". It was found by the owner in 1988. St. Louis County, Missouri. *Jeff Anderson collection, Indiana.* $125.00.

Paleo rectangular blade or square knife, 3⅝", mixed Upper Mercer. It was purchased by the owner in 2000, at an estate sale. Chandlersville area, Muskingum County, Ohio. *Jesse Weber collection; photograph by Norman's Photo, Newcomerstown, Ohio.* $150.00.

Paleo rectangular blade or square knife, 3⅝", mottled Upper Mercer flint. This was obtained by the owner at an estate sale in 2000. Chandlersville area, Muskingum County, Ohio. *Jesse Weber collection; photograph by Norman's Photo, Newcomerstown, Ohio.* $350.00.

Paleo square knife, 2⁹⁄₁₆", purchased by the owner at a farm sale. The material is Upper Mercer gray, and the piece came from Licking County, Ohio. *Jesse Weber collection; photograph by Norman's Photo, Newcomerstown, Ohio.* $50.00.

Rectangular blade or square knife, 3" long, Upper Mercer flint. Ex-collection Vietzen, the artifact was obtained at auction. Ohio. *Jesse Weber collection; photograph by Norman's Photo, Newcomerstown, Ohio.* $300.00.

Paleo knife, parallel flaking, long edge with secondary retouch. It is probably of Flint Ridge in two colors, and its length is 3⅜". Coshocton County, Ohio. *Jesse Weber collection; photograph by Norman's Photo, Newcomerstown, Ohio.* $75.00.

Clovis knife, chert, No. 702 in Peck's North Carolina fluted survey. It is ¾" x 1⅜" and was found by the owner in Buncombe County, North Carolina. *Collection of and photograph by Gary Henry, North Carolina.* $30.00.

Lerma-like blade, 1¼" x 4⅜", from Goodflint.com. It is ex-collection McIntosh and was found in Logan County, Kentucky. *Doug Goodrum collection, Kentucky.* $75.00.

Paleo knife, mottled pale blue Upper Mercer, 3⁹⁄₁₀". The blade is ex-collection Winegardner and came from Licking County, Ohio. *Mike Diano collection, Florida.* $200.00.

Paleo square knife or rectangular blade, 3" long, dark Upper Mercer flint. It has a possible shaft-scraper on one edge. The owner found this example in Hocking County, Ohio. *Mike Diano collection, Florida.* $125.00.

Paleo blade, 3⅘", mottled blue Upper Mercer. It is ex-collection Wilkens and was found in Richland County, Ohio. *Mike Diano collection, Florida.* $175.00.

Knife, possibly Paleo, heavily patinated light tan chert. It measures 1⅜" x 2⁵⁄₁₆" and is very thin. Found by the owner, it came from Wayne County, North Carolina. *Michael Womble collection, North Carolina.* $40.00 – 60.00.

Knife, probably Paleo, light tan chert, 1⁵⁄₁₆" x 2¹³⁄₁₆". The example is quite thin and was found by the owner in Wayne County, North Carolina. *Michael Womble collection, North Carolina.* $60.00 – 85.00.

Stemmed blade, possibly Paleo, 1³⁄₁₆" x 2½", flint in banded shades of gray. It was found by the owner in Wilson County, North Carolina. *Michael Womble collection, North Carolina.* $45.00.

Stemmed blade, Late Paleo, 1⅛" x 2⅞". The material is light green flint for this knife, which has a excurvate edge and off-center tip. It was found by Sam Womble in Wayne County, North Carolina. *Michael Womble collection, North Carolina.* $40.00.

Knife, probably Paleo, 2¾". Gray flint was used for the artifact, found by the owner in Stone County, Missouri. *Curtis Chisam collection, Missouri.* $10.00.

Paleo blade or preform, 2¾" long, patinated Knife River flint. The ovate form and wide, long flake scars suggest the Paleo origin. Morton County, North Dakota. *Brian Blotsky collection and Larry Bumann scan, both North Dakota.* Unlisted.

Paleo blade or preform, Knife River flint with milky patination on some ridges. It came from Morton County, North Dakota. *Collection of and scan by Larry Bumann, North Dakota.* $75.00.

Knife, probably Paleo, 3¼" long and ⁵⁄₁₆" thick. Made of white flint, this was found by the owner in Stone County, Missouri. *Curtis Chisam collection, Missouri.* $35.00.

Paleo knives or preforms, Knife River flint, from Morton County, North Dakota. Left, large obverse flaking. $100.00. Right, overshot flake on much of obverse face. $150.00. *Collection of and scan by Larry Bumann, North Dakota.*

329

Paleo blade or point preform, some patination, Knife River flint. This piece came from Burleigh County, North Dakota. *Brian Blotsky collection and Larry Bumann scan, both North Dakota.* $150.00.

Uniface Paleo knife or tool, Indiana hornstone, 3½". It has a large perforator or graver tip, and the excurvate edge is sharpened for knife use. Ex-collection Tolliver, it is from Hocking County, Ohio. *Don Casto collection.* $100.00.

Paleo curved knife or dagger, 3¾", glossy light-colored mixed flint. It was found in the Midwest. *Don Casto collection.* $75.00.

Simpson blade, 5½", Hillsborough Basin flint. It was found by O. W. Moody Sr. near the Alafia River. Hillsborough County, Florida. *Bill Moody collection, Massachusetts.* $500.00.

Rectangular Paleo blade, 3⅜", well chipped in translucent creamy orange Flint Ridge. An excellent specimen, it was found in Fairfield County, Ohio. *Don Casto collection.* $200.00.

Paleo general-purpose blade, 1½" x 3⅞", mixed blue Coshocton (Upper Mercer) flint. The owner has a very similar blade that is fluted. This example has several flute-like basal thinning flake scars. Richland County, Ohio. *Lar Hothem collection.* $50.00.

Paleo rectangular blade, 3" long, mottled blue Upper Mercer. The excurvate edge is resharpened, while the opposite and straighter edge is "backed," or flattened, probably for handle attachment. The owner found this knife in Fairfield County, Ohio. *Don Casto collection.* $50.00.

Paleo curved knife, Upper Mercer gray-tan and blue, 3½" long. It was found by the owner in Fairfield County, Ohio. *Don Casto collection.* $65.00.

Rectangular blade, 3⅝", Mill Creek chert. Examples like this, with incurvate side edges, have been found in Ohio, Kentucky, and elsewhere. Eastern Midwest. *Dwight Wolfe collection.* $125.00.

Rectangular blade or Paleo square knife, 1⁵⁄₁₆" x 2⅞", pinkish-cream chert. It was found in Alexander County, Illinois. *Bybee collection, Kentucky; Tom Davis photograph.* $65.00.

Rectangular blade or square knife, 1⅜" x 2⅝". The material is Fort Payne chert, and the piece came from Hardin County, Kentucky. *Bybee collection, Kentucky; Tom Davis photograph.* $30.00.

Paleo knife, black Kanawha flint, ¹⁵⁄₁₆" x 2⅜". It came from an Ohio River site in West Virginia. *Private collection; Rodney Roberts photograph.* $25.00.

Paleo knife, base flute, unknown pale green flint with light tan spots, 1¼" x 1¾". It was found on an Ohio River site, West Virginia. *Private collection; Rodney Roberts photograph.* $20.00.

Paleo knife, green and tan flint, light grinding on lower blade edges. This piece is 1⅛" x 2⁵⁄₁₆" and came from an Ohio River site. West Virginia. *Private collection; Rodney Roberts photograph.* $20.00.

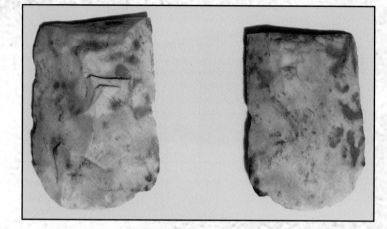

Rectangular blade, white chert or flint with dark inclusions. It measures 1⅛" x 1⅝" and was picked up on a site along the Ohio River. West Virginia. *Private collection; Rodney Roberts photograph.* $25.00.

Paleo knife, tan flint with darker inclusions, ground lower blade edges and base. The knife is 1⁵⁄₁₆" x 2⅝" and came from the Ohio Valley area. West Virginia. *Private collection; Rodney Roberts photograph.* $40.00.

Paleo rectangular blade, 3⅝", unusual Flint Ridge moss agate that is translucent despite medium thickness. It came from near Midway Mall, Lorain County, Ohio. *Dwight Wolfe collection.* $125.00.

Paleo knives or preforms, both made of Knife River flint and both from Emmons County, North Dakota. *Collection of and scan by Larry Bumann, North Dakota.* Unlisted.

Paleo Indian knives, Knife River flint with different degrees of patination. All were found in Emmons County, North Dakota. Top left, bipointed, patinated. $250.00. Top right, excurvate edge. $200.00. Bottom left, heavily patinated. $200.00. Bottom right, bipointed. $150.00. *Collection of and scan by Larry Bumann, North Dakota.*

Paleo bipointed blade or preform, Knife River flint with milky patination. It has large percussion flake scars, several of which appear to be typical overshot (one edge to another). It was found in western North Dakota. *Collection of and scan by Larry Bumann, North Dakota.* $200.00.

Paleo knife, at least one basal graver tip, 3³⁄₁₆". The material used is both unusual and unknown. Fairfield County, Ohio. *Dan Casto collection.* $50.00.

Lanceolate point or blade, 1³⁄₈" x 3", tan and gray Upper Mercer flint. This fine and thin example is ex-collection McKnight and is from Pickaway County, Ohio. *Private collection.* $600.00.

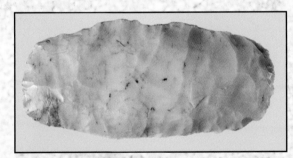

Rectangular blade, translucent Flint Ridge. It has a flute on the reverse about 1¹⁄₁₆" long, and its overall length is 2¹⁵⁄₁₆". Ex-collection Hooks, Richland County, Ohio. *Don Casto collection.* $150.00.

Paleo lamellar flake knife, both long edges sharpened, Florence permian flint. Found by the owner, it came from Jefferson County, Nebraska. *Jim Horst collection, Nebraska.* $25.00.

Paleo semi-lunate knife, excurvate working edge, size as indicated and provenance unlisted. *Jim Horst collection, Nebraska.* $125.00.

Paleo knife, sharpened on two long edges, possible graver tip. Provenance unlisted. *Jim Horst collection, Nebraska.* $50.00.

Paleo rectangular blade, ex-collection Robertson, creamy-tan Burlington. It measures 2⅜" x 5¼" and was found in Jefferson County, Missouri. *Dwight Wolfe collection.* $200.00.

Paleo knife, angled baseline, blue Upper Mercer mixed flint. The blade is 3⅝" and came from Ohio. *Dwight Wolfe collection.* $60.00.

Fluted point or knife, 3½". Ex-collection Beer, the material is yellow-brown quartzite. Northeastern Ohio. *Frank Meyer collection.* Unlisted.

Paleo curved knife, Kanawha flint, ground basal chipping platform. The knife is 4¹⁄₁₆" long, from Ohio. *Don Casto collection.* $75.00.

Paleo knife, flute-like basal thinning, 3⁹⁄₁₆". Dark Upper Mercer was used for this piece, found by the owner in Guernsey County, Ohio. *Jesse Weber collection; photograph by Norman's Photo, Newcomerstown, Ohio.* $100.00.

Paleo rectangular blade or square knife, 3½" long, Delaware County flint. The knife was found in Auglaize County, Ohio. *Jesse Weber collection; photograph by Norman's Photo, Newcomerstown, Ohio.* $100.00.

Clovis preform, early stage Paleo point or blade, Burlington chert. This piece is 3⅜" x 6⅛", and even though it is a preliminary stage of manufacture, not many Paleo artifacts are this large. It came from the Western Bluff area of Jersey County, Illinois. *Gregory L. Perdun collection, Illinois.* $75.00 – 100.00.

Paleo dagger, fluted obverse base, 5⅜" long. Approximately 1¼" wide, this knife is made of Upper Mercer flint and came from Guernsey County, Ohio. *Jesse Weber collection; photograph by Norman's Photo, Newcomerstown, Ohio.* $350.00.

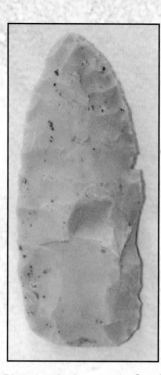

Ovoid uniface knife, Burlington chert with part of the rust-colored original surface, 3¼" long. It was found in the Western Bluff area, Jersey County, Illinois. *Gregory L. Perdun collection, Illinois.* $65.00.

Clovis blade, milky Burlington chert, 2⅞". This artifact was salvaged from a broken tip. Western Bluff area, Jersey County, Illinois. *Gregory L. Perdun collection, Illinois.* $250.00 – 450.00.

Clovis preform or knife, fluted only on the obverse, Chouteau flint. It is 3½" long and came from the Western Bluff area, Jersey County, Illinois. *Gregory L. Perdun collection, Illinois.* $175.00 – 250.00.

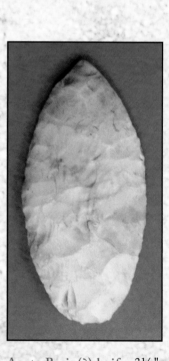

Notched ovoid knife, 5⅛", rare and well made. The owner has seen hundreds of fluted points but only two notched ovoids, of which this is one. Western Bluff area, Jersey County, Illinois. *Gregory L. Perdun collection, Illinois.* Museum grade.

Agate Basin(?) knife, 3⅛", Burlington chert. It has exceptionally fine workstyle and finish. The owner bought this, in 1991, from the farmer who found it. Southern Knox County, Illinois. *Fred Smith collection, Illinois.* $125.00 – 150.00.

336

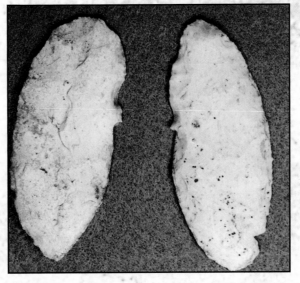

Square-end knife, with side spoke-shave, probably Paleo, 3⅜" long. The material is Moline chert, and the blade came from McDonough County, Illinois. *Fred Smith collection, Illinois.* $30.00 – 40.00.

Ovoid knives, with graver spurs in one side, Burlington chert, each 3¾" long. Very similar in size and style, they were found by the owner about six miles apart. Warren County, Illinois. *Fred Smith collection, Illinois.* Each, $30.00 – 50.00.

Paleo squareback rectangular blade, glossy and translucent Flint Ridge in many muted colors, 3⅝". This fine knife is pictured in *Flint Ridge Artifacts* and came from Delaware County, Ohio. *Len and Janie Weidner collection.* $900.00.

Rectangular blade, probably patinated Flint Ridge or Delaware County flint in light tan, 4½" long. This Paleo knife is ex-collections Max Shipley and Dick Coulter. Licking County, Ohio. *Private collection.* Unlisted.

Knife, probably Paleo, light purple translucent Flint Ridge, 4⅞". It is ex-collection Coffman, from Crawford County, Ohio. *Len and Janie Weidner collection.* $800.00.

Paleo rectangular blade, jewel Flint Ridge, flute attempt at base center to left. This example is 3⅜" long, ex-collections Champion and Haskins. Knox County, Ohio. *Lar Hothem collection.* $150.00.

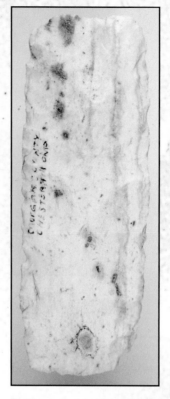

Paleo rectangular blade, unknown cream and gray flint with brown inclusions, 5" long. It is ex-collections Coulter and Goodwin and came from near Chesterville, Morgan County, Ohio. *Jim Beckman collection, Ohio.* $700.00.

Paleo knife, beautiful yellowish brown patinated Upper Mercer, one end fluted. The large blade is 6½" long and is ex-collection Kley. Licking County, Ohio. *Terry Elleman collection, Ohio.* $1,500.00.

Lanceolate blade, golden tan patinated flint, 3⅛" long. This Late Paleo artifact was found in Highland County, Ohio. *Terry Elleman collection, Ohio.* $200.00.

Paleo knife, black Zaleski flint, 4¾" long. The blade was a personal find of the owner in Miami County, Ohio. *Terry Elleman collection, Ohio.* Unlisted.

Lanceolate knife, 3" long, found by the owner. The excurvate edge was carefully retouched from both faces, while the opposite edge has few such signs. Fairfield County, Ohio. *Don Casto collection.* $75.00.

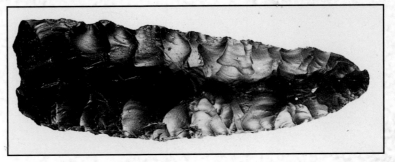

Paleo curved blade, flute-like basal thinning, 4 1/16" long. The material is solid coal-black Zaleski flint, and the knife has a median ridge. Fairfield County, Ohio. *Don Casto collection.* $175.00.

Paleo knife, with basal flutes, 4 3/16" long. A gray and green variety of Upper Mercer, it is ex-collection Casto. Perry County, Ohio. *Jim Beckman collection, Ohio.* $150.00.

Lanceolate knife, Late Paleo, 3 7/8". This blade with a median ridge is made of blue Upper Mercer and was found by the owner. Southcentral Ohio. *Don Casto collection.* $150.00.

Paleo knife, found by the owner on a Paleo site in 2001, Knife River flint. It is 3 1/16" long, and was pictured in *Indian Artifact Magazine.* Brookings County, South Dakota. *Harlan Olson collection, South Dakota.* $100.00.

Paleo general purpose blade, light brown Delaware County flint. 3 7/8" long. It has the usual long excurvate edge and offset tip. Fairfield County, Ohio. *Lar Hothem collection.* $125.00.

Paleo knife, banded Upper Mercer flint colored blue and tan, 4¹/₃₂". The obverse broad basal flute is 1¾" long. Coshocton County, Ohio. *Lar Hothem collection.* $175.00.

Lanceolate, excurvate sides and ground chipping platform at base, 2¹⁵/₁₆". Gray banded Upper Mercer was used for this point or blade, found in Coshocton County, Ohio. *Lar Hothem collection.* $35.00.

Paleo knife, snapped base that forms a chipping platform for thinning, 3⅝" long. Dark blue Upper Mercer was used for this artifact, found in Fairfield County, Ohio. *Lar Hothem collection.* $30.00.

Paleo blade, honey-colored flint, 1" x 2⅞". Found by the owner's father-in-law, Sam Jenkins, it came from an Ohio River site. West Virginia. *Private collection; Rodney Roberts photograph.* $20.00.

Paleo semi-lunate knife, beveled straight edge, ⅞" x 2⅛". It is made of translucent blue Flint Ridge and was found by the owner's father-in-law, Sam Jenkins. The two men have been surface hunting since 1987. West Virginia. *Private collection; Rodney Roberts photograph.* $60.00.

Clovis knife, Early Paleo, basal obverse flute, 4¹¹/₁₆". Made of gray chert, this blade is ex-collections Speer, Lilljedahl, and Walter. Central Texas. *Dr. Guy H. Gross collection, Texas.* $650.00.

Field hunters know that in terms of Paleo points, the most common finds are broken examples. And when an artifact fragment is picked up, it is usually the base. This is because most prehistoric sites are known due to location and flint or chert chips (also known as debitage). It is thought that when a point was broken on the hunt, the base and wooden shaft were brought back to camp. The shaft alone was well worth saving, and perhaps the broken point as well.

This is evidenced by three ways in which broken Paleo points were commonly treated. If broken near the original tip, the point might be retipped and so continue in use. Or the broken portion might be made into another tool form, like a graver or shaft-scraper. Or perhaps the basal portion was too short for salvage of any kind and was simply discarded. Often the remaining point portion — whether tip, midsection, or base — will have signs that it continued functioning as a tool. Good material in the Paleo era was treated as a valuable commodity.

Just as the Paleo people respected broken parts, so do collectors today. Due to the typical fine workstyle and high-grade material, and the mere fact that the artifact is Paleo, collectors place them in frames or at least do not throw them away. For example, the bases of fine fluted points, incomplete "heartbreakers" or "weepers" that they are, can bring hundreds of dollars. Generally, the more of a point that is present, the more the piece is worth.

Along with such pieces, one acquires not only a solid bit of prehistory, but a sad appreciation regarding what the point must have once been. The bases of exceptional fluted points or lance points are one of the great "if only" aspects of artifact collecting, especially when found by the collector.

Clovis base, well-fluted on both faces, two-tone gray flint. It is 1½" long and was found by the owner in 1999. St. Joseph County, Indiana. *Paul Weisser collection, Indiana.* $45.00.

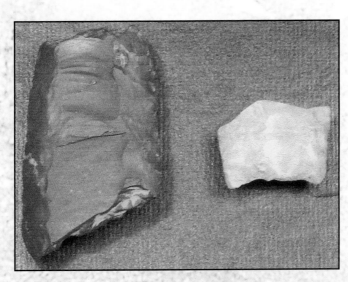

Paleo artifacts. Left, red jasper point(?) section, fluted both faces, obverse double-fluted full length, 1⅛" x 1¾". Right, gray chert, ⅝" x 15⁄16" wide, ⅛" thick. Both were found by the owner in Hunterdon County, New Jersey. *Bob Bronish collection, New Jersey.* Unlisted.

Clovis point base, heavily patinated chert, base converted to side-scraper, 15⁄16" x 1⅜". This piece is shown as No. 656 in Peck's North Carolina fluted point survey. It was found by the owner in Buncombe County, North Carolina. *Collection of and photograph by Gary Henry, North Carolina.* $30.00.

Dalton base and point, high-grade chert. Both were found by the owner in Buncombe County, North Carolina. Left, ¾" x 15⁄16". $10.00. Right, ¾" x 1¾". $40.00. *Collection of and photograph by Gary Henry, North Carolina.*

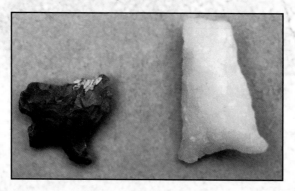

Quad, tip damage, 2¼" long. It was found by the owner in Rush County, Indiana. *Jeff Anderson collection, Indiana.* $100.00.

Paleo points, both found by the owner in Buncombe County, North Carolina. Left, Hardaway side-notch, chert, ¾" x ¾". $5.00. Right, point, distal end missing, quartzite, ¾" x 1⅛". $10.00. *Collection of and photograph by Gary Henry, North Carolina.*

Clovis base, Early Paleo, milky quartz with a touch of yellow, 13⁄16" x ⅞". No. 576 in Peck's North Carolina fluted point survey, it was found by the owner in 1997. Buncombe County, North Carolina. *Collection of and photograph by Gary Henry, North Carolina.* $5.00.

Dalton variety base, Late Paleo, dark chert, ⅞" x 1⅛". This piece was found by the owner in Buncombe County, North Carolina. *Gary Henry collection, North Carolina; Nick Lanier photograph.* $5.00.

Hardaway side-notch, mixed chert, ⅞" x 1". Found by Harwood, it is from North Carolina. *Collection of and photograph by Gary Henry, North Carolina.* $20.00.

Fluted point, chert, 1³⁄16" x 2³⁄16". Found by Harwood, the broken point came from Greene County, Tennessee. *Collection of and photograph by Gary Henry, North Carolina.* $20.00.

Clovis fluted tool, Early Paleo, found by L. Murphy. This highly unusual artifact is 1⅜" x 2½", and its provenance is unlisted. *Doug Goodrum collection, Kentucky.* $150.00 – 400.00.

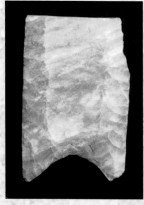

Clovis basal portion, 2¹⁄16", gray Upper Mercer. It was reworked in ancient times to form a side-scraper at the upper right edge. Ex-collection Col. Vietzen, it is from Ohio. *Bill Moody collection, Massachusetts.* $85.00.

Fluted point bases, both found by the owner on a site that has produced many Paleo artifacts. The left example, 1⅝", is made of translucent amber flint, while the base on the right is of black Upper Mercer. Fairfield County, Ohio. *Don Casto collection.* Unlisted.

Unfluted Paleo point lower section, 2½" long. It is made of "burnt sugar" quartzite and is colored a rich reddish black. While the source of this material is uncertain, the piece was found near Bremen, Ohio. *Don Casto collection.* Unlisted.

Clovis basal portion, gray hornstone(?), broken across upper flute and with possible graver tip at upper right corner. It is 1¹⁵⁄₁₆", ex-collection Col. Vietzen. Logan County, Kentucky. *Bill Moody collection, Massachusetts.* $65.00.

Paleo knife, incurvate baseline with possible graver spur on one corner, 3¼". Of Upper Mercer mixed flint, it came from Fairfield County, Ohio. *Don Casto collection.* $75.00.

Clovis point base, ⅝" x ⅞", ³⁄₁₆" thick. Flutes on both faces are ⅝" long, and edges are ground bull length. Of tan transparent agate, it was a 1992 find by the owner in Franktown, Colorado. *Mark Boswell collection, Colorado; photograph by Infocusphotography.com, Colorado.* $50.00.

Clovis body, ¾" x 1¾", ¼" thick. It is randomly flaked and fluted for ¾" on both faces. Gray, tan, and red quartz was used for the point, found in Crowley County, Colorado. *Mark Boswell collection, Colorado; photograph by Infocusphotography.com, Colorado.* $125.00.

Dalton preform, broken in manufacturing, Burlington with good parallel flaking. It is 3⅜" long and was found in the Western Bluff area, Jersey County, Illinois. *Gregory L. Perdun collection, Illinois.* $15.00 – 25.00.

Clovis fluted point base, broken by a posthole digger into two pieces, artifact 2" long. It came from the Western Bluff area, Jersey County, Illinois. *Gregory L. Perdun collection, Illinois.* $40.00.

Clovis base, 1⅛" x 1⁷⁄₁₆", ¼" thick. It is fluted for the full length, and the material is gray and tan quartz. Both flutes and flaking are well done, and the base was found in Crowley County, Colorado. *Mark Boswell collection, Colorado; photograph by Info cusphotography.com, Colorado.* $50.00.

Hardaway Dalton point, with basal damage, chert, 1" x 1½". It was picked up in 1987 by the owner. Buncombe County, North Carolina. *Collection of and photograph by Gary Henry, North Carolina.* $30.00.

Hardaway Dalton point, with basal protrusion missing, quartz, 1⁵⁄₁₆" x 1⁹⁄₁₆". Found by the owner in 1986, it is from Richmond County, North Carolina. *Collection of and photograph by Gary Henry, North Carolina.* $20.00.

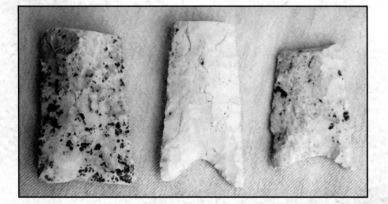

Dalton bases, Late Paleo, various grades of Burlington. The longest example is 2¼". Jersey County, Illinois. *Gregory L. Perdun collection, Illinois.* Each, $5.00 – 15.00.

Hardaway Dalton point, with basal ear damage, Late Paleo, chert, ⅞" x 1⁵⁄₁₆". The owner found this resharpened piece in 1998. Buncombe County, North Carolina. *Collection of and photograph by Gary Henry, North Carolina.* $40.00.

Hardaway Dalton point, with damaged basal ears, Late Paleo, quartz, 1" x 1⅜". Found by the owner in 1988, it is from Buncombe County, North Carolina. *Collection of and photograph by Gary Henry, North Carolina.* $30.00.

Hardaway Dalton point, missing tip, Late Paleo, ⅞" x 1¼". Made of quartz, it was found by the owner in 2002. Haywood County, North Carolina. *Collection of and photograph by Gary Henry, North Carolina.* $20.00.

Beaver Lake base, Late Paleo, 1³⁄₁₆" x 1⁵⁄₁₆". The owner found this piece, made of chert, in 2001. Madison County, North Carolina. *Collection of and photograph by Gary Henry, North Carolina.* $7.00.

Hardaway Dalton point, distal end missing, crystal quartz, ¹¹⁄₁₆" x 1". This was found by the owner in 1995. Buncombe County, North Carolina. *Collection of and photograph by Gary Henry, North Carolina.* $10.00.

Fluted point, Early Paleo, broken Redstone-like type. Made of cream and blue Upper Mercer, it has wide and shallow flutes on both faces. Size is 1¼" x 1⅝". Probably Tuscarawas County, Ohio. *Private collection.* Unlisted.

Fluted point, light gray unknown flint with dark gray stripes, 1⅞". The reverse lower face is also fluted, and tip damage appears to be recent. Ex-collection Hogue, Coshocton County, Ohio. *Private collection.* $100.00.

Preform lance section, Late Paleo, basal thinning platform on obverse. It is made of gray and cream streaked Upper Mercer and is 1¾" long. The broken areas were used as tool tips and edges. Coshocton County, Ohio. *Private collection.* Unlisted.

Lance point or blade, broken tip, black Upper Mercer, light basal grinding. The artifact is ⅞" x 3⅛" and was found by the owner's father-in-law, Sam Jenkins. A good piece for restoration, it is from the Ohio River Valley. West Virginia. *Private collection; Rodney Roberts photograph.* Unlisted.

Dalton point, tip damage, 2¼", white chert. It was found by the owner in Ozark County, Missouri. *Curtis Chisam collection, Missouri.* $15.00.

Broken Dalton section, with a spokeshave, 1⅛" x 1⅞". Made of Burlington chert, it was found in Montgomery County, Missouri. *Bob Rampani collection, Missouri.* $20.00.

Salvaged Dalton blade, lower portion with a large spokeshave, 1⅛" x 2½". It is made of Burlington and was surface found by the owner. Lincoln County, Missouri. *Bob Rampani collection, Missouri.* $50.00.

Fluted point, fire cracked at upper blade, gray-tan patinated Flint Ridge. It is 2¼", and the obverse flute is ⅞" long. The off-center indentation on the baseline has been seen on a number of fluted Paleo points and may have had a purpose. This example was found by T. Linger in Fairfield County, Ohio. *Private collection.* $50.00.

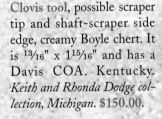

Clovis tool, possible scraper tip and shaft-scraper side edge, creamy Boyle chert. It is ¹³⁄₁₆" x 1¹⁵⁄₁₆" and has a Davis COA. Kentucky. *Keith and Rhonda Dodge collection, Michigan.* $150.00.

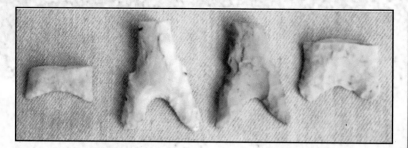

Dalton bases, large type variety, longest 1⅜". Made of Burlington chert, the center two are deeply concave. All are from Jersey County, Illinois. *Gregory L. Perdun collection, Illinois.* Each, $5.00 – 15.00.

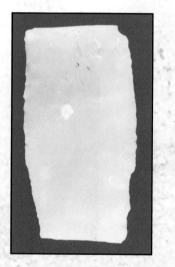

Dalton bases, Late Paleo, center and left Burlington, right example Chouteau flint. Such authentic examples are key study pieces for determining authentic artifacts. The largest example is 2⅝" long. Jersey County, Illinois. *Gregory L. Perdun collection, Illinois.* Each, $5.00 – 15.00.

Clovis base and angled midsection, possibly used as a tool, speckled light-colored hornstone. The fragment is fully fluted and the original flute length is unknown. The piece is 1" x 1½" and was found by the owner in Hardin County, Kentucky. *Collection of and photograph by Clint Basham, Kentucky.* Unlisted.

Fluted point, with broken tip, length 3⅜". The obverse flute is full length, and the reverse flute is 2¾". Of blue and purple unknown flint, it was found in Morgan County, Ohio. *Len and Janie Weidner collection.* Unlisted.

Lance midsection, with probable graver corners, 2½". Translucent blue-gray Flint Ridge, it has very fine chipping and was found by the owner in Licking County, Ohio. *Joel Embrey collection.* Unlisted.

Late Paleo lance section, blue-purple Flint Ridge, 2¼". It has a shaft-scraper on one side, and graver tips at each end of the large break area. Central Ohio. *Private collection.* $20.00.

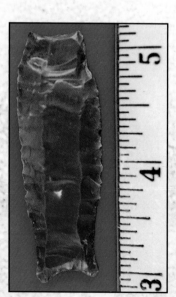

Cumberland point salvaged into a tool, long main flute and tip flute, probably Kentucky hornstone. (Hillsdale chert from West Virginia is sometimes this color, but has some fossil inclusions). The Cumberland has two probable graver spurs at the distal end. Harlan County, Kentucky. *Craig Ferrell collection.* $250.00.

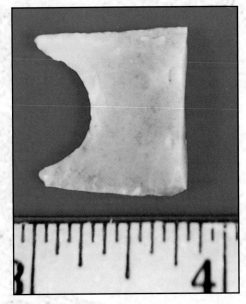

Debert-like Clovis base, Hughes River chalcedony, finely chipped. It was picked up in Putnam County, West Virginia. *Craig Ferrell collection.* Unlisted.

Cumberland point base, Fort Payne chert. A large and beautifully made section; a collector can only marvel at what the point once was. Pulaski County, Kentucky. *Craig Ferrell collection.* $200.00.

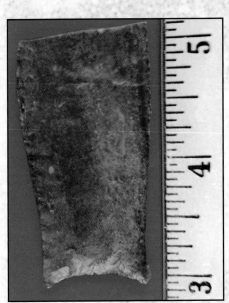

Clovis base, Sonora chert, possibly broken during fluting of the second face. Note the presence of fluting nipple or projection at base center. It came from Lyon County, Kentucky. *Craig Ferrell collection.* Unlisted.

Clovis point, found broken on a dirt road, Hillsdale (Greenbrier) chert. Fluted, the point came from Boone County, West Virginia. *Craig Ferrell collection.* $100.00.

Fluted point base and midsection, small flutes, size as indicated. It is made of light-colored Crooksville chert and came from Putnam County, West Virginia. *Craig Ferrell collection.* $25.00.

Bases of Paleo points, some fluted, various high-grade materials. Bases rather than point tips tend to be found on Paleo sites. Find locations unknown. *Glenn F. Witchey collection.* Unlisted.

Paleo fluted point midsection, unknown striped flint. Workstyle suggests this was once part of an exceptional point. Mason County, West Virginia. *Craig Ferrell collection.* Unlisted.

347

Fluted point body, 1¾", Nellie chert. It was found in Ohio. *Glenn F. Witchey collection.* $50.00.

Fluted point base and midsection, 1⅞" long, dark flint. The break area may be an impact fracture. Tennessee. *Glenn F. Witchey collection.* $75.00.

Fluted point base, 1⅜", dark Upper Mercer. It is from Knox County, Ohio. *Glenn F. Witchey collection.* $50.00.

Clovis preforms, broken in early manufacturing state, Burlington chert. The largest two pieces are 1¾" long. Western Bluff area, Jersey County, Illinois. *Gregory L. Perdun collection, Illinois.* Each, $10.00 – 20.00.

Clovis preforms, fluted both lower faces, broken in manufacturing by end shock. They are made of Burlington chert, and the longest is 2⅛". The find site contained many more broken points than whole. Western Bluff area, Jersey County, Illinois. *Gregory L. Perdun collection, Illinois.* Each, $10.00 – 20.00.

Clovis preforms, broken on the second flute attempt with reverse hinges through the point, Burlington chert. Each is about 1¾" long. They came from the Western Bluff area, Jersey County, Illinois. *Gregory L. Perdun collection, Illinois.* Each, $10.00 – 20.00.

Clovis preform bases, broken when the flute reverse hinged. The largest piece is 2⅛" long. These were found on the same knapping site and came from the same chert (Burlington) core. Western Bluff area, Jersey County, Illinois. *Gregory L. Perdun collection, Illinois.* Each, $10.00 – 20.00.

Clovis preform bases and tips, broken on a Paleo lithics manufacturing site, largest piece 3" wide. They were found in the Western Bluff area, Jersey County, Illinois. *Gregory L. Perdun collection, Illinois.* Each, $5.00 – 10.00.

Paleo lance, tip missing, 2¼" long. It is made of Nellie chert and was found in Ohio. *Glenn F. Witchey collection.* $20.00.

Paleo point, damaged tip, 1¾" long. Made of mixed unknown flint, it was found in Van Wert County, Ohio. *Glenn F. Witchey collection.* $50.00.

Fluted point basal section, dark flint, 1" long. This was a personal find by the owner in Medina County, Ohio. *Glenn F. Witchey collection.* Unlisted.

Hardaway Dalton base, Late Paleo, misty chalcedony, ¾" x ¹⁵⁄₁₆". It was found by the owner in 1987 and came from Buncombe County, North Carolina. *Collection of and photograph by Gary Henry, North Carolina.* $5.00.

Hardaway side-notch base, frosty chalcedony, ⁹⁄₁₆" x ¾". This was once a spectacular artifact; this piece was found by the owner in 1989. Buncombe County, North Carolina. *Collection of and photograph by Gary Henry, North Carolina.* $5.00.

Dalton point, 2" long, tip damage. Made of white flint, it was found by the owner. Ozark County, Missouri. *Curtis Chisam collection, Missouri.* $10.00.

Paleo knife, portion with long basal flute, pink banded flint, 1⅞" long. Only ¼" thick, this artifact was found by the owner in Stone County, Missouri. *Curtis Chisam collection, Missouri.* $15.00.

Fluted point base, near-black fire-marked Upper Mercer, 1¼". Found in 1962, it is ex-collection Witzman and is illustrated in *Survey of Ohio Fluted Points* No. 10, page 9. Wayne County, Ohio. *Glenn F. Witchey collection.* $50.00.

Clovis base, multiple flutes, glossy green flint that may be Van Port. It is 1¹⁄₂₀" long and was found in Chautauqua County, New York. *Dave Summers collection, New York.* $55.00.

Ross County type fluted point salvaged as a knife, of gray, tan, and green Coshocton (Upper Mercer) flint. It is 2³⁄₂₀" and was resharpened to a pentagonal outline. Chautauqua County, New York. *Dave Summers collection, New York.* $350.00.

Lanceolate section, with scraper edge, of gray, blue, and tan Onondaga, 2¾", ex-collection Whipple. Niagara County, New York. *Dave Summers collection, New York.* $70.00.

Hardaway Dalton, green-gray Deepkill flint, 1⅖". It came from the Lower Hudson Valley, New York. *Dave Summers collection, New York.* $60.00.

Paleo point, unknown pink and white chert, 1" x 2½". It was found by the owner in Monroe County, Indiana. *Collection of and photograph by Jon Hunsberger, Indiana.* $40.00.

Fluted point base and midsection, blue unknown flint, 2" long. It was picked up in Tennessee. *Glenn F. Witchey collection.* $75.00.

Fluted point tool (Clovis end-scraper), 1⅜" long, dark golden flint, The point "hinged through" while being fluted, and was salvaged as a tool. The example has a Dickey COA and came from Putnam County, Tennessee. *Back to Earth.* $125.00.

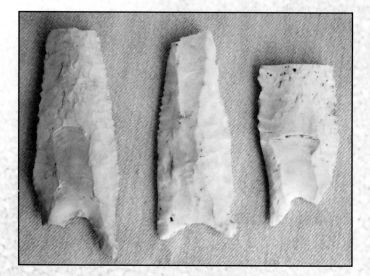

Fluted point base, used as a tool, graver tip at top left. While the exterior has patinated to purple, the break area indicates the original flint was near-black. The base is 2⅜" long and came from Knox County, Ohio. *Gilbert Cooper collection.* Unlisted.

Dalton family fluted points, damaged, longest 3". The center example is of special interest because it is tip fluted. All are Burlington chert and from Jersey County, Illinois. *Gregory L. Perdun collection, Illinois.* Each, $10.00 – 35.00.

PALEO POINT TYPES

One of the reasons for collecting Paleo points across North America is acquiring as many different types as possible. Each region has special forms and materials, and many of the types have been officially named.

Special thanks from the author are due Gregory Perino, well-known archaeologist and artifact authenticator, for permission to reprint Paleo type names from his book series. The series includes volumes 1, 2, and 3 of *Selected Preforms, Points and Knives of the North American Indian*. The books are wide-ranging and accurate, and are highly recommended for amateur archaeologists and serious collectors.

The points in this chapter are listed in alphabetical order, and each listing has four sections. First is the point type name, followed by the Paleo period (Early, Late, or general), the North American geographic region, and a brief description of the point.

Agate Basin
Late Paleo
Most of U.S. except easternmost states
Narrow to wide, lanceolate, tapered stem, finely chipped

Alberta
Late Paleo
Canada, High Plains
Rectangular stem, angular to rounded base corners

Allen
Late Paleo
West
Lanceolate, concave baseline, rounded basal corners

Angostura
Late Paleo
Western states
Tapered lower blade, serrated edges, slightly concave baseline

Anzick
Paleo
West and Midwest
Large, fluted, triangular, straight baseline

Appomattox River
Late Paleo
Virginia
Thin, small points with incurved baselines

Arkabutla
Late Paleo
South
Widest at base corners, small ears, concave baseline

Barber
Late Paleo
Texas and Oklahoma
Deeply concave baseline, contracting lower portion

Barnes
Late Paleo
Eastern Midwest from Canada to Arkansas
Narrow blade with long flutes, concave baseline

Beaver Lake
Late Paleo
Eastern Midwest, Southeast
Tapered waist, extended ears, concave baseline

Belen
Late Paleo
New Mexico and Texas
Small and thin, squared base with slightly incurvate baseline

Browns Valley
Late Paleo
Northern Midwest
Lanceolate, widest at middle, baseline averages straight

Bull Brook
Paleo
Extreme East
Somewhat triangular, fluted, moderately concave baseline

Cactus Hill
Early Paleo
Virginia and Pennsylvania
Pre-Clovis, short lanceolate with incurved baseline

Clovis
Early Paleo
Most of North America
Variable fluting, many configurations and sizes

Cody (knife)
Late Paleo
Western U.S. and Canada
Stemmed, often single-shouldered, angled blade

Colbert Dalton
Late Paleo
Southeast
Stemmed, edges serrated, some beveled

Colby
Paleo
Wyoming, possibly elsewhere
Rounded basal lobes, indented baseline, fluted

Coldwater
Late Paleo
South
High and wide shoulders, constricted lower blade

Crescent (knife)
Paleo
Great Basin
Semi-lunate in shape, no notches or stems

Crowfield
Late Paleo
Northeast
Wide and very thin, excurvate edges, wide or narrow flutes

Cumberland
Late Paleo
Watersheds of the Cumberland, Tennessee, and Ohio
Long and narrow, thick, ears, long flutes

Dalton
Late Paleo
Rocky Mountains to the Atlantic
Flared ears, stemmed, serrated

Debert
Late Paleo
Maine, Nova Scotia, probably elsewhere
Baseline deeply indented, fluted

351

Denbigh
Early Paleo
West Coast of Alaska
Various shapes, ultra-fine ribbon flaking on some

Eden
Late Paleo
Plains states
Squared base with stem, long and narrow

Fayette
Late Paleo
Central Midwest
Tapered stem, incurvate baseline, some with serrations

First View
Late Paleo
Texas, New Mexico, Colorado
Squared base, slight stem, median ridge, fine flaking

Folsom
Late Paleo
Plains states (mainly)
Wide and long flutes, delicate edge retouch, thin, concave baseline

Frederick
Late Paleo and Early Archaic
Plains states
Triangular, with median ridge, slightly incurved baseline

Golondrina
Late Paleo
Texas and northern Mexico
Concave base, indented lower sides, ears

Goshen
Late Paleo
Montana, Wyoming, the Dakotas
Thin, straight to concave baseline, some with needle tips

Greenbrier
Late Paleo
Eastern Midwest and South
Incurvate baseline, side notches, varied widths and lengths

Greenbrier Dalton
Late Paleo
Upper Southeast
Shallow side-notches, serrated edges

Hardaway
Late Paleo into Early Archaic
Carolina Piedmont and adjacent regions
Triangular, wide for size, small side notches

Hardaway Dalton
Late Paleo into Early Archaic
Southern Appalachians and adjacent regions
Triangular, flared basal lobes

Haw River
Early Paleo
Southeast
Widest at base, incurved baseline, may be pre-Clovis

Hazel
Paleo
Eastern Midwest and South
Large, with flat facial flaking and long narrowed waist

Hell Gap
Late Paleo
High Plains
Lanceolate with long stem and wide shoulders

Hempstead Dalton
Late Paleo
Missouri, Arkansas, Oklahoma
Triangular, wide and shallow side notches, flared ears

Hi-Lo
Late Paleo
Western Great Lakes
Short and wide, fluted or with rudimentary side notches

Hinds
Late Paleo
South
Short and wide, shallow side notches, stemmed appearance

Holcombe
Late Paleo
Western Great Lakes region
Thin and small, pointed basal ends, excurvate sides

Holland
Late Paleo
Upper Midwest and elsewhere
Lanceolate, stemmed, serrated edges, some with ears

Jeff
Late Paleo
South
Wide, lower sides slightly constricted, straight baseline

Kimmswick
Paleo
Missouri, Illinois
Long and tapered, concave baseline, short flutes

Kisatchie
Late Paleo
West and South
Short and wide, slightly stemmed, widest at baseline

Levi
Paleo
Texas
Long and narrow, parallel sides, incurved baseline

Lovell
Late Paleo into Early Archaic
High Plains region
Concave or straight baseline, lower sides constricted

Mesa
Paleo
Great Plains, Alaska, and western Canada
Lanceolate, median ridge, concave baseline

Meserve Dalton
Late Paleo
Rocky Mountains to Illinois
Shallow V-shaped baseline, beveled edges

Midland
Late Paleo
High Plains region
Thin and small, not fluted, basal thinning

Milnesand
Late Paleo
Plains states
Parallel sides, fairly straight baseline, unfluted

Nansemond Dalton (knife)
Late Paleo
North Carolina and Virginia
Indented baseline, shallow side notches, ears

Northumberland
Late Paleo
Upper East
Lanceolate, excurvate edges, full-length flute on one face

Ovoid (knife)
Paleo
Midwest and elsewhere
Double ended, one side edge may be beveled

Owl Cave
Late Paleo
Idaho and adjacent states
Lanceolate, straight to excurvate baselines

Pelican
Late Paleo
West and South
Small, pointed ears, fluted, somewhat stemmed

Pike County
Late Paleo
Midwest
Long, narrowed waist, ears

Plainview
Late Paleo
Plains states
Lanceolate, slightly incurved baseline

Quad
Late Paleo
Eastern Midwest and upper South
Fairly wide, distinctive extended ears, narrowed waist

Ragged Island
Late Paleo
Southeast
Wide, with incurvate baseline and varied shapes

Redstone
Late Paleo
Alabama and Tennessee
Widest at base, very triangular, long and wide flutes

Ross County
Early Paleo
East
Wide and flat facial flake scars, wide and short flutes

San Patrice
Late Paleo into Early Archaic
Western portions of the South
Short with wide stems, tapered ears, several varieties

Santa Fe
Late Paleo
South
Widest at base, incurved baseline, basal thinning

Scottsbluff
Late Paleo
Plains and adjacent areas
Stemmed, short and abrupt shoulders, baseline somewhat excurvate

Simpson
Late Paleo
Florida and nearby states
Incurvate baseline, stemmed but not shouldered

Sloan Dalton
Late Paleo
Upper Mississippi Valley
Large, incurvate baseline, occasional transverse flake scars

St. Louis
Paleo
States east of the Rockies
Very large, excurvate sides, or long and narrow

Stringtown
Late Paleo
Ohio and probably neighboring states
Lanceolate, stemmed, with base corner protrusions or gravers

Suwannee
Late Paleo
Florida and nearby states
Incurvate baseline, narrowed waist, eared basal corners

Tallahassee
Late Paleo
Florida and nearby states
Triangular, incurved baseline, serrated edges

Tulare Lake
Late Paleo
California
Small flutes or large thinning flakes, varied shapes

Vian Creek
Late Paleo
Western portions of the South
The "Dalton Fishtail," constricted base, flared ears

Victoria
Late Paleo
Texas
Long and narrow, constricted waist, incurved baseline

Wheeler
Late Paleo
South
Triangular, incurvate baseline, several varieties

Windust
Late Paleo
Oregon, Washington
Wide and stemmed, concave baseline, several configurations

Withlacoochee
Late Paleo
Florida and adjacent states
Triangular, incurved baseline, large facial flake scars

Zella
Late Paleo
Texas
Lanceolate, long, rounded and narrowed base

PALEO ARTIFACT FINDS

It is a big moment in the life of the average surface hunter when a fine Paleo artifact is picked up. If that find is a prize fluted point, it is more than a big moment — it is a great event. Most collectors and amateur archaeologists who have experienced this have the occasion implanted in their minds forever. They could locate the find spot within a few feet, and relate the time of year and the weather that day.

Important Paleo finds have been made over the past several centuries and as recently as yesterday. Years ago, before the importance of Paleo artifacts was fully understood, the artifacts were simply considered Indian relics and collected along with other artifact types. Gradually, it was recognized that Paleo points and tools were distinctive and beautiful and scarce.

Thousands of fine Paleo artifacts have been found, and many specimens receive no publicity. There is a certain amount of secrecy involved, in that many collectors do not wish to let others know about prime surface hunting areas. In fact, even finds that are reported are often only provenanced to a county or township level, and not an exact site. This is especially true for early finds, when both Paleo artifact rarity and site importance were not fully realized, and detailed information was not always written down.

This of course has changed, and now collectors document most finds and tend to keep accurate records. Here are examples of some Paleo finds made over the years.

A large and fine Scottsbluff made of blue chert was discovered in the Cabool area, Missouri. With slightly expanding stem, it measured 7" long.
(Editor. *Prehistoric American*, Genuine Indian Relic Society, Vol. XXXVI No. 1, 2002, p. 11.)

One of the largest Agate Basin (Late Paleo) points came from Winnebago County, Wisconsin. The lower two-fifths of the point or blade had ground edges, and the artifact was 8⅛" long. The material was a light tan sugar quartzite.
(Editor. *The Redskin*, Genuine Indian Relic Society, Vol. II No. 4, October 1967, p. 141.)

Fluted to the tip on both faces, an exceptional Cumberland was found about 1930, appropriately enough along the Cumberland River in Kentucky. Gray flint was used for the point, which was 5⅛" long.
(Editor. *Central States Archaeological Journal*, Vol. 17 No. 2, April 1970, p. 96.)

Years ago, a cache of lanceolate blades from the Late Paleo was found in Licking County, Ohio, near the small town of Alexandria. The nine points or blades were made of either Flint Ridge or Walhonding Valley materials, and the six Flint Ridge specimens were up to 5" long.
(Hothem, Lar. *Flint Ridge Artifacts*, Hothem House Books, Lancaster, Ohio, 2004, p. 33.)

Sometime in the 1930s a gem-quality Agate Basin point, made of translucent Knife River flint, was picked up in a wind blowout. From the North Dakota–Minnesota state lines area, it was 1" x 4⁷⁄₁₆" long.
(Editor. *Central States Archaeological Journal*, Vol. 48 No. 3, July 2001, p. 130.)

About 2¼" long, a Folsom point came from Knox County, Illinois, one of at least 20 found in the state. The point, fully fluted on the obverse, had pointed basal ears.
(Perino, Gregory. "Recent Discoveries of Folsom Points in Illinois." *Artifacts*, Vol. 4 No. 2, 1974, pp. 14, 15.)

A cache of nine lanceolate Paleo points was found in Erie County, Ohio, west of Huron. The artifacts were made of gray to black flint and were up to 5" long.
(Vietzen, Col. Raymond C. *From the Earth They Came*. White Horse Publishers, 1978, p. 283.)

Sugar quartzite in light tan was used for a slender fluted point found in Wisconsin. The point was 4⅛" long and had a U-shaped baseline.
(Editor. *The Redskin*, Genuine Indian Relic Society, Vol. III No. 1, January 1968, p. 17.)

A large and fine Clovis point was recovered in Oceana County, Michigan. It was made of glossy Norwood flint colored blue-gray, rusty orange, and cream with dark gray stripes. The Clovis was 4⅜" long.
(Baldwin, John. "The Spooner Norwood Clovis." *Central States Archaeological Journal*, Vol. 34 No. 2, April 1987, pp. 92, 93.)

Buffalo River chert was used to make an exceptional fluted Cumberland, later found near Savannah, Tennessee. Fluted on one face for 4⅓", the point itself (with small tip portion missing) measured 5¾".
(Whitt, Ellis. "The Hardin County Cumberland." *Prehistoric American*, Genuine Indian Relic Society, Vol. XXXVI No. 2, 2002, p. 51.)

A large Paleo point found in Clark County, Ohio, had the Clovis-like concave base but was unfluted, and basal edge grinding gave an appearance of mild stemming. The point was made of brown jasper and measured 1½" x 5³⁄₁₆". It was once in the well-known Dr. Kramer collection.
(Vietzen, Raymond C. *The Ancient Ohioans and Their Neighbors*. Ludi Printing Company, 1946, p. 338.)

Sometime in the mid-1940s, one of the longest and finest Agate Basin points from the Midwest was pocketed by a man while rabbit hunting. Made of mottled dark Upper Mercer, the tapered and concave-base point came from along the White River, Orange County, Indiana. At 1¼" x 6¾", the point had no damage.
(Walsman, Larry. "Noble's Spear Point." *Central States Archaeological Journal*, Vol. 48 No. 4, October 2001, p. 37.)

A Ross County fluted point was found in Scioto County, Ohio. Made of black Upper Mercer flint, it measured 1⁷⁄₁₆" x 3¹⁵⁄₁₆".
(Prufer, Olaf H. *Survey of Ohio Fluted Points No. 5*, September 1961, Cleveland Museum of Natural History, p. 3.)

Gray Coshocton flint was used for a fine Clovis point that came from Delaware County, Ohio. The point was 1" x 3⅝", and the obverse flute was about half of the point length.
(Editor. *Prehistoric American*, Vol. XXXIII No. 4, 1999, p. 14.)

A large white chert Paleo blade found in Jackson County, Arkansas, was very finely chipped and had a concave baseline. Exposed by a farmer's disc, the blade was 11" long.
(Editor. *The Redskin*, Genuine Indian Relic Society, Vol. IV No. 1, January 1969, p. 14.)

Made of an unknown but attractive and highly translucent yellowish flint or chert, a Clovis point came from Gibson County, Indiana. The fluted point was about 4" long.
(Editor. *Central States Archaeological Journal*, Vol. 46 No. 3, July 1999, p. 138.)

A fine fluted point in tan flint or chert was surface found in Preble County, Ohio. It was 3⅞" long and the secondary chipping was uniface and delicately done.
(Editor. *The Redskin*, Genuine Indian Relic Society, Vol. XI No. 3, 1976, p. 108.)

A top-grade Sloan Dalton made of quality Burlington chert came from Greene County, Arkansas. Uniform transverse flaking was present, and the color combinations were cream and caramel with brown. The artifact measured 2" x 7".
(Pfeiffer, Leslie S. "A Classic Sloan Dalton From Northeast Arkansas." *Prehistoric American*, Genuine Indian Relic Society, Vol. XXXI No. 2, 1997, pp. 18, 19.)

An excellent Cumberland point with flutes on both faces was picked up in 1976. It was made of gray flint with pale red, and came from Tennessee. The point was 4½" long.
(Editor. *Central States Archaeological Journal*, Vol. 24 No. 1, January 1977, p. 48.)

Pope County, Minnesota, produced a superior fluted Clovis 4¾" long. Once in the famous Judge King collection, in New Jersey, the Clovis was made of unknown glossy translucent flint in creamy pink, dark red, paprika red, and white.
(Baldwin, John. "King Clovis." *Prehistoric Art/Archaeology '83*, Genuine Indian Relic Society, Vol. XVIII No. 3, 1983, pp. 88, 89.)

In 1968, a long and narrow fluted point was found in Franklin County, Missouri. Made of light-colored flint or chert, it was just over 5".
(Editor. *Central States Archaeological Journal*, Vol. 16 No. 2, April 1969, p. 81.)

Three concave-base Paleo points were found at a site in Oak Harbor, northern Ohio. These averaged a little over 1½" in length; two had basal fluting, and all were made of gray chert. An additional larger fluted point from the same site was made of black flint.
(Vietzen, Col. Raymond C. *From the Earth They Came*. White Horse Publishers, 1978, p. 225.)

A beautiful Clovis with Enterline multiple fluting on one face was discovered in Gordon County, Georgia. Made of highly translucent dark amber flint, it was 1⁷⁄₁₆" x 4⁹⁄₁₆" long.
(Beutell, Tommy C. "The Firelane Clovis." *Prehistoric American*, Genuine Indian Relic Society, Vol. XXXII No. 1, 1998, p. 18.)

Thin and widest at midsection, a remarkable fluted point was found in Scioto County, Ohio. Fluted on both lower faces, it was made of mixed blue flint and measured 4" long.
(Editor. *Artifacts*, Vol. 5 No. 3, 1975, p. 28.)

An outstanding fluted Clovis came from near Fitchburg Furnace, Kentucky. It was made of translucent streaked dark orange Carter Cave flint and was 3¾" long.
(Editor. *Central States Archaeological Journal*, Vol. 45 No. 1, January 1998, p. 2.)

One of the most impressive fluted Cumberland points came from Stewart County, Tennessee. It had slight restoration, and its length was 6¼".
(Editor. *The Redskin*, Genuine Indian Relic Society, Vol. III No. 2, April 1968, p. 77.)

Bollinger County, Missouri, was the discovery area of a large and fine Sloan Dalton, found about 1975. It had exceptional chipping, was made of tan Burlington, and was 7⅝" long.
(Editor. *Prehistoric American*, Genuine Indian Relic Society, Vol. XXXII No. 1, 1998, p. 20.)

Orange, purple, and yellow Flint Ridge material was used for a slender fluted point, found in a rock shelter. Both faces were fluted for about one-third of total length, 4⅜". The point came from Rockcastle County, Kentucky.
(Editor. *Central States Archaeological Journal*, Vol. 27 No. 3, July 1980, p. 145.)

Approximately 6¾" long, a fine Late Paleo unstemmed lance was found in Crawford County, Missouri. It was made of brown material that had lighter clouding.
(Editor. *The Redskin*, Genuine Indian Relic Society, Vol. XII No. 3, 1977, p. 95.)

A large and fine St. Louis type Clovis came from Grayson County, Kentucky. Made of glossy and patinated chert, the fluted point or blade was 2¼" x 6".
(Editor. *Prehistoric American*, Vol. XXIX No. 2, 1995, inside front cover.)

In 1930, two clovis-like points were discovered in a sand pit associated with mammoth bones near Greeley, Colorado. One point, made of white agate, was 3¼" long. The other, of brown jasper, was 4⅝".
(Editor. *Central States Archaeological Journal*, Vol. 18 No. 1, January 1971, p. 28.)

Knife River flint was the dark translucent material used for a fine large fluted Clovis from Perry County, Indiana. The point was very thin and 5" long.
(Editor. *The Redskin*, Genuine Indian Relic Society, Vol. II No. 2, April 1968, p. 44.)

One of the largest Dalton points or blades was made of white chert and came from Jackson County, Illinois. It had a V-shaped baseline and was 10" long.
(Editor. *Prehistoric American*, Genuine Indian Relic Society, Vol. XXV No. 4, 1991, p. 11.)

A stemmed lanceolate from the Late Paleo was found in Franklin County, Ohio. Picked up in 1961, the material was a nodular flint from Kentucky. Well-chipped, the artifact was just over 6" long.
(Editor. *Ohio Archaeologist*, Vol. 12 Nos. 1-2, January-April 1962, front cover, p. 1.)

Made of gray-brown Edwards Plateau flint, a scarce Folsom point was found on the South Plains of Texas. It had fine flaking reminiscent of an Angostura (oblique parallel), and the point still retained the central basal protrusion used for fluting. At 2" long, the point weighed about 10 grams. Two other complete Folsoms and eight broken examples had earlier been found at the same site.
(Parker, Wayne. "An Unfluted Folsom from Crosby County, Texas." *Central States Archaeological Journal*, Vol. 25 No. 2, April 1978, pp. 82, 83.)

A superb fluted Clovis with a deeply indented baseline was picked up about 1970 in Independence County, Arkansas. Made of what was probably patinated Burlington chert, the point was 1⁵⁄₁₆" x 5⅛".
(Hathcock, T. Roy. "The Georgia Montgomery Clovis." *Prehistoric American*, Genuine Indian Relic Society, Vol. XXXI No. 2, 1997, inside back cover.)

Kentucky produced a top Clovis point in 1968; it was fluted on both lower faces and made of light-colored chert. Very carefully chipped, the Clovis was 4¹³⁄₁₆" long.
(Grimsley, Tom. "Happiness: Finding a Rare Paleo Point." *Central States Archaeological Journal*, Vol. 16 No. 3, July 1969, pp. 126, 127.)

Apparently also found in Kentucky, one of the largest Clovis (St. Louis variety) points or blades had a deeply concave baseline. It was 8" long and made of dark flint or chert.
(Young, Col. Bennett H. *The Prehistoric Men of Kentucky*, Filson Club Publications No. 25, Louisville, 1910, p. 161.)

An Agate Basin variant from Hancock County, Ohio, exhibited exceptional form and workstyle. It had a small straight base and excurvate edges from base corners to blade tip. Made of dark glossy mottled flint, it was 6³⁄₁₆" long.
(Editor. *Prehistoric American*, Genuine Indian Relic Society, Vol. XXVI No. 3, 1992, p. 3.)

Dark flint was used to make a lanceolate, found near the Elkhart River, Indiana, in 1983. It was well shaped and the lower blade edges were ground; length was almost 4".
(Weiner, Gary. "Personal Field Finds." *Ohio Archaeologist*, Vol. 36 No. 1, Winter 1986, p. 42.)

Pike County, Illinois, was the find area for a large undamaged Dalton in light-colored chert. Found in a cornfield, it was 1½" x 7⅜" long.
(Schultz, Terry A. "The Find of a Lifetime." *Prehistoric American*, Genuine Indian Relic Society, Vol. XXIX No. 2, 1995, p. 12.)

Guernsey County, Ohio, was the find site for one of the longest fluted points from the state. Dark Flint Ridge was used for the point, which measured 5⅛" long. The obverse was fluted for about half of length.
(Hothem, Lar. *Flint Ridge Artifacts*. Hothem House Books, Lancaster, Ohio, 2004, p. 41.)

A Paleo point or blade from St. Louis County, Missouri, had characteristics of both Early and Late Paleo design. The general shape was lanceolate (Late), while the baseline was V-shaped and the lower face had a short flute (Early).
(Editor. *Central States Archaeological Journal*, Vol. 18 No. 4, October 1971, p. 152.)

Found in Franklin County, Ohio, a Late Paleo stemmed lance was made of tan chert with several other colors. The point or blade was 6" long and had a relatively short stem.
(Editor. *The Redskin*, Genuine Indian Relic Society, Vol. III No. 1, January 1968, p. 9.)

An excellent Redstone fluted point made of dark Fort Payne chert was discovered in Madison County, Alabama. The triangular point with barbed base corners was 4" long.
(Editor. *Prehistoric American*, Genuine Indian Relic Society, Vol. XXVIII No. 1, 1994, inside front cover.)

A rare cache of fluted points was unearthed in northern Ohio. The caption for sketches of the group reads: "Cache of 12 Paleo-Indian spearheads found on Portman farm at South Amherst, Ohio....Artifacts were plowed up near the creek. All are of dark gray Onondaga chert and range from 2½" to 3" in length. Found about 1900. Circa 10,000 B. C."
(Vietzen, Col. Raymond C. *Yesterday's Ohioans*. 1973, p. 32.)

Perry County, Indiana, was the discovery area for a superb fluted point, found in 1987. Made of dark flint, it was picked up in a tobacco field along the Ohio River. It measured 1⅝" x 5".
(Editor. *Prehistoric Artifacts*, Genuine Indian Relic Society, Vol. XXII No. 1, 1988, p. 10.)

A cache of eleven Late Paleo points or blades was found in Knox County, Ohio. One of the best examples, carefully chipped, was made of blue Upper Mercer flint and measured 6⅝" long.
(Hothem, Lar. *First Hunters — Ohio's Paleo-Indian Artifacts*. Hothem House Books, Lancaster, 1990, p. 96.)

An exceptionally large and well-made fluted point was found on farmland in Van Buren County, Michigan. Made of Flint Ridge material, the Clovis was 2" x 6½". One flute was 3¾" and the other almost as long, and the St. Louis type artifact was patinated to a mixed tan-brown.
(Baldwin, John. "Chalcedony Clovis." *Central States Archaeological Journal*, Vol. 49 No. 4, October 2002, p. 170.)

Two Late Paleo lance points were found together around 1990 in Delaware County, Ohio. The examples were about 6" long, very narrow, and beautifully chipped. They resembled the dagger form, which may be the scarcest Late Paleo artifact type in the Midwest. Only a few other examples have been seen, and most (as were these two) were made of translucent blue-gray Flint Ridge.
(Hothem, Lar. Various sources.)

A fine Clovis fluted point was found on a farm in Tuscarawas County, Ohio. Made of black Warsaw (Upper Mercer) flint, it was 4½" long. Another high-grade fluted Clovis 4¼" long came from Todd County, Kentucky. The example was made of yellow-gray unknown material. And a fluted Clovis picked up near Newark, Ohio, measured 4⅝". Quite thin, it was made of milky white chalcedony from Flint Ridge.
(Vietzen, Col. Raymond C. *The Old Warrior Speaks*. White Horse Publishers, 1981, pp. 174, 178.)

Northeast Texas produced one of the finest Scottsbluff points found. It was made of translucent root beer Edwards chert, and the size and workstyle were far above average. The point or blade was 1¼" x 6¾".
(Pfeiffer, Leslie S. "A Scottsbluff Point from Northeast Texas." *Prehistoric American*, Genuine Indian Relic Society, Vol. XXX No. 4, 1996, p. 15.)

Over 4" long, an exceptional fluted point was found in Licking County, Ohio. Made of patinated Flint Ridge, it was colored blue, gray, and pink. One face was single fluted for ¹⁵⁄₁₆", while the opposite had multiple fluting for 1½".
(Editor. *Ohio Archaeologist*, Vol. 10 No. 4, October 1960, p. 134.)

Only a few true Folsom points have come from east of the Mississippi River, but a classic specimen did turn up in Morgan County, Illinois. Made of light-colored chert, it was fluted full-length on one face and nearly to the tip on the other. The Folsom was 2⅝" long.
(Perino, Gregory. "Early Projectile Points Found." *Central States Archaeological Journal*, Vol. 14 No. 3, July 1967, p. 104.)

Holmes County, Ohio, produced a cache of 144 Paleo artifacts, but no type description was given. The artifacts were made of black Coshocton (Upper Mercer) flint.
(Vietzen, Col. Raymond C. *Prehistoric Indians — From Darkness into Light*. White Horse Publishers, Elyria, Ohio, 1995, p. 44.)

Many different materials were used for fluted Clovis points, but perhaps the most unusual was clear crystal quartz. One point made of this transparent material was 1¾" long and came from Harnett County, North Carolina.
(Editor. *Prehistoric American*, Genuine Indian Relic Society, Vol. XXX No. 2, 1996, p. 18.)

The Kreitchfield cache, from near Loudonville, Ohio, contained a large number of lanceolate points or blades from Late Paleo times. At least 18 complete specimens were recovered, one of which was 4⅜" long, and many others were broken and not picked up. All the artifacts had a coating of red ochre.
(Hothem, Lar. *First Hunters — Ohio's Paleo-Indian Artifacts*. Hothem House Books, Lancaster, Ohio, 1990, p. 143.)

One of the largest and best Agate Basin points was found in the Florissant Valley, St. Louis County, Missouri. Made of medium-dark chert, it was finely chipped and 7" in length.
(Editor. *Central States Archaeological Journal*, Vol. 25 No. 1, January 1978, p. 41.)

Nine Late Paleo lances were in a cache found west of Huron in Erie County, Ohio. Dark flints, perhaps Upper Mercers, were used for the lanceolates, and the site was on the shore of Lake Erie. [By coincidence, the Copeland cache from Licking County, Ohio, also held nine lanceolates.]
(Vietzen, Col. Raymond C. *From the Earth They Came*. White Horse Publishers, 1978, p. 283.)

An unusual Late Paleo knife or point made of colorful Carter Cave (KY) flint came from the eastern Midwest. With very slight and short stemming, the wide artifact was ex-collections Shipley and Saunders, and 5½" long.
(Editor. *The Redskin*, Genuine Indian Relic Society, Vol. X No. 1, 1975, p. 16.)

A small-stemmed ovoid Paleo knife was found in Perry County, Illinois. Made of chert, the knife was about 7" long. (Editor. *Central States Archaeological Journal*, Vol. 34 No. 1, January 1987, p. 15.)

In 1911, when a waterline was being dug in Portsmouth, Ohio, a lanceolate blade was found 4½' deep. Broken by a digger's pick, both parts were kept and the artifact was reassembled. It was made of pink translucent flint and was 3" wide and 18" (1½') long. It was the longest Paleo point or knife known to have been found. (Kramer, Leon M. D. "The Saga of the Great Portsmouth Spear." *Ohio Indian Relic Collectors Society*, Bulletin No. 24, June 1950, pp. 36 – 40.)

Found in 1965, a large Late Paleo Scottsbluff with a short stem was 4¼" long. It was picked up in Washita County, Oklahoma. (Editor. *The Redskin*, Genuine Indian Relic Society, Vol. VIII No. 3, 1973, p. 115.)

Delaware County, Ohio, produced a classic fluted Clovis point made of mixed gray Coshocton (Upper Mercer) flint. Fluted on both faces, the point was 1" x 3⅝". (Editor. *Prehistoric American*, Genuine Indian Relic Society, Vol. XXXIII No. 4, 1999, p. 14.)

A cache of Late Paleo points or knives came from Decatur County, Tennessee. The Greenbrier Dalton type had indented baselines, wide and shallow side notches, and needle tips. Of the five examples, the longest was 5½". (Editor. *Central States Archaeological Journal*, Vol. 47 No. 3, July 2000, p. 137.)

Northern Ohio contained a mysterious cache of fluted points, one that has left few traces. "The cache of Paleo fluted points on Beaver Creek, near South Amherst, Lorain Co., Ohio, was the best I have ever heard of and now it has disappeared and perhaps will never be seen intact. I never saw all specimens together...and it seems I can go no farther. It seems all who knew of the cache are now dead." (Vietzen, Col. Raymond C. *Prehistoric Indians — From Darkness into Light*. White Horse Publishers, Elyria, Ohio, 1995, pp. 17, 20.)

Two of the largest fluted points in existence were classed as subtype 3 Clovis. Lengths were, respectively, 7" and 8". (Editor. "Prehistoric Art." *The Redskin*, Genuine Indian Relic Society, Vol. XIV No. 3, 1979, pp. 30, 39.)

Perhaps the finest fluted Cumberland point to come from the region was picked up in Cumberland County, Kentucky. Made of semi-translucent pale tan flint, it was beautifully shaped and chipped. It measured 1⅗" x 5½". (Brooks, H. B. "The Finding of the Cole Cumberland." *Central States Archaeological Journal*, Vol. 20 No. 1, January 1973, pp. 40 – 43.)

Honey-colored quartzite was used for a fluted Clovis point, found in Adams County, Ohio. The point was just over 3" long, and the obverse flute in the difficult-to-chip material was over 1" long. (Editor. *Ohio Archaeologist*, Vol. 10 No. 2, April 1960, p. 39.)

An exceptional fluted Clovis came from Alabama, and it was distinctive both for size and flute length. Made of translucent Bangor flint, the point had a deeply concave baseline, and was 2 1/16" x 5⅜". Fluted on each face, the obverse flute was 4 5/16" long. (Moore, Charles E. "The Belgreen Clovis." *Central States Archaeological Journal*, Vol. 45 No. 3, July 1998, p. 150.)

A stemmed Late Paleo lance, made of black Flint Ridge material, was picked up in Perry County, Ohio. The point or knife was 5¾" long. (Editor. *The Redskin*, Genuine Indian Relic Society, Vol. III No. 2, April 1968, p. 57.)

One of the finest Crowfield fluted points was found in Pennsylvania and was made of jasper. It was 1¼" x 4½", and ¼" thick. Crowfields tend to be wide and thin, with multiple long and narrow flutes. (Pfeiffer, Leslie S. "The Crowfield Fluted Point." *Prehistoric American*, Genuine Indian Relic Society, Vol. XXXIII No. 2, 1999, p. 18.)

A fluted Clovis with deeply concave baseline in the Dr. Glass collection came from Mason County, Kentucky. Made of blue-gray chert, it measured 1⅜" x 4½". (Editor. *The Redskin*, Genuine Indian Relic Society, Vol. VIII No. 1, 1973, p. 38.)

Found by a farmer in 1927, a fine fluted point came from near Hinckley, Medina County, Ohio. It was almost 4" long, and each lower face was fluted for about 2". The material was black Coshocton (Upper Mercer) flint.

(Vietzen, Col. Raymond C. *Prehistoric Indians — From Darkness into Light*. White Horse Publishers, Elyria, Ohio, 1995, p. 43.)
Fayette County, Illinois, was the first home for an outstanding fluted point that was triangular and had excurvate edges. It had a deeply incurvate baseline, was made of medium-dark flint, and was 5⅝" long.
(Editor. *Central States Archaeological Journal*, Vol. 40 No. 3, July 1993, p. 131.)

A regional type, Bull-Tongue Simpson points are sometimes found in Florida. An extraordinary find in dark chert was made in Putnam County. The Late Paleo example had a tapered narrow base and measured 2¹⁵⁄₁₆ x 7⅝", with a thickness of only ¹¹⁄₃₂".
(Tatum, Jim and Carlos. "Longest Known Bull-Tongue Simpson," *Prehistoric American*, Genuine Indian Relic Society, Vol. XXXIV No. 2, 2000, p. 17.)

Found in 1975, an exceptional Agate Basin point came from Adams County, Illinois. Made of white chert, it was 4¼" long.
(Editor. *The Redskin*, Genuine Indian Relic Society, Vol. XI No. 2, 1976, p. 50.)

One of the largest and best Folsoms was found in North Dakota and was made of patinated Knife River flint. About 3" long, both faces were fluted nearly to the tip.
(Editor. *Central States Archaeological Journal*, Vol. 41 No. 2, April 1994, p. 103.)

A superb Agate Basin in white Burlington chert was discovered in Jersey County, Illinois. It measured 1" x 6⅜" and had a long collecting history.
(Editor. *Prehistoric American*, Genuine Indian Relic Society, Vol. XXXV No. 1, 2001, p. 10.)

Made of dark flint or chert, a large Ross County fluted point was uncovered in a rock shelter. From Van Buren County, Arkansas, the point was 5" long.
(Editor. *Central States Archaeological Journal*, Vol. 33 No. 3, July 1986, p. 155.)

A very large St. Louis type Clovis was found in Hickman County, Kentucky, about the year 1917. Made of Dover chert, the undamaged point or knife was 2" x 7½" and had the typical deeply concave baseline.
(Rogers, Dwain. "A Kentucky Giant... 'The Robinson Clovis.'" *Central States Archaeological Journal*, Vol. 47 No. 3, July 2000, pp. 114, 115.)

An exceptional Paleo point with a shallow V-shaped baseline was found in the West, probably in South Dakota. Finely chipped and with smoothed basal edges, the point was 4" long. The same campsite produced the bases of two other Paleo points.
(Ferguson, Les. "Collections." *The Redskin*, Genuine Indian Relic Society, Vol. X No. 4, 1975, pp. 152, 153.)

Made of jasper in many colors, an extremely fine fluted Clovis was picked up in a Kansas waterway. The length of this unresharpened artifact was 4¹³⁄₁₆".
(Fox, Dan. "The Kansas Fox Clovis Point." *Prehistoric American*, Genuine Indian Relic Society, Vol. XXXIII No. 4, 1999, pp. 4 – 6, front cover.)

A fine fluted point, probably made of Logan County chert, was found about 1942. The point was thin and well chipped, with ground basal edges. The point, from Van Wert County, Ohio, was 3¾" long.
(Mohr, Bob. *Ohio Archaeologist*, Vol. 47 No. 4, Fall 1997, p. 10.)

A cache of six square knives was found about 1900 in Douglas County, Kansas. The largest blade, 9" long, was broken in prehistoric times and the pieces notched near the break for repair and continued use.
(Shewey, Charles. "A Rare Paleo Square Knives Cache." *Prehistoric American*, Genuine Indian Relic Society, Vol. XXXV No. 1, 2001, pp. 30, 31.)

Made of black Flint Ridge material, an extraordinary fluted point was found in Guernsey County, Ohio. It was 5⅛" long, and the obverse flute was half the overall point length.
(Editor. *The Redskin*, Genuine Indian Relic Society, Vol. IV No. 4, October 1969, p. 131.)

Illinois, in 1962, produced an outstanding example of a rare Paleo point or knife, the St. Louis. Made of light and dark banded Dongola (Cobden) chert, the artifact was 1¾" x 5¹⁵⁄₁₆". It was fluted for over 3" on one face and just over 1" on the other.
(Pfeiffer, Dr. Leslie. "The St. Louis Fluted Variety Clovis from Logan County, Illinois." *Central States Archaeological Journal*, Vol. 47 No. 4, October 2000, pp. 202, 203.)

Complete Clovis point finds are unusual, but a cache of the type is very unusual. However, five Clovis points were found together in a rock shelter, with the largest example 4¾". They were discovered in Randolph County, Illinois.
(Editor. *Central States Archaeological Journal*, Vol. 46 No. 1, January 1999, p. 29.)

A rare First View Paleo point was picked up north of Laredo, Texas. Made of patinated Edwards Plateau flint, it had heavy basal grinding, and its length was 4½".
(Editor. *Prehistoric American*, Genuine Indian Relic Society, Vol. XXXI No. 3, 1997, inside back cover.)

From southwestern Ohio came a Paleo knife in creamy tan Flint Ridge with gray-white and purple veining. The knife had an incurvate baseline and one excurvate and one straight edge. One face had a basal flute that measured ¾" x 1¾", and the overall knife size was 1¼" x 5⅞".
(Hart, Steven. "An Ohio Transitional Period Knife." *The Redskin*, Genuine Indian Relic Society, Vol. X No. 2, 1975, pp. 74 – 75.)

Yellow translucent Kaolin was used for a remarkable fluted point found in Jackson County, Illinois. Patinated and with a moderately deep U-shaped baseline, the point measured 1⅛" x 4⅝".
(Pfeiffer, Leslie S. "Three Southern Illinois Fluted Points." *Prehistoric American*, Genuine Indian Relic Society, Vol. XXXI No. 4, 1997, p. 20.)

A very large and fine Clovis point, 6" long, was found in Upton County, Texas. Made of light-colored chert or flint, it was basally fluted on the obverse for more than half of length.
(Editor. *Central States Archaeological Journal*, Vol. 46 No. 1, January 1999, p. 5.)

In Benton County, Tennessee, a large fluted point was found along Eagle Creek. Chipped in brown flint with touches of blue and gray and with reddish inclusions, the Clovis had a straight base and sides that were excurvate from base to tip. The artifact was 6¾" long.
(Editor. *The Redskin*, Genuine Indian Relic Society, Vol. XI No. 3, 1976, pp. 96, 97.)

A concave-base Paleo point from Spencer County, Indiana, was fluted to the tip on one face. Made of gray chert, the point was 3¾" long.
(Editor. *Central States Archaeological Journal*, Vol. 12 No. 2, April 1965, p. 88.)

An exceptional Holland-like point or blade came from Ralls County, Missouri. It had light stemming and an incurvate baseline. The artifact, once in the Hoke collection, was made of light-colored chert and measured about 1¾" x 5+".
(Editor. *The Redskin*, Genuine Indian Relic Society, Vol. XII No. 4, 1977, p. 154.)

A fine Paleo point with shallow fluting came from Portage County, Ohio, and was found in the early 1900s. With a moderate waist, the base corners were pointed and the baseline incurvate. It was 4¼" long, and "medium dark slate-grey flint..."
(Prufer, Olaf H. *Survey of Ohio Fluted Points No. 1*, Cleveland Museum of Natural History, May 1960, p. 6.)

A fine uniface blade made of hornstone, pointed at one end and rounded at the other, was 4⅞" long. It was picked up in Hart County, Kentucky.
(Editor. *Artifacts*, Vol. 14 No. 2, 1984, p. 58.)

Light tan Flint Ridge was the material used for a Late Paleo lance 6¼" long. It came from Darke County, Ohio, and was found in 1966.
(Hothem, Lar. *Flint Ridge Artifacts*. Hothem House Books, Lancaster, Ohio, 2004, p. 39.)

Fluted to the tip, a Cumberland point of dark chert or flint was found in Hardin County, Tennessee. It was 4¼" long, and the bases of two other Cumberlands came from the same site.
(Editor. *The Redskin*, Genuine Indian Relic Society, Vol. IV No. 1, January 1969, p. 24.)

Two fluted Clovis points from St. Louis County, Missouri, were made of Knife River flint. One measured 1⅜" x 4½", while another (a St. Louis type) was 2⁷⁄₁₆" x 6⁷⁄₁₆".
(Perino, Gregory. "Early Projectile Points Found." *Central States Archaeological Journal*, Vol. 14 No. 3, July 1967, pp. 102 – 106.)

Cedar Hill chert was used for a fine fluted Clovis found in Illinois. With a V-shaped baseline, the point was 1¼" x 4⅜".
(Editor. *Prehistoric American*, Genuine Indian Relic Society, Vol. XXXVI No. 1, 2002, p. 7.)

A superb Scottsbluff, just over 5" long, was found in southwestern Arkansas. It had a short stem for size, and the material was dark flint with light clouding.
(Editor. *The Redskin*, Genuine Indian Relic Society, Vol. I No. 1, July 1966, p. 12.)

Peoria County, Illinois, produced a large Paleo knife made of patinated reddish Avon chert. It was pointed at each end, and one edge was beveled due to resharpening. The blade was nearly 8" long.
(Editor. *Central States Archaeological Journal*, Vol. 49 No. 3, July 2002, p. 143.)

One of the best lanceolates from the region was found in Adams County, Ohio. The point or blade was made of dark Upper Mercer flint and was parallel flaked for much of the length, 5¾".
(Editor. *Artifacts*, Vol. 10 No. 1, 1980, p. 1.)

The organizations and publications cited in this chapter are enormously helpful in recording America's prehistoric past. Membership is encouraged, and the associated publications deserve shelf space in all collectors' libraries.

Archaeological Society of Ohio
(Publishes *Ohio Archaeologist*)
138 Ann Court
Lancaster, OH 43130

Central States Archaeological Societies, Inc.
(Publishes *Central States Archaeological Journal*)
11552 Patty Ann
St. Louis, MO 63416-5471

Genuine Indian Relic Society, Inc.
(Publishes *Prehistoric American*)
1811-B North Berkeley Blvd.
Goldsboro, NC 27534-3333

The spirited bidding at an auction is usually a good indication of how much certain Paleo artifacts are worth. This chapter provides recent auction figures. All are courtesy Jan Sorgenfrei, Owner/Manager of Old Barn Auction, 10040 S. R. 224 West, Findlay, Ohio, 45840 (phone: 419/422-8531).

For these listings, the item name and description is followed by the auction date and the final bid amount. Please note that the monetary figure includes the 10% buyers' premium.

Agate Basin, 2¾", agate, Utah.
15Feb2003 $209.00

Dalton Drill, 1⅞", light-colored chert, provenance unknown.
18May2002 $66.00

Fluted point, barbed ears, 2½", Howard County, Missouri.
8Dec2001 $770.00

Dalton, 2½", Randolph County, Illinois.
20Jul2002 $143.00

Stemmed lance, 3½", Williams County, Ohio.
24Jun2000 $159.50

Fluted point, striped flint, 2¾", Trimble County, Kentucky.
20Jul2002 $302.50

Fluted point, 3", Onondaga, deeply concave baseline, Massachusetts.
8Dec2001 $1,595.00

Paleo point, 4", thin, some plow damage, Twigg County, Kentucky.
22Nov2003 $440.00

Suwannee, 1⅞", Chipola River, Jackson County, Florida.
4Nov2000 $143.00

Clovis fluted point, 2¾", Macon County, Tennessee.
15Mar2003 $357.50

Fluted point, 3⅞", ex-Townsend, Muskingum County, Ohio.
8Dec2001 $2,090.00

Lanceolate, 3¼", Upper Mercer flint, Knox County, Ohio.
22Nov2003 $66.00

Dalton point, fluted, 3¼", Missouri.
24Jun2000 $209.00

Stringtown stemmed lance, 5⅛", Ross County, Ohio.
15Mar2003 $176.00

Fluted point, 3½", fine, Gasconade County, Missouri.
28Apr2001 $1,045.00

Dalton, exceptionally large and fine, 7¾", Missouri.
22Nov2003 $2,750.00

Square knife, 3¾", Defiance County, Ohio.
24Jun2000 $154.00

Paleo lanceolate blade, 4⅜", Richland County, Ohio.
23Aug2003 $231.00

Fluted point, Indiana Green flint, 2¼", De Kalb County, Indiana.
24Jun2000 $302.50

Fluted Clovis, Flint Ridge, 2¾", Delaware County, Ohio.
15Mar2003 $660.00

Fluted Point, 3" long, Monroe County, Michigan.
24Jun2000 $319.00

Cumberland, fine, Davis COA, 3⅞", Tennessee.
22Nov2003 $2,530.00

Fluted point, 2⅞", ears, Kentucky.
8Dec2001 $275.00

Fluted point, 2⅞", bull's-eye hornstone, Williams County, Ohio.
24Jun2000 $1,430.00

Paleo point, hornstone, thin, 2½", Indiana.
23Aug2003 $297.00

Cumberland, 3½", fluted, Jefferson County, Kentucky.
24Jun2000 $907.50

Fluted point, 3¾", Flint Ridge, excellent, Pickaway County, Ohio.
18May2002 $7,700.00

Scottsbluff, parallel-flaked, agate, 3¼", Colorado.
16Jun2001 $660.00

Dagger, probably Paleo, 7⅛", provenance unknown.
18May2002 $440.00

Paleo knife, dagger shape, 6⅝", Delaware County, Ohio.
9Mar2002 $2,310.00

Eden-like point, glossy flint, 3" long, Indiana.
11Jan2003 $220.00

Scottsbluff, transverse flaking, 3¼", Jefferson County, Missouri.
27Jan2001 $770.00

Agate Basin, 6⅝", near-white chert, Perry County, Indiana.
21Jun2003 $660.00

Uniface square knife, 3¾", Wyandot County, Ohio.
11Jan2003 $225.50

Fluted point, dark flint, 4½", Mason County, West Virginia.
21Sep2002 $2,750.00

Stemmed lance, 4⅛", Bayport chert, St. Clair County, Michigan.
22Nov2003 $192.50

Plainview, 2⅝", Zwolle area, Louisiana.
4Nov2000 $220.00

Late Paleo blade, Flint Ridge, 5⅛", Franklin County, Ohio.
9Mar2002 $495.00

Fluted point, 3" long, Maury County, Tennessee.
27Oct2001 $852.50

Dalton point, 4⅞", found in Illinois.
22Nov2003 $220.00

Fluted point, 2⅝", thin, Steuben County, Indiana.
24Jun2000 $302.50

Fluted point, 4¹⁄₁₆", dark flint, Texas.
4Nov2000 $797.50

Square knife, 4½", ex-Shipley, Licking County, Ohio.
18May2002 $660.00

Lanceolate, 3¼", X-Hill, Upper Mercer, Delaware County, Ohio.
22Nov2003 $209.00

Fluted point, barbed ears, 2⅛", Mason County, Kentucky.
20Jul2002 $3,576.50

Fluted point, light-colored flint, 3⅞", Kentucky.
16Jun2001 $797.50

Crowfield, fluted, 2⅜", Muskingum County, Ohio.
15Feb2003 $522.50

Square knife, 5⅛", ex-Walters and Munger, Indiana.
27Oct2001 $357.50

Clovis point, 2" long, Clark County, Kentucky.
15Mar2003 $302.50

Square knife, 3⅞", Lenawee County, Michigan.
26Oct2002 $203.50

Fluted point, 1⅞", De Kalb County, Indiana.
24Jun2000 $242.00

Lanceolate, parallel-flaked, 4⅝", thin, Tennessee.
23Aug2003 $302.50

Knife, quartzite, lanceolate form, 6½", Wisconsin.
23Dec2002 $1,320.00

Fluted point, Burlington, 3⅜", Pike County, Illinois.
17May2003 $550.00

Fluted point, 3¾", ex-Whipley, Posey County, Indiana.
26Oct2002 $357.50

Dalton, 4½", light tan chert, Morgan County, Illinois.
21Sep2002 $121.00

Fluted Clovis, 3⅜", Jackson COA, barbed, unknown provenance.
27Jan2001 $687.50

Lanceolate, Flint Ridge, 3", ex-Copeland, Delaware County, Ohio.
22Nov2003 $660.00

Paleo point, incurvate baseline, triangular, 3¼", Kentucky.
26Oct2002 $165.00

Lanceolate, 5⅜", from near Marysville, Union County, Ohio.
24Jun2000 $880.00

Clovis, small, fluted, dark flint, 1½", Clark County, Kentucky.
15Mar2003 $192.50

Fluted point, gray agate, 2", from near Lamar, Colorado.
27Oct2001 $412.50

Fluted point, 2⅜", Sullivan County, Tennessee.
23Aug2003 $253.00

Dalton, large at 6", Missouri.
16Jun2001 $632.50

Lanceolate, ex-Copeland, 3¼", Clinton County, Ohio.
22Nov2003 $302.50

Fluted point, parallel flaking, 5¼", Saline County, Missouri.
8Dec2001 $1,988.00

Cumberland, fluted, 2⅛" long, Kentucky.
26Oct2002 $275.00

Paleo point, 2¼", dark flint, Indiana.
25Aug2001 $88.00

Dalton, large at 5¼", ex-Murray, Fulton County, Illinois.
22Nov2003 $3,850.00

Fluted point, 4½", Pettis County, Missouri.
4Nov2000 $137.50

Lanceolate, Carter Cave flint, 4" long, Adams County, Ohio.
23Aug2003 $165.00

Stringtown stemmed lance, 4", Williams County, Ohio.
24Jun2000 $198.00

Fluted point, 3⅛", Belmont County, Ohio.
20Jul2002 $1,155.00

Scottsbluff, 4¼", brownish flint, Edwards County, Texas.
4Nov2000 $550.00

Paleo point, 3⅞", light-colored chert, Boone County, Missouri.
22Nov2003 $132.00

Fluted point, 3½", found 1988 in De Kalb County, Tennessee.
24Jun2000 $1,017.50

Dalton-Hemphill, 3⅞", Lincoln County, Missouri.
22Nov2003 $412.50

Fluted point, 3½", ex-Townsend, Knox County, Ohio.
8Dec2001 $2,090.00

Uniface blade, 1¾" x 6½", Todd County, Kentucky.
15Mar2003 $440.00

Lanceolate, incurved baseline, 4", Pennsylvania.
26Oct2002 $495.00

Dalton, quartzite, 4⅛", slender for size, Wisconsin.
22Nov2003 $264.00

Dalton point, 2½", Humphrey County, Tennessee.
16Jun2001 $198.00

Fluted point, 2¼", light-colored flint, Branson area, Missouri.
4Nov2000 $247.50

Uniface knife, triangular, 4¼", Miami County, Ohio.
21Jun2003 $49.50

Beaver Lake, 3½", Carter Cave, Bracken County, Kentucky.
28Apr2001 $302.50

Paleo knife, wide, 4¾", Upper Mercer, Union County, Ohio.
21Jun2003 $330.00

Fluted point, 3⅝", light-colored flint, Delaware County, Ohio.
9Mar2002 $3,300.00

Holcombe, 1¼", Perino COA, Brown County, Ohio.
22Nov2003 $99.00

Cumberland, unfluted, thin, 3⅜", Kentucky.
26Oct2002 $467.50

Fluted triangular point, 2⅛", Elkhart County, Indiana.
24Jun2000 $330.00

Dalton, white chert, 2⅝", Missouri.
15Mar2003 $165.00

Fluted point, 3⅜", Union County, Kentucky.
24Jun2000 $550.00

Lanceolate, Indian Green, 3¾", provenance unknown.
23Aug2003 $154.00

Scottsbluff, 3⅞", parallel flaking, Missouri.
16Jun2001 $247.50

Dalton point, 3¾", Greenup area, Illinois.
26Oct2002 $110.00

Fluted point, tip missing, 4¾", provenance unknown.
15Feb2003 $1,540.00

Fluted point, ears, 2⅛", De Kalb County, Indiana.
24Jun2000 $253.00

Dalton, 3⅞", incurvate baseline, St. Clair County, Illinois.
26Oct2002 $121.00

Dalton point, 2³⁄₁₆", Davis COA, Arkansas.
21Jun2003 $71.50

Fluted point, without tip, 5⅞", Monroe County, Illinois.
15Feb2003 $1,210.00

Paleo point, flared ears, hornstone, 2", Todd County, Kentucky.
9Mar2002 $165.00

Stemmed lance, 4¼", dark material, Massachusetts.
8Dec2001 $187.00

Paleo uniface point, 2¾", hornstone, Meigs County, Ohio.
22Nov2003 $132.00

Fluted point, slender, 3⅞", Barren County, Kentucky.
21Sep2002 $825.00

Lanceolate, 3½", Upper Mercer flint, Brown County, Ohio.
15Mar2003 $187.00

Paleo point, hornstone, 2⅜", Logan County, Kentucky.
9Mar2002 $297.00

Fluted point, 3", sugar quartzite, Kenosha County, Wisconsin.
27Jan2001 $1,705.00

Holland point, parallel flaking, 4½", Missouri.
21Jun2003 $687.50

Lanceolate, Upper Mercer flint, 4½", Pickaway County, Ohio.
18May2002 $990.00

Fluted point, 3⅜", mixed flint, Twigg County, Kentucky.
21Jun2003 $770.00

Paleo point, 2⅞", Indiana Green, tip break, Jay County, Indiana.
20Jul2002 $220.00

Dagger, probably Paleo, 4⅞", Flint Ridge, Franklin County, Ohio.
18May2002 $660.00

Fluted point, Ft. Payne chert, 3¼", Kentucky.
24Jun2000 $715.00

Fishtail Dalton, 5⅛", Berner COA, Pike County, Missouri.
23Aug2003 $660.00

Fluted point, 2¾", light-colored chert, Adams County, Illinois.
27Oct2001 $209.00

Fluted point, 4", restored tip, Meade County, Kentucky.
15Feb2003 $550.00

Dalton, light-colored chert, 3¼", Missouri.
26Oct2002 $93.50

Cumberland, fluted, 2¼", Mason County, Kentucky.
17May2003 $104.50

Dalton, parallel flaking, 5¾", Illinois.
15Feb2003 $2,200.00

Fluted point, 1¾", Monroe County, Michigan.
23Aug2003 $143.00

Dalton, 2¾", barbed ears, Lyon County, Kentucky.
27Jan2001 $176.00

Fluted point, fine, Carter Cave, 2⅞", Union County, Ohio.
15Jun2002 $2,970.00

Beaver Lake, 2⅛", Davis COA, Tennessee.
22Nov2003 $275.00

Dalton, serrated edges, 5¾", Pettis County, Missouri.
26Oct2002 $170.00

Stemmed blade, 5" long, Hudson River area, New York.
4Nov2000 $176.00

Fluted point, quartzite, 3¼", Adams County, Wisconsin.
21Sep2002 $440.00

Dalton point or blade, large and fine, 7¾", Missouri.
17May2003 $825.00

Fluted point, slight restoration, 3⅞", Clinton County, Kentucky.
21Sep2002 $412.50

Cumberland, fluted, 2⅛", glossy flint, Allen County, Ohio.
23Dec2002 $1,210.00

Quad point, fluted, 2¼", Crescent chert, Fulton County, Illinois.
17May2003 $440.00

Fluted point, light-colored flint, ex-Frank, 5", Illinois.
4Nov2000 $302.50

Paleo point, tapered waist, incurvate baseline, 2", Indiana.
23Aug2003 $159.50

Lanceolate, 3⅞", Atascosa County, Texas.
27Oct2001 $66.00

Dalton-Hemphill, 4¾", glossy chert, Boone County, Missouri.
22Nov2003 $209.00

Paleo type knife, 6", Florissant area, Missouri.
27Jan2001 $187.00

Paleo point, ears, 1⅞", Carter Cave, provenance unknown.
15Feb2003 $192.50

Dalton, 4⅝", light-colored chert, Pike County, Illinois.
26Oct2002 $165.00

Dalton point, fluted, ears, 2", Stoddard County, Missouri.
15Jun2002 $154.00

Hemphill Dalton, slight stem, 4½", Tennessee.
16Jun2001 $132.00

Stemmed lance, Carter Cave, 5¼", Clermont County, Ohio.
15Jun2002 $577.50

Dalton point, 3¼", Calhoun County, Illinois.
21Sep2002 $93.50

Dalton, 2½", dark flint, Harrison County, Kentucky.
27Jan2001 $192.50

Agate Basin, 5⅞", Hudson River area, New York.
4Nov2000 $412.50

Greenbrier-Dalton, 2¼", Humphrey County, Tennessee.
22Nov2003 $192.50

Fluted point, 2⅝", light-colored flint, Illinois.
27Jan2001 $242.00

Fluted point, one face with two flutes, 2⅝", provenance unknown.
23Aug2003 $550.00

Scottsbluff, 4¼", parallel flaking, Arkansas.
4Nov2000 $1,320.00

Dalton, light-colored chert, 5" long, Calloway County, Missouri.
27Jan2001 $522.50

Clovis point, slight restoration, 2⅛", Indiana Green, Indiana.
17May2003 $385.00

Lanceolate blade, 5" long, Allegheny County, Pennsylvania.
4Nov2000 $148.50

Stemmed lance, 3¾", excurvate sides, Knox County, Ohio.
23Aug2003 $165.00

Paleo point, finely chipped, 3¼", Mason County, Kentucky.
27Oct2001 $440.00

Fluted point, 3½", Berner COA, Ross County, Ohio.
15Feb2003 $1,430.00

Dalton point, 4½", light-colored chert, Boone County, Missouri.
21Sep2002 $297.00

Folsom point, 1" x 1½", Winkler County, Texas.
27Oct2001 $2,530.00

Fluted point, barb tip missing, 3⅞", Wayne County, Michigan.
23Aug2003 $132.00

Lanceolate, tapered, 4", Pendleton County, Kentucky.
27Jan2001 $1,045.00

During research for this book, useful information was found that adds dimension and interest to the study of Paleolithic cultural items. Even these facts and observations offer only a small window into an ancient world.

This is a concise summary of why collectors want artifacts from Paleo times: "Paleo period flint relics are by far the most sought after artifacts for most collectors. The reason for this is two-fold. The Paleo period is the oldest period in North America, which makes Paleo artifacts the oldest North American relics available to collectors. Additionally, the quality manufacturing and unique style of the 'fluted' base, found only on Paleo period relics, makes it an extremely collectible item. In our free market system the law of supply and demand works well, and thus Paleo period relics realize by far the highest market prices due to their high collectibility and low availability."
(Bennett, James R. *Relics & Reproductions — Identifying Reproductions & Altered Ancient American Artifacts*. Homestead Publishing Company, Polk, Ohio, 2003, p. 67.)

At times and with certain artifacts, it is difficult to determine if an example is positively and only from Paleo times. Certain classes — like gravers, rectangular blades, plain end-scrapers — indeed originated in the Paleo, but the simplicity and efficiency of the tools caused them to be continued into the Archaic and sometimes even later. The only certain way to know if some of these artifacts are indeed Paleo is if they are found on a single-component Paleo site.
(Hothem, Lar. Various sources.)

Professor Warren K. Moorehead, who lived at a time when fluted points were not widely recognized as being very old, still understood that they were something special. At one time, most fluted points were referred to as Folsoms after the Western discovery site. Some fluted points were Pennsylvania discoveries, as Moorehead noted when recording a 1916 archaeological excursion; "Four very fine knife-like points of the Folsom type have been found within three miles of Lock Haven. The writer does not claim there are any large number of Folsom Points in the Susquehanna Valley."
(Moorehead, Warren K. *A Report of the Susquehanna River Expedition*. The Andover Press, Andover, Massachusetts, 1938, p. 79.)

Some 409 Clovis-like points were reported in a survey of North Carolina. One large and fine fluted point came from Granville County and was about 5" long. It was made of silicified shale.
(Peck, Rodney M. *Clovis Points of Early Man in North Carolina*. The Piedmont Archaeological Society, Vol. 6, 1988, pp. 1, 11.)

Paleo end-scrapers are often found across North America, and they tend to be distinctive. "If all the facets on the dorsal face of a long narrow chip show that all the previous chips were struck off in the same direction as the one that detached this chip from the core, it is a true blade if large or a bladelet if small....The Paleo-Indian scraper is nearly always made from a short true blade, while the later scrapers were made from an ordinary flake. Most of the Paleo-Indian scrapers were made on a blade made by slightly resolved flaking [flake that is thinnest at the bulb or percussion end], which gave them a concave ventral surface and so made a more efficient tool."
(Smith, Arthur George. "The Old Sarge Says." *Ten Years of the Tennessee Archaeologist Selected Subjects, 1954 – 1963*, Vol. XVIII No. 2, pp. 448 – 456.)

At the Hanson site, Wyoming (Folsom culture), a specialized tool form was sometimes made. Large chert flakes, and sometimes biface artifacts, were struck a blow near the center. Breakage lines radiated away from the point of impact, and this produced a number of triangular-shaped pieces. The tips of these pieces evidently were used as gravers to score or groove bone for making other tools.
(Frison, George C. and Bruce A. Bradley. *Folsom Tools and Technology at the Hanson Site, Wyoming*. University of New Mexico Press, Albuquerque, 1980, pp. 97 – 99.)

The face of a Paleo point may have tip fluting, a long and relatively narrow flake scar that runs from the tip down the face. This is often called "impact fluting," but there are usually no signs, such as irregular breaks or crushing at the tip, of striking an object. Instead, these flutes were purposefully done by ancient flint knappers. Tip fluting is usually on resharpened examples, and may even be on both upper faces. While the purpose is not known, the result thinned the tip and upper blade portion. This may have contributed to more effective point or knife use. Note that this form of tip thinning by fluting is not the same as true fluting for shaft attachment; that was done from the tip, not the base.
(Hothem, Lar. Various sources.)

One old-time collector in Wrens, Georgia, found "ten or fifteen beautiful fluted points." These apparently were from the Briar Creek headwaters, and the collector acknowledged they came from one site. The man, also a preacher and the father of writer Erskine Caldwell, never divulged where he had found the points.
(Waring, Antonio J. Jr. "Paleo-Indian Remains in South Carolina and Georgia." *The Waring Papers*. The Peabody Museum, Cambridge, Massachusetts, 1968, p. 237.)

The Olsen-Chubbuck site, in southeastern Colorado, was once a Late Paleo killing ground for a species of now-extinct bison. The animals were contained in a narrow gully, or arroyo, where they were then speared and butchered, leaving behind a bone bed that stretched for just over 170 feet. Some expertly chipped projectile points were found with the bones. These were of the Scottsbluff (slightly stemmed), Eden (straight-sided, ripple-flaked), and Milnesand (wide, random-flaked) types. Despite being three dis-

tinct point forms, all were apparently used at the same time.
(Wheat, Joe Ben. "A Paleo-Indian Bison Kill." *Early Man in America, Readings from Scientific American.* W. H. Freeman and Company, San Francisco, CA, 1951/1973, pp. 80, 82, 83.)

Fluted points were used from about 12,000 BC to 10,000 BC. Lanceolate points were used thereafter, from about 10,000 BC to 8000 BC or so. Large, now-extinct animals (megafauna) probably disappeared around 10,000 BC, so later fluted-point people probably hunted modern and still-existing animals like deer, buffalo, caribou, and elk (wapiti), plus smaller food animals. The temperature increase from late in the glacial period (Pleistocene) to warmer times (Holocene) was about 12 degrees. The once-glaciated landscape gradually changed from evergreens and shrubs to mixed hardwood forests and some grasslands, much like the natural world today.
(Hothem, Lar. Various sources.)

At the Parrish Village site in Kentucky, excavators in 1939/1940 uncovered a lower Paleo occupation. Earlier, a fluted point about 3" long had been surface collected. Fluted on both lower faces, it was made of light-colored chert. A fluted point, which somewhat resembled a Redstone, also had been found, and an additional point was Cumberland-like. During excavation, a fluted point, a lightly notched point, and two fluted point bases were revealed, plus numerous tools.
(Webb, William S. *The Parrish Village Site/Hopkins County, Kentucky.* Reports in Archaeology Vol. VII No. 6, February 1951, University of Kentucky, Lexington, pp. 410, 434 – 438.)

There are several problems involved when attempts are made to identify the material or source of flint or chert used for Paleo artifacts. Early Paleo artifacts, especially, are often made of materials gathered at a distance from the find. Or, the material may be from a minor source or quarry that is either difficult to locate or may even have disappeared due to recent or modern construction activity. Too, the great age of Paleo cultural debris means that the artifacts are often weathered and patinated beyond recognition. The interior flint or chert is then extremely difficult to identify precisely.
(Hothem, Lar. Various sources.)

Plainview points, named after a site near Plainview, northwestern Texas, have been found over most of western North America. They are somewhat like Clovis points but lack fluting and have irregular flaking. In addition to a Plains distribution, Plainviews have been found from Alaska to Mexico.
(Wormington, H. M. *Ancient Man in North America*, 4th edition. The Denver Museum of Natural History, Denver, 1957, pp. 107, 110.)

Life in Paleo times may have been subsistence-oriented, but a few artistic or ritual works were made. Known as the Malakoff Heads, they were found in the Trinity River Valley from 1929 to 1939. Weighing from 60 to 135 pounds each, the limestone concretions had the rough features of human heads. They came from a terrace that contained the bones of extinct animals such as mastodon,

horse, camel, and ground sloth. The purpose of the ancient stone carvings is unknown.
(Newcomb, W. W. Jr. *The Indians of Texas.* University of Texas Press, Austin and London, 5th printing, 1980, pp. 11, 12.)

Enterline fluting of Paleo points has been described based on examples found at the Shoop site, located near Enterline, Pennsylvania. Artifacts from the site, technically known as the Enterline Chert Industry, included points fluted in a special way. The method was a form of multiple fluting, whereby two long and narrow flutes were driven from the lower face sides, followed by the removal of a large central flute. At times, the large flute took away traces of the earlier flutes.
(Wormington, H. M. *Ancient Man in North America*, 4th edition. The Denver Museum of Natural History, Denver, 1957, pp. 67, 68 – 71.)

What may have been a very large Agate Basin point or blade was found in Wisconsin. "Another very fine example...is made of a shiny, cream colored flint marked in places with pink and purplish tints and having tiny reddish specks scattered over its surface. On one side of the blade a broad, bright yellow streak extends from its base to the point of the blade. Its point has received a slight injury, otherwise this specimen is in perfect condition. It measures 9¾" in length, is one inch in width at its base, and nearly 2½" in width at its widest part, about 4" from its point. The weight is seven ounces. It was found in Sec. 4, Town of Manitowoc Rapids, Manitowoc County, being secured by its present owner from a man who obtained it in payment of a saloon debt."
(Brown, Prof. Charles E. "Ceremonial Knives." *The Archaeological Bulletin*, The International Society of Archaeologists, Vol. 6 No. 2, March-April 1915, Somerset, Kentucky, pp. 30, 31.)

Besides the Clovis family, four other fluted point types occur with some frequency in the Great Lakes region. The Barnes has a narrow base and is Cumberland-like, with at least one flute and basal ears. It is medium size. The Crowfield is thin and wide, with multiple flutes. The Gainey point is Clovis-like, thick and with parallel sides. The Holcombe is small and thin, with excurvate sides and pointed basal tips.
(Hothem, Lar. Various sources.)

The Adkins site is located in the Magalloway Valley of northwestern Maine, and one incomplete and one complete fluted point came from there. Other artifacts, including flakes, totaled 415. A unique feature of the site was a probable meat cache, consisting of large rocks, some inward leaning. Spaces between large rocks were closed with smaller ones, and the deboned meat from 11 to 14 caribou could have been stored in the enclosure. Interestingly for a small Paleo site, 14 different varieties of raw material were used for the artifacts.
(Gramly, R. M. *The Adkins Site — A Palaeo-Indian Habitation and Associated Stone Structure.* Persimmon Press, New York, 1988, pp. v, 15 – 17.)

Paleo fluted points usually have typical shaft-attachment fluting, done only from the base whether on one or both faces. However, when a flute runs full-length, a few scarce examples have fluting that began at the tip. Proof of this can be seen in the ripple patterns that remain here and there in the flute scar or channel. A rare fluting technique, seen only on a few examples, was fluting from both the base and tip of the point to create a full-length flute. Yet another point, perhaps one of a kind, seen by the author was fluted full length (part from the base, part from the tip). This was done on both faces.
(Hothem, Lar. Various sources.)

Years ago, hints were given for surface hunting Paleo points in western (Wyoming) regions. "Many collectors hunt for sand blows and blow outs. Many people prefer to go out just after a hard rain or wind storm. They consider the side from which the wind usually blows to be the better location. Here the wind usually blows from the southwest, moving the sand to the northeast. Thus the southwestern part of a blow would be the better place to look because it would be covered up on the northeastern side."
(Russell, Virgil Y. *Indian Artifacts of the Rockies*. Douglas, WY, 1945, p. 25.)

Drills made by the Late Paleo lanceolate people in Ohio had three different basal shapes. These were expanded or T-shaped, expanded and rounded, and tapered but not expanded. At the Sawmill site, almost 90% of the artifacts were made of Walhonding and Coshocton flints.
(Prufer, Olaf H. and Raymond S. Baby. *Palaeo-Indians of Ohio*. The Ohio Historical Society, Columbus, 1963, pp. 32, 34.)

In a brief research listing by the author, unpublished until now, 76 Paleo rectangular blades (square knives) found in Ohio were tallied. Lengths were available for 65 of the examples. The average length was 3.57 inches, and extreme lengths were 2⅜" to 5⅝". Typical materials were dark Upper Mercer flint from eastern Ohio in blues, blacks, and grays.
(Hothem, Lar. Various sources.)

An easily recognized Paleo tool is the combination spokeshave and scraper, and a number were found on the Williamson site, Virginia. "Note that where a blade has two spokeshaves, they are never exactly opposite each other. Early man was planning ahead, for he knew that if they were placed opposite, the blade would become weakened, especially after resharpening. The most interesting aspect of this tool type is that they give us an indication of the diameter of Paleo man's lance shafts (that is, assuming that they were used to shape and smooth lance shafts). The width of the shave gives us diameter, the depth gives us radius or half the diameter."
(Painter, Floyd. "Paleo Man's Tool Kit." *The Williamson Site, Dinwiddie County, Virginia*. Rodney M. Peck, Editor, 1985, pp. 21, 23.)

The Debert site in Nova Scotia, along with many other artifacts, produced a total of 140 projectile points, 10 of them complete. As with the Vail site in Maine, fluted point baselines tended to be deeply incurvate. Of a 25-point sample, 60% were fluted on both faces, 20% were fluted on one face, and 20% were unfluted.
(MacDonald, G. F. *Debert — A Paleo-Indian Site in Central Nova Scotia*. Persimmon Press, New York, 1985, pp. 70 – 72.)

Microblades are known to be associated with Paleo times (though they were also used later), and they have been found at a few North American sites. "Microblades are present in Paleolithic complexes in Siberia, and some have been found in the Blackwater Draw locality in New Mexico under circumstances that suggest an age of some 11,000 or 12,000 years."
(Wormington, H. M. and Richard G. Forbis. *An Introduction to the Archaeology of Alberta, Canada*. Denver Museum of Natural History, Proceedings No. 11, Denver, 1965, p. 14.)

Some Paleo points in the eastern Midwest look like fluted points except that they lack the flute. They tend not to be as well made as fluted points, have basal thinning instead of true flutes, and are generally smaller than fluted points. Sometimes found with fluted points, they may be the last of the fluted point tradition.
(Prufer, Olaf H. *The McConnell Site — A Late Palaeo-Indian Workshop in Coshocton County, Ohio*. Scientific Publications of the Cleveland Museum of Natural History, Vol. 2 No. 1, January 1963, p. 17.)

Early observers, before scientific knowledge of Paleo points was widespread, were yet aware of their distinctive shapes and comparative scarcity. One photo grouping ("quite rare") of nine Paleo points was described in this way: "Points of one of these standard forms are exactly alike as to size, shape, distinguishing characteristics, and generally as to material. In such investigations, it is quite easy to observe that certain type forms have a wide distribution and form about the same per cent of the whole number, in one county as in another county, perhaps two hundred miles away..."
(Funkhouser, W. D. and W. S. Webb. *Ancient Life in Kentucky*. The Kentucky Geological Survey. Frankfort, KY, 1928, pp. 215, 216.)

In 1926, when fluted points were discovered near Folsom, New Mexico, they created an immediate sensation in the archaeological and collecting worlds. Both groups were impressed by the association of the points with extinct animal (bison) bones, which pushed back the certain date of human occupation in North America by thousands of years. Soon every fluted point came to be called a Folsom, or Folsom-like or Folsomoid. Artifact dealers quickly supplied such artifacts, and a 1935 advertisement by G. I. Groves of Chicago offered Folsoms at $3.00 each.
(Editor. *North American Indian Relic Collectors Association/Official Bulletin*, Vol. 1 No. 7, December 1935, back cover.)

Shape or outline of fluted points is not always reliable in determining a type. Resharpening changes the shape, and unfinished points may be substantially different from completed points.
(Roosa, William B. "Some Great Lakes Fluted Point Types." *The Michigan Archaeologist*, Vol. 11 Nos. 3-4, Sept.-Dec. 1965, p. 90.)

While large Paleo uniface blades are widely known, a narrow and different bladelet form sometimes goes unrecognized. Triangular in cross-section, these are often 2" to 3" long and about ⅜" across one face. Paleo bladelets are sturdy and have sharp edges. Probably hafted in bone or antler handles, they were likely multi-purpose tools for cutting tasks. Most are slightly to moderately curved. The high ancient breakage rate indicates they received rough use.
(Hothem, Lar. Various sources.)

Very recent information (via DNA results) about when pre-Clovis people came to what is now North America sets a general time date of 18,000 years ago or 16,000 BC. Clovis is now average-dated at about 11,600 BC, so the earlier peoples would have had about 4,400 years to make artifacts of some sort.
(Wade, Nicholas and John Noble Wilford. "DNA Study Puts Siberians in New World 18,000 Years Ago." *The Columbus Dispatch*, Ohio, July 27, 2003, p. A-6.)

By the beginning of 1982, North Dakota had 192 Paleo points recorded. The three most numerous types were: Folsom, 45; Agate Basin, 34; and Scottsbluff, 27. Of the total Paleo points found, 77% were made of Knife River flint, probably from western North Dakota.
(Schneider, Fred E. "A Preliminary Investigation of Paleo-Indian Cultures in North Dakota." *Manitoba Archaeological Quarterly*, Vol. 6 No. 4, October 1982, p. 35.)

Other than the basics of physical form — like shape, workstyle, size and material — two other amazing things can be learned from Paleo points and tools. Sometimes, on artifacts over ten thousand years old, minute traces of blood remain. The blood can be identified as to the kind of animal that was killed or butchered. Even traces of human blood have been noted, probably the result of accidental cuts. Also, microwear analysis using electronic microscopes, along with comparisons of edges created by experimental manufacturing, can provide evidence of how a tool was used. This can be so exact that differences between working fresh hide and dry hide can be determined.
(Hothem, Lar. Various sources.)

The Vail site in western Maine produced 79 whole or fragmentary fluted points of a type similar to those found at the Debert site, Nova Scotia. These fluted points are notable for having a very deeply concave baseline, somewhat U-shaped. Drills, 56 in number, had both fluted and unfluted bases. Many other artifacts — scrapers of several forms, limaces or uniface scrapers that are slug-shaped, cutters and hammer-anvils — were also found. Over ten thousand worked specimens were recovered from the habitation site and associated caribou-killing ground. The Vail site dates to 9120 BC +/- 180 years.
(Gramly, Richard Michael. "The Vail Site: A Palaeo-Indian Encampment in Maine." Bulletin of the Buffalo Society of Natural Sciences, Vol. 30, Buffalo, New York, 1982, pp. x, 23 – 45.)

One of the top authenticators in the country, John F. Berner, made a record of point and blade types most commonly reproduced by modern knappers. Of the thirteen types listed, and totaling 100%, six or nearly half were types from the Paleo period. They were: Clovis, 22.0%; Agate Basin, 8.7%; Dalton, 7.0%; Cumberland, 4.8%; Scottsbluff, 4.2%; and, Folsom, 2.7%.
(Berner, John F. "The Popularity of Reproduction Styles." *Prehistoric American*, Genuine Indian Relic Society, Vol. XXXII No. 3, 1998, p. 10.)

Clovis points are known to have served as projectile points, whether fixed to hand-held spears or Atl-atl javelins that were sized somewhere between spears and arrows. However, the majority of fluted points do not have extremely pointed tips, and many are somewhat rounded or even blunted. It would seem that a less pointed tip was preferred over a very pointed tip. But, a more pointed tip is more prone to breakage than a rounded and slightly thicker tip. Prehistoric flint-knappers and hunters seemed to have struck a careful projectile tip compromise that worked.
(Hothem, Lar. Various sources.)

Northern Ohio was evidently a major hunting-foraging region for Early Paleo people. A group of fluted Clovis points from the region was made from a variety of high-grade materials, and lengths were from 2" to 4".
(Vietzen, Col. Raymond C. *Indians of the Lake Erie Basin*. Ludi Printing Company, 1965, p. 241.)

Across the country, notched points are generally considered to be Archaic and later, but a few are known to be from Paleo times. "Another development in the Plains area concerns notched points. Until a few years ago, there was a belief that all such forms were of fairly recent age....At the Simonsen site near Quimby, Iowa, were found the remains of more than twenty-five bison of a variety larger than modern buffalo, probably Bison occidentalis. The projectile points recovered were large triangular side-notched forms with concave bases. A radiocarbon date of 8,430 +/- 520 years ago (6480 B.C.) was obtained here. The points from the Simonsen site are very similar to those found at the Logan Creek site in Burt County, Nebraska..." [Recent recalibration of radiocarbon dates now would make the site much older.]
(Wormington, H. M. and Richard G. Forbis. *An Introduction to the Archaeology of Alberta*, Canada, Denver Museum of Natural History, Proceedings No. 11, Denver, 1965, pp. 23, 24.)

Most of the famous Folsom points of the American West are isolated finds, but one site contained chipped artifacts besides fluted points. The Lindenmeier site in northern Colorado had scrapers of the snubnose type, plus side-scrapers "...and a few implements difficult to classify because they combine several features." One end-scraper variety is of special interest. "The removal of several long flakes from the top produced a fourth subform, one with a quadrangular cross-section. The latter also resulted from the removal of a single, long, broad flake, which produced a fluting similar to that on the projectile points."
(Roberts, Frank H. H. Jr. "A Folsom Complex," *Smithsonian Miscellaneous Collections*, Vol. 94 No. 4, Washington, June 20, 1935, pp. 22 – 30.)

Most measurements of flute length are done on flutes that exist on a finished point. However, since the original fluting process began on a straight (or even convex) baseline, the actual flute in most cases was considerably longer. The length of the original as-made flute can be determined by measuring from a line drawn between the two ear tips.
(Mason, Ronald J. *Late Pleistocene Geochronology and the Paleo-Indian Penetration into the Lower Michigan Peninsula*, University of Michigan Anthropological Papers No. 11, Ann Arbor, 1958, p. 14.)

Sixty years ago, mainly due to wide publicity given to Folsom and Clovis sites, it was believed that fluted points were mainly found in the western U.S. As more finds were made, 30 years ago it was thought that more fluted points were found in the U.S. Southeast. New information and surveys, however, now indicate that areas of major fluted point concentrations are in the eastern Midwest and the Northeast.
(Hothem, Lar. Various sources.)

Late Paleo chipped adzes from the Dalton people tend to be oval or pear shaped and fairly large. The beveled working edges at one end, straight to excurvate, often have striations that indicate they were used to cut charred wood.
(Yerkes, Richard and Linda M. Gaertner. "Microwear Analysis of Dalton Artifacts." *Sloan — A Paleoindian Dalton Cemetery in Arkansas*. Smithsonian Institution Press, Washington, DC, 1997, pp. 58, 63 – 65.)

Artifact collectors in North America have an immediate understanding of the word *Paleo*, also spelled *Palaeo*. The word itself means "old." And the word is sometimes combined with *lithic*, meaning "stone," so Paleolithic means "Old Stone Age." Also, a Paleolith is a stone implement (artifact) from Paleo times. More fully, Paleolithic (especially in Europe) refers to Ice Age cultures that are apparently much older than those in North America.
(Hothem, Lar. Various sources.)

The Quad site in Alabama had many Paleo combination tools. Examples were scraper-gravers, knife-gravers, knife-scraper-gravers, scraper-knives, and knife-graver-spokeshaves.

(Soday, Frank J. "The Quad Site, A Paleo-Indian Village in Northern Alabama," *Ten Years of the Tennessee Archaeologist Selected Subjects/1954 – 1963*, Vol. X No. 1, pp. 14, 15.)

At the Naco Mammoth site, Arizona, eight fluted Clovis points were associated with the bones of a mammoth. Comparing this point placement with that of a Texas find, there were similarities. "Assuming that there was little or no shifting of the points since the death of the animals, the angle and place of penetration was about the same in each case, from the upper right side of the elephants and at the base of the skull, the spot in the elephant's anatomy where the spinal cord was most vulnerable....It is worth noting that all the points recovered at Naco were between the skull base and fore part of the rib cage."
(Haury, Emil W. "Artifacts with Mammoth Remains, Naco, Arizona," *American Antiquity*, Vol. XIX No. 1, Society for American Archaeology, July 1953, pp. 1, 5 – 7.)

One Paleo artifact form often seen is the snapped blade. These are examples of points or blades that are broken, though there is disagreement as to whether such examples are accidental or purposeful, or perhaps both at different times. If the break was clean, it left two long and sharp working edges, and these often have smoothness or chippage from use. Also, depending on the angle of the break across the main body of the artifact, one or two pointed corners were produced for heavy-duty graver work. These tips show use dulling quite often. Such "secondary" or salvage tools are quite common and simply require close study (a 10-X glass is helpful) for identification.
(Hothem, Lar. Various sources.)

A tool used to roughen edges of projectile points and other chipped tools often goes unrecognized. Tools of this kind are cobbles of quartzite, sometimes also used as hammerstones, but with a distinct difference. The stones were broken or split about in half, and the split, or fresh, surface was used as a grinder for flint edges. These ultra-hard artifacts in this shape were found on the Williamson site, and the flattened split surfaces had elongated smoothing marks worn into them.
(Painter, Floyd. "Split Cobble Abraders — An Important Item in Paleo Man's Tool Kit." *The Williamson Site, Dinwiddie County, Virginia*. Rodney M. Peck, Editor, 1985, pp. 79 – 85.)

A Late Paleo site in southern Alberta contained bison bones and projectile points. These were stemmed types, mainly Alberta and Scottsbluff. Compared to the latter, the Albertas had less-pointed tips and longer stems. Other artifacts found were scrapers, choppers, and flakes with graver tips.
(Forbis, Richard G. "Fletcher: A Paleo-Indian Site in Alberta." *American Antiquity*, Vol. 33 No. 1, January 1968, The Society for American Archaeology, pp. 1 – 9.)

There is good evidence that some fluted projectile points were also used as knives, and at least one factor may be important in

determining such use. "Lateral grinding usually extends for a third to a half the length of the point. That the shortest specimens are often those with most lateral grinding respective to length lends support to the belief that many, if not all, of the shorter points are the result of reworking originally longer blades. Evidence of the secondary utilization of fluted blades as knives is most often to be secured from these shorter specimens."
(Mason, Ronald J. "Indications of Paleo-Indian Occupation in the Delaware Valley." *Pennsylvania Archaeologist*, Vol. XXIX No. 1, April 1959, pp. 12, 13.)

In terms of animals sometimes killed and processed by Paleo hunters, the two largest were the mastodons and mammoths. Mastodons tended to be forest dwellers, leaf and shrub eaters, and were found mainly in the eastern U.S. but occasionally elsewhere. Mammoths lived more on the Plains and prairies of the western U.S. and were mainly grass eaters. Their teeth had grinding surfaces.
(Hothem, Lar. Various sources.)

Of four fluted projectile points found at the Colby site in Wyoming, three had distinctive basal outlines. The base corners were rounded and the base bottom center, relatively small, was incurvate and U-shaped. The fourth point appeared to be a typical Clovis. They were found near two large piles of mammoth bones.
(Frison, George C. and Lawrence C. Todd. *The Colby Mammoth Site*. University of New Mexico Press, Albuquerque, 1986, pp. 46, 91 – 93.)

An excellent example of the Northumberland fluted knife type is shown in a book by Col. Vietzen. Illustrated is a classic lanceolate form with full fluting on one face only. Made of Carter Cave flint from Kentucky, the lance is carefully chipped. It was found in western Pennsylvania, a state that has produced most of the few specimens found. The combination of fluting and the lance shape suggests a time placement somewhere in the Late Paleo era.
(Vietzen, Col. Raymond C. *Prehistoric Americans*. White Horse Publishers, 1989, p. 27.)

The largest numbers of tool types at the Adams site, Kentucky, were uniface scrapers. These were end-scrapers, 137; side-scrapers, 166; and combination end- and side-scrapers, 93. Together they formed some 32% (nearly one-third) of the total artifacts studied.
(Sanders, Thomas Nolan. *Adams: The Manufacturing of Flaked Stone Tools at a Paleoindian Site in Western Kentucky*. Persimmon Press, Buffalo, NY, 1990, p. 63.)

On the Plains, Clovis fluted points are generally associated with mammoth remains, as at Blackwater Draw, New Mexico. Folsom fluted points (Lindenmeier site, New Mexico) are often found with extinct bison remains. And Hell Gap knives and Frederick knives sometimes have a beveled cutting edge.
(Irwin, Henry T. and H. M. Wormington. "Paleo-Indian Tool Types in the Great Plains." *American Antiquity*, Vol. 35 No. 1, January 1970, Society for American Archaeology, pp. 24, 25, 29.)

There can be some confusion involving two named artifact types, these being the Ross and the Ross County. While both were named after Ross County, Ohio, where examples were found, they are otherwise completely different artifacts both in time and origin. The Ross County is a fluted Paleo point distributed over much of the eastern U.S., and it has large flattened flake scars on the faces. The Ross is Middle Woodland, a large Hopewellian stemmed blade, probably used for ritual purposes.
(Hothem, Lar. Various sources.)

A cache of Paleo artifacts was discovered in southwestern Oklahoma. Called the Anadarko cache, there were 4 core chipping tools, 2 discoidal choppers, 26 prismatic blades, and other knife forms. Blade surface polish indicated that they had been used to cut meat, and hence were butchering tools.
(Hammatt, Hallett H. "A Paleo-Indian Butchering Kit." *American Antiquity*, Vol. 35 No. 2, April 1970, Society for American Archaeology, pp. 141 – 151.)

For collectors, there is a sort of dividing line for fluted points in terms of length and desirability. Assuming that other factors, such as condition and material, are about equal, the elusive length factor comes into play. Depending on the individual collector, this line is somewhere between 3" and 4". Fluted points under 4" are scarce, while those over 4" are very scarce. There is also a large value disparity between under-4" and over-4" fluted points, and a difference of half an inch can be significant.
(Hothem, Lar. Various sources.)

Mesa points, found on a site in northern Alaska, greatly resemble Agate Basin points from the Late Paleo period. Mesas are lanceolates with tapered stems and incurvate baselines, just like some other Agate Basin forms.
(Perino, Gregory. "Points and Barbs." *Central States Archaeological Journal*, Vol. 46 No. 2, April 1999, p. 103.)

At the Midland site, Texas, blow-out localities numbers two to five produced 74 artifacts. Late Paleo, there were seven fluted Folsoms, 20 unfluted Folsoms, a Meserve, and a Milnesand. In addition to 24 fragmentary artifacts, there were 19 scrapers or knives and two manos, or seed-grinding stones.
(Wendorf, Fred, et al. *The Midland Discovery*. University of Texas Press, Austin, 1955, pp. 43 – 65.)

From a collecting point-of-view, the most difficult fluted point type to acquire (other than large complete blades like the Anzick and St. Louis) is probably undamaged Folsom. Not only were relatively few made, but the large flutes and overall thinness made Folsoms quite fragile and prone to breakage during manufacture and use. Even fragmentary examples are considered highly collectible. Per weight, they are undoubtedly the most valuable chipped prehistoric artifacts in North America.
(Hothem, Lar. Various sources.)

A major Paleo site in Jersey County, Illinois, contained many tool

types in addition to numerous fluted points. Such tools were scrapers (end, side, thumb, and hafted), gravers, gouges, fluted blades, preforms, and hammerstones.
(Perdun, Gregory L. "Ready's Paleo-Indian Site." *Central States Archaeological Journal*, Vol. 35 No. 3, July 1988, pp. 134, 135.)

One type of elongated blade in the eastern Midwest is believed to be from the Late Paleo. Long, narrow and flattened, one or both ends have angular corners, and the ends are wider than the central blade portion. They are made of flints commonly used in Late Paleo times.
(Smith, Arthur George. "A Peculiar Knife Type." *Ohio Archaeologist*, the Archaeological Society of Ohio. Vol. 9 No. 4, October 1959, p. 140.)

In Alaska's Brooks Range, a site produced broken fluted points and other artifacts associated with the Paleo period. Three points had basal flutes and parallel sides, and a narrow lance-like point was also found. Split bifaces were recovered, also uniface scrapers, gravers, burins, cores, and broken bladelets.
(Alexander, Herbert L. *Putu — A Fluted Point Site in Alaska*. Department of Archaeology, Simon Fraser University, Burnaby, British Columbia, 1987, pp. 12 – 36.)

The presence of so many artifacts with graver tips provides indirect proof that many other artifacts were made that no longer exist. The tips are on flakes, damaged points, complete points, multipurpose tools and end-scrapers. It is believed that gravers were used to make narrow channels in bone, antler, and ivory so that these organic materials could be broken into useful parts. The parts in turn were probably made into projectile points, perforators, awls, and needles. Very few of these artifacts have survived to the present, but they must have been common in Paleo times.
(Hothem, Lar. Various sources.)

A rare Paleo blade form is the egg-shaped knife, wide and with a relatively small and rounded stem at one end. Usually large, up to 8½" long, the knives are quite thin for size. Two examples from Illinois were 4⅜" (Scott County) and 4⅞" (Jersey County). At times, one or both edges were beveled due to resharpening.
(Perino, Gregory. "A Little about Ovoid and Tanged Knives." *Central States Archaeological Journal*, Vol. 19 No. 3, July 1972, pp. 101 – 104.)

Two forms of fluted Folsom points are known. One tends to be short and wide, with rounded shoulders located between the mid-section and tip. The other form is relatively long and slender, with a tapered tip. The two forms have full flutes, and pointed basal corners. Both are thin and side edges have small and delicate chipping scars.
(Roberts, Frank H. H. Jr. "A Folsom Complex." *Smithsonian Miscellaneous Collections*, Vol. 94 No. 4, Washington, June 20, 1935, p. 15.)

An extinct bison butchering and kill site in northwestern Nebraska contained between 500 and 600 sets of animal remains, and a number of Paleo artifacts. Stemmed Alberta (Late Paleo) points were excavated from the bone bed, and broken Albertas and butchering tools were also found.
(Ferguson, Les. "The Hudson-Meng Bison Kill Site." *The Redskin*, Genuine Indian Relic Society, Vol. X No. 3, 1975, pp. 90 – 92.)

Fluted points are very much a hallmark of Paleo times. They, along with spurred end-scrapers, seem to be found only on Paleo sites or as isolated surface finds. Fluted points have not been found in Asia, which is assumed to be the jumping-off region for North America. All indications are that true fluted points were a distinctly American development or invention. They were not made before Paleo times, and they were not made after.
(Hothem, Lar. Various sources.)

Nearly 100 whole or fragmentary fluted points were recovered from the Bull Brook site, Massachusetts. The fluted points ranged in length from 1¾" to 3¾", and had nearly parallel sides and concave bases. Other flint artifacts included scrapers, drills, gravers and knives.
(Editor. *The Redskin*, Vol. X No. 2, 1975, pp. 64 – 69; reprint from *Bulletin of the Massachusetts Archeological Society*, Vol. 34 Nos. 1 & 2, 1972 – 1973, pp. 1 – 6.)

Most known Clovis kill sites involve mammoth bones and a few mastodon bones. However, a Clovis point found in Harper County, Oklahoma, provided evidence that Clovis people also hunted bison. The point was discovered at Jake Bluff, along the Beaver River.
(Editor. "Newsbriefs." *Illinois State Archaeological Society/Bulletin*, Fall-Winter 2002.)

When reference is made to a "flute," as a kind or type of artifact, collectors know what that means — a fluted point. However, Paleo Indians fluted three different artifacts. One, and the best known, is indeed the fluted projectile point, and this was done for a smaller hafting arrangement for deep penetration. Knives were also sometimes fluted, as were some long end-scrapers. Apparently, knives and scrapers were fluted for a tighter hafting fit. The flutes on some end-scrapers are the flake scars from previous large flakes struck from a core, though some were obviously made later. In fact, some end-scrapers have a core-flute along the shaft and another flute that begins about the middle of the end-scraper edge.
(Hothem, Lar. Various sources.)

Whether the result of cultural disparity or the kinds of flint available, there is a difference in fluted point lengths in the eastern Midwest. Sample lengths: Michigan, 2.06 inches; Ohio, 2.68 inches; Indiana, 2.67 inches; Kentucky, 3.03 inches.
(Editor. *The Redskin*, Genuine Indian Relic Society, Vol. IV No. 3, July 1969, pp. 84 – 86.)

Chipped artifacts with small to tiny needle-like tips have been found on many Paleo sites. Commonly referred to as gravers, their

actual purpose may sometimes have been for tattooing. Complete examples average three such tips, but on individual specimens the number is from one to six or more. As for pigment, hematite and graphite materials have been found on many Paleo sites.
(Painter, Floyd. "Possible Evidence of Tattooing by Paleo-Indians of Eastern North America." *The Williamson Site, Dinwiddie County, Virginia*. Rodney M. Peck, Editor, 1985, pp. 87 – 93.)

A unique Late Paleo knife form in the West probably goes unnoticed by many collectors. "The channel flakes from typical Folsom points were not always discarded. Several examples show that they were used as knives. Close inspection of the edges reveals minute retouching, which perfected the cutting qualities of the stone and made a serviceable tool from one of the by-products of the process of point manufacture. There is extreme variation in the length of these objects. This may be attributed to their thinness and liability to breakage. Specimens range from 23 to 46 mm in length, 13 to 17 mm in width, and 1.5 to 2 mm in thickness.
(Roberts, Frank H. H. Jr. "A Folsom Complex." *Smithsonian Miscellaneous Collections*, Vol. 94 No. 4, Washington, June 20, 1935, pp. 27 – 28.)

The size range of Paleo fluted points is considerable. As a class the St. Louis is the largest, being both long (up to 6" or more) and wide. Found in the central U.S., examples are few. The Holcombe averages between 1½" and 2" long. It is found in the western Great Lakes region. Of these, of course, retipped examples are shorter, and resharpened examples are more narrow.
(Hothem, Lar. Various sources.)

The Barnes point may be a Cumberland variant and in general is smaller than a Cumberland. It also may have a more northern distribution, and the types are probably different enough to warrant separate type names.
(Fogelman, Gary L. "Let's Talk About the Barnes Fluted Point Type." *Central States Archaeological Journal*, Vol. 47 No. 2, April 2000, pp. 94, 95.)

While it is generally assumed that the fluting of a Clovis point was the final manufacturing step (aside from basal/lateral edge dulling), this was not always the case. In a discussion of two finds, the Willcox Playa point and the Texas Canyon point: "From an examination of the chipping, it would appear that the Clovis Fluted points from southeastern Arizona were first shaped and then fluted on both sides before they were chipped into a final shape, inasmuch as the conchoidal depressions caused by the final chipping were found to overlap the margin of the conchoidal depression of the flute."
(DiPeso, Charles C. "Clovis Fluted Points from Southeastern Arizona." *American Antiquity*, Vol. XIX No. 1, July 1953, Society for American Archaeology, pp. 82 – 85.)

The farthest north for fluted point finds is Alaska. However,

much of the Paleo occupation there seems to have produced various lanceolate forms. Current thought is that fluted point technology probably moved northward into Alaska, rather than south from the Alaska region.
(Hothem, Lar. Various sources.)

In Michigan, the Holcombe site (a series of small Paleo emplacements on a sand ridge) produced some 393 artifacts. Of these, eight were non-Paleo. Of Paleo origin were 318 bifacials, 62 unifacials, and five possible cores or fragments. Bifacially worked artifacts included preforms, 6 complete points, and 178 point fragments (102 bases), uniface scrapers, and uniface gravers. Many of the artifacts were made of Bayport chert in light or dark gray, and white.
(Fitting, James E., et al. *The Paleo-Indian Occupation of the Holcombe Beach*, University of Michigan Museum of Anthropology No. 27, Ann Arbor, MI, 1966, pp. 1, 36, 39, 41, 48.)

The materials from which Paleo artifacts were made tend to generate speculation and debate. In collector terminology, if the material is rather drab, has lower-grade inclusions, and is non-glossy, it is called chert. If the material is glossy or colorful and has some translucency, it is called flint. This is not necessarily the way a geologist would differentiate the two, but the word usage is fairly standardized. These definitions imply that most Paleo artifacts are made of flint. Chalcedony suggests highest grades, with few inclusions, a glossy surface, some color, and high translucency. Agate is more a western U.S. term and implies similar materials and sometimes color bands. Also western and from the Rockies to the West Coast is obsidian, opaque to translucent, in dark colors. This is volcanic glass. Jasper is opaque and colored yellow through red. Rock crystal or crystal quartz is clear, and quartzite can be subdivided into clear and colored varieties. In general, and with some exceptions, Paleo workers selected the highest possible cryptocrystalline substances for their tools and weapons.
(Hothem, Lar. Various sources.)

If the availability of information about Ohio fluted points applies to other states, most fluted point finds are not precisely useful for a scientific study. For every point that has a solid provenance, three others have no such documentation.
(Prufer, Olaf H. *Survey of Ohio Fluted Points No. 8*. Cleveland Museum of Natural History, November 1962, pp. 1, 2.)

Over half a century ago, Clovis sites in North America could be classed in two ways. Campsites were determined to have fluted points and other varieties of flint tools like choppers, gravers, knives, and scrapers. Kill sites had fluted points, animals bones, and either flint tools or no other tools.
(Haynes, C. Vance Jr. "Elephant Hunting in North America." *Early Man in America, Readings from Scientific American*. W. H. Freeman and Company, San Francisco, 1951/1973, p. 50.)

Six types of Paleo points have been noted in Indiana. They are Clovis points, with fluting generally less than half of length; fluted points widest at the base; Cumberland or "fishtailed" points; fluted leaf-shaped points widest at mid-length; pentagonal fluted points; and small triangular fluted points.
(Dorwin, John T. *Fluted Points and Late-Pleistocene Geochronology in Indiana*, Indiana Historical Society, Vol. IV No. III, December 1966, Indianapolis, pp. 153 – 156.)

Dozens of Paleo point types or forms exist, but the one most likely to be found in a fragmentary condition is the Folsom. "The rarity of perfect specimens has been commented upon in various articles on the subject of Folsom points. A large majority consists of broken examples. There was only one complete blade in the group of 19 found at Folsom, and the proportion at other sites has been even smaller. This may be attributed, as has frequently been suggested, to the brittleness caused by the fluting. The removal of the longitudinal flakes so thinned the points that they became extremely fragile."
(Roberts, Frank H. H. Jr. "A Folsom Complex," *Smithsonian Miscellaneous Collections*, Vol. 94 No. 4, Washington, DC, June 20, 1935, p. 17.)

A Paleo knife form in the eastern Midwest can be recognized by certain characteristics. It is made on a large, thick flake, and one end tapers to a point. All edges are worked. "On inspection of the edges, one is impressed with the care manifested in producing the cutting edge, in contrast to the remainder of the flake, which in most cases was left rough."
(Webb, William S. *The Parrish Village Site/Hopkins County, Kentucky, Reports in Archaeology* Vol. VII No. 6, University of Kentucky, Lexington, February 1951, pp. 443, 445.)

Burin flaking has been seen on some Paleo points in both the East and West. This is a specialized edge-chipping process, apparently done by indirect percussion using a punch and mallet or hammerstone. Burin flaking or faceting drove off a long and narrow sliver of flint, in essence making two parallel edges instead of the single original edge. Burin flaking was done on one or both sides of the tip or from the base corner, rarely both. The purpose of burin flaking or burin faceting is not known, but when done at the tip, it created a graver. When done at the base, it formed a thicker edge. Burins have been found on both Early and Late Paleo points, and the practice continued into the Archaic period.
(Hothem, Lar. Various sources.)

Folsom hunters (Late Paleo) in the Southwest tended to select highest-grade materials for their fluted points. These materials included lavender Flattop chalcedony (from Colorado sites) and Alibates and Edwards Plateau (from Texas).
(Pfeiffer, Dr. Leslie. "The Folsom Culture." *Central States Archaeological Journal*, Vol. 47 No. 3, July 2000, pp. 142, 143.)

Fluting on Paleo points seems to have had two purposes. One was purely for hafting, or offering a secure fit for the wooden shaft. The other purpose was to permit a narrowed and smaller shaft end for point attachment. This allowed the deepest penetration possible of a prey animal. There was a delicate balance — large enough for good strength yet small enough for efficient striking.
(Hothem, Lar. Various sources.)

There is firm proof that humans in North America were associated with now-extinct Pleistocene animals. These were: Mammoth, mastodon, two types of ground sloth, three kinds of bison, two kinds of camel, two kinds of horse, musk-ox, and four-horned antelope. There is also some evidence of association with a number of other animals, including peccary, short-faced bear, and dire wolf.
(Harrington, Mark Raymond. *Gypsum Cave, Nevada, Southwest Museum Papers No. Eight*, Los Angeles, CA, 1933/1963, pp. 184, 185.)

Some fascinating comments on collecting artifacts more than a century ago were made by the prolific Professor Moorehead. (As Paleo artifacts were not recognized as such at the time, many fine fluted points would have been as available to collectors as more common types.)
"I receive many letters from students requesting information as to where they can purchase specimens, and as to the best localities for field searching, buying of farmers, etc. ... the best way to enlarge a cabinet is to visit a rich territory and carefully canvass it. Wheeling [bicycling] is out of the question in many places; a horse and buggy being necessary, for the roads are rough.
"Small collections are in the hands of farmers, doctors, store keepers and boys...Some want much, others can be bought for dollar or so. There are no set values and the cost of a rare object or of a collection depends on two things: how keen the purchaser is to possess it, and the price desired by the owner. Most of the more valuable collections have been bought by museums. Single rare objects may be had of the three or four dealers of good reputation."
(Moorehead, Warren K. *Prehistoric Implements*. The Robert Clarke Company, Cincinnati, OH, 1900, p. 175.)

One of the striking things about fluted points when they are handled has to do with great amounts of time and incredible events. It is a fact that long ago these carefully made yet fragile objects could and did kill large animals, including elephant-like creatures. This is part of the reason fluted points in particular attract collectors, for the points were designed to be used in dangerous times for survival. The drama is all there, frozen forever in a bit of flint. The untold story contained in a single fluted point is beyond knowing, almost beyond imagining.
(Hothem, Lar. Various sources.)

One of the few non-chipped artifacts known from Paleo times came from the Lindenmeier site (Folsom) in northern Colorado. This was a paint palette, an oval stone with a depression on one face that held traces of red paint. Also found in the deposits were bits of hematite that had been rubbed, suggesting that they were the source of pigments used with the palette.
(Roberts, Frank H. H. Jr. "A Folsom Complex." *Smithsonian Miscellaneous Collections*, Vol. 94 No. 4, Washington, June 20, 1935, pp. 30, 31.)

Waller knives appear to be specialized blades from Paleo and later times. They are essentially elongated uniface blades with small offset tangs or expanded stems at or near one end. Another description is that they are hafted flake knives. Mainly from Florida and the southeastern states, many have been river finds.
(Gutierrez, Dr. Albert and Alex. "Waller Knives, A Unique Florida Knife Form." *Central States Archaeological Journal*, Vol. 50 No. 1, Winter 2003, p. 11.)

Mr. Virgil Russell was the premier collector of Late Paleo Yuma (now known as Eden) points. He was the author of *Indian Artifacts of the Rockies* and of *Indian Artifacts*, a book that had many reprintings. He briefly described his collection to a fellow collector: "I am 62 years old & have been stressing yumas. Have about 200 yumas — 10 folsoms & one corner tang knife. That's my collection. Each piece is in a 5" x 7" white plastic frame — on white & black velvet. Each frame is in a special made box — labeled 'Russell Yuma Collection' — then have five such cases, 40 in a case. Have each piece written up with its history, etc. Have sold approximately eighty also. I am sure I have the biggest and best yuma collection in existence. Yumas are hard to get..."
(Personal two-page handwritten letter from Virgil Y. Russell to Charles Hyman, dated Oct. 11, 1956; Hothem collection.)

Years ago, collectors were fascinated with Mound Builder artifacts, and anything having to do with mounds was eagerly sought. Today, much interest has settled on Paleo artifacts. There is an overall focus on the first known people to roam the Americas, and on the objects they left behind. This is indicated by professional conferences and publications, collector talk and activity, and values for Paleo artifacts.

Along with this increased interest and demand, values for better Paleo artifacts have shot up and are reflected by listings in this book. It should also be noted that some of the highest prices paid for top-grade Paleo points never receive any publicity. This is because these are private collector-to-collector arrangements, either by trade or payment or a combination.

There are half a dozen ways to acquire Paleo artifacts today besides the traditional surface hunting or walk-and-look. And one welcome aspect of collecting Paleo artifacts is that there is a complete price range. End-scrapers can bring $10, uniface blades $100, and points all range of values. The collecting field truly provides something for everyone.

The Internet is fast becoming a part of everyday life, and almost anything is available there. This includes Indian goods and many offerings of Paleo artifacts. Some persons who sell online are reputable dealers who may also provide catalogs or set up at artifact shows. Others seem to have little or no established history as business people.

Some Paleo artifacts are offered with a money-back guarantee, while others are sold as-is, with no proof of authenticity, and *buyer beware*. Since a purchase (whether at an online auction or from a dealer's set-price stock) is based on an electronic image, it is often not possible to get a good idea of what the artifact really is. Sometimes there is only a grace period of a few days to return an item if it proves unsatisfactory, and that is not enough time to allow for in-mailing or shipment, study or authentication, and out-mailing or shipment.

In short, the Internet is a growing force, and knowledge of how to use it wisely for collecting needs to grow along with it. One thing to do is talk with Internet-experienced collectors in order to learn about different sites and how reputable they are.

Auctions have long been the method of choice for both selling collections and purchasing artifacts from such collections. There are established auctions that specialize in Indian artifacts and have large mailings that bring together collectors for the sale. Some auctions have experienced people look over the sales inventory before auctions and remove any questionable pieces.

While some Paleo artifacts can sell for many thousand dollars due to spirited bidding, the chances are also high that the arti-facts are authentic. There is usually a range of Paleo types and quality, so that a bidder can acquire almost anything for a collection, whether something inexpensive or a frame centerpiece.

Indian artifact shows are periodic get-togethers of dealers and displayers, buyers and lookers, all with a great interest in things prehistoric. Depending on where the shows are held, and which dealers or displayers attend, shows are a great opportunity to learn more about Paleo artifacts from different regions and the materials from which they were made.

A collector can also compare price and quality, and do a personal examination of what is being offered. Many shows have regulations stipulating that fake or questionable artifacts must be so marked or removed from the display tables. This pre-screening provides a certain level of protection to collectors. So do shows that have a policy requiring money back with the return of any artifact to the seller for the duration of the show.

Shows (and auctions) are wonderful learning experiences, and are a good way to meet other collectors and exchange information and knowledge. It is simply amazing how many differences there are within the somewhat limited classes of Paleo artifacts. In Clovis forms alone, there are dozens of shapes and sizes, and hundreds of materials.

Collectors often establish a working relationship with dealers and purchase artifacts from them. Dealers may have the history of a piece, who owned it, and where it was found. Such facts make up the provenance or collecting history of an artifact, and help establish its authenticity.

Dealers are usually quite knowledgeable about market conditions and price their artifacts accordingly. They are often aware of certain collections or artifacts that are for sale or might become available. In this way, a collector might be able to obtain Paleo artifacts that he or she might not be able to locate on his or her own.

Other collectors are a main avenue for artifact exchanges or purchases. Such persons are familiar with what they have, and informal trades and purchases or sales are often made. Many collectors have known one another for years, and levels of trust ensure that most deals are straightforward and that the artifacts are as they are said to be. If any problems arise, these are settled quickly and amicably due to the friendship factor.

Of course, there are many kinds of collectors, from those who want mainly self-found pieces to those who desire the best of the best. No matter what level or interest direction of the collector, Paleo artifacts tends to be among the most sought after and admired in the entire field of Indian artifacts. In fact, it is common for high-grade non-Paleo artifacts to be traded for medium-grade Paleo artifacts.

All collectors search and hope for that situation or opportunity that comes only occasionally in a lifetime. That is when an old-time collection becomes available at a reasonable price. Such collections have often been put away for many years by the family of a now-gone collector and have had nothing added or removed. This almost always means that the collection has few or no fake pieces, and probably contains quite a few Paleo artifacts.

Since most people now have at least a general idea of what such groupings are worth, if the collector can afford an approximate fair market price, he or she has a real find. Most or all of the artifacts are not known to the collecting community, and interest tends to be high. Since some basic information will accompany the collection, this adds to Paleo knowledge, especially if the collection was found or obtained in a local area.

In all of the six Paleo artifact collecting methods briefly mentioned, a steady theme is the emphasis on authenticity. Visit any major gathering of flint knappers in this country, and you will note the great skill of the more advanced replicators. Also to be noted is the great number of Paleo points being turned out. In the process of modern artifact chipping, and in a sort of reverse-technology analysis, much has been learned about how Paleo knappers made, or could have made, their artifacts.

However, not all replicators mark their creations. And some sign their work with diamond-tipped pens; such marks can be ground off. While modern makers sell their work as modern, somewhere along the way the origin often seems to become lost. Eventually, either by intent or wishful thinking, many artifacts began to be treated as truly old. One of the great mysteries is how, in a couple of years, a modern artifact can accelerate backward in time ten thousand and more years. This is not faster than the speed of light, but it is faster than the speed of time.

In some cases, a Paleo point that is correctly made of the proper material receives additional treatment. There are various methods for aging an artifact to give it at least the superficial appearance of being quite old. There are many means of doing this, including putting a piece in a rock tumber, giving it acid baths, adding use marks, attempting to add patination, adding organic and mineral deposits, staining, and so forth. The end result is a Paleo artifact that can often mislead the average collector.

Some modern and artificially aged Paleo artifacts may be promoted with other attempts to deceive. There is always a story of how such a piece was found or collected, and some stories are quite convincing. False information, including old dates, stickers, and collector marks, may be marked on the piece. The latest trick seems to be forged COAs, especially those copied from well-accepted authenticators.

The problem of fake Paleo artifacts is so prevalent that for high-priced points, collectors like to see more than one certificate of authenticity (COA) from respected authenticators. Some Paleo points now have three or four "papers" that accompany them, and this trend is growing.

Interest in Paleo artifacts, especially points, has brought a great increase in values. Ten years ago, a long lanceolate might sell for one hundred dollars. Today, the same artifact could easily bring one thousand. A dealer, asked about his stock of Paleo points, remarked, "If it's fluted, it's sold." Still, now is the time to acquire solid and authentic Paleo artifacts. Collecting in this field was indeed easier ten years ago, but just consider what it will be like ten years from now.

Thanks are due the many collectors who contributed photographs for this book, and their names are credited to the photographs. Without their kind help, this book would not have been possible.

Special thanks also to Dennis Arbeiter (Rainbow Traders, P.O. Box 566, Godfrey, IL 62035) for auction photographs and results. And the following businesses and individuals contributed photographs: Back to Earth, Old Barn Auction, Gilbert Cooper, Earthworks Artifacts, Dave Summers, H. B. Greene II, John and Susan Mellyn, Michael Hough, Len and Janie Weidner, and John Baldwin.

For more information and products, the following publications and businesses are recommended:

Indian Artifact Magazine
245 Fairview Road
Turbotville, PA 17772-9063

Prehistoric Antiquities Quarterly
P.O. Box 296
North Lewisburg, OH 43060

Artifact Display Frames
Indian River Display Case Company
13706 Robins Road
Westerville, OH 43081

Lar Hothem has been a collector of Indian artifacts for 50 years, and a student of prehistoric lifeways for nearly as long. He is a member of many archaeological societies, including Central State Archaeological Society, Genuine Indian Relic Society, Archaeological Society of Ohio, and American Society for Amateur Archaeology. Lar is the author of over 700 articles on historic and pre-historic subjects. When not writing or taking pictures, he enjoys surface hunting for artifacts in the eastern Mid-west, attending Indian artifact shows, and traveling with his wife, Sue. *Paleo-Indian Artifacts* is his 32nd book.

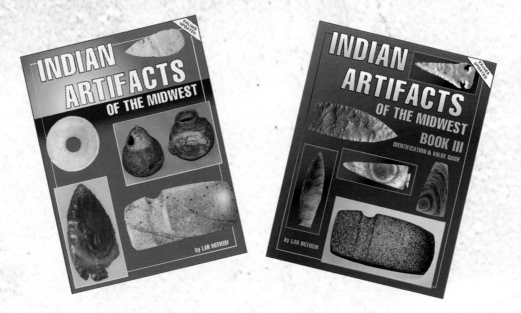

INDIAN ARTIFACTS of the Midwest

Lar Hothem

These collectors' handbooks are loaded with thousands of artifacts of all types found in the Midwest. They give the necessary facts about each item featured, such as important details, size, dates, location found, and of course, current collector values. The Paleo, Archaic, Woodland, and Mississippian Periods are covered, accompanied by hundreds of detailed photographs, with no repeats from any of the other books in the series. Collecting tips and a section on artifact authentication services are also provided. Lar Hothem, widely known for his research and expertise in the field of Indian artifacts and arrowheads, emphasizes the more common, readily available types.

Book I • Item #2279 • ISBN: 0-89145-485-3
8½ x 11 • 208 Pgs. • PB • 2001 values • $14.95
Book III • Item #4870 • ISBN: 0-89145-782-8
8½ x 11 • 344 Pgs. • PB • 2001 values • $18.95
Book IV • Item #5685 • ISBN: 1-57432-197-8
8½ x 11 • 360 Pgs. • PB • 2003 values • $19.95
Book V • Item #6231 • ISBN: 1-57432-326-1
8½ x 11 • 448 Pgs. • PB • 2003 values • $24.95

INDIAN ARTIFACTS: The Best of the Midwest

Lar Hothem

Lar Hothem, author of the bestselling series, *Indian Artifacts of the Midwest,* is widely known for his research in the field of Indian artifacts. His latest book, complete with nearly 2,300 color photographs, showcases items from some of the finest collections of Midwestern artifacts, many of them never before published. Artifacts from all prehistoric periods are covered: Paleo, Mississippian, Archaic, and Woodland. States featured are Kentucky, Ohio, Indiana, Illinois, Michigan, Wisconsin, Missouri, and Iowa. Descriptions, type, material, time period, size, location, and current collector value are given for every piece. Classes include boatstones, pendants, axes, plummets, bannerstones, birdstones, and fluted points. 2004 values.

Item #6463 • ISBN: 1-57432-390-3 • 8½ x 11 • 464 Pgs. • HB • $29.95

ARROWHEADS & Projectile Points

Lar Hothem

Projectile points of American Indians are the focus of this book, which has hundreds of photos, information about geographic origin, methods of production and sizes, and a special section on detecting fakes. The author is well known for his extensive knowledge of Indian artifacts of the Midwest. 2004 values.

Item #1426 • ISBN: 0-89145-228-1 • 5½ x 8½ • 224 Pgs. • PB • $7.95

INDIAN TRADE RELICS

Lar Hothem

The first of author Lar Hothem's books to be featured entirely in color, this volume boasts over 1,150 photographs of actual artifacts hundreds of years old, each with accurate and detailed captions. Emphasizing what was traded long ago, what exists today, and what can still be collected, the book is an introduction to the subject of historic trade goods, from glass beads, cloth, and ornaments to knives, firearms, traps, and axes. There are also gunflints, arrowheads, tomahawks, kettles, and miscellaneous trade goods. 2003 values.

Item #6130 • ISBN: 1-57432-303-2 • 8½ x 11 • 320 Pgs. • HB • $29.95

FISHING LURES, GUNS & KNIVES

6469	Big Book of Pocket Knives, 2nd Ed., Stewart & Ritchie	19.95
6225	Captain John's Fishing Tackle Price Guide, Kolbeck & Lewis	19.95
5355	Cattaraugus Cutlery Co., Stewart & Ritchie	19.95
5906	Collector's Encyclopedia of Creek Chub Lures & Collectibles, 2nd Ed., Smith	29.95
5929	Commercial Fish Decoys, Baron	29.95
5683	Fishing Lure Collectibles, Vol. 1, Murphy/Edmisten	29.95
6141	Fishing Lure Collectibles, Vol. 2, Murphy	29.95
5912	The Heddon Legacy – A Century of Classic Lures, Roberts/Pavey	29.95
6028	Modern Fishing Lure Collectibles, Vol. 1, Lewis	24.95
6131	Modern Fishing Lure Collectibles Vol. 2, Lewis	24.95
6132	Modern Guns, 14th Ed., Quertermous	14.95
5603	19th Century Fishing Lures, Carter	29.95
5166	Std. Gde. to Razors, 2nd Ed., Ritchie/Stewart	9.95
6031	Standard Knife Collector's Guide, 4th Ed., Ritchie/Stewart	14.95

ARTIFACTS, TOOLS & PRIMITIVES

1868	Antique Tools, Our American Heritage, McNerney	9.95
1426	Arrowheads & Projectile Points, Hothem	7.95
6021	Arrowheads of the Central Great Plains, Fox	19.95
5362	Collector's Guide to Keen Kutter Cutlery Tools, Heuring	19.95
4943	Field Gde. to Flint Arrowheads & Knives of N. Amer. Indian, Tully	9.95
1668	Flint Blades & Projectile Points, Tully	24.95
2279	Indian Artifacts of the Midwest, Book I, Hothem	14.95
3885	Indian Artifacts of the Midwest, Book II, Hothem	16.95
4870	Indian Artifacts of the Midwest, Book III, Hothem	18.95
5685	Indian Artifacts of the Midwest, Book IV, Hothem	19.95
6130	Indian Trade Relics, Hothem	29.95
2164	Primitives, Our American Heritage, McNerney	9.95
1759	Primitives, Our American Heritage, Series II, McNerney	14.95

TOYS & CHARACTER COLLECTIBLES

2333	Antique & Collectible Marbles, 3rd Ed., Grist	9.95
5900	Collector's Guide to Battery Toys, 2nd Ed., Hultzman	24.95
5150	Cartoon Toys & Collectibles, Longest	19.95
5038	Collector's Guide to Diecast Toys & Scale Models, 2nd Ed., Johnson	19.95
5169	Collector's Guide to T.V. Toys & Memorabilia, 1960s & 1970s, 2nd Ed., Davis/Morgan	24.95
6471	Collector's Guide to Tootsietoys, 3rd Ed., Richter	24.95

4945	G-Men & FBI Toys & Collectibles, Whitworth	18.95
5593	Grist's Big Book of Marbles, 2nd Ed.	24.95
3970	Grist's Machine-Made & Contemporary Marbles, 2nd Ed.	9.95
6128	Hot Wheels, the Ultimate Redline Guide, Vol. 1, Clark/Wicker	24.95
6230	Hot Wheels, the Ultimate Redline Guide, Vol. 2, Clark/Wicker	24.95
4950	Lone Ranger Collector's Reference & Value Guide, Felbinger	18.95
6466	Matchbox Toys, 1947 – 1998, 4th Ed., Johnson	24.95
5830	McDonald's Collectibles, 2nd Ed., Henriques/DuVall	24.95
1540	Modern Toys, 1930 – 1980, Baker	19.95
5365	Peanuts Collectibles, Id. & Value Guide, Podley/Bang	24.95
5619	Roy Rogers and Dale Evans Toys & Memorabilia, Coyle	24.95
6237	Rubber Toy Vehicles, Leopard	19.95
6340	Schroeder's Collectible Toys, Antique to Modern Price Guide, 9th Ed.	17.95
6239	Star Wars Super Collector's Wish Book, 2nd Ed., Carlton	29.95
5908	Toy Car Collector's Guide, Johnson	19.95

FURNITURE

3716	American Oak Furniture, Book II, McNerney	12.95
6012	Antique Furniture — A Basic Primer on Furniture	12.95
1118	Antique Oak Furniture, Hill	7.95
3720	Collector's Encyclopedia of American Furniture, Vol. III, 18th & 19th Century Furniture, Swedberg	24.95
6474	Collector's Guide to Wallace Nutting Furniture, Ivankovich	19.95
5359	Early American Furniture, A Practical Guide for Collectors, Obbard	12.95
3906	Heywood-Wakefield Modern Furniture, Rouland	18.95
6338	Roycroft Furniture & Collectibles, Koon	24.95
6343	Stickley Brothers Furniture, Koon	24.95
1885	Victorian Furniture, Our American Heritage, McNerney	9.95
3829	Victorian Furniture, Our American Heritage, Book II, McNerney	9.95

PAPER COLLECTIBLES & BOOKS

5902	Boys' & Girls' Book Series, Jones	19.95
5153	Collector's Guide to Children's Books, Vol. II, Jones	19.95
1441	Collector's Guide to Post Cards, Wood	9.95
5031	Collector's Guide to Early 20th Century American Prints, Ivankovich	19.95
4864	Collector's Guide to Wallace Nutting Pictures, Ivankovich	18.95
5926	Duck Stamps, Chappell	9.95
2081	Guide to Collecting Cookbooks, Allen	14.95
6234	Old Magazines, Clear	19.95
2080	Price Guide to Cookbooks & Recipe Leaflets, Dickinson	9.95

3973	Sheet Music Reference & Price Gde., 2nd Ed., Guiheen/Pafik . . .19.95
6041	Vintage Postcards for the Holidays, Reed 24.95

OTHER COLLECTIBLES

5916	Advertising Paperweights, Holiner/Kammerman 24.95
5838	Advertising Thermometers, Merritt 16.95
5814	Antique Brass & Copper, Gaston .24.95
5898	Antique & Contemporary Advertising Memorabilia, 2nd Edition, Summers 24.95
1880	Antique Iron, McNerney 9.95
3872	Antique Tins, Dodge 24.95
5030	Antique Tins, Book II, Dodge 29.95
5251	Antique Tins, Book III, Dodge 29.95
4845	Ant. Typewriters & Office Collectibles, Rehr 19.95
4935	W.F. Cody – Buffalo Bill Collector's Guide, Wojtowicz 24.95
6345	Business & Tax Guide for Antiques & Collectibles, Kelly . . .14.95
5151	Celluloid, Collector's Ref. & Val. Gde., Lauer/Robinson 24.95
5152	Celluloid Treasures of the Vict. Era, VanPatten/Williams 24.95
3718	Collectible Aluminum, Grist 16.95
6342	Collectible Soda Pop Memorabilia, Summers 24.95
5060	Collectible Souvenir Spoons, Book I, Bednersh 19.95
5676	Collectible Souvenir Spoons, Book II, Bednersh 29.95
5666	Collector's Encyclopedia of Granite Ware, Book 2, Greguire . .29.95
6468	Collector's Ency. of Pendant & Pocket Watches, Bell 24.95
5836	Collector's Gde. to Antique Radios, 5th Ed., Slusser/Radio Daze .19.95
4857	Collector's Guide to Art Deco, 2nd Ed., Gaston 17.95
5820	Collector's Guide to Glass Banks, Reynolds 24.95
4736	Collector's Guide to Electric Fans, Witt 16.95
3966	Collector's Guide to Inkwells, Badders 18.95
4947	Collector's Guide to Inkwells, Book II, Badders 19.95
5681	Collector's Guide to Lunchboxes, White 19.95
5836	Collector's Guide to Antique Radios, 5th Ed., Slusser 19.95
5278	Collector's Guide to Vintage Televisions, Durbal/Bubenheimer .15.95

6475	Complete Price Guide to Watches, No. 24, Shugert/Engle/Gilbert .29.95
5145	Encyclopedia of Advertising Tins, Vol. II, Zimmerman 24.95
6328	Flea Market Trader, 14th Edition, Huxford 12.95
5918	Florence's Big Book of Salt & Pepper Shakers 24.95
6458	Fountain Pens, Past & Present, 2nd Ed., Erano 24.95
6459	Garage Sale & Flea Market Annual, 12th Edition, Huxford . . .19.95
3819	General Store Collectibles, Wilson 24.95
5044	General Store Collectibles, Vol. II, Wilson 24.95
2216	Kitchen Antiques, 1790 – 1940, McNerney 14.95
5991	Lighting Devices and Accessories of the 17th – 19th Centuries, Hamper 9.95
2109	Personal Antique Record Book 4.95
1301	Personal Doll Inventory 4.95
6104	Quilt Art 2004 Engagement Calendar 9.95
5835	Racing Collectibles, Racing Collector's Price Guide 19.95
2026	Railroad Collectibles, 4th Ed., Baker 14.95
3443	Salt & Pepper Shakers IV, Guarnaccia 18.95
6339	Schroeder's Antiques Price Guide, 22nd Edition 14.95
5007	Silverplated Flatware, Revised 4th Ed., Hagan 18.95
6138	Standard Antique Clock Value Guide, Wescot 19.95
5058	Std. Encyclopedia of American Silverplate, Bones/Fisher . . .24.95
6139	Summers' Gde. to Coca-Cola, 4th Ed 24.95
6324	Summers' Pocket Gde. to Coca-Cola, 4th Ed. 12.95
5057	Treasury of Scottie Dog Collectibles, Vol. I, Davis/Baugh 19.95
5369	Treasury of Scottie Dog Collectibles, Vol. II, Davis/Baugh 19.95
5837	Treasury of Scottie Dog Collectibles, Vol. III, Davis/Baugh . . .24.95
5144	Value Guide to Advertising Memorabilia, 2nd Ed., Summers . .19.95
3977	Value Guide. to Gas Station Memorabilia, Summers/Priddy . .24.95
4877	Vintage Bar Ware, Visakay 24.95
5925	The Vintage Era of Golf Club Collectibles, John 29.95
6010	Vintage Era of Golf Club Collectibles Collector's Log 9.95
5999	Wilderness Survivor's Guide, Hamper 12.95

This is only a partial listing of the books on antiques that are available from Collector Books. All books are well illustrated and contain current values. Most of these books are available from your local bookseller, antique dealer, or public library. If you are unable to locate certain titles in your area, you may order by mail from COLLECTOR BOOKS, P.O. Box 3009, Paducah, KY 42002-3009. Customers with Visa, Master Card, or Discover may phone in orders from 7:00 a.m. to 5:00 p.m. CT, Monday – Friday, toll free 1-800-626-5420, or online at www.collectorbooks.com. Add $3.00 for postage for the first book ordered and 50¢ for each additional book. Include item number, title, and price when ordering. Allow 14 to 21 days for delivery.

www.collectorbooks.com

1-800-626-5420
Fax: 1-270-898-8890